Retail Marketing Management

Retail Marketing Management

David Gilbert

FINANCIAL TIMES
Prentice Hall

An imprint of **Pearson Education**

Harlow, England · London · New York · Reading, Massachusetts · San Francisco · Toronto · Don Mills, Ontario · Sydney
Tokyo · Singapore · Hong Kong · Seoul · Taipei · Cape Town · Madrid · Mexico City · Amsterdam · Munich · Paris · Milan

PEARSON EDUCATION LIMITED

Edinburgh Gate
Harlow
Essex CM20 2JE
England

and Associated Companies around the world

Visit us on the World Wide Web at:
http://www.pearsoneduc.com

First published in 1999

© Pearson Education Limited 1999

The right of David Gilbert to be identified as Author
of this Work has been asserted by him in accordance
with the Copyright, Designs and Patents Act 1988.

ISBN 0 273 63019 9

British Library Cataloguing in Publication Data
A CIP catalogue record for this book can be obtained from the British Library

10 9 8 7 6 5 4 3 2
04 03 02 01 00

Typeset by Tech Set Limited, Gateshead
Printed and bound in Great Britain by Redwood Books, Trowbridge, Wiltshire

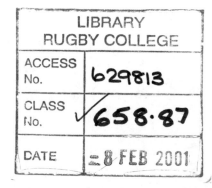

Contents

About the contributors

David Gilbert, BA, MA, DipM, PhD, is a Reader in Marketing in the School of Management Studies for the Service Sector at the University of Surrey. Prior to working in academia he was employed as a marketing manager for Rank Leisure. He also has experience of working with Littlewoods on various aspects of their strategic planning and was retained as a Research Director of major studies into image, promotion awareness and change of corporate identity. He has extensive consultancy experience, having worked on assignments to locate a number of travel agencies in England and to improve the sales of retail outlets in museums, zoos and other leisure attractions. Dr Gilbert has published extensively in leisure marketing journals and is very interested in the fields of tourism marketing, consumer behaviour and customer satisfaction measurement.

Joshua Bamfield, MA, MPhil, MBCS, is Director of the Centre for Retail Research based in Nottingham and Professor of Management. He has carried out consultancy over the last twenty years for a range of large and medium-sized retailers, mainly dealing with EPOS and IT as well as strategic innovation. He has also conducted a number of studies into the costs of crime and the use of technology to combat theft.

James Bell, BA, CertEd, MBA, is a Lecturer in Retail Management in the School of Management Studies for the Service Sector at the University of Surrey. Before starting an academic career, he worked for a number of years in food retail operations. Current research interests include the management of retail service quality and of consumer co-operatives.

Hayley Myers, BA, PhD, is currently Senior European Retail Editor with the Corporate Intelligence Group. Previously she spent three years as a Lecturer in Retail Management in the School of Management Studies at the University of Surrey, where her teaching and research interests included the international activity of retailers, location management and the social responsibility of retailers. Prior to this she completed a PhD which focused upon the internationalisation of European food retailers.

Preface

Retailing occupies a pre-eminent position in the economies of all modern societies. The retail sector is changing at an ever-increasing rate and this is leading to greater competitor activity. Such activity leads to a need to improve the way companies approach retail marketing. In short, to gain success, retail management has to be developed within the context of a marketing approach. The aim of this book is to help students and managers to develop by getting them to consider different ways of approaching the retail marketplace, to learn a set of retail marketing principles and to feel more confident about practical uses of retail marketing.

Retail Marketing Management grew out of a retail marketing course run at the University of Surrey for Sears' managers. The content reflects what Sears' senior people deemed to be the most important aspects of retail management to be communicated to their up-and-coming managers. Sears wanted a course built on the strength of a marketing framework so that this could form the integrating system for the inputs. The recent blurring of areas of retail with the growing importance of catering outlets, financial services and electronic retailing, places a fresh need on creating greater emphasis of services marketing within the approach to retail marketing management. Also, retailing is becoming much more international and therefore an individual UK retail management approach would be too restrictive for the managers of tomorrow.

This content of the original Sears' programme was subsequently improved, based upon the feedback gained from a number of leading retail management academics. As such the text is an attempt to create a comprehensive application of marketing concepts to the discipline of retail management. We believe because it started with an industry led demand for particular sections that it offers a different formula to many other books dealing with retail marketing. In fact it is believed this book is much closer to the essence of a contemporary retailer's need for marketing than many others purporting to offer an applied marketing approach.

Today no undergraduate or postgraduate retail course would be complete without the inclusion of material which helped the student to understand the applications of marketing to retail management. This text was written to prepare students for a career in retailing whether they are approaching the subject for the first time or are already working in the industry. Marketing is an increasingly important area requiring retailers to look at the business through the customer's eyes. The trend to understand the business from the customer's perspective underlies the emphasis of this book. The incorporation of chapters which investigate some aspects of marketing to greater depth than other texts was a conscious effort to fit in with industry's need to ensure retailers have a wider knowledge of marketing and its retail applications. The book is written to encourage the reader to feel comfortable with the detail and content as much of the text includes practical examples, especially those of the *Financial Times* and *The Economist*.

It is believed some of the content of this book opens up new ground for retail management. The detailed coverage of the management of brands, consumerism and social responsibility, and consumer behaviour has not been covered as comprehensively in previous retail marketing books.

All this could not have been produced without the help of many others prime amongst whom are James Bell, Hayley Myers and Joshua Bamfield. I am also indebted to Jane Powell, my publisher, who helped with many aspects of the material contained in this book. My thanks are due to the staff of the School of Management Studies at the University of Surrey. Principal among these include Haiyan Song, Michael Howley, Phil Dawes, Joanne Traves and my secretary Gillian Chubb who organised much of my other work in order to create time for me on this book. In addition, I should mention Peter Newman and Jean Gilbert who managed to find some time for reading the draft chapters, making a high number of improvements to the text, and Professor David Airey whose level of energy for administration helped relieve my postgraduate co-ordinator duties. I am also indebted to the former Group Marketing Director of Littlewoods, Prodip Guha, who remains the most enlightened and dynamic marketing person I have had the personal benefit of working for.

May I also thank those who worried about my intake of coffee and managed to restrict my caffeine needs. The publisher was also very patient in waiting for the final drafts as the many other University responsibilities I had delayed its progress for several months. And last but not least, I thank my family and friends for the tolerance shown due to less socialising than would be normal if the pressure of finishing the book had not intervened.

David Gilbert

1 An introduction to retailing as an activity

This chapter should enable you to understand and to explain:
- the importance of the retail industry;
- what retailing is;
- the theories underpinning the study of retail management;
- the structure of retailing in the UK.

THE RETAIL ENVIRONMENT

It is often stated that the only constant in retailing is change and it is certainly true that the pace of development within retailing appears to be accelerating. More than ever before, at the close of the twentieth century, we are witnessing the emergence of new forms of retailing, in part in response to demand from increasingly sophisticated consumers. The market is becoming more segmented with retail formats focusing on the needs of particular consumer groups. The result of this is the development of a more complex retail environment.

Where once it was manufacturers' brands that were all important, the 1990s have seen the power of retailers' brands challenging the position of suppliers. The traditional forms of independently owned small businesses and co-operatives have lost significant market share and, in developed economies, the retail sector is now characterised by large-scale multiple chains run by powerful and sophisticated organisations.

The increasing size of retailers and intensifying rates of competition in the markets in which they are operating has led retailers to search for new ways in which to grow their businesses. During the late 1980s and 1990s we witnessed retailers moving away from their core businesses into such areas as financial services. Similarly, an acceleration of retail internationalisation occurred resulting in familiar logos, liveries, store fascias and retail formulas being found throughout the world. All this illustrates that retailing is a dynamic industry.

THE GROWING IMPORTANCE OF THE RETAIL INDUSTRY

Retailing is not only an integral part of our economic structure but also shapes, and is shaped by, our way of life. While the trading of goods has always been a part of traditional societies, in recent times the buying and selling of products has become a much more formalised and brand-dominated activity. Even as relatively recently as the

1

1960s retailing was predominately seen as having a smaller and significantly less important role than other industries such as manufacturing. However, the retail sector is increasingly being viewed as an important activity in the economy and its impact on society in general is readily acknowledged. This acceptance of its importance is a reflection of a number of factors; for example, retailing accounts for a significant proportion of GDP, it employs a large proportion of the workforce, and retailers are among the largest and most sophisticated of organisations.

The power of individual retail organisations is growing; they are now comparable with, and even bigger than, many manufacturers. For example, the six largest retailers in Europe are comparable with only two European manufacturers (*The Economist*, 1995), an indication of the growing dominance of retailers within the supply chain. Certainly the annual turnovers achieved by retailers are comparable with the largest companies in other service industries. If the retail sector is compared with organisations within the hospitality sector, and indeed with major corporations outside the service sector, the relatively powerful position of retailers is clear. For example, in 1997 the UK's largest food retailer, Tesco, had a turnover of £14 984 million compared with £3198 million for the hospitality group Whitbread and £7980 million for the pharmaceutical giant Glaxo–Wellcome. The amount is also higher than that of Unilever, which is a major company in the UK (*see* Table 1.1).

Table 1.1 Annual turnovers for a variety of corporations, 1997

Company	Sector	Turnover 1997 (£m)
Tesco	Food retailing	14 984.0
Unilever	Manufacturing	13 632.0
Marks & Spencer	Variety retailing	8 243.3
Glaxo–Wellcome	Pharmaceuticals	7 980.0
Whitbread	Hospitality	3 198.0

Sources: Company annual reports

The increasing importance of the retail sector is reflected in its contribution to GDP. In the UK the retail and wholesale sector accounted for a substantial 12 per cent of GDP in 1997 (adapted from National Accounts, 1998). This implies that a very significant proportion of the economy is linked to retailing, hence public policy tends to recognise its importance as a driving force and aims to promote its sustained growth.

A significant historical reason underlying the perceived increasing importance of retailing is that its contribution to the economy is much more visible in the modern era than it was in the past. In less developed economies the retail structures are less developed and are dominated by informal retailing, such as markets. In such environments bartering may be an important way of trading, making it very difficult to estimate transactions. Even when currency is used, informal retailing methods are much less likely to include the recording of transactions in a systematic way, in part due to the sellers not being faced with the same regulations as formal retailers. As a retail structure becomes increasingly developed, characterised by large multiple chains rather than small-scale independent retailers, retailers' accounts become more sophisticated, and hence turnover and profit are more visible. The formalisation and growing importance of distribution channels has resulted in the retail sector's contribution to economic vitality becoming more obvious – a matter of public record. This has resulted in healthy returns on capital employed, as can be seen in Table 1.2.

Table 1.2 Top 20 UK retailers: return on capital employed, 1997/98

	Company	Capital employed (£ mn)	Pre-tax profit (£ mn)	ROCE (%)
1	WH Smith	585.0	254.0	+43.4
2	Argos	321.5	128.4	+39.9
3	Arcadia	602.1	165.9	+27.6
4	Kingfisher	2 111.8	520.5	+24.6
5	John Lewis Partnership	633.2	152.6	+24.1
6=	Marks & Spencer	5 303.1	1 168.0	+22.0
6=	Boots	1 961.0	431.9	+22.0
6=	Littlewoods	866.4	191.1	+22.0
9	Dixons	1 016.0	218.7	+21.5
10	Wm. Morrison	809.2	151.4	+18.7
11	GUS	3 347.3	623.7	+18.6
12	Tesco	4 726.0	728.0	+15.4
13	ASDA	2 780.5	404.9	+14.6
14	J. Sainsbury	5 123.0	719.0	+14.0
15	Safeway	2 844.6	340.2	+11.9
16	Somerfield	1 005.3	114.2	+11.4
17	Iceland	393.3	43.5	+11.1
18	CWS	809.3	78.2	+9.7
19	Sears	1 236.9	−115.7	−9.4
20	Kwik Save	na	na	na

Source: Retail Intelligence, 1998a, p. 84

Another indication of the important role retailers play in today's society is their status as employers. It is estimated that the retail industry employs more than ten per cent of the UK workforce. Not only do retailers employ a significant proportion of the overall workforce, but they are extremely important employers of particular groups. Notably, the retail sector has higher levels of female employees than many other sectors; indeed it is estimated more than two-thirds of the retail labour force are female. Also more than half of retailing employees are employed on a part-time basis (Labour Market Trends, 1998), in part due to the need to maintain a highly flexible workforce capable of adapting to the differing labour demands. In the past the retail sector has had a reputation for not supporting its employees and for having lower pay and longer hours than other sectors. However, increasingly there are examples of retailers implementing innovative and supportive working conditions. For example, the DIY retailer B&Q has marketed itself to both its workforce and consumers as an organisation supportive of part-time and older employees.

Retailers are becoming increasingly important in their role as gatekeepers within the channel of distribution. In the past, when suppliers were dominant, retailers supplied the merchandise that was on offer and consumers selected from this. However, as retailers have become significantly more powerful they are more able to exert their power over suppliers and stock only the brands they wish to sell, depending on their overall retail strategy and supplier relationships. The effect of this is that consumers are able to purchase only what is selected and offered to them by retailers, as opposed to manufacturers, and so retailers may be considered to be shaping consumer demand. For example, if organic produce is difficult to obtain or is sold at a relatively high price, sales are likely to be limited – the retailer thus shaping consumer purchasing behaviour. Further, as retailer own brand lines take an increasingly large proportion of the market, retailers are also influencing the development of new products.

This issue brings into question the concept of the social responsibility of retailers. It has been suggested that the only responsibility of businesses is to make profits (Friedman, 1970), although the late Lord Sainsbury had put it more succinctly and fairly by leaving room for ethical concern, seeing profit as 'a first motive for a commercial business'. However, such is the current lack of trust of the public in large business that the degree of social responsibility taken by retailers is being questioned more and more. In some cases regulations are brought in to try and make the retail environment a fairer one for competition. In addition, retailers are increasingly using the idea of self-regulation and social responsibility as a marketing tool (*see* Chapter 11).

Large retail multiple chains are increasingly looking for new opportunities – new areas in which to grow their business. This is especially the case in markets with highly developed retail structures where competition is fierce and regulation often restricts the development of further stores. One strategy of expansion has been for retailers to move away from their core business and into broader retail activities; for example, moving from the food sector to the DIY or clothing sector, or diversifying into financial services. It is in part a reflection of the high esteem in which retailers are held that many of the personal banking services are proving to be a success. Customers seem to be displaying increasing loyalty to the retailer fascia or brand rather than manufacturer brands. It appears that consumers are willing to trust J. Sainsbury or Marks & Spencer with their financial needs in part because they trust their retail offer and organisational culture. In fact many companies are moving from a self-concept of being a trader to one of being committed to the development and marketing of a brand. This market-led approach requires the development of a sophisticated set of marketing programmes, as exemplified in some later chapters of this book. By strong brand positioning and image creation a retailer can improve trade rather than trading itself being the main business focus. The rise in competitive pressure in the industry has led to an endless search for competitive advantage – currently based on the precept that it is much cheaper to retain an existing customer than to acquire a new one. This has led to the development of loyalty card schemes which offer more intimate service while providing the benefit of valuable market data for the retailer.

Increasingly retailers are also expanding their businesses by moving internationally. Although there have long been examples of international retailers, they have focused mainly on the luxury goods markets; it was not until the late 1980s that the process of retail internationalisation occurred on any significant scale. Furthermore, it is a process that is increasing at an accelerating rate: not only are more retailers operating internationally, but they are moving into an increasing number of markets and expanding into more geographically and culturally distant markets. For example, the ten largest European retailers all operate in at least four different international markets, with some in significantly more (Retail Intelligence, 1998b). Thus, whereas in the past retailers were essentially domestic operations, but often dealing with multinational suppliers, by the end of the 1990s many were operating as multinational companies, thus strengthening their negotiating position.

MINICASE 1.1

The Co-op and the competitive nature of the retail marketplace FT

A diversion, was how executives at the Co-operative Wholesale Society described attempts in 1997 to break up the 130-year-old mutual and return cash to its members. But, in fact, Andrew Regan's £1.2bn takeover bid was exactly what the CWS needed if it is to survive as a co-operative in the 21st century. The result was a wide-ranging review of the business and a realisation that the co-operative movement would have to re-learn the lessons of co-operation. For never has the Co-op been more divided, and the effects of this on the movement's retail businesses have been severe. The Co-op is made up of 50 mutual retail societies, of which the 15 largest account for more than 90 per cent of the movement's trade. Until as recently as 1985, the co-operative movement as a whole could boast it was the UK's leading grocery retailer, as well as a banker, insurance provider, funeral services group, and agricultural operator. However, it is in food retailing where the effectiveness of mutuality has been questioned. While the supermarket chains such as Tesco, J. Sainsbury, Asda and Safeway have invested heavily in store development, delivering a consistent product range to customers, the Co-op's individual societies have been left to stagnate. From first place in grocery retailing, the Co-op as a whole has now been pushed down to fifth place, according to Verdict, the retail consultants. 'We have long argued that the members of the co-operative movement needed to co-operate much more closely with each other to make the most of their combined power,' Verdict argues in its report on the food sector. 'Such co-operation, however, seems further away than ever.' The CWS, one of the two largest societies in the co-op movement, admits that the independence of the individual societies has been a problem. Yet, attempts have been made to develop a national approach to product ranges and retail disciplines such as buying procedures, stock, and store investment. The biggest success appears to have been the ethical stance adopted by most societies on issues such as product labelling and animal testing. This strategy has proved successful for the Co-op Bank, and should be a natural for the food business, says Verdict. 'Few bottom line focused retailers take so strong a position,' the consultant says. Len Fyfe, chairman of CWS, says 65 per cent of the movement now has a unified approach. But the remaining 35 per cent is still hesitant. 'It has been discussed but people want to retain their independence,' he says. 'Both employees and members want to remain part of a smaller organisation and co-operative rather than be absorbed into a bigger one.' Nevertheless, this weakness should also be one of the movement's strengths, he argues. It makes co-operative retailers more responsive to local needs and so ensures that they are in closer touch with the communities they serve. Even the big operators have acknowledged that local communities could represent the next significant opportunity in food retailing.

Tesco, Sainsbury and Safeway have all recently introduced smaller high street formats aimed at the growing convenience market. 'Consumers are changing their eating habits and hence their shopping requirements,' says Verdict. The pattern today is a society which has less time to spend shopping for and preparing meals. Thus, there is an opportunity for local retailers to provide not just the traditional emergency purchase, but immediate and attractive meal solutions. Moreover, even the superstore operators have acknowledged that consumers are tiring of the faceless corporate. All the big operators are seeking to recreate their own version of the old-style high street with in-store bakeries, butchers and take-away counters. CWS has been forced to undertake a wide-ranging re-evaluation, and has opted to focus on convenience retailing. The strategy sits well with its mainly small neighbourhood stores and its image as a concerned and ethical retailer, says Verdict. But Co-operative Retail Services, which is a larger food retailer than CWS, but a smaller company, has decided to take on the big boys by focusing on the superstore arena. This, says Verdict, could be a fatal mistake. CRS has only 19 superstores and does not generate enough cash to fund the required investment, it claims.

Source: Peggy Hollinger, *Financial Times*, 10 March 1998

> **Factors illustrating the growing importance of the retail sector**
>
> - large and increasing contribution to GDP
> - economic importance more visible
> - major employer
> - retailers as gatekeepers
> - retailers diversifying their activities
> - organisations growing on an international scale
> - blurring of areas of retail to include wider area of business activity
> - size of operations allowing for supply chain control

THE STUDY OF RETAILING

Interest in the study of retailing has to some extent mirrored the growth and increasing prominence of the retail industry. Retailing has emerged from a number of interrelated disciplines: geography, economics, planning and, more recently, management and marketing. In the past it has not been acknowledged as a subject area in its own right, indeed Potter (1982, p. 2) described the academic study of retailing as 'the Cinderella of the Social Sciences'.

Increasingly retailing is being focused upon as an accepted area of academic debate, in part a reflection of the industry's growing importance and visibility as a contributor to national economic development. Brown (1992) has suggested that the development of the study of retailing may be considered as following the wheel of retailing (*see* discussion below of cyclical theories of retail change). Changes in academia have also resulted in the development of the subject area. University research centres focused on retailing have become established and professorial appointments in retailing have been made. One outcome of the recognition of the study of retailing is the fact that academic journals focusing on retailing are being published as well as specific retail industry consultancy reports.

As marketing and management disciplines have become more established, degree courses specialising in retailing have been developed in North America, the UK and elsewhere within Europe – in part in response to calls from industry for significant increases in graduate recruitment in the retail sector. Although retailers may have been considered to be behind other industries in terms of recruitment, they are becoming more sophisticated as organisations and they are realising the importance of appropriate recruitment. As a result, they are beginning to use similar procedures and offer employees employment packages that compete favourably with those of established blue chip organisations in the market for graduates.

RETAIL DEFINITION

There are many approaches to understanding and defining retailing; most emphasise retailing as the business activity of selling goods or services to the final consumer. We have defined retail as:

> **any business that directs its marketing efforts towards satisfying the final consumer based upon the organisation of selling goods and services as a means of distribution.**

The concepts assumed within this definition are quite important. The final consumer within the distribution chain is a key concept here as retailers are at the end of the chain and are involved in a direct interface with the customer. However, the emphasis on final consumer is intentionally different from that on customer: a consumer is the final user of a purchase whereas a customer may have bought for their own use, as a present or as part of their own business activity. Purchases for business or industrial use are normally not retail transactions. Additionally, retailing includes more than the sale of tangible products, involving services such as financial services, hair cutting or dry cleaning.

Retailers are often referred to as 'middlemen' or 'intermediaries'. This suggests they occupy a middle position, receiving and passing on products from producers and wholesalers to customers. This is accomplished by the addition of service and the provision of the store in a convenient location to provide a successful channel of distribution. The key objective for any successful channel is to ensure availability of the right product, in the right quantity, at the right time. All marketing channel decisions need to be related to ensuring the customer is a focal point for the selection and display of stock so as to make the sales operation as effective as possible.

In demand-led Western economies we usually consider retailing as providing a necessary service and a positive contribution to the economy. This is due to the effectiveness of the retailer in supporting manufacturing by buying in bulk (either directly from the manufacturer or through a wholesaler) on the basis of knowing what the consumer requires. However, in supply-led economies such as the former centrally planned economies (CPEs) of Eastern Europe, retailing has traditionally been viewed as an unnecessary and unproductive link in the channel of distribution (Myers and Alexander, 1997).

The actual term 'retailing' is thought to be derived from the old French word '*retailler*' which means 'a piece of' or 'to cut up' (Brown, 1992). This implies the breaking of bulk function of the retailer – that is, the acquiring of large amounts of the products they sell and dividing it up into smaller amounts to be sold to individual consumers.

Thus a retailer carries out a specific service and this should not be confused with the wholesaler. Retailers and wholesalers are different in nature and perform distinct functions. Some specific differences between them are listed below.

1 The interface with the customer is predominately service based, with social interaction and interpersonal sales techniques masking the sophistication of computer-based ordering, stocking and transaction systems.

2 Retailers sell small quantities of items on a frequent basis unlike wholesalers who sell in bulk but on a less frequent basis.

3 Retailers attempt to provide convenience in terms of location, payment and credit facilities, range of merchandise, after sales service, etc.

4 Retailers offer selection – an assortment of merchandise related to the target market in order to provide choice.

5 Retailers set up in business to trade with the general public whereas wholesalers may restrict the general public from purchasing from their warehouses.

6 Retailers normally charge higher unit prices than would a wholesaler.

7 A retailer's pricing policy tends to be simpler than that of the wholesaler, with less use of a discounting structure.

8 The retailer bears a different kind of risk to the manufacturer and wholesaler.

THE DYNAMIC NATURE OF RETAIL CHANGE

Retailing may be said to be dynamic. One of the areas of retailing that has been addressed by authors is the way in which the retail environment changes. Brown (1987) has reviewed the research in this area and suggests that theories of retail institutional change may be classified into three groups: environmental, cyclical and conflict theories. Environmental theories seek to explain developments in the retail industry as resulting from changes in the wider environment such as variations in lifestyle patterns. Cyclical theories, allied to the business cycle, suggest there are patterns of development which may predict changes in the retail industry, just as cycles can be seen in general economic conditions. Conflict theories propose that institutional retail change is an outcome of the relationships between, and competitive behaviour of, retailers.

Environmental theory

A whole array of factors shape the nature of retail environments; factors of an economic, social, political, regulatory, cultural and demographic nature all impinge upon the environment in which retailers operate. The problems of the department store in the 1980s perhaps show how important it is to ensure that adaption takes place to suit changing environmental trends. It is easy to see direct links between some environmental conditions and retail change: for example, the impact of a relaxation in regulations governing store opening hours is obvious. Other changes in the wider environment may be less direct but still play a fundamental part in shaping the nature of retail development, for example, increasing acceptance of female waged labour influencing lifestyle and consumer purchasing patterns (Myers, 1996). Changes in government planning guidelines may provide further examples of significant environmental factors.

There are specific examples illustrating how environmental factors have directly influenced the development of particular types of retail format. For example, Appel (1972) suggested that the success of the import of the self-service format from the USA to Europe in the 1940s was due – in part – to environmental conditions. The format was based on price competitiveness which made it particularly appropriate in a time of economic downturn. Some consumer groups were characterised by increasing rates of car and refrigerator ownership, which meant there was a growing demand for less frequent bulk buying. More recently superstores have transformed the grocery retailing marketplace in the UK and now account for the majority of expenditure each week by UK consumers. The development of superstores are a means by which the leading grocery retailers have grown their market shares. Customers have switched to this relatively new form of grocery retailing, moving away from smaller local stores. Superstores (sales areas greater than 25 000 square feet) have grown to what could be a saturation point for the market as there are now over one thousand such outlets. Figure 1.1 indicates the growth patterns of these stores in the UK.

Environmental theories have taken a 'Darwinian' approach and suggest that only retailers with the most appropriate organisational structure and formats will survive (Gist, 1968; Davidson et al., 1983; Brown, 1987). This implies that if retailers expand into new markets where there are different environmental conditions in terms of, for example, economy and culture, they may need to adapt in order to succeed. It also suggests that if retailers are to survive over time they must respond appropriately to the evolution of market conditions or otherwise face the possibility of extinction.

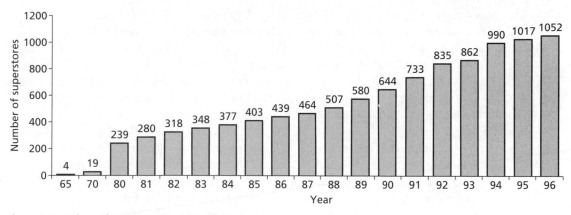

Fig. 1.1 Number of UK superstores, 1965–96

Source: Institute of Grocery Distribution, 1997

The major environmental factors

1 Changes related to the consumer:
 ● demographic changes – increases or decreases in population numbers, age groups, racial groups, socio-economic groups, etc.;
 ● attitudes and preferences to purchasing, brands and products;
 ● changes in lifestyle, whereby time is more important and therefore fast food, telephone banking, credit card payments are becoming important;
 ● economic influences based upon real incomes, confidence, numbers of women working, etc.

2 Changes in technology:
 ● microwave cookers, food freezers, motor cars, the Internet, computer applications to business, just-in-time delivery systems, and so on.

3 Changes in competition:
 ● the competitive strength or otherwise of actual or alternative channels of distribution, depending upon the nature and type of the retail organisation.

Cyclical theories

The wheel of retailing

One of the original theories addressing the issue of retail institutional change is the wheel of retailing (McNair, 1931, 1958). This concept proposes 'a more or less definite cycle', as follows. When retailers enter a market they compete by offering goods at the lowest possible price or 'the bold new concept, the innovation', in order to attract customers. As retailers develop their experience and gain capital, they tend to increase their level of service and quality – and therefore their price. This success allows mature retailers to move steadily into an upmarket position. However, retailers in this position may become vulnerable due to high costs, declining efficiency and, perhaps, stagnating management strategies which culminate in a downturn in sales. If this is the case the retailer may plunge into decline and even be forced to withdraw from the market. The consequence of this move around the wheel of retailing is that a gap is left at the bottom end of the market – an opportunity for a new retailer to enter.

An example of this process is provided by changes within the UK food retail sector. In the 1970s the main players were very much price oriented, illustrated by Tesco's sales cry of 'pile it high, sell it cheap'. However, throughout the 1980s the main grocery retailers moved to a higher quality and service orientation, operating larger stores from more accessible sites. This trend has resulted in further consolidation of the market during the 1990s and a considerable gap being left at the lower end of the market. This opportunity has been seized by the Continental hard discounters who have moved into the UK market. For example, German retailers Aldi and Lidl are following an aggressive expansion strategy, rolling out smaller scale stores and offering heavily discounted limited lines relying on high volumes and an efficient operation to make their money.

In the classic phases of the wheel of retailing there are three stages: entry; trading-up; and vulnerability. At the entry stage a retailer enters the market as a low-price, low-status competitor with operating expenses reduced to a minimum. This is reflected in restricted services, low rent locations, modest store shopping atmosphere and limited product mix. As the retailer becomes successful, and accepted, others emulate the original business. The retailer then trades-up through success to improved facilities, and offers enhanced services and improved or additional product lines. With maturity, the retailer becomes more vulnerable due to an inability to adapt, producing a decline in the rate of return from the business. The entry of new lower price innovators signals decline for the mature business.

In practice the wheel of retailing can explain some of the changes in the UK retail marketplace. The changes from corner store to supermarket as price vulnerability occurred fits the model. However, the factors in modern retailing such as size of operation of leading retailers, the importance placed on branding and loyalty schemes, and a continual drive for efficiency by all personnel create highly competitive operations. The basic difficulty in utilising the wheel of retailing approach is the timescale. It can vary extensively, depending on the speed of economic, social and technological change.

The retail accordion theory

The retail accordion theory suggests that retailers initially enter a market as a general retailer; with experience they focus down on particular product sectors and/or consumer groups. Over time they begin to diversify their offer in order to grow, but again will revert to specialisation. The premise of the retail accordion is that the changes in retail operations are related to strategies that alter the width (selection) of the merchandise mix. An example of this type of pattern is the establishment of small-scale specialist food retailers such as grocers or bakers followed, over time, by the takeover of the food retail sector by large-scale superstores with diverse product ranges. We are now witnessing the next stage in this pattern: the re-emergence of the small store in the guise of convenience formats such as Tesco's Metro and Sainsbury's Local with limited ranges for a different market but trading under the same name, brand and reputation.

We can see this specialisation occurring due to:

- store sizes in some locations being unable to accommodate greater variety in order to compete and therefore specialisation occurs;
- greater disposable income and large urban populations allowing for profitable segmentation;
- the importance of the specialist shopping experience and convenience stores;
- established retailing brands wanting to obtain more specialist coverage of the market.

MINICASE 1.2

The values behind retailing

Sir Richard Greenbury (chairman of Marks & Spencer in 1998) was born in 1936 and he joined Marks & Spencer in 1953 as a junior management trainee. He became a director in 1972, managing director in 1978 and chief executive officer in 1988. 'My approach is what I call the three Ps – people, product and property. I have what I describe as an obsession with the product. There really isn't a line in this business which I couldn't tell you about – who made it, the kind of business we do on it, what the raw materials are, and so on. I have an encyclopaedic knowledge of the product. That is what retail is about. It was John Sainsbury, I think, who coined the expression "retail is detail". It is no use having a wonderful vision for the next century if you don't have the product right next week. I know the suppliers very well. All new lines are sent to me every week for sampling. I do sample them and express my views about them. There are times when I see things other people can't because they are too close to it. Sometimes I get things right. Sometimes I don't. If I see what is happening, I extrapolate from that. Good judgement is everything. That is why I always put people before everything else. I believe that I am very privileged because I can't think of any other staff in the retail world which has more commitment. This is a business that encourages you to be ambitious. Ambition, as long as it is not at the expense of everyone else, is a very healthy thing. Ninety-five per cent of the senior people in this business have been in it for many years.

There are great advantages to knowing the business extremely well. At my level, we have what we call a divine discontent. We must never allow ourselves to be satisfied. We must never get complacent. Customers have no loyalty, nor should they have. We are as good as last season's performance in the same way that an entertainer would say he was as good as last night's performance. I am very tolerant of failure. I want people to be courageous with buying decisions. If every time they get it wrong they get a real earbashing, it is not the way to encourage people. One mistake is fine. I am not too happy with two mistakes but I will live with it. But if I see someone make the same mistake time and time again, then I will get abrasive.'

Source: Vanessa Houlder, *Financial Times*, 16 February 1998

The trend to become more general may also be noted as being due to:

- expansion of complementary lines as part of the retail offer;
- a skimming policy – that is, carrying more of the profitable lines and creaming these off from those of the competition;
- a move to increase the density of shoppers in-store by providing a complete range offering. Marks & Spencer adopted this policy with their expansion into a range of foods;
- the growth of large shopping centres having outlets which allow for expansion of lines and ranges.

The retail life cycle theory

The retail life cycle theory suggests that retail developments pass through stages. At birth (termed the embryonic stage in the context of industry life cycles), there are slow rates of growth due to limited resources and experience. This is followed by a time of rapid growth as efficiency and experience increase. Eventually growth will level off into the mature stage due to increased costs and competition and reduced efficiencies. In a mature market the competition remains intense, growth slows and profits begin to fall. A continued decrease in market share and profitability will eventually cause the development to decline and, if the situation worsens, ultimately to withdraw from the market. The less competitive companies, which have previously entered the market, will be forced out early as the market goes through a shake-out period. An example of a company which has had problems in relation to the life cycle is Woolworths. In an attempt to remain competitive its range was expanded to a point where the offer became undefined and it became a store of last resort. It recognised it was not adequately providing for the needs of the contemporary consumer and survived only because it recognised the value of adopting a focus strategy. Figure 1.2 illustrates the way a retail business may grow from the embryonic stage into a period of maturity and, perhaps, to final decline.

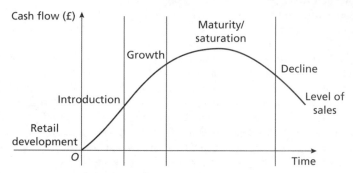

Fig. 1.2 The retail life cycle

Conflict theory

Competition between retailers causes changes in the nature of the retail environment. However, it is not so much the day-to-day competition between companies that causes institutional change, but rather the imbalance caused by innovations. Brown (1987) states that a response to innovation follows a process of four stages. Initially retailers are in shock at the innovation; second, they deny the threat by means of defensive retreat; they thirdly then move into a stage of acknowledgement and assessment; and finally develop a strategy of adaption.

Types of retailer response to innovation

- shock
- defensive retreat
- acknowledgement and assessment
- adaption

The question is the timescale and strategy requirements which may occur as a result of the call for adaption. There is a need to understand the type of change needed, the cost of any adaption and the resultant profitability of a change.

An example of retail innovation as a catalyst for change is the introduction of self-service supermarkets. As the supermarket developed and increasingly took market share from the traditional specialist retailers a direct reaction by the independents was necessary; in order to remain competitive, they formed themselves into voluntary groups and buying alliances. As part of their strategy companies such as Spar copied the trend by offering self-service. The buying alliances also helped the independents to remain in touch with the prices offered by the developing supermarket chains.

Theories of retail institutional change – a summary

1 environmental
2 cyclical:
   - the wheel of retailing
   - the retail accordion
   - the retail life cycle
3 conflict

THE STRUCTURE OF RETAILING IN THE UK AND EUROPE

A number of structural changes in the retail environment have become evident during the post-war era. These developments have occurred throughout Europe, although they are apparent to differing extents in different markets. Three fundamental and interrelated transitions have occurred in the European retail environment: first, the balance of power has shifted along the distribution channel from the manufacturers to the retailers; secondly, traditional independent retailers and co-operatives have lost market share to multiple chain organisations; and thirdly, markets have become increasingly consolidated and concentrated. Table 1.3 indicates the sales of some of the major UK retailers with foreign operations.

Table 1.3 Major UK retailers with foreign operations, 1996–97

Retailer	Operations	Worldwide sales (£bn)
Tesco	Grocery multiple	14.9
J. Sainsbury	Grocery multiple	13.4
Marks & Spencer	Mixed goods and grocery	8.2
Kingfisher	Mixed goods, DIY and electrical	5.7
Great Universal Stores	Mail order and clothing	2.1
Littlewoods	Mail order and mixed goods	1.9
Sears	Clothing, footwear, sports	1.8
WH Smith	Mixed goods, books, music	1.8

Sources: Retail Intelligence, 1998b; company reports.

These structural trends are intrinsically linked. Retailers have been able to use their power against suppliers, in part, due to the growth of multiple organisations. Multiples have grown dominant due to being more competitive and achieving economies and efficiencies of scale, in turn due to their enhanced negotiating position because of their power over suppliers.

Structural trends in European retailing

● increasing dominance of retailers over suppliers

● increasing market share held by multiples and associated loss by independents and co-operatives

● increasing rates of market concentration

● technical superiority of the big players providing cost-effectiveness

All of the trends occur to differing extents throughout Europe. The most advanced markets have the most power held by retailers, highest proportion of multiple chains and the highest levels of market concentration.

The extent of the domination of the market by multiples varies throughout Europe. The highest levels of concentration and multiple dominance are in the structurally advanced markets of the UK and Germany, where the top three to five players account for almost half the market share in the grocery sector. This trend decreases slightly in the structured markets of France and the Netherlands, while in intermediary and traditional markets such as Spain, Italy, Portugal and Greece small-scale independent retailers still maintain a strong market presence. However, even in these markets the trend is towards market dominance by multiples. Just as we can follow these structural trends since the 1960s and 1970s, so we can trace geographical trends.

Independent and co-operative retailers have fought to maintain their market share. To varying degrees throughout Europe public policy has favoured them, for example by restricting the development of new stores or controlling mergers and acquisition of large companies. They have also attempted to fight back strategically by joining together in voluntary groups and alliances and by providing a complementary retail offer to the multiples. For example, small grocery stores may be unable to compete with the range of merchandise of a superstore but they can increase their competitiveness by locating in neighbourhoods rather than out-of-town sites and offering longer opening hours for local consumer convenience.

Retailers are constantly having to assess the changing environment in which they operate and adapt accordingly. One outcome of this has been the way in which retailers have altered their store format, size and location. Outcomes of environmental changes are the dichotomous trends in store size, the development of dominant formats in national markets, and locational issues such as the move of stores to out-of-town sites.

CONCLUSION

Retail organisations have grown in size dramatically, particularly in the food sector. This has mirrored a growth in store size, for example, the emergence of the superstore in the UK and the hypermarket in France. At the same time as food retailers have been increasing the size of new stores, they have also been selling off the smaller stores in their portfolio. These older smaller stores are typically located on the high street and in town centres, while the new very large stores tend to be on out-of-town sites. Thus the upgrading of store size has altered the locational strategy of food retailers from within towns to their outskirts. The major players have consolidated their positions with the use of improved branding, relationship marketing schemes, own-brands and improved retail environments.

Store size may be considered in terms of the polarisation model. While on the one hand large-scale formats are becoming increasingly large in order to benefit from economies and efficiencies of scale, they have left a gap at the other end of the market for small-scale stores. While we are seeing fewer specialists, small-scale convenience stores are very much in evidence. Not only are these operated by independent retailers and voluntary chains, but even the multiple retailers have recognised an opportunity for small scale stores that complement their large-scale operations – as exemplified by Tesco's Metro and Sainsbury's Local fascias.

Similarly, though the hard discounters have entered the UK market to fill a gap at the lower end of the pricing structure, their entry may also be viewed in terms of polarisation of store size and location. Whereas the superstores are increasing their size and moving to out-of-town locations, the discount supermarkets and convenience stores are of a significantly smaller scale and tend to be located in town centres – in part because they are able to find sites of adequate size, unlike the superstores which need very large sites and in part because they are focused on consumer demand within retail centres, not the need for 'one-stop' shops.

Retailers have tended to move towards large-scale retailing, in terms of multiple chains and store size, in order to gain from efficiencies and economies of scale. However, small-scale operators do have certain advantages. First, they often benefit from supportive public policy, for example, legislation limiting the development of large out-of-town stores. Second, they attempt to gain their own economies by developing voluntary groups and buying alliances. Third, small-scale retailers may benefit from clustering in town centres and thus creating a critical retail mass to attract and more easily satisfy consumers.

It is interesting to note that in terms of large-scale food retailing different formats are apparent in various markets. For example, the UK food sector is dominated by the quality and service oriented superstore; in contrast the French market is characterised by the large-scale, out-of-town hypermarket that is price oriented and has a high ratio of non-food ranges. Germany has a mix of hypermarkets and discount supermarkets, while in the Netherlands and the Benelux countries the high street supermarket format is dominant. This begs the question: is the development of these dominant formats in markets a reaction by retailers to national consumer demand or have retailers imposed particular retail conditions upon consumers?

EXERCISES

The exercises that follow help to place the information in this chapter in a practical context. We suggest they are worked through before you move on to Chapter 2.

1 What is a retailer and what is their function? Which retailers would fall into the categories outlined in the grid below? Add your responses in the spaces in the grid.

Retailer that has developed through cyclical theory change	Who:	How:
Retailer that has developed through accordion theory change	Who:	How:
Retailer that has developed through conflict theory change	Who:	How:

Of the theoretical approaches you have considered, which one offers the clearest understanding of change and why?

2 Think about the trends that have occurred in your local high street. Read Minicase 1.1 about the Co-op. What are the main problems affecting the Co-op and how does this information fit with any theory you have read relating to the changes in the retail marketplace?

3 Consult the statistics on the performance of different types of retail businesses (e.g. Internet, DIY stores, superstores, corner shop grocers, department stores, bespoke tailors, mail order). You then need to provide a breakdown by company of at least three areas from this list with at least three years' figures. Now comment on what are some of the important statistics you have found and the changes which may occur in the next decade. Also comment on the ways the big players may perform against their competitors.

REFERENCES AND FURTHER READING

Appel, D. (1972) 'The supermarket: early development of an institutional innovation', *Journal of Retailing*, 48, 39–53.

Brown, S. (1987) 'Institutional change in retailing: a review and synthesis', *European Journal of Marketing*, 21 (6), 5–36.

Brown, S. (1992) *Retail Location: a micro-scale perspective.* Aldershot: Avebury.

Davidson, W.R., Sweeney, P.J. and Stampfl, R.W. (1983) *Retailing Management.* 5th edn. New York: John Wiley.

The Economist (1995) 'Retailing survey', *The Economist*, 4 March, 6–16.

Friedman, M. (1970) 'The social responsibility of business is to increase profits', *The New York Times Magazine*, September, 13.

Gist, R.R. (1968) *Retailing: Concepts and decision.* New York: Wiley and Sons.

Hollinger, P. (1998) 'Survey – future of mutuality: the Co-op: Members urged to co-operate, *Financial Times*, 10 March.

Houlder, V. (1998) 'Never be satisfied and never become complacent', *Financial Times*, 16 February.

Institute of Grocery Distribution (1997) *Grocery Retailing 1997: The market review*, July. Watford: IGD Business Publications.

Keh, H.T. and Park, S.Y. (1997) 'To market, to market: The changing face of grocery retailing', *Long Range Planning*, 30 (6), 836–46.

Labour Market Trends (1998) 'Employee jobs', *Labour Market Trends*, June, S. 21.

McNair, M.P. (1931) 'Trends in large scale retailing', *Harvard Business Review*, 10, 30–9.

McNair, M.P. (1958) 'Significant trends and developments in the post war period', in Smith, A.B. (ed.) *Competitive Distribution in a Free High Level Economy and its Implications*. Pittsburgh, PA: University of Pittsburgh.

Myers, H.A. (1996) 'Internationalisation: The impact of the European Union. A study of the food retail sector'. Unpublished PhD thesis. School of Management Studies, University of Surrey.

Myers, H.A. and Alexander, N. (1997) 'Food retailing opportunities in Eastern Europe', *European Business Review*, 97 (3), 124–33.

National Accounts (1998) *Annual Abstract of Statistics 1997*. London: The Stationery Office.

Potter, R.I.B. (1982) *The Urban Retailing System: Location, cognition, behaviour*. Aldershot: Gower.

Ratchford, B.T. (1998) 'Introduction to the special section: Economic perspectives on retailing', *Journal of Retailing*, 74 (1), 11–14.

Retail Intelligence (1998a) *UK Retail Report No. 95*. London: Retail Intelligence.

Retail Intelligence (1998b) *The European Retail Handbook – 1998 edition*. London: Retail Intelligence.

2 An introduction to retail marketing

This chapter should enable you to explain:

- the origins of marketing;
- business philosophies and the differences between the production, sales and marketing eras;
- definitions, concepts and functions associated with marketing;
- the differences between marketing and sales and what constitutes a marketing orientation.

RETAILING AND MARKETING

Retailing was introduced in terms of its function and structure in Chapter 1 and why it is so visible in our everyday lives. However, not everyone may be clear that retailing involves the activity of shopping, purchasing by means of the Internet, dealing with financial services or even visiting a local fast food outlet or hairdresser. This daily involvement is interpreted in different ways and underlies the complexity of retail marketing operations. For a fuller understanding we require a framework of concepts to ensure we have a basic knowledge of what may constitute retail marketing.

Retailing in its various guises can be traced back for centuries but because the elements of retailing and conditions of the marketplace have changed substantially there has been a requirement for a corresponding change in both techniques and approaches. Retailing comprises all the activities involved in the marketing and distribution of goods and services. Therefore, marketing is a core area for any retail operation as the success or failure of retailers is based upon how well they understand and serve the needs of their customers.

Change in consumer behaviour is constantly occurring. For example there has been increasing pressure on people's time given the growth in the number of families with both partners working; more children arrive home to organise their own cooking or purchases; and extra time is being spent on leisure activities, including shopping as a leisure pursuit. This has led to a number of segments which have higher disposable income but little discretionary time for more routine purchasing. Such changes produce intense competition among retailers. These changes are so dramatic, we are witnessing major shifts in the way that consumers interact with some of the more traditional areas of the retail sector – prime among these are the financial service providers. Changes in consumer lifestyles have required elements of the banking relationship to be handled in a more convenient manner and more economically. This has led to the development of banking services using automated teller machines (ATMs), the post, telephone or by electronic means. Non-branch banking is an important development which reflects the needs of the modern consumer.

This trend, known as *disintermediation*, is even more pronounced in the insurance sector. The traditional use of an insurance broker to organise car, house or personal insurance has given way to a major growth in direct marketing. The use of telephone sales and other methods of marketing has transformed both the distribution and the cost structure of the industry. This has been made possible not only by rapid and focused technological development but also by consumers' acceptance of the new services and their price advantage. However, at the same time as we are witnessing these changes, there is growing pressure from some consumers to retain local banks in order to counteract concerns about the exclusion of certain sections of society from financial services provision.

NEED FOR A STRATEGIC APPROACH

Any change that occurs has to be underpinned by an appropriate marketing strategy if it is to be successful. As part of the development of retail marketing there is a need to ensure that both the positioning of any offer, and the image of that offer, are sound and logically linked. *Positioning* as a marketing concept is based upon a market position of image, price and quality rather than geographical position. It is where a retailer will decide on the 'placing' of their business in a market position where it will be able to compete favourably with other similar retail outlets. This position should be perceived clearly by the consumer so that the retailer gains some advantage, either through being different from others in the mind of the consumer or more clearly identified as offering a particular type of retail offer by the choice of that position. This type of approach can provide a positive image of the retailer. For example a recent success story in positioning is Toys Я Us, which has positioned itself in a 'category'. Category retailers dominate through specialising in very large-scale, high volume formats with value-for-money pricing and strong branding. The success of such outlets has led to the coining of the term 'category killers', so called because the concept destroys or snuffs out various parts of a traditional chain and dominates an entire category of merchandise. This late twentieth century retail marketing approach has led to the early domination of some areas of the market for toys, sports goods, electrical goods and DIY needs.

The approach of many retailers is to aim for growth and domination of their chosen position in order to create leadership. Leadership in the marketplace cannot be gained overnight. Even Wal-Mart, now the world's largest retailer, had only 50 stores and sales of $50 million in the 1970s. We should, however, be aware that there is a reverse to these successes; a high number of ventures end in failure. In the USA in 1993, Sears announced that – after 107 years – the company would no longer offer its mail order catalogue. This was due to increasing competition through the penetration of retailers such as Wal-Mart stores into rural areas, changes in the use of the car, and changing consumer purchasing patterns. However, many other catalogues were doing far better than that of Sears. The problems of companies such as Sears may be related to their inability to squeeze sales from mature markets and the need to improve their retail marketing approach.

The maturation of the retail marketplace has led to the development of schemes which allow improved relationship building with the customer. There is a recognition that relationship marketing schemes will reduce the long-term costs of attracting customers due the retention benefits they provide. Therefore, recent developments in retail marketing have been associated with building customer loyalty (*see* Chapter 5 for definitions and a full discussion of retail loyalty schemes). The ability of a retailer to enhance and build customer loyalty is highly dependent on identifying and understanding the target market, and offering the right type of reward or scheme to ensure the retention of the bulk of their custom over the long term. Just as customers may be unique in their demands, there is a need for different types of loyalty building. Sopanen (1996) carried out research for the SOK group and found there are six different kinds of loyalty:

1 *monopoly loyalty* – where no choice is available;

2 *inertia loyalty* – where customers do not seek alternatives;

3 *convenience loyalty* – attributed solely to the location of a retail outlet;

4 *price loyalty* – where customers believe in seeking out low prices, but will shift if lower prices are identified elsewhere;

5 *incentivised loyalty* – based upon loyalty reward schemes for accumulating benefits;

6 *emotional loyalty* – found in brand loyalty, this is the most elusive to create.

Each of these is important and requires attention by marketing people to establish the future direction with regard to providing competitive prices, offering the appropriate loyalty schemes and developing stronger branding. The current use of relationship marketing can be seen to be in direct contrast to transaction marketing approaches which have been the traditional approach to markets; Fig. 2.1 provides a clear comparison of their differences in approach. As can be seen, relationship marketing has a longer-term perspective, emphasising the retention of the customer.

Gengler *et al.* (1997) carried out research into relationship marketing and found that, because of the importance of repeat business and measuring attitudes, it is a vital tool for retail businesses. Loyalty schemes have recently been extended to include improved targeted groupings such as OAPs, students, families with children, etc. The schemes now offer air miles, extra loyalty points linked to seasonal promotions and financial services. The benefit of these schemes to a retailer is that they can carry out data-mining of the information collected in order to provide improved promotional and targeting benefits.

Transaction marketing	Relationship marketing
• short-term orientation	• long-term orientation
• 'me' oriented	• 'we' oriented
• focus on result of a sale as the sale is the end of the process	• focus on retention and repeat sales
• emphasis on persuasion to buy	• stress on creating positive relationships
• need to win, manipulation	• providing trust and service
• stress on conflict inherent in achieving a transaction	• partnership and co-operation to minimise defection and provide longer-term relationships (with customers or strategic alliances, joint ventures, vendor partnering, etc.)

Fig. 2.1 Transaction and relationship marketing – a comparison
Source: Gilbert, 1996

An important business need of modern retailing is to do things better than the competition, in the case of loyalty schemes to offer better types of incentives or relationship clubs. This fits with the need to develop sustained competitive advantage, with each aspect of the business being improved to a level which gives a superior position to that of the competition. This will be related to decisions over retail location and design, service provision or merchandise selection, technology, financial cost-control, and communication plans.

Communication programmes are especially important for retailers. It will not have been long since you last saw a promotion for either a fashion product, brand of food or discounted good. We are continuously bombarded with advertising and sales material. Each day the post brings yet another letter containing one type of retail offer or another. There are numerous advertisements placed in the media each day and all shops have a myriad of promotional messages. We are surrounded by invasive messages and communication paid for out of marketing budgets. However, as we shall see later in this chapter, marketing is far more than the promotion of a retail product – this constitutes only one aspect of marketing. Promotion is often used to build brand image and we are witnessing a great deal more activity or investment in stronger branding at the end of the 1990s. This may be in relation to the retailer's name or the own-brand products which cover a wide spectrum of price and quality positioning. Improvement of brand image creates more added psychological value to the retail operation.

The background to these changes is a continuous rise in the potency of retail companies. Over a relatively short period of time the retail industry has developed enormous power and is now exercising considerable control over manufacturers. This change has occurred alongside a continuing concentration of the retail business into fewer large international companies. This is especially the case in food retailing; in the UK, for example, five chains account for the major share of the market. Many of the recent changes in the size of organisations has led to the creation of a widening gulf between managers of the business and consumers. A consequence of the distance which has been created is the lack of first-hand knowledge of the consumer's wants and needs. Where marketing thinking has been adopted, the emphasis is on developing a full understanding of the dynamics of consumer behaviour. We should be aware that organisations which use marketing are influenced by historical changes such as the change of power from the manufacturer to the retailer, and the change in perception of consumers and their resultant behaviour.

Gabor (1977) in McGoldrick (1990) lists three major indicative trends in the transfer of power to the retailer in the UK:

1 The abolition of resale price maintenance (RPM) in 1964 in the UK, in most product sectors. This represented a significant landmark in the shift of power, although pressures for change existed well before the legislation. This process has been ongoing. In 1997 the Monopolies and Mergers Commission decided to support a ban on recommended retail prices (RRPs) across a wide range of electrical goods. This means large electrical manufacturing companies cannot refuse to supply discount retailers.

2 The spread of own brands, which accounted for nearly 22 per cent of retail sales and 25 per cent of food sales by 1986. Ten years later in 1996 own-brand sales represented over 50 per cent of grocery sales (ACNielsen, 1997).

3 Increased retail concentration – which is both an effect and a cause of further retail power. By 1986, large multiple chains (ten or more outlets) held almost 60 per cent of retail trade in Britain. This concentration has increased as the leading grocers increase their retail offers with financial services, new store developments, and a broadening of the product range.

Retail concentration in grocery retailing is clearly illustrated in Figs 2.2 and 2.3.

The changes represented in Fig. 2.3 need to be placed in the context of the 1960s, when business in the UK had become increasingly uncompetitive by world standards. This was identified to be a failure of management and new courses were set up

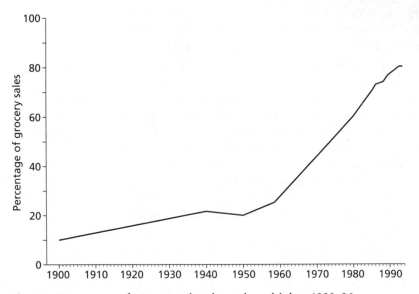

Fig. 2.2 Percentage of grocery sales through multiples, 1900–94

Sources: ACNielsen, 1997; Board of Trade

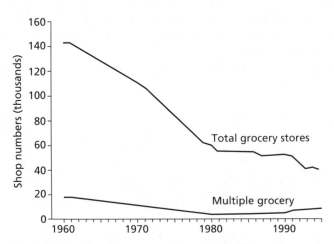

Fig. 2.3 Number of grocery outlets, 1960–95

Source: ACNielsen, 1997

introducing the concepts and applications of marketing to a new breed of managers. However, changes have often been slow to materialise. Within the marketplace the companies that have adapted most successfully to contemporary changes are those which have directed management resources to supporting research into market and consumer trends, and to improving channels of distribution and communication campaigns. The stress is shifting to brand building and involves the development of own-labels. This dates from as late as the 1980s due to the retail industry being one where custom and tradition have been particularly strong, based upon an emphasis on trading or buying. According to Wileman and Jary (1997), in most retail companies a marketing function does not exist; even if it does, they point out, it is likely to be subordinate to the trading function. McGoldrick (1990) indicated the marketing concept was late in its application to the retailing industry and that even though there had been a use of marketing it did not mean the concept had been properly or fully applied. The interpersonal sales, trading service aspects of the industry have created styles of interaction with customers which only began to alter in the late 1990s. As with many other industries in the service sector this sales mentality has preserved the customary, long-established ways of doing business. The need for change has been forced upon the industry by the changes which have occurred in relation to the consumer and market forces. Modern retail marketing has emerged as a business reaction to changes in the social and economic environment, with the most successful companies having demonstrated a keen sense of providing the right organisation structure and complete package offer for the retail consumer. This emergence relies as much on an approach or attitude to business or the market as it does to specific management expertise. Marketing is, therefore, a philosophy which initially relies on the art and science of different management approaches.

THE DEVELOPMENT OF MARKETING

We have discussed some of the important retail changes which may be associated with marketing. If we state that we live an era of marketing, what does this mean? One method for perhaps understanding the development of marketing is to treat it as the development of ideas and trace what has been written about them. Unfortunately, while historical accounts show that trade has always existed, the term marketing was only used as a noun in the first part of the twentieth century. The use of the word marketing in the early stages of the twentieth century was associated with a number of factors which were loosely related to the activity of achieving a sale. Therefore, marketing as it is known at the end of the twentieth century must be considered to be a recent development.

One way of attempting to answer a question about the meaning of marketing is to look at the definition which is presented later in this chapter. It is very easy to describe, using a definition, what is meant by marketing; but it is far more difficult to describe the practice of marketing. This is because central to marketing is the body of underlying concepts which forms the general guide for organisational and managerial thinking, planning and action. Therefore, to achieve a comprehensive understanding of marketing, it is necessary to master the underlying concepts.

Marketing has evolved against a background of economic and business pressures which have required an increased focus on adopting a series of managerial measures based upon satisfying consumer needs. Key to the importance of marketing within retail has been the level of economic growth throughout the twentieth century – growth which has led to improvements in living standards, enlargement of the population, a dramatic improvement in educational standards and increases in the discretionary time of consumers. Such changes enabled the Disney management to launch the Disneyland theme park concept and McDonald's to open their first fast-food restaurant, in the USA in 1955. Not all retail management was well conceived. Early retailing followed a passive supply-led approach; markets were assumed to exist and the retailer only had to provide an acceptable outlet, or means, for the consumer to make a purchase (channel management). At the early stage of retailing there was only minimal branding and competitive advantage was gained through creating efficiencies in operational costs.

The development of marketing is fashioned as the outcome of social and business pressures. The most widely accepted account of the development of marketing is that proposed by Keith (1996) outlining the 'production to sales, to marketing' evolvement of the Pillsbury company in the USA. In 1960 Keith argued that the growing recognition of consumer orientation would 'have far reaching implications for business, achieving a virtual revolution in economic thinking'. He inferred that, at the time of writing, consumer orientation was only just beginning to be accepted as a business concept. A survey of the literature reveals an account of the history of marketing and modern business practice as having developed in three distinct stages: the production era, the sales era, and the marketing era.

1 *The production era.* During this stage there was a belief that if products were priced cheaply enough they would be bought. Therefore, it was important to plan supply to the marketplace, with the emphasis on consistently reducing costs. The focus of management was on increasing the efficiency of production, which involved an inward, product-oriented emphasis to reduce unit costs rather than an outward, market-oriented emphasis. The overriding objective for management was standardisation of the production of the offer, in order that it could be sold at the lowest price to the market.

2 *The sales era.* This is an evolvement phase where companies attempted to sell the products they believed in. If the consumer did not agree with the company's assessments – and so did not buy – there had to be a search for more effective means of selling. As competition increased, companies realised they could not survive without knowing more about different markets and improving their sales techniques. Therefore, the attempts of companies to influence demand and tailor it to meet their supply – in terms of retail product and outlet – characterised a sales era.

3 *The marketing era.* This is the phase that characterises the end of the twentieth century and is dominated by a reversal of the preceding philosophy. Companies started to provide the products or merchandise they could sell – the goods people wanted – rather than trying to sell what they had. They adopted a consumer-led approach and concentrated on improving the marketing mix. It was recognised that customer needs and satisfaction were the most effective basis for planning and that a company has to be outward looking to be successful. With this approach, customer needs are key: the starting point for retail business processes.

There are continuing arguments as to the dates encompassed by the above eras, or even whether they can be treated as discreet periods. For our purposes, in the majority of texts the marketing era is identified as having been established from the 1950s onwards. For a full discussion, *see* Gilbert and Bailey (1990). The important factors, which have ushered in the marketing era during the late twentieth century, are discussed in some detail in the following paragraphs.

First, the increases in demand were occurring at a lower rate than the rises in productivity. This culminated in an oversupply of retail outlets serving similar markets and too many companies in the marketplace. The increase in competition, coupled with the risks associated with the retail marketplace, has led to greater reliance on the use of marketing. Selling strategies can only dominate when there is a lack of competition. As competition increases, the weaker competitors are squeezed or bought out of the marketplace. Concentration, contraction and mergers produce a 'battlefield' for retailers and provide the incentive to adopt marketing as a superior business philosophy. With the growth in market concentration, the larger companies are able to benefit from increased negotiating and buying strength.

The retail business system may be viewed as an organism which is concerned solely with survival and a wish for proliferation. Following this argument, when a business system is threatened it will take functional steps to improve the situation. The reaction by competitors, such as Sainsbury and Safeway, to Tesco's launch of their loyalty card is an example of the way change occurs through competition and the need to develop marketing to suit new environments. This response did not stop Tesco creating a competitive advantage from the launch of its Clubcard in 1995 or Clubcard Plus in 1996, nor did it halt Tesco's rise to the position of the UK's most important grocery retailer. Marketing may provide for tactical change and modification of the system in times of risk, oversupply or market saturation. When the marketplace is competitive, marketing assumes a much more important role.

Second, the consumer was becoming more affluent and, therefore, it was possible to develop retail products which could be sold using a range of non-price attributes. This has required the development of methods of creating, and changing, consumer attitudes and beliefs; it is noticeable that promotion and image, managing quality and services, improving store/retail atmosphere have all become significantly more important.

Third, the distance between the retailer and consumer had been continuously increasing. This led to a need for marketing research in relation to the gathering of information on market trends, evaluating levels of satisfaction, and understanding consumer behaviour. This has been compounded by the centralisation of retail decision making away from individual unit or store managers and into head office. This development was fuelled by the need for retailers to take advantage of the economies of scale of central buying. However, retail technology has provided much more detailed information about customers and their buying habits along with increased operational efficiency in such areas as checkout processes, and shelf and inventory replenishment. Thus retailers felt the need to get close to their customers again and their own size and technical development has allowed this.

Fourth, as society developed, the mass market splintered into a number of sub-markets while at the same time methods of reaching the mass market became increasingly difficult. This was due to the increase in specialist media and the potential for a whole range of new retail products. The changes required improved expertise in the segmentation of markets and the formulation of different marketing mix strategies which would maximise demand for individual segments. Segmentation in retailing can take a number of different approaches. These are often based upon customer groups, product groups and shopping/usage occasions.

MINICASE 2.1

A potted history of retailing

For much of this century retailing was a Cinderella business even though in many countries it was – and remains – the largest single industry, employing between 7% and 12% of the workforce. It also counts almost everyone, everywhere, among its customers. Retailers were seen as simple and parochial businesses requiring little management skill, as fusty as the stock that gathered dust on their shelves. No longer. In the past 15 years, retailing has undergone a many-sided revolution from which it has emerged as a leader in business innovation and the management of complexity. Top retail firms are now run by polished professionals. They exert enormous power and influence over manufacturers and consumers – and over urban, suburban and rural environments the world over. Retailers have grown, first at home and then increasingly abroad, into some of the world's largest companies, rivalling or exceeding manufacturers in terms of global stretch. Wal-Mart, a discount chain that has become the world's top retailer and has bigger sales than any of its main suppliers. It is Procter & Gamble's largest single customer, buying as much as the household-products giant sells to the whole of Japan. The retail business carries clout in many different ways. Each of Europe's top half-dozen food retailers has bigger sales than any of the continent's food manufacturers except Nestlé and Unilever.

At the heart of this retailing revolution lie two things. One is the rise in disposable incomes since the Second World War, first in the industrialised countries and more recently in parts of Asia and Latin America. More people had more money with which to go shopping, so more and more shops were built to meet this demand. The second is more recent, and arises from changes in the way goods and services reach the consumer. This distribution chain used to be controlled by manufacturers and wholesalers. The retailer's role was to buy goods from a range offered by the wholesaler or other intermediaries, and sell them on to the consumer. His main competitive advantage lay in merchandising – his skill in choosing the assortment of goods for sale in the store. He had a second potential advantage – closeness to the customer – but its only use, if any, was to beat his rival retailer across the street. For it was manufacturers who decided what goods were available, and in most countries at what price they could be sold to the public. That distribution system is now being turned upside down. The traditional supply chain, powered by manufacturer 'push', is becoming a demand chain, driven by consumer 'pull'. In most countries resale price maintenance – which allows suppliers to fix the price at which goods can be sold to the final customer – has been either abolished or by-passed. Retailers have won control over distribution not just because they decide the price at which goods are sold, but also because both individual shops and retail companies have become much bigger and more efficient. They are able to buy in bulk and to reap economies of scale, mainly thanks to advances in transport and in information technology.

Source: Reid. © *The Economist*, London, 4 March 1995

The four factors discussed on page 25 have combined to force retailers and suppliers (manufacturers or providers) to work even closer with one another in an effort to provide for the precise needs of the customer. Both retailers and suppliers are combining their talents in areas such as product design and research and development to ensure systems, services and goods will continue to satisfy current and future customers.

DEFINITIONS AND CONCEPTS OF MARKETING

Any conceptual definition of a business discipline is, by nature of its condensed form, a limited abstraction of values, techniques and practices which are the focus of its activity. Therefore, no single definition can be comprehensive enough to describe the true essence or complexity of marketing. Various definitions of marketing have been offered based upon the values prevalent at the time. Early definitions, reflecting the business philosophy and environment of the time, stressed the importance of selling. A popular definition utilised for many years stressed marketing being a managerial process of providing the right product, in the right place, at the right time and at the right price. This definition is mechanistic and stresses the provision of the product offer without due regard to those involved in the process.

No modern definition of marketing can ever disregard the importance of Philip Kotler, who has established himself as the most widely referenced proponent of general marketing theory. Kotler *et al.* (1999) define marketing as:

> a social and managerial process by which individuals and groups obtain what they need and want *through creating and exchanging products and value with others.*

Kotler *et al.* argue the definition is built on the main concepts of wants, needs, demands and satisfaction through exchange, transactions and relationships because these aspects are central concepts to the study of marketing. In 1984 the British Chartered Institute of Marketing defined marketing as:

> the management process responsible for identifying, anticipating and satisfying customers' requirements profitably.

A comparison of both definitions reveals there are significant core similarities. On further examination it is found both stress marketing as a management process. In addition, the British Chartered Institute clarifies the management responsibility as being one of assessment of consumer demand through the identification and anticipation of customer requirements. This denotes the importance of research and analysis as part of the overall process. One important difference is that Kotler's definition is more appropriate to not-for-profit organisations where there is free entrance or a subsidisation towards the cost of a service. However, the most important implication which should be at the heart of any definition is the emphasis which is placed on the consumer's needs as the origin of all of the company's effort. The marketing concept has been expressed in many succinct ways, from Burger King's 'Have it your way' to the 'You're the boss' of United Airlines. This is the basis of the modern marketing concept which holds that the principal means of success is based upon not only identifying different consumer needs but also in delivering a retail product, the experiences of which provide sets of satisfactions which are preferable to those of the competitors. In addition, these satisfactions have to be delivered with attention to their cost-effectiveness as marketing has to be evaluated on the basis of its expenditure.

Understanding the retail experience from a marketing perspective is extremely important. However, the marketing concept – where the consumer is the driving force for all business activities – must not be confused with a sales approach. The next section ensures that difference is understood and then we will introduce you to the notion of marketing orientation.

THE DIFFERENCES BETWEEN MARKETING AND SELLING

By now it should be obvious to the reader that marketing and selling are not synonymous. Levitt (1960) described the difference as follows:

> Selling focuses on the need of the seller; marketing on the needs of the buyer. Selling is preoccupied with the seller's need to convert his product into cash; marketing with the idea of satisfying the needs of the customer by means of the product and the whole cluster of things associated with creating, delivering and finally consuming it.

Current changes in the retail marketplace, from Internet e-commerce to telephone banking, have placed greater emphasis on the use of marketing rather than selling.

Retailing is much more than a sales transaction. Marketing has led us to focus on the full experience of the customer. Even though shopping may take place in a number of different types of retail setting, each offers a unique set of diverse experiences. Whether a shopper goes to the convenience store as opposed to an upmarket boutique in a shopping mall, or a fast-food outlet rather than a sandwich bar, there is a *total retail experience* of the occasion. This includes everything about the purchase, from the journey and parking until the checkout or payment and leaving. The total retail experience involves all elements of the retail offering which provide satisfactions or dissatisfactions to that retail episode. This will include the number and type of salespeople, and their level of service and demeanour; the displays on the floor and in the window; the merchandise – by brands, depth and width; and the atmosphere of the retail outlet in terms of music or other factors which will affect the senses. Marketing has to consider these and many other variables in order to ensure that each and every experience by the consumer is as satisfactory as possible. In fact, the marketing management team have to exceed customer expectations if they are to provide a 'wow' factor to the whole experience. All this is very important because satisfied consumers return and will tell others; they act as advocates of the retailer if their experience is consistently good.

The contrast between the sales and the marketing approaches highlights the importance of marketing planning and analysis related to customers and the marketplace (*see* Fig. 2.4 for a summary comparison of the two concepts). The sales concept focuses on the merchandise or goods being offered, and uses selling and promotion to achieve profits through sales volume. The underlying weakness is that the sales concept does not necessarily satisfy the consumer and may only culminate in short-term, rather than long-term company success. If the customer does not value the product, more resources and effort will have to be provided at the sales stage in order to achieve the sale. The marketing concept, on the other hand, has as its focus customer needs and it stresses the requirement for an integrated marketing effort throughout the company to achieve profits through customer satisfaction. Thus we begin to see the importance of the pervasive influence of marketing for the whole of the company.

Adherence to the marketing concept has rewarded IKEA with a major return on its investments. IKEA, the Swedish home furnishings retailer, started in 1958 with one store and now operates in 27 countries with over 130 stores and plans for further expansion. Its

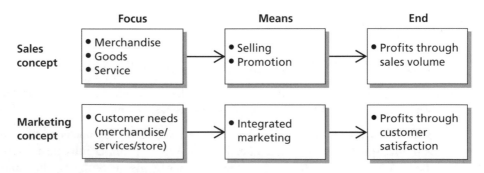

Fig. 2.4 The sales and marketing concepts compared

international marketing success is the envy of other retailers. The brand is a recognised concept based upon customer needs, including: ease of parking, stock availability and self assembly take away packs, modern designs, good value, children's play areas, and the offer of a leisure day out experience. In addition products are constantly updated to match changing consumer lifestyles. Emphasis is placed upon in-store service and staff training programmes. Given the description of IKEA's retail operation, the adoption of the marketing concept (as outlined above) can be identified as central to the company's success.

MARKETING MANAGEMENT TASKS

A marketing orientation relies on a series of management responsibilities. To clarify the situation, marketing can be seen to provide for a business to customer interface with responsibility for specific management tasks. These tasks are more clearly explained in Chapter 5 which provides a discussion of the marketing mix. It should be made quite clear here, however, that retail companies without a proper commitment to a marketing orientation have little likelihood of effectively executing the marketing function. Moreover, they will have an even lower expectation of success if their competitors adopt and commit themselves to a marketing orientation.

The full retail marketing function requires a combination of many activities. Whether they are those involving staff, producers or customers, they are all focused on facilitating and expediting transaction exchanges. The tasks listed in Fig. 2.5 ensure potential buyers and sellers will be able to offer value to each other, be informed and communicate with each other. Surrounding this set of tasks is the requirement for all activity to be focused on creating customer satisfaction.

Task	Marketing function
1 identifying customers' needs and buying patterns for a store's retail offer	• marketing research and EPOS datamining
2 analysing marketing opportunities	• analysis and selection of target markets (segmentation) and understanding buyer/supplier relationships
3 translating needs into products (assortments and store layouts)	• retail product planning and formulation as well as merchandise and stock management
4 determining the retail product's value to the customer at different seasonal periods	• pricing policy – management to provide value
5 making the product available	• establish distribution outlets, inventory systems, location analysis
6 informing and motivating the customer	• promotion (selling and advertising, relationship marketing schemes), signage and in-store display

Fig. 2.5 The business to customer interface of marketing functions

The marketing function may, therefore, be treated as a system which is designed to be an interface with the customer. This marketing system is illustrated in Fig. 2.6.

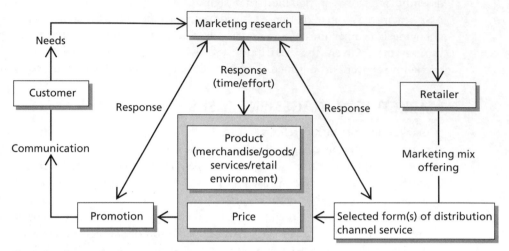

Fig. 2.6. The marketing system

THE ADOPTION OF MARKETING

There are numerous examples within retail of a change to a marketing orientation resulting in success. The retail industry, due to its high service-based content, has been characterised by a history of custom and tradition rooted in trading practice. Until recently there has been a lack of vision in the industry which has resulted in the demise of many of the traditional companies during the final twenty-five years of the twentieth century. During this period we have seen a growing concentration and power shift towards retailers. However, there are weaknesses in historical trends which are still pertinent now. For example, O'Reilly's (1984) comments are apposite and still relevant; they are based on some areas of concern:

1 surplus floorspace capacity arising from rapid geographical expansion may cause space productivity to fall;

2 the intensification of competition as retailers' strategies converge in terms of locations, retail formats, assortments and private brands;

3 a possible serious decline in high street property values, especially as new technology reduces the financial institutions' reliance on large networks of branches;

4 the sheer scale of retailers' investment in stores, distribution systems, information systems, etc. could make them less flexible and more vulnerable to those offering new formats, improved economies and superior systems to the market.

As the marketplace becomes ever more complex, there is a need to ensure that the marketing function is attuned to current customer requirements. It would seem a simple change to listen to customers and provide what they say they want. If we examine the service marketing mentality of a very important piece of leisure equipment – a television – we can see that it began to change as late as the 1980s and 1990s. If you want to rent a TV, or have one repaired, there is a history of intractability and inflexibility of the suppliers who work to their own delivery and work schedules. This leads to consumers having to wait in after taking days off work, or cancelling social arrangements, or reorganising the children's travel to or from school. By 1989, Radio Rentals had finally recognised the advantage of offering to install or repair televisions and a range of other equipment at a time when it was convenient to the consumer. This was further improved – albeit almost a decade later – with the use of larger vans to carry spares, mobile telephones, and flexible hours to suit the client which include various times at weekends and/or evenings. As installations take only minutes and because repairs more often than not involve the replacement of a complete circuit board or parts, the time costs to the company are not excessive. At the same time, the company is able to build customer loyalty and stabilise the number of accounts it holds.

THE MARKETING ENVIRONMENT OF THE COMPANY

In 1995 Argyll (ASDA) tried to reinvent itself to counteract the way it had been caught in the increasingly competitive environment of grocery retailing. The Safeway supermarket group announced 124 store closures and 4800 job losses (Cope, 1995) as part of a major restructuring intended to allow the company to become more competitive with the market leaders Sainsbury and Tesco. At the time, the chairman Sir Alistair Grant said, 'I want Safeway to be a leader rather than a follower so that we are in a better position to come up with new initiatives.' The environmental forces of competition and change can be seen to have caused major problems for the group.

These environment forces affect each individual retail enterprise as well as the total retail market structure. This environment is made up of different levels of influence which will affect the opportunities and marketing decisions that need to be made as a consequence of their actual or forecast pressures. Historical conditions affecting competition and rivalry in company markets; the values of stakeholder groups; and the political, economic, social and technological changes of the wider environment – these all affect the likely performance of the company and its brands. These influences are discussed in greater detail in Chapter 7, which deals in detail with marketing planning.

The company marketing environment can be considered to be related to four levels (*see also* Table 2.1):

- Retail marketing operates as a demand management function within an organisational context (*level 1*) and as such it needs to be adequately resourced and managed in order to be effective.

- A small retailer may have grown (*level 2*) through supplying to a local consumer market and using superior service and knowledge of customer needs over the competitors. However, later growth may require a more sophisticated development of new markets and a fuller understanding of the range of customer requirements. Retail is predominantly an intermediary service which, like any other market type, will be affected by the market environment in which the company operates. Therefore, competitors are as important as the customers served. As a result of the price-led strategies of companies new to the UK, such as Aldi (Germany) and Netto (Denmark), considerable growth was achieved in a relatively short time period. In fact the price-led discounters' marketplace changed rapidly and by 1996 it accounted for 8 per cent

Table 2.1 Four levels of marketing environment affecting the company

Level 1: The company	Level 2: Company markets	Level 3: Company stakeholders	Level 4: The wider environment
Marketing sub-functions need to be well organised and integrated with other company functions. Marketing has to communicate the needs of the market environment as described in levels 2, 3 and 4; and marketing thinking needs to dominate its strategy formulation.	The existing distribution systems and trends in specific forms of retail selling or outlet will affect the retail marketplace. The degree of rivalry, extent of consumer sophistication and the intensity of competitive activity will affect market activity choice.	Interest groups will affect the context of decision making, e.g. shareholders, competitors, customers, employees, unions, government, suppliers, debtors, local community, banks, etc. – all of whom may have conflicting values but all of whom have a stake in the company.	Analysis is required of various forces: ● political ● economic ● social ● technological. Interrelationships of these different forces and changes in them are powerful market environment determinants.

of the grocery sector (*Retail Week*, 1996). The most significant casualty at that time, due to the environmental changes, was J. Sainsbury. For the first time in twenty years Sainsburys announced a fall in profits from £809 million in 1994 to £765 million in 1995.

● The stakeholder system (*level 3*) involves all those participants in the company's value chain – a system within which different relationships have to be carefully fostered and reinforced. The power of stakeholder influence can be harnessed in a positive way to ensure a greater likelihood of competitive advantage in brand management, company reputation, product and service acceptability, etc.

● The wider macro-environment (*level 4*) places pressures on a company which are beyond the control of management. The broad categories of Political, Economic, Social and Technological (mnemonic PEST analysis) involve a series of different levels of aggregation – regional, national and international – related to business constraints and opportunities. (See page 186 for further discussion.)

All retailers need to take account of the environment and its likely effects on business. The influences and pressures of the different levels will be taken into account by those companies following a market-led business philosophy. The following section helps to clarify further what a company marketing approach is, describing the market-led company in terms of a business philosophy.

ALTERNATIVE BUSINESS PHILOSOPHIES

Marketing is a business philosophy which places the consumer and their needs at the forefront of all activities. For example, at Mens Wearhouse in the USA customers are not given less service because it is a discount outlet with prices up to 30 per cent below those of department stores; they are offered added services: free pressing and alteration of any suit bought in the outlet. In addition, a telephone call after 15 days is made to ensure the suit fits properly. Shoppers need to feel they are getting added value for a purchase even though it may be discounted. A valuable knowledge of the process related to the purchase of men's suits only occurs when someone bothers to identify the key needs of the shopper.

While it is important to recognise the importance of structuring any organisation so that the focus is the customer, there are a number of alternative philosophies which can be recognised. Each of these philosophies acts as a guiding orientation and a system of approaching the market. Figure 2.7 illustrates an important set of approaches, especially for those retail companies creating their own-brand products. In order to follow these philosophies it is important to understand the initial starting point within each chain system. This is because the first stage in the sequence of events more clearly demonstrates the locus of the company's approach to effecting exchange transaction relationships.

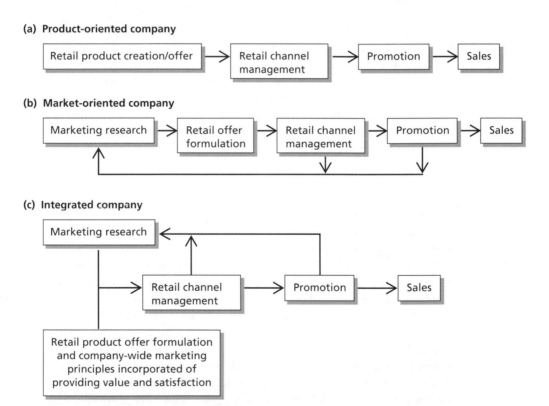

(a) Product-oriented company

Retail product creation/offer → Retail channel management → Promotion → Sales

(b) Market-oriented company

Marketing research → Retail offer formulation → Retail channel management → Promotion → Sales

(c) Integrated company

Marketing research ← Retail channel management → Promotion → Sales

Retail product offer formulation and company-wide marketing principles incorporated of providing value and satisfaction

Fig. 2.7 Three possible business philosophies

The product-oriented company (*see* Fig. 2.7(a)) may be ineffective due to problems encountered in having the wrong retail product or store layout for the market, and therefore having to waste extra resources on promotion and selling in order to achieve a sale. With this business type it is normal to find companies believe their products to be acceptable and all that is required for sales to occur is the identification of prime markets and methods of selling. Such an approach to the marketplace by retailers who make, as well as buy in, products is associated with a lack of understanding of the true needs of the customer. A focus and emphasis on the merchandise as product, rather than an understanding of the benefits the consumer is seeking, is still the basis of a great deal of current marketing. Being product focused is misguided because the retailer should offer benefits such as:

- the promise of attractive looks, not simply a stress on clothes;

- good looking feet and pleasure from walking, not simply a stress on the offer of shoes,

- hours of pleasure and the benefit of knowledge, not simply a stress on books or magazines;

- the 'snob' effect of certain brands – where richer groups purchase expensive merchandise in order to manipulate the management of their impression on others.

In short, the retailer is not selling simply 'things'; the sale has to incorporate aspirations, benefits, pleasure and new emotions.

Retail managers should take heed of success stories such as that of Wal-Mart; the late Sam Walton argued he had one abiding principle: to give customers what they wanted. In addition the strategy was to discount, concentrate on small town locations and aim for excellent employee relations. A product-focused philosophy is acceptable when there is a shortage or during boom times which are characterised by little competition. However, this approach usually indicates inward-looking management which concentrates on improvement within the company rather than outward-looking management, concentrating on the consumer and emerging retail needs.

The examples in Fig. 2.7(b) and (c) offer the ideal approach to organising business in the modern retail marketplace. They are driven by research which creates an understanding of the consumer, the business and the marketplace. Research will be both secondary and primary. Information has to be collected from within and outside the company in order to establish a clear picture of the marketing environment. The integrated approach provides for a sequence of events which commences with an understanding of the consumer, the competitors, the types of product that the company is capable of providing and a system which sensitises the whole company to a marketing orientation. The integrated system helps to ensure methods of improving the satisfaction levels of the consumer are incorporated into each department's objectives. Within these two examples of company philosophy, it can be seen that the feedback process allows the marketing department to develop products – as well as different forms of promotion – which are right for the consumer. This establishes a more effective means of ensuring products are successful and that marketing budgets are used more efficiently. Marketing starts with the consumer and the market; the sovereignty of the consumer is clear. This has to be the correct strategy as it is the consumer alone who can dictate what they may want from tomorrow's retail marketplace. The retail industry is spending vast sums of money on developing new promotions, improving products, building or refurbishing new outlets and investing in technology. The only way for the risk level to be kept to a minimum is through the adoption of a marketing philosophy which provides products related to the needs of consumers.

MARKETING ORIENTATION

Markets are ever changing and characterised by risk and threat; retail marketing, therefore, requires an appreciation of the types of decision required in relation to the complexity of situations faced by the company. The factors creating complexity are:

- the need to consider a vast number of changing situations related to the scale of the modern retail market and its competitive forces;
- the uncontrollable nature of the above forces, and the unstable and unpredictable character of markets;
- the scarcity of reliable and comprehensive information;
- the continual improvement in marketing by competitors;
- the changing nature of consumers.

In order to deal with markets in a systematic way marketing has introduced a number of key approaches. These have been developed to capitalise on the many different sales and marketing opportunities in the retail industry. The industry has thrown off many of the traditional attitudes it had towards the customer, largely due to a realisation of the importance of a marketing orientation. Five main areas can be identified which offer a truly marketing based approach and these are discussed below.

1 It is a management orientation or philosophy

When a company is truly marketing oriented, the focus of company effort is placed on the consumer and this then leads to an integrated structure and customer focus within the company. There is the recognition that the conduct of the organisation's business must revolve around the long-term interests of the customers it serves. It adopts an outward-looking orientation which requires responsive action in relation to external events. The overriding philosophy is to maximise customer satisfaction. This is achieved through offering merchandise or ways of purchasing which provide benefits of satisfaction through the buying process, as well as through use and possession of different items. The utilities delivered can be both perceived and real, as store image, sales techniques and branding can all affect the overall satisfaction level of the consumer. The focus of retailers in the 1980s and early 1990s was on new ways to satisfy consumers. This is characterised by Curry's, large DIY retailers and the superstores which pioneered out-of-town developments. The late 1990s have witnessed a focus on new product development, loyalty schemes, a concern with branding, and the broadening of retail channels. This has culminated in grocery retailers moving into petrol forecourts, own-brand developments and smaller, city-centre formats. In addition, the Internet is in the process of rapid development for appropriate types of product and, where more direct methods of selling are the norm.

2 Encourages exchange transactions

This involves affecting the attitudes and decisions of consumers in relation to their willingness to make purchases. Marketers have to develop innovative methods to encourage exchange to take place. They also need to ensure the service offers value for money which may have to be linked to building intrinsic value into the retail offer. This can be related to the retailer's decisions over the intrinsic qualities of design, workmanship, materials used and features of the merchandise they offer. The customer will be looking for quality, suitability, value and acceptability. Marketers are required to ensure that they understand what the consumer values in order to create high levels of exchange transaction. Relationship marketing is a more refined aspect of this, with marketers attempting to retain the customer over longer periods of time through club or loyalty programmes.

3 Long- and short-term planning

This concerns strategic planning and tactical activity. There is a need for the efficient use of resources and assets for the long-term success of a company, while tactical action will be required to keep plans on course. All retail planning needs to create some match between the differences in consumers' purchasing and usage needs on the one hand, and the retailer's buying and selling requirements on the other. This may involve merchandise planning, trading area and store planning, market targeting, merchandising techniques, own-product development, as well as sales and tactical promotions (*see* Chapter 7 for a marketing planning approach to business). Such planning is used to create innovative formats or to target niche markets. The retailing success stories for the late 1990s are those of:

- B&Q Warehouse – a DIY 'category killer';
- Crazy George's – Thorn's recent format offering household goods to low income groups;
- Daisy and Tom – children's superstores;
- Disney Store – character merchandising and toy retailer;
- Internet Bookshop – the first UK bookseller to utilise cyberspace;
- MVC – music retailer offering discounted CDs, magazines and videos to its members.

4 Efficient cost-effective methods

Marketing's principal concern with any company has to be the delivery of maximum satisfaction and value to the customer at acceptable or minimum cost to the company, in order to ensure long-term profit. A large marketing budget may achieve a great deal but this may not constitute an acceptable cost to the retailer. Retailers have to be able to judge the operational and financial performance of their business in relation to the level of marketing expenditure. The productive use of any marketing budget relies on the knowledge and expertise of those employed in the marketing department and varies according to the type of trade involved, for example fashion, food or DIY.

5 The development of an integrated company environment

The company's efforts and structure must be matched with the needs of the targeted customers. Everybody working for the company must participate as much as they can in an holistic, total corporate marketing environment, with each retail department maximising the satisfaction level of consumers. Integration is not just a smile or politeness; the emphasis has to be on creating assured quality and the highest standards of service (*see* Chapter 3 for a full discussion of this important area). Any company barrier to satisfying the customer or improving service must be removed. The onus is on the company to provide organisational structures which are responsive and are flexible enough to undergo change to suit changing customer needs.

CONCLUSION

From the discussion in this chapter it should be abundantly clear that retail marketing involves a number of special characteristics, as outlined below.

1 Marketing is a philosophy with the overriding value that the decision-making process of any company has to be led by the consumer's needs, the marketplace, and the company's assets and resources.

2 Successful marketing requires a specific type of organisation structure which supports the belief in integrating the principles of consumer orientation throughout the company.

3 It requires innovative methods of thinking and planning so that new ideas are generated to take advantage of opportunities or to improve existing methods of marketing. As such, retailers need to create clear propositions of their retail offer. The clear differentiation of a Sainsbury's from an Aldi or that of a 7–Eleven from a Marks & Spencer are examples of the clarity of retail marketing thinking and planning.

4 The retailer has to create the right environment, additional advantages and value, or loyalty schemes in order to ensure the customer is offered a complete package of benefits.

Retail marketing has evolved due to the different business and social changes which have occurred throughout the twentieth century. This chapter emphasises that marketing has developed as a reaction to the different conditions which impinge on business operations. While we can identify different business philosophies, clarify the marketing concept and describe the benefits of a marketing orientation, the heart of marketing lies in the way marketing management functions in an attempt to create consumer satisfactions.

EXERCISES

The exercises that follow help to place the information given in this chapter in a practical context. We suggest they are worked through before you move on to Chapter 3.

1 Discuss the way you believe marketing is being used by the retailer types listed in the top left-hand box of the grid below:

Major grocery chains Banks and building societies Petrol stations Chemists Others (provide types)	**What is the marketing emphasis?**
Can you identify any trends or emphases by type of retailer?	**What are they and do they seem successful?**

2 Ask some of your colleagues or friends what they believe retail marketing to be. Also ask them what marketing people are responsible for. Now explain the philosophy and concepts of retail marketing, highlighting the differences between the theory you have read in textbooks and the ideas of those to whom you have spoken.

3 Think about the contemporary pressures from the wider environment and list all those which you believe will have an impact on a retail company's business. Are these being addressed by companies? If not, what action should be taken for retail companies to react to the most important changes you have identified? What, if any, are the wider and more general implications of the environmental changes you have identified?

REFERENCES AND FURTHER READING

ACNielsen (1997) *The Retail Pocketbook*. Oxford: NTC Publications.

Business Week (1993) 'History collides with the bottom line', *Business Week*, 8 February, 34.

Cook, D. and Walters, D. (1991) *Retail Marketing: Theory and practice*. Hemel Hempstead: Prentice Hall.

Cope, N. (1995) 'Kwik Save starts price war', *Independent*, 3 May, 34.

Drucker, P. (1974) *Management Tasks, Responsibilities, Practices*. London: Heinemann.

Gabor, A. (1977) *Pricing, Principles and Practices*. London: Heinemann.

Gengler, C.E., Leszczyc, P. and Popkowski, T.L. (1997) 'Using customer satisfaction research for relationship marketing: a direct marketing approach', *Journal of Direct Marketing*, 11 (1), 23–9.

Gilbert, D.C. (1996) 'Relationship marketing and airline loyalty schemes', *Tourism Management*, 17 (8), 575–82.

Gilbert, D.C. and Bailey, N. (1990) 'The development of marketing – a compendium of historical approaches, *Quarterly Review of Marketing*, 15 (2), 6–13.

Keith, R.J. (1960) 'The marketing revolution', *Journal of Marketing*, January, 35–8.

Keith, R.J. (1996) 'The marketing revolution', in Enis, B.M. and Cox, K.K. (eds) *Marketing Classics*. 8th edn. London: Allyn & Bacon.

Kotler, P., Armstrong, G., Saunders, J. and Wong, V. (1999) *Principles of Marketing*. 2nd European edn. Englewood Cliffs, NJ: Prentice Hall.

Levitt, T. (1960) 'Marketing myopia', *Harvard Business Review*, July/August, 45–56.

Lusch, R.F., Dunne, P. and Gebhart, R. (1993) *Retail Marketing*. Ohio: South-Western Publishing Co.

McGoldrick, P.J. (1990) *Retail Marketing*. Maidenhead: McGraw-Hill.

O'Reilly, A. (1984) 'Manufacturers versus retailers: The long-term winners?', *Retail and Distribution Management*, 8 (2), 55–8.

Reid M. (1995) 'Survey of retailing (1): Change at the check-out – economies of scale and information technology have given top retailers awesome power. But can they keep it?', *The Economist*, 334, 4 March.

Retail Week (1996) *Retail Week*, November, 18–20.

Sivakumar, K. and Weigand, R.E. (1997) 'Model of retail price match guarantees', *Journal of Business Research*, 39 (3), 241–55.

Sopanen, B. (1996) 'Enhancing customer loyalty', *Retail Week*, December, 21–4.

Wileman, A. and Jary, M. (1997) *Retail Power Plays*. London: Macmillan.

3 Consumer behaviour and retail operations

This chapter should enable you to understand and explain:

- the benefits of studying consumer behaviour;
- the decision-making process as part of buying behaviour theory;
- motivation theory and Maslow's hierarchy of needs;
- the content of consumer behaviour models;
- the influence of demographics and family roles on retail purchase behaviour.

CONSUMER BEHAVIOUR IN THE RETAIL CONTEXT

It is important to realise that management cannot be effective unless it has some understanding of the way retail consumers make decisions and act in relation to the consumption of retail products. There is, therefore, a need to understand the different ways in which consumers choose and evaluate alternative retail services. While the term 'consumer' would seem to indicate a singular concept of demand, the reality is there is a wide diversity of consumer behaviour – with decisions being made for a range of reasons. We need to study consumer behaviour to be aware of:

- the needs as well as the purchase motives of individuals;
- how demographic change may affect retail purchasing;
- the different effects of various promotional tactics;
- the complexity and process of purchase decisions;
- the perception of risk for retail purchases;
- the different market segments based upon purchase behaviour;
- how retail managers may improve their chance of business success.

Many variables will influence the way consumption patterns differ. These will change based upon the different types of retailers in the marketplace and the way individuals have learnt to approach purchase opportunities. The variations are countless and, therefore, it is more practical to deal with general behavioural principles which are often discussed within a framework that includes the disciplines of psychology, sociology and economics.

The principles that apply will help explain retail purchases – whether they are from a store, a catalogue, or some other form of retail offer. A market-based system assumes that individuals enter the marketplace with money to spend. Consumer spending is directly related to an individual or household's income, the first call upon which will be for necessities such as food, rent, insurances, energy and home costs. The amount of money someone has left after paying for necessities and their taxes is known as *discretionary income*. From this discretionary income individuals may purchase luxury items. However, discretionary income is not an easy concept to pin down because some individuals and households treat particular purchases as necessities while others treat them as luxuries.

First, we should all be aware that there is a process of purchasing which takes into account the needs, wants and demands for products; Table 3.1 describes this process for the purchase of clothes.

Table 3.1 Needs, wants and demand functions for the purchase of clothes

Motivation	Characteristics
Needs	Basic human requirements for warmth, covering, social status
Wants	Potential to purchase occurs as the individual feels a drive to satisfy those needs
Demands	Those wants for which the customer is able to pay

The simplest of models of buying generated from the states of motivation outlined – needs, wants and demands – is illustrated in Fig. 3.1. This process is based upon the response to a stimulus. The decision to buy the clothes may be linked to feeling a need to impress friends at a party, that something is wearing out, that there is a need for more fashionable clothes and knowing where to go to purchase the favoured brand.

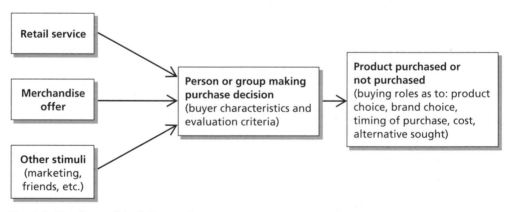

Fig. 3.1 Simple model of the purchase process

Buyer characteristics (*see* Table 3.1 and Fig. 3.1) will influence the type of purchases made. For example, the culture, social class, age, occupation, personality and beliefs of the individual will affect the types of product they purchase. Also the buyer will be attempting to establish his or her self-worth by buying products as part of impression management. The purchase process has been influenced by marketers to ensure that products and brands are chosen to create a social comparison between the purchaser and others. This is based upon the symbolic meaning that brands have built up over a period of time. Nevertheless, the final choices made by consumers are by no means simple.

Snyder and Fromkin (1980) explained the dichotomy of individuality and conformity in fashion adoption. According to this theory, humans strive towards individuality (uniqueness) and conformity in appearance. Through a social comparison process individuals evaluate their level of uniqueness in relation to others, resulting in both emotional and behavioural reactions. It would appear that individuals have the most positive reactions when they perceive their appearance to be moderately similar to others. The most negative reactions occur when individuals perceive themselves as either dissimilar or very similar to the comparison individual or group. Consequently change occurs towards similarity when perceived similarity is low, and towards dissimilarity (uniqueness) when perceived similarity is high. Accordingly, fashion merchandising and sensible stock levels at perceived realistic prices can satisfy the need both for individuality as well as for conformity.

The purchase of fashion items and accessories can also be seen to follow Veblen's notion of *conspicuous consumption*: the theory that consumption often takes place as a means of displaying one's wealth. It could be argued that some forms of conspicuous consumption are declining as those individuals with the wealth to purchase extravagantly deliberately adopt more frugal lifestyle purchases. However, when dressing in styles associated with the working classes or urban groups, as has occurred with jeans, there is still the opportunity to achieve the 'snob effect' of purchasing designer or expensive brand labels. The wealthier groups, or those who have been willing to pay higher amounts for clothing, have remained important as it is the *trickle-down* effect of reference group influence which may account for the adoption of different products by less wealthy individuals. Sometimes the fashion product is created in large numbers to bring down unit price and thus enable trickle down; at other times products, such as mobile phones or electronic diaries, are accepted at the height of their pricing.

Choices over purchase are subject to a vast number of forces acting collectively. As part of the way the whole process is influenced we also need to realise that there are different roles – initiator, influencer, decider, buyer, user – which individuals may play in the buying process (*see* Table 3.2). Within these roles the potential consumer exhibits varying types of purchase behaviour. This will be based upon the nature and importance of the decision to be made and who needs to be consulted prior to purchase. Buying a wedding present for a best friend will probably involve all the above buying role types and may involve a number of people.

Table 3.2 Buyer roles

Buyer role	Characteristics
Initiator	First individual who suggests product/service should be evaluated/purchased
Influencer	Provides views and advice which are valued and can influence the final decision
Decider	The individual who will take the decision in the buying process as to what, how, when, etc.
Buyer	The individual who actually makes the purchase
User	The individual who consumes or uses the service/product

The next question that needs to be asked is: how free are individuals to make purchase decisions? Some would argue that behaviour is conditioned and that it is possible through effective marketing to persuade individuals to adopt specific purchase behaviour. The question remains as to how rational human beings are in the purchase process. The assumptions of how consumers may approach retail purchases are well summed up by Ajzen and Fishbein (1980):

> Generally speaking, human beings are usually quite rational and make systematic use of the information available to them. We do not subscribe to the view that human social behaviour is controlled by unconscious motives or overpowering desires, rather people consider the implications of their actions before they decide to engage or not engage in a given behaviour.

However, it is still debated whether consumers act in a rational way by consideration of the alternatives or whether they are more compulsive in action. The difficulty we have in understanding this is that individuals have expressed conscious rationalisations as well as having unexpressed attitudes to purchase. The analysis of the different patterns that take place – and why – is therefore complex.

COMPARISON OF BEHAVIOURIST AND COGNITIVIST APPROACHES

The study of consumer behaviour as a whole can be found to lie either within or between two major approaches: the behaviourist approach and the cognitivist approach. It is not always clear from the literature the approach that any one author is taking. To enable you to have a clearer idea of the difference in perspective the differences between the two approaches, simplified key points are listed in Table 3.3.

Table 3.3 Behaviourist and cognitivist perspectives

Behaviourist	Cognitivist
• Observed behaviour is all important	• What goes on in a person's mind is the key to comprehension
• Behaviour is predictable	• Behaviour is not predictable
• People are information transmitters	• People are information generators
• People are all alike	• Each person is unique
• Behaviour is rational	• Behaviour is irrational
• Human characteristics can be studied independently	• People must be studied as a whole
• Emphasis is on what a person is and does	• Emphasis is on what a person can be
• Behaviour can be understood	• Behaviour can never be completely understood

As with most polar opposites, reality probably occurs somewhere between the two extremes of these views. Behaviour is predictable to a certain extent, yet can never be completely understood. Decisions are made that have both rational and irrational elements. The importance of identifying both extremes is that it sets a framework within which to work and helps us to understand the more extreme stances taken by some theorists. What we do know is that socio-economic, demographic, social and psychological buying decision variables will affect the purchase patterns of consumers. These influences are examined later in the chapter; first, there is an explanation of some of the main theories of consumer behaviour.

THE MAIN THEORIES OF CONSUMER BEHAVIOUR

Perhaps the most fruitful approach to an understanding of retail demand is to identify and evaluate the broader theories of consumer behaviour linked to purchase behaviour. This is far from simplistic as we are faced with a proliferation of research within a discipline which has displayed significant growth and diversity. The discipline of consumer behaviour has borrowed a range of concepts from the quantitative and behavioural sciences in order to generate integrated models of action. Because of the difficulties which are involved in proving that one model is superior to another, we are confronted by a range of models which rely on a correspondence of belief rather than any logical proof that they are right or wrong. Theories can only be assessed on the contribution they make to our understanding of the purchase process. Complex models may never be proven or validated beyond any doubt; they can offer only intuitive criteria based upon existing knowledge to predict the likely process of decision making. However, behaviour is not totally random or beyond our comprehension due to the patterns of consumer behaviour which may be predicted.

Models of behaviour are a useful means of organising disparate bodies of knowledge regarding social action into a somewhat arbitrary yet plausible process of intervening psychological, social, economic and behavioural variables. The early major theories were those of Engel *et al.* (1968); Engel *et al.* (1986); Howard and Sheth (1969); and Nicosia (1966). These models can be found to share several commonalities:

1 they all exhibit consumer behaviour as a decision process. This is integral to the model;

2 they provide a comprehensive model focusing mainly on the behaviour of the individual consumer;

3 they share the belief that behaviour is rational and hence can, in principle, be explained;

4 they view buying behaviour as purposive, with the consumer as an active information seeker – both of information stored internally and of information available in the external environment. Thus the search and evaluation of information is a key component of the decision process;

5 they believe that consumers limit the amount of information taken in, and move over time from general notions to more specific criteria and preference for alternatives;

6 they all include a notion of feedback – that is, outcomes from purchases will affect future purchases.

A brief overview of some models will provide a better understanding of the decision-making process.

The Engel–Kollat–Blackwell (EKB) model

The Engel, Kollat and Blackwell (EKB) model has been widely referenced and is acknowledged as one of the most comprehensive explanations of consumer behaviour. The original model has undergone three major revisions since 1968 and the current model, while retaining some of the fundamentals, has become more sophisticated in definitional and explanatory aspects and therefore varies from the original version. This reflects the progress made in knowledge which required some adaptation to the original model for its continued survival.

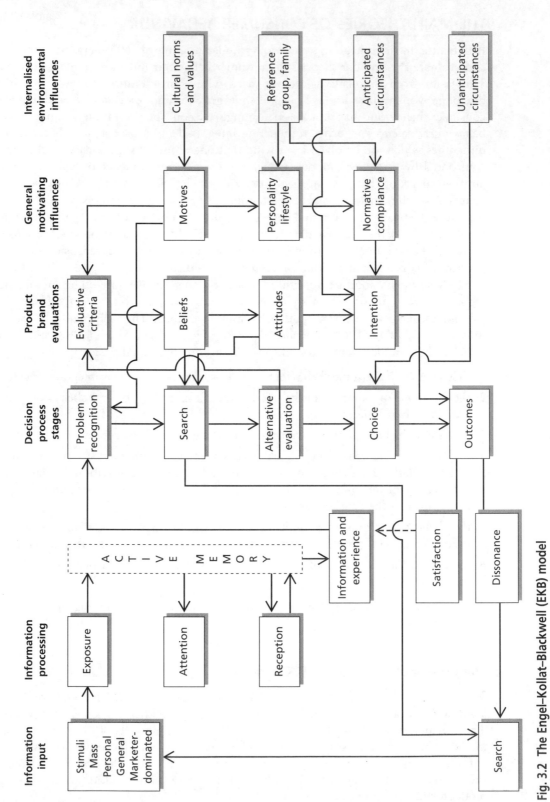

Fig. 3.2 The Engel–Kollat–Blackwell (EKB) model

Source: Engel, Kollat and Blackwell, 1968

The EKB model (*see* Fig. 3.2) takes a broad view, incorporating inputs such as perception and learning which are discussed in great detail. A key feature of the EKB model is its incorporation of the differences between *high* and *low involvement* as part of the buying process.

High involvement is normally present in the decision-making process when the perceived risk in the purchase is high. This element of risk is higher when the consumer is unsure about the outcome of his or her purchase decision. This arises when:

- information is limited;
- the buyer has low confidence;
- the price relative to income is high.

This has obvious connections to demand. Engel, Blackwell and Miniard (EBM) in 1986 stated that limited problem solving (LPS) activity takes place when there is little perceived risk that a wrong decision will be made. As they also point out, most consumer decisions are of the LPS type. However, when present, extended problem solving (EPS) affects the amount of effort put into the search to reduce the perceived risk. This will involve a great deal more external searching.

The EKB model has the decision process as pathways of convergence passing through various stages of processing prior to any choice being made. The central process can be seen to incorporate five stages:

1 problem recognition/arousal;
2 internal search – alternative evaluation;
3 external search – alternative evaluation;
4 choice/purchase;
5 outcomes as dissonance or satisfaction.

The environmental factors, such as cultural norms and values, motives, etc. which influence these stages are important. The model incorporates influence which moves from the general to the specific, which is from the macro level (reference group, social class, norms) to the micro level (belief, intention, attitude).

Minicase 3.1 (overleaf) illustrates the importance of culture, beliefs and reference groups to consumers' shopping behaviour.

Sheth's family model of behaviour

Quite often the purchase decision process is investigated in terms of the individual; for example, some models have stressed the individual as the single focus of attention. It is clear that for the purchase of high price items the decision process involves a high level of risk that the decision may be a poor one. It also often involves the preference resolution of more than one individual. This creates a complex situation whereby, more often than not, the purchase has to satisfy the divergent needs of the group. Obviously a family decision involves multiple influences from its members. Within the theory of family buying behaviour there is the concept of role structure, that is, individual members of the family take on roles such as collecting information, deciding on the available budget, etc. Whatever way a family makes its final decisions we have to realise

MINICASE 3.1

Is the mail order market related to class in Britain?

Offering customers the ability to shop from the convenience of their own homes is no longer something which British retailers can afford to ignore. A recent study by retail systems experts, ICL, found that almost 50 per cent liked the idea of making their purchases from home via a personal computer or television. The rapid rise of the cash-rich and time-constrained consumer is forcing retailers not just in the UK, but in continental Europe, to rethink the ways they get products to customers. Most are exploring the potential of electronic shopping, which one leading German mail order group, Quelle, estimates will account for 10 per cent of its sales by 2005. But, in reality, on-line shopping is an embryonic market and most observers forecast that it is unlikely to account for much more than 1 per cent of Europe's $2 trillion in retail sales over the next decade. Mail order continues to be the traditional method of home shopping in the region, although characteristics of the markets vary from country to country. In the UK, the market has historically served lower income consumers attracted by the credit they

could not get elsewhere. The sector has long been dominated by Great Universal Stores and Littlewoods, which have placed almost as much importance on their finance businesses as on building retail brands.

In France and Germany, however, mail order has been far less class conscious, according to Mike Hawker, managing director of Empire Stores, the UK group owned by La Redoute of France. In part this is due to history. In Germany where shopping hours are severely restricted, mail order provides much needed access to products. In France, mail order was born from the demise of the textile industry, and was always acceptable to a broader range of customers. 'La Redoute is a perfectly acceptable alternative shopping route for the middle class French consumer,' says Mr Hawker, 'whereas GUS is not acceptable to middle class Britain.' Mr Hawker argues, the big players in the UK have been slow to introduce specialist catalogues to the niche markets which are driving most of the growth in mail order throughout Europe.

Source: Peggy Hollinger, Financial Times, 17 March 1998

we are not dealing with a homogeneous unit but with a collection of individuals with different goals, needs, motives and interests.

The Sheth model of the family decision process (Fig. 3.3), provides one of the few examples of an attempt to replicate the behaviour of group decision making. The problem with the schema of Sheth is that aspects of search, motives, beliefs and predispositions occur in tandem with each member of the group prior to there being a resolution of the group to a final decision, whereby joint or autonomous outcomes occur. While we have to applaud Sheth for breaking away from an overreliance by theorists on individual decision models, we may need to question the reality of his model as to how groups bargain and trade off parts of the larger decision, especially in relation to products shared by members of the family.

THE BUYING DECISION PROCESS AND THE IMPLICATIONS FOR RETAIL MANAGEMENT

Whatever approach is taken it is normally agreed that the act of buying retail products is characterised as a process of different stages. As part of this approach, the buying decision is the involvement of some or all of the stages outlined in Fig. 3.4 and listed on pages 48–50.

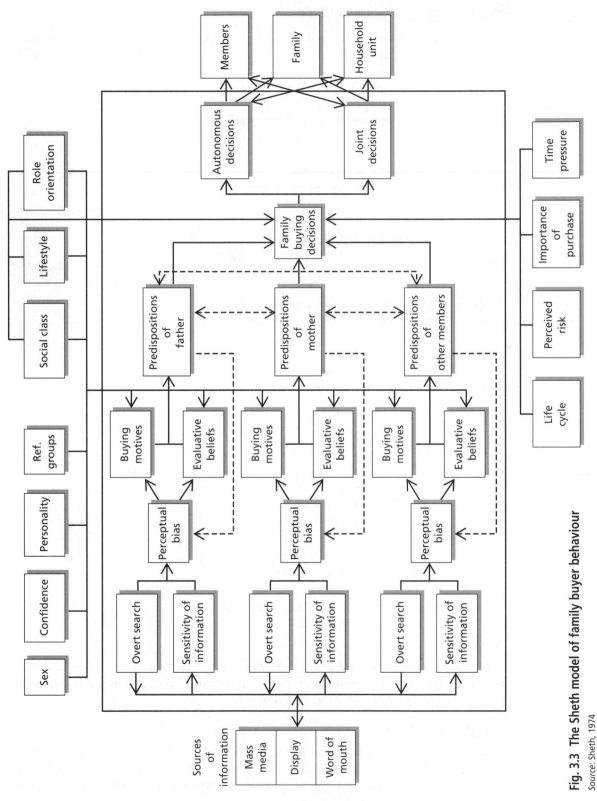

Fig. 3.3 The Sheth model of family buyer behaviour
Source: Sheth, 1974

The retail buying process outlined

The starting point is where a need is recognised and the individual is energised into becoming a potential customer.

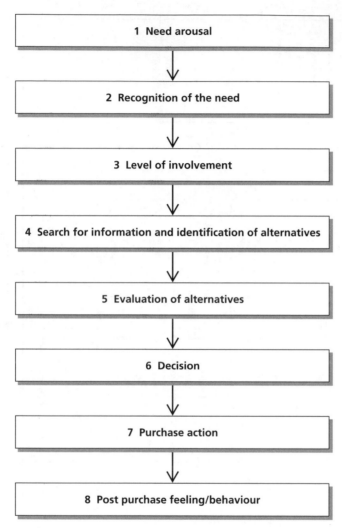

| 1 Need arousal |
| 2 Recognition of the need |
| 3 Level of involvement |
| 4 Search for information and identification of alternatives |
| 5 Evaluation of alternatives |
| 6 Decision |
| 7 Purchase action |
| 8 Post purchase feeling/behaviour |

Fig. 3.4 Eight-stage model of the retail buying process

1 Need arousal

The buying process is triggered by the emergence of an unsatisfied need. The stimulus for this is a *cue* (social or commercial) or a *drive* (physical, when the senses are stimulated) which motivates or arouses the individual to act.

2 Recognition of the need

This is the prerequisite stage based upon the recognition of the need to perhaps replenish the stock of food or a need for new clothes because of a forthcoming function or holiday. Retailers can affect this stage using good window displays, advertising and promotion, and stimulating in-store merchandise displays. The stimulation of demand is important given many shopping trips are simply to browse.

The recognition may be that other secondary needs emerge. For example, the desire for a holiday may require new luggage and leisurewear. A new suit may also be part of a complex need that includes buying a shirt, tie and shoes as well. Good retailers recognise the opportunity to group complementary products or to provide cues as to what else the customer may require. The marketing-oriented retailer will present a total merchandise package to the consumer but also will train their staff to prompt the customer to think about his or her accessory requirements.

3 Level of involvement

This is the amount of time and effort invested in the decision process, for example the depth of search for information. Involvement will differ based upon the complexity of the product, the individual customer perceptions and the buying situation in which the purchase is to be made. This is discussed further below in the context of simple or complex decision making.

4 Search for information and identification of alternatives

Brands which initially come to mind when considering a purchase are referred to as the *evoked set*. However, friends, shop assistants, merchandise, leaflets, magazine adverts, etc. may provide a consideration set. The search for information occurs on an internal and external basis. Individuals will draw upon memory as to which products and/or stores will satisfy their needs best. Clearly any brands or stores which come to mind – evoked sets – are going to achieve a distinct advantage over competitors. The promotional campaigns of brands or products, as well as peer group influence, will also have a major impact on what is to be considered for purchase.

Some customers who enjoy shopping will search more than those who do not enjoy shopping. The individual who enjoys shopping is more likely to spend time in shops assessing the alternatives and gathering information from different sales staff. It is important to realise that if this type of buyer does not obtain the required information from one retailer they will visit another for more appropriate information. There are those customers who are more self-confident and as such will be found to search less. In addition there are the routinised shoppers who know in advance what they want to spend and where to find the products they want. The situational factors which affect search phases are the number of competing brands and stores available and the time pressure within which the purchase has to be made. Typically, the potential customer will continue to collect information until the point when he or she is satisfied that the risk of their intended purchase is acceptable.

5 Evaluation of alternatives

Comparisons are made of the salient attributes based upon the criteria of the potential purchaser. This could be based upon criteria such as cost, reputation or performance expectation. This is a complex stage based upon comparing attributes within the context of brand beliefs and attitudes. As they come to their final choice customers will form some ranking of preference among the alternatives. Also, the consumer may be trying to satisfy both functional needs related to the performance of the product as well as psychological needs associated with the gratification shoppers obtain in terms of self-image. For example, a designer label shirt may not be functionally as good as another shirt but may be chosen because it will say something about the wearer. Usually the customer will form a purchase intention at this stage but they could also seek additional information or delay the purchase if they remain unsure of the outcome.

6 Decision

Choice is made as part of a problem-solving exercise to select on the basis of the overall balance of evaluation, with the most favoured offer, brand and method of purchase being selected.

7 Purchase action

This may be affected by the available merchandise: for example, colours or size. It may also be affected by the type of transaction, based upon credit facilities or payment methods.

8 Post purchase feeling/behaviour

This is the feeling the individual experiences after the purchase. Quite often with important purchases the purchaser will doubt the wisdom of their choice or have some dissatisfaction; they may have a need for reassurance to reduce what is known as *cognitive dissonance* or disequilibrium. This state is when tension results from holding two conflicting ideas or beliefs at the same time. If the doubt over purchase is high, it may affect use of the product or result in a decision not to repurchase. This psychological state of anxiety is reduced by the means of guarantees, telephone helplines to deal with queries, or as 'no-quibble' return policies such as those operated by Marks & Spencer. It is also reduced through advertising which reinforces the wisdom of having made the purchase. The post-purchase process is related to how well the customer has been satisfied on the basis of their expectations of the product and store.

The buying decision process can be simple or complex

In the case of high risk purchases such as expensive items, medicinal cures or presents for those we care about, the purchase is often of a complex nature where an individual will be likely to go through each of the eight stages outlined. This type of purchase routeing is sometimes termed a *complex* or *'high involvement'* purchase. We have already touched upon this with the EKB model of consumer behaviour. As part of the high involvement process, customers will spend more time and effort to seek out information and evaluate alternative products. Customers who are trying to satisfy important needs may require, or be reassured by, in-store merchandise displays which reduce uncertainty and risk. For example, a purchase of a bed to help with a bad back may require a cutaway mattress to show how the springs will provide support. The provision of in-store videos, brochures and leaflets to explain the merchandise and describe its specifications – in terms that the customer understands – will assist in the sale of merchandise.

For routine, habitual or normal day-to-day purchase items, however, the process is more elementary and often termed *simplistic* or *'low involvement'*. The phases at 3, 4 and 5 above are often ignored or skipped through. For example, the purchase of regular items such as salt, sugar and matches will be low involvement. As a general rule goods that are purchased more frequently, are less expensive and perform functional roles are related to a simplified process of purchase. With low involvement the customer relies more on personal knowledge due to successful prior experiences; even if the purchase is expensive, through prior satisfaction the process may be simplistic. The consumer may be brand or store loyal because they have been highly satisfied with previous purchases and, therefore, may adopt a low involvement route of purchase.

Store loyalty exists when consumers habitually visit the same store because they are satisfied with the shopping experience and products on offer. Store loyalty may be enhanced by selecting the right location, offering breadth and depth of merchandise selection, creating the right sales ambience or atmosphere, promoting goods intelligently, providing optimum service standards and rewarding frequent customers through loyalty schemes.

We can examine the product categories of retail to understand the links to different characteristics of the purchase (*see* Table 3.4).

Table 3.4 Product categories and level of purchase involvement

Product category	Characteristics of purchase
Convenience	There is frequent purchase with little effort exerted to compare or judge alternatives – the typical process is low involvement
Shopping	Price, quality and value comparisons are made – the typical process is medium involvement
Speciality	Due to the specialist aspects of the purchase, the perception of quality and value are relevant. Given ignorance often exists regarding the product, the risk is higher. The typical process is therefore high involvement
Fashion	Fashion products are highly susceptible to peer and reference group influences. However, some fashion products have slower rises to popularity than others with gradual declines – the typical process is medium to high involvement

The different aspects of perceived risk

The retail service encounter can be characterised as a moment of self-realisation; that is, the customer assesses the quality of the service encounter as well as his or her own personal feelings about the possible purchase. Retail purchases are associated with:

● some risk of the decision making leading to a negative physical or tangible consequence;

● the uncertainty of the decision with regard to subjective consequences.

Uncertainty is often associated with personal reservations and risk. Therefore, there is a requirement placed on retailers to understand its complexity. Retail has developed rapidly over the past few decades, led by a marketing thrust which has created diversity of supply, focused on important consumer segments and stimulated high levels of demand. Within this development, marketing has often concentrated more on improving the product than understanding the consumer and the complexity of their decision processes.

Retail products may involve complex decision making because the purchase is often personal and thus often of relatively high risk. This is promulgated on the basis of worries about the *economic*, *physical*, *psychological* and *performance* aspects of the purchase.

Economic risk

The risk can be *economic*, involving the purchaser in the problem of deciding whether or not the product offer is of good value or not. Consumers face economic or financial risk when they purchase retail products which they are not sure will deliver the desired benefits. Retail sometimes involves the purchase of an expensive product which cannot be easily assessed prior to purchase and being taken home. This type of risk is heightened for those with low levels of disposable income for whom the purchase represents a major expenditure.

Physical risk

Some products may be perceived to be dangerous such as children's toys or electrical goods which have unknown brand names. It may be the case that some people have a fear of electrical goods or medicines, irrespective of what brand they purchase.

Psychological risk

Status can be lost through patronising the wrong stores or using companies which have a poor image. The fear is that the peer group of the consumer may ask, 'Where on earth did you buy this?' This risk occurs when the potential customer feels the purchase may not reflect the self-image they wish to portray.

Performance risk

This risk is experienced where the effectiveness of different brands cannot be assessed in advance. This type of risk is associated with feelings that the product may not deliver the desired benefits. For those who made a bad purchase such as a poor holiday or an uncomfortable new bed, there is unlikely to be an opportunity to make up for it by attempting to have another, better holiday or to replace the bed in the same year. Most consumers do not have the additional money or holiday entitlement to make good the purchase if it goes wrong.

From a marketing point of view these risks have to be minimised through product and promotion strategies. Creating and delivering communication campaigns helps to convince the potential customer of the reliability of the company and will lessen the feeling of risk. By acquiring information the consumer builds up mental pictures and attitudes which create the expectation of positive benefits from the retail or consumption experience.

Consistency of offering will allow the consumer to learn to worry less about risk. It is therefore important for retailers to have an understanding of how expectations will affect the service experience. The development of brand or store loyalty is far easier if the consistency of service is managed properly. If this is successful, the resulting reputation will lead to risk-reduction perceptions.

Influences on the consumption process

The consumer decision processes can be found to fall within a simplified framework of influence. These influences have been researched by many different authors. It can be found that investigation has centred on the following four areas.

1 *Energisers of demand*. These are the forces of motivation which lead a potential consumer to decide upon a shopping visit or to seek out a product.

2 *Filterers of demand*. Even though motivation may exist, demand is constrained or channelled due to: economic factors (social class and disposable income), sociological factors (reference groups, cultural values), and psychological factors (perception of risk, personality, attitudes).

3 *Effecters*. The consumer will have developed ideas of a product or brand from its promotion, development of image, and information which is generally available (learning, attitudes, associations). These effecters will heighten or dampen the various energisers which lead to consumer action. In addition an effecter could be the position, display and type of merchandise which creates an impulse purchase. For example, grocery items which are located at end-of-aisle displays, and placed at eye level, often exhibit increased demand.

4 *Roles*. The important role is that of family member who is normally involved in the different tasks of the purchase process and the final resolving of decisions about when, where, and how the group will consume the retail product (family influence, cultural influence).

Energisers or motivational forces – the need and involvement stage

The classic dictionary definition of motivation is derived from the word 'motivate' which is to cause (a person) to act in a certain way due to compelling forces; or to stimulate interest. There is also reference to the word 'motive' which is concerned with initiating movement or inducing a person to act. As would be expected, the concept of motivation offers insight as one of the major determinants of consumer behaviour.

Tauber (1972) suggested shoppers utilise six categories of personal motivation:

1 *role playing* – shopping may be a learned and expected behaviour pattern which, for some, becomes an integral part of their role;

2 *diversion* – shopping may provide an escape from the daily routine, a form of recreation; it can provide a diversionary pastime for individuals or free entertainment for the family;

3 *self-gratification* – the shopping trip may represent a remedy for loneliness or boredom, with the act of purchasing being an attempt to alleviate depression;

4 *learning about new trends* – includes a desire for continuation of personal education. Many people enjoy shopping as an opportunity to see new things and get new ideas;

5 *physical activity* – the exercise provided by shopping is an attraction to some, especially those whose work and travel modes provide little opportunity for exercise;

6 *sensory stimulation* – the shopping environment may provide for many forms of stimulation, through light, colours, sounds, scents and through handling the products.

In addition to the above it was identified that shopping activity is also characterised by the following five social motives.

1 *Social experiences outside the home.* In a similar way to the social setting of the traditional market, the shopping area can provide the occasion for social interaction – meeting friends or simply 'people watching'.

2 *Communication with others having a similar interest.* Hobby, sports and even DIY shops allow the opportunity to associate with staff and shoppers with similar interests.

3 *Peer group attraction.* Using a particular store may reflect a desire to be associated with the group to which one chooses or aspires to belong. This may be particularly significant in patronising a store which is seen to be associated with a high status or a 'trend' image.

4 *Status and authority.* In the stores that seek to serve the customer – especially when they are contemplating high-cost, comparison purchases – some shoppers enjoy being 'waited on' while in the store.

5 *Pleasure of bargaining.* Some derive satisfaction from the process of haggling or from shopping around to obtain the best bargains.

As with most of the authors dealing with motivation the research is qualitative; therefore, the proportion of shopping which would exhibit one type of motivation rather than another is difficult to judge. What we do know is that the patronage of a retail outlet will be based upon certain common motives. These are:

- its *convenience* in terms of the time required to reach the outlet, perhaps park, walk around to find the product and then pay;
- the *reputation* of the retailer as judged by self, friends and other retailers;
- *retail environment characteristics* such as ambience, decoration, displays, lighting, heating or air conditioning. Many customers seek to browse and explore the retail outlet offerings;
- *service encounter expectations* of the friendliness of the staff, their knowledge, return policy arrangements, the efficiency and courteousness of the transaction, the after-sales service. The expectation of queues and other shopper numbers;
- *expectations of the merchandise* – that the variety, value for money, quality and brands will fulfil the needs of the visit;
- *expectations of value* – value for money through fair pricing, loyalty rewards, guarantees.

If the retail outlet image, or service delivery policy, corresponds to the customer's need priority then improved loyalty is a likely result. If the priority is convenience, then a customer will be willing to patronise an outlet which is close but perhaps more expensive. We should be aware that convenience in terms of the ease of shopping and paying is becoming more important. This is because, due to social pressures, the time that an individual is willing to allocate to shopping has been declining – explaining the popularity of convenience stores. Alternatively some customers may value the shopping experience and want better levels of service. This is why some retailers play music in stores to encourage longer browsing times and the higher probability of a sale. Once a consumer has found a retail experience which suits him, or her, repeat visits and store loyalty are more likely.

There are different types of shopping trip. A number of studies have identified that households have a routine of supermarket shopping which includes one weekly main trip and other secondary purchases. The main trip is planned to cover most of a household's grocery needs. In the USA nearly all supermarket trips are by car whereas in the UK about 80 per cent are by car. Larger outlets are able to draw in customers from longer distances as consumers are willing to spend more time travelling to utilise these stores because of the wider range of merchandise on offer and ancillary services such as an integral snack and coffee bar.

UNDERSTANDING MOTIVATION – MASLOW'S HIERARCHY MODEL

It could be argued that due to its simplicity, Maslow's need hierarchy is probably the best known theory of motivation. It is used in industrial, organisation and social science texts on a regular basis. The theory of motivation proposed by Abraham Maslow is in the form of a ranking, or hierarchy, of individuals' needs (1943). Maslow considered the factors which led to an ultimate goal of achieving self-actualisation or fulfilment. He argued that if some of the higher needs in the hierarchy were not satisfied, then the lower needs – the physiological ones – would dominate behaviour. If a lower need, or needs were satisfied, however, they would no longer motivate and the individual would be motivated by the next level in the hierarchy. He initially proposed that the individual would endeavour to satisfy the needs of each level on a sequential basis but later accepted that individuals would attempt to satisfy needs at more than one level simultaneously.

The model shape given to Maslow's series of motivations is normally triangular which seemingly indicates a narrowing toward a higher level set of motivations. Alternatively it is illustrated by way of five steps. There seems little empirical evidence to suggest why any of these shapes – as opposed to, say, overlapping Venn diagrams which blur the changes in motivation – is more accurate as a representation. Therefore, the following hierarchy list, rather than a model, is offered.

High	5	**Self-actualisation** – self-fulfilment and realisation, enriching experiences
	4	**Esteem** – ego needs, success, status, recognition, accomplishments
	3	**Belongingness** – acceptance, affection, giving and receiving love
	2	**Safety** – security, shelter, freedom from fear and anxiety
Low	1	**Physiological** – hunger, thirst, sex, rest, sleep, activity

Maslow (1968) identified that there are two motivational types of sequence mechanism in motivation. These can be greatly simplified as:

- deficiency or tension reducing motives;
- inductive or aroused seeking motives.

Maslow maintained that his theory of motivation is holistic and dynamic and can be applied to both work and non-work spheres of life. Despite his claims, Maslow's hierarchy of needs has received no clear support from research.

Maslow treats his need levels as universal and innate. However, he accepts that they have inherent weakness due to instinctual reasons; they can be modified, accelerated or inhibited by the environment. He also states that while all the needs are innate, only those behaviours which satisfy physiological needs are unlearned. While a great deal of demand theory has been built upon Maslow's approach, it is not clear from his work why he selected five basic needs; why they are ranked as they are; how he could justify his model when he never carried out applied observation or experiment; and why he never tried to expand the original set of motives. His theory was developed out of a study of neurotic people and he argued that he was not convinced that the selective use of its application elsewhere (in organisational theory) was legitimate (1965).

The early humanistic values of Maslow seem to have led him to create a model where self-actualisation is valued as the level 'man' should aspire to. It is not as if Maslow has been extended or distorted by behaviour theorists but simply that he has provided a convenient set of containers which can be relatively easily labelled. The notion that a comprehensive coverage of human needs can be organised into an understandable hierarchical framework is of obvious benefit for authors. If individuals are satisfying basic needs and seeking self-fulfilment, then retailers have to understand the need to offer products which allow consumers the opportunity to fulfil their higher needs of self-improvement, the attainment of individuality, provide status and give some deeper meaning in life. Some exclusive brands achieve this but many other brand strategies set out to create these associations.

Within Maslow's model human action is connected to predetermined, understandable and predictable aspects of action. This is very much in the behaviourist tradition of psychology as opposed to the cognitivist approach, which stresses the concepts of irrationality and unpredictability of behaviour. However, Maslow's theory does allow for people to transcend the mere embodiment of biological needs, an ability which set them apart from other species.

To some extent the popularity of Maslow's theory can be understood in moral terms. It suggests that, given the right circumstances, people will grow out of their concern for the materialistic aspects of life and become more interested in 'higher' things. In examining the needs that Maslow has isolated, we should question some of those that may be absent. For example, individuals often strive for dominance or abasement, for intrinsic as well as extrinsic reward, and they often sublimate one need for another.

One trend which may be loosely linked to Maslow's need for improvement in self-esteem is the *compulsive shopper*. In recent years there has been the identification of the deviant pattern of compulsive shopping. This type of shopper has been identified in Europe and in other countries. In the USA about 6 per cent of shoppers are thought to exhibit some form of this trait. The characteristic is associated with the purchase of a range of clothes, shoes and goods that are not required and may never be used. The situation can be a psychological difficulty, becoming a financial problem and causing great distress. The behaviour often occurs among individuals who are unhappy and are suffering emotional difficulties. Compulsive buyers obtain emotional release or improved mood states when they purchase. The urge to purchase is stronger than their decision not to purchase. It is found compulsive buying is mainly carried out by women who have low self-esteem. They are usually trying to reward themselves through conspicuous consumption and, to gain recognition, will often talk about their purchases.

There are other shoppers who have been identified as definite behavioural types. There is the *economic consumer* who is oriented to be as careful as possible in the use of their finances and time. This consumer is focused on the value of purchases. The *befriending consumer*, sometimes referred to as 'personalising', likes to develop strong personal attachments with store employees as a substitute for social contact. This type of shopper seeks out more intimate store types. The *ethical consumer* is happiest shopping in a small business and wants to help out local store merchants, particularly the 'little guy'. The *apathetic consumer* does not like to shop. Convenience is paramount to minimise the time and trouble of shopping. The *habitual shopper* goes 'grazing' in the field of shops on a very regular basis. He or she cannot think of anything else to do with their time and derives a comfort feeling in making regular purchases.

Motivations are an important clue to the purpose and type of shopping individuals will undertake. This helps retailers position their store to appeal to the different preferences based upon merchandise, price and quality. This leads to decisions in terms of which type or types of shoppers to attract and how many of them are able to be targeted.

DEMOGRAPHIC FACTORS

Demographic factors which influence demand are based upon the aggregate of individual social patterns within society. These factors may not be subject to dramatic change but account for powerful effects on the volume and nature of demand for different products. Demographic factors form the bedrock of the way individuals adopt different forms of lifestyle in their own social worlds.

Population size, growth rate and projections	Age structure profile Distribution by gender Birth/death rates Life expectancy	Types of shopping trip, given age and mobility of shopper
Geographic density of population	Location by different demographic variables, migration patterns	Geographic shifts and transit patterns by region and city. Ethnic groups, location and trends
Household size Family size	Patterns of child rearing: single parents, child minding, extended family, etc.	Trends of marriage/divorce/ cohabitation and family life cycle (FLC) needs
Income and wealth distribution	Population who are working or unemployed, pensions, unearned income	Levels of disposable income and ability to purchase at different price levels
Socio-economic groups	Social groups, occupational groups, retirement patterns, reference groups, peer groups	Patterns of educational attainment and changing values and culture

Fig. 3.5 Demographic factors which influence patterns of demand

Based upon Fig. 3.5, the changes over the past decades are creating both problems and opportunities for marketers. Most countries are experiencing changes now and facing predicted and projected ones.

Demographic changes – problems and opportunities

Slowing birth rate

Predictions in some countries are indicating the total population will decline. However, with smaller families the first born still requires the baby-related goods of furniture, clothes and additional items which are normally passed on to other siblings. Age is an important demographic variable as many purchases, such as those for babies and children, are age dependent. The trends are linked to important changes in relation to the baby, youth and mature markets. Retailers are keen to influence children under 12 years of age rather than treat them as passive in the consumer behaviour process. This is because children influence their parents' consumption patterns, constitute a very large annual purchasing market, they are tomorrow's adult consumer and learn to know how to buy for themselves and their future dependants.

Average life expectancy

Average life expectancy for both males and females is continuing to increase. This, in combination with lower birth rates, is creating an ageing population – the so-called grey market. In the UK male life expectancy rates rose from 48 years in 1901 to 73 years in 1991 and for females from 52 years to 78 years in the same period. By 1985 15 per cent of the UK population were over 65 years of age. Such trends will have an impact on those companies with products targeted on specific age groups. Many of the older generation, for a number of reasons, did not pay into pension schemes and consequently their pensions and benefits barely keep up with inflation. These groups and the unemployed are likely to adapt their lifestyle to basic activities linked to the home and family. However, the mature market of the 45 years plus groups offers significant profit potential due to its spending power now and better future pension entitlements.

The actual and projected UK population by age (1971–2031) is provided in Table 3.5. The predicted percentage change in the UK population by age is illustrated graphically in Fig. 3.6.

The social structure

The UK's social structure may develop into a polarised society based upon the rich becoming richer while the poor become poorer. There are other divisions such as the

Table 3.5 Actual and projected UK population by age, as a percentage of the total population

	1971	1981	1991	1995	2001	2011	2021	2031
Under 16	25	22	20	21	20	18	18	17
16–34	26	29	29	27	25	24	23	22
35–54	24	23	25	26	29	29	26	25
55–64	12	11	10	10	10	12	14	13
65–74	9	9	9	9	8	9	11	13
75+	5	6	7	7	7	7	8	11
Total (millions)	55.9	56.4	57.8	58.6	59.5	60.5	61.1	60.7

Source: Office for National Statistics, 1997

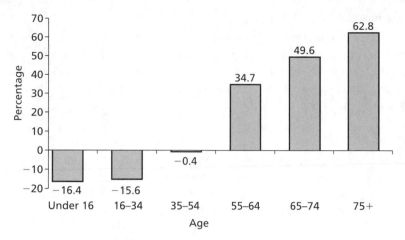

Fig. 3.6 Projected percentage changes in UK population by age, 1995–2031
Source: Office for National Statistics, 1997

healthy or unhealthy, the technologically literate or technologically illiterate, those who are mobile or immobile, and those who are time-rich or time-poor. The implications are that those who are time-rich but money poor will have to be careful with their budgets and will need to shop around for the lowest prices. This social category may well include the retired as well as disadvantaged groups. However, lack of mobility and the high cost and/or unavailability of public transport may restrict the money poor to shop nearer home. If the majority of the middle and older aged groups are technologically illiterate then penetration of the Internet and their use of other means of IT-based home shopping will be limited.

The target group for retailers will be the money rich and time-poor group, as this segment will demand quality products for which they will be prepared to pay a premium. This group are also more likely to embrace IT as a solution to overcome the problems of time constraints and the offer of greater convenience of shopping. The average household expenditure on food – per person per week – increased by 5.4 per cent to £15.63 in 1995. While this increase may be in part linked to inflation according to the Institute of Grocery Distribution (1997) it is also attributable to changing consumption patterns. It is argued this is based upon convenience purchases and higher priced premium products. The report also indicates lifestyle trends – such as vegetarianism, eating out, snack foods, healthier eating and preferences for foreign or ethnic foods – have created purchase behaviour changes.

Delay of marriage

Couples are continuing to wait until they are older than previous generations before they marry. They also wait longer to have their children. This will mean a trend toward more compact housing units, smaller food packaged items, etc. It also means there are higher levels of disposable income prior to child rearing. This allows for the sale of more luxury items and a higher preponderance to consume leisure products. The term often used for these households is 'dinky' (dual income, no kids yet) and relates to a group with higher than average consumption patterns due to their joint incomes and freedom from the time and money constraints of supporting children.

Value of education

There is a desire among young people to obtain a good education and a greater number than ever before are entering higher and further education. This means individuals are entering the workforce later and are often in debt, with sizeable student loans to pay off. Occupation trends are for more white collar jobs which places an emphasis on the purchase of formal styles of clothing.

Number of households

The number of households is increasing due to single occupancy and parents living separately from their children. As consumption units become smaller there is more purchase for personal rather than group use (*see* Table 3.7 for an indication of household size in the section, Role and family influence).

Working women

More women are working outside the home and they are predominately entering the service sector or becoming the sole bread winner. The rise in the number of females in the workforce has to be assessed in conjunction with their traditional roles of wife/partner and mother. This means they are more likely to spend higher amounts of money on labour-saving devices in the home, be more independent in their purchases, and have higher levels of disposable income for leisure activities. However, time constraints will be important and retailers may have to extend their hours of operation and their product range to ensure that they serve the needs of the working woman.

Population mobility is increasing

The younger groups under 35 years of age are the most mobile. In addition companies relocate or expand on an international basis. The implication for retailers is that well-known chains or franchises will be more successful, especially if they take the opportunity to expand by way of franchising or licensing.

Ethnic groups

The interests of ethnic groups are becoming more important due to their percentage increase share of the population. In 1996 the estimated ethnic minority share of the British population was 6 per cent of the population or around 3.3 million people (Institute of Grocery Distribution, 1997). Because in Britain the ethnic minorities group is generally younger than the rest of the population, the difference in birth rates and family composition lead to different retail and product demands. All this means there is potential profit for those companies which can target their promotions to this growing segment. In the USA Sears, McDonald's and Kmart have attempted to appeal more to the ethnic market by the use of African American models in various of their promotions, or by the introduction of special merchandise. In the UK WH Smith have stocked ethnic greetings cards and BT advertise in Hindi to promote long distance phone calls. In addition many food manufacturers and multiple retailers have responded to demand in areas with large ethnic communities by stocking and promoting ethnic foods.

SOCIO-ECONOMIC CATEGORIES

A main division of consumer groups is that of socio-economic or class division. The groups listed below are based upon type of employment of a head of household. The middle class groups are categorised as those in the groups A, B and C1.

A	Upper middle class	– higher managerial/professional, e.g. doctor, director
B	Middle class	– intermediate manager or professional ABs are 17.6 per cent of the population
C1	Lower middle class	– supervisory/clerical/junior managerial C1s are 26.6 per cent of the population
C2	Skilled working class	– skilled manual worker C2s are 21.5 per cent of the population
D	Working class	– semi-skilled or unskilled worker Ds are 15 per cent of the population
E	Lowest level of subsistence	– pensioners, casual worker and others Es are 19.3 per cent of the population

While social class is often used to describe the readership or viewing patterns of various media it is probably not as relevant as an understanding of lifestyle, demographics and cultural values for segmenting markets or positioning products. There are interesting trends toward more home-based working; more women working, especially in managerial roles; more occupations being classified as middle class; etc. A number of changes make it difficult to adhere to traditional methods of designating class.

1 While class position may have provided fairly clear demarcations of buying power prior to the 1960s, increases in disposable and discretionary income by occupational group type has blurred the class groups.

2 Class is treated as being relatively permanent whereas people's careers and jobs may change – which affects the basis of the measure of current or past status.

3 Class groups are treated as if they are homogeneous and individuals are expected to behave like each other. If a broader set of measures are used incongruence may arise, with an individual registering high on one measure and low on another.

4 The number of women working and the type of work they do will affect the definition and measurement of the 'head of the household's' occupation. An indication of trends is the forecast that in the UK and America women will soon represent almost 50 per cent of the workforce. The impact of more women working and the consequent lack of family shopping time is likely to result in:

- increased sales of labour-saving appliances and equipment;
- women having more independence over purchase decisions, with the seeking of identity from purchases;
- leisure time taking on increased importance with the resultant need for leisurewear and related products;

- shopping being skewed more to evening and extended opening hours or perhaps being increasingly based upon direct purchasing. Once attracted to the store, consumers will require the retailer to ensure there is good, clear signage and labelling in order to facilitate quicker shopping. Limited time may lead to more opportunities for telesales or Internet sales functions;

- limited time leading to greater opportunity for pre-prepared and convenience foods or quick service restaurants or takeaway outlets. Retailers may need to examine the need for more self-service and pre-packaging of various products. There may also be a greater demand for reductions in payment and checkout time functions;

- service companies (repairs, etc.) having to ensure that services are offered outside normal work hours or at weekends;

- the purchase of more luxury items due to an increase in affluence among some families;

- advertisers promoting more heavily to the employed female, as a segment, and this may be based on evening television commercials and the daily press.

As indicated above the attitudes of the general public to health and leisure are changing. These values are reflected in the type of clothing and fashions which are based upon leisure related activity. Minicase 3.2 reflects this trend and touches on the concern about the future market problems due to the decline in the number of younger people.

MINICASE 3.2

Consumer change – growth in sports-related retail products

Sales of sports goods in the UK have grown by an average of just under 7 per cent annually, compared to just under 5 per cent for all retail sales. There has been a growing interest among consumers in most forms of sport both as participants and spectator/fans. Favourable domestic economic conditions has led to the emergence of sportswear brands as fashion brands in their own right. In addition, aggressive promotion of the top brands by global giants such as Nike, Adidas and Reebok, have all combined to fuel demand for sports goods and clothing. The biggest beneficiaries in the UK have been the multiple retailers, led by (in descending order of market share) Sports Division, JJB Sports, Allsports, Blacks Leisure and JD Sports. It is predicted the value of the UK sports and outdoor goods market will grow from £2.9bn in 1997 to £3.5bn by 2001. However, those same analysts warn that the sales growth rate in the sector will begin to slowly decline in coming years for a variety of reasons. Perhaps the main, and certainly longest-term, concern is a demographic one: the numbers of 20–34 year olds in the UK are on the decline, which means the group responsible for the bulk of demand in the sports group market is shrinking, and quite rapidly. However, the retailers are confident they can counteract any negative effects of this demographic trend by either selling more goods and clothing to existing customers – British consumers have a long way to go before they match their US counterparts in terms of how many pairs of trainers they own.

A plausible threat to the sports retailers' peace of mind comes from the dreaded 'F' word: fashion. There is always the possibility that more trend-conscious consumers will desert the main sports brands for newer, non-sporting names – which is not good news for specialist retailers. In the US, for example, sales of Nike sports shoes have suffered in the past year from the rising popularity of so-called 'brown shoes' as brands such as Caterpillar and Rockport have become more fashionable among young consumers. If the sports retailers are not to lose out, they will have to become more attuned to trends in the fashion world.

Source: Patrick Harverson, *Financial Times*, 17 March 1998

The changes occurring in society are dynamic and will lead to further changes in men's and women's roles. Men will often do the shopping and it may be the female who is the main 'bread winner'. Such changes may produce different patterns of retail use, shopping habits and responsibilities. The opening up of higher education in the UK and the increased level of foreign travel will influence further changes. Consumers are more knowledgeable and sophisticated in their tastes. The degree of education of younger people is leading them to be less conforming, open to less pressure to follow different fashion trends and to be more confident over purchases. However, they are also aware of their rights and, therefore, will expect more attention to be given to quality control. In addition their early schooling will have implanted in them the values of protecting the environment and seeing the resources of the earth as in need of being sustained. Issues of developing new retail sites, purchasing products which do not misuse the earth's resources, or the questioning of the exploitation of workers in Third World countries may become more important. Some retailers are accepting this trend and changes to methods of doing business have already been championed by The Body Shop.

The changing values of households and the ability to purchase create a pattern for ownership of a range of consumer durables. Increasing affluence and the importance of technology, linked to purchases based upon leisure activity and help with household chores, can be gauged from the household purchasing patterns outlined in Table 3.6. Many of these trends are linked; for example, the microwave may supplement or replace the cooker but it also ensures the future of the freezer.

Table 3.6 Ownership of consumer durables, Great Britain, 1972–94

Households with:	1972 (%)	1979 (%)	1985 (%)	1987 (%)	1989 (%)	1991 (%)	1994 (%)
Home computer	–	–	13	18	19	21	24
Colour TV	–	66	86	90	93	95	97
Video recorder	–	–	31	46	60	68	77
CD player	–	–	–	–	15	27	47
Washing machine	66	74	81	83	86	87	89
Dishwasher	–	3	6	8	12	14	19
Microwave	–	–	–	30	47	55	67
Telephone	42	67	81	83	87	88	91
Car or van	52	57	62	64	67	67	69

Source: General Household Survey, 1994

ROLE AND FAMILY INFLUENCE

As the fundamental social unit of group formation in society, the influence of a family on retail demand is extremely important. A family act as the purchasing unit which may be supplying the needs of perhaps two or more generations. In addition it socialises children to adopt particular forms of purchasing and acts as a wider reference group. Given the importance of family behaviour in the purchase of products we may want to question the preponderance of literature which treats consumer behaviour as a model of individual action.

The concept of family life cycle (FLC) helps us to understand how situation-specific life stage conditions exert a great influence on buying behaviour. The FLC is not just a progression by phase or age but represents likely fluctuations in disposable income and changes in social responsibilities. For example, the bachelor stage represents an individual living away from home with few responsibilities but with the need for affiliation with others and the likelihood of purchases of leisure and entertainment, personal care items and clothes. As we grow older our preferences for products and activities change in relation to the different demands placed on income and time. In addition, as we grow older we will have accumulated durable goods, such as furniture, which we do not replace unless necessary. Wells and Gubar (1966) have conceptualised the life cycle of families in the USA, from the bachelor to solitary survivor stage, as follows:

1 **Bachelor stage:** young single people not living at home.

2 **Newly married couples:** young, no children.

3 **The full nest I:** young married couples with dependent children.

4 **The full nest II:** married couples with dependent children over six.

5 **Full nest III:** married couples with dependent children.

6 **The empty nest I:** older married couples with no children living with them. Head of household in labour force.

7 **Empty nest II:** as above, but head retired.

8 **The solitary survivor I:** older single people in labour force.

9 **Solitary survivor II:** as above, but retired.

Many of these different stages represent attractive market segments for those who market and retail products and services such as: insurance, banking, children's wear, etc. However, the trends in divorce, delayed-child marriages and single parent family households indicate a large number of individuals do not easily fit into the above life-cycle pattern. In order to take account of social trends and ensure the above model remains applicable, the definition of 'married' needs to be relaxed to include any couple living together who are in a long-term relationship.

Each member of a family fulfils a special role within the group. They may act as husband/father, wife/mother, son/brother or daughter/sister. Family decision making assigns roles to specific members of the family. Decision making may be shared or decisions may be made by one person. One member of the family may be the facilitator, while information may be gathered by another. The family acts as a composite buying unit with the different role patterns leading to particular forms of retail product purchase.

We should not expect family decisions to be taken easily. Olsen and McCubbin (1983) suggest that it should be assumed there is disagreement and a lack of congruence among family members rather than assume the family is an integrated and highly congruent group of individuals. Indeed, while much research has been conducted in order to determine the differentiation and distribution of roles within the family in relation to purchasing behaviour, there has been little theoretical endeavour to determine the effects of lack of consensus on family decision making. Olsen claims that family decision making moves away from egalitarian preferences towards a more centralised structure as families move along the stages of the life cycle.

In addition to particular commodities that are linked with joint decision making, Sheth (1974) defined certain situations where joint decisions are made. He identified that where the level of perceived risk in buying is high then joint decisions are more likely in order to reduce individual risk; similarly, where the purchasing decision is important to the family as a whole or where there is high involvement in the purchase, joint decisions are also probable. Finally, where there are few time pressures, consensus decision making may be seen as more appropriate (a shortage of time will usually encourage one member to make a quick decision). Certain demographic groups are identified as more syncratic, e.g. middle-income groups, families in the early stages of the life cycle, childless families, and families where only one parent is employed.

There are other classifications of consumers by life cycle, with each system taking a slightly different approach in its emphasis. This is because the concept of a family or household is dissimilar within different countries. For example, the age at which we define a child or adult as having reached adulthood varies widely throughout the world – even within the EU.

Table 3.7 Percentage of people in UK households by sex, age and family type, 1996

Age/sex	One person	Couple, no children	Couple, with children	Lone parent, with dependent children	Lone parent, with non-dependent children only
Males					
under 16	0	–	78	22	–
16–24	15	7	64	8	7
25–34	21	22	51	1	5
35–44	14	12	69	2	3
45–54	12	27	57	1	3
55–64	16	57	25	–	2
65–74	21	68	9	–	2
75 and over	34	59	4	–	3
Females					
under 16	0	–	78	22	–
16–24	14	11	55	14	5
25–34	12	20	51	15	2
35–44	7	11	67	13	2
45–54	11	32	47	4	5
55–64	21	58	15	1	5
65–74	40	50	5	–	4
75 and over	68	25	1	–	5

Source: Office for National Statistics, 1997

Table 3.7 indicates the number of single person households and the resultant opportunity to develop smaller packs and single servings to reduce the price to the consumer and wastage. In particular, elderly women and males aged between 25 and 34 are increasingly likely to live alone.

UK households with one person have changed from 22 per cent of all households in 1981 to 28 per cent in 1996. Four or more people in a household has declined in the same period from 29 per cent to 22 per cent of all households.

The company CACI (CAC Inc. International) has provided a national breakdown, placing each UK household into a classification group. It was found that a database system of splitting the different residential neighbourhoods into segments could have predictive power for the market targeting of different products. This system known as Acorn (a classification of residential neighbourhoods) identified 40 variables from census data in order to describe the different types of people living in each enumeration district. This was further refined to take into consideration postcode matches to address and housing type. This information is used in different ways based upon lifestyle groups to provide profiles of consumption patterns for food, drink, car ownership, central heating, kitchen equipment, etc. There are several levels of abstraction of the data with the most simple illustrated in Table 3.8. Table 3.8 is based upon small group classification of no more than 150 homes and then aggregated to form the different Acorn types. The assumption is that neighbours, due to the similarity in housing type, will purchase similar products.

Table 3.8 CACI Acorn profile of Great Britain, 1997

ACORN category	Percentage of population (16+)		ACORN group	Description	Percentage of population (16+)	
	1991	1997			1991	1997
A Thriving	20.17	20.37	1	Wealthy achievers, suburbia	15.18	15.35
			2	Affluent greys, rural communities	2.35	2.37
			3	Prosperous pensioners, retirement areas	2.64	2.65
B Expanding	10.85	10.89	4	Affluent executives, familiy areas	3.46	3.47
			5	Well-off workers, family areas	7.39	7.42
C Rising	8.41	8.31	6	Affluent urbanites, town and city areas	2.41	2.39
			7	Prosperous professionals, metropolitan areas	2.25	2.24
			8	Better-off executives, inner city areas	3.75	3.68
D Settling	24.49	24.5	9	Comfortable middle agers, mature home owning areas	13.78	13.85
			10	Skilled workers, home owning areas	10.71	10.65
E Aspiring	13.93	13.88	11	New home owners, mature communities	9.91	9.88
			12	White collar workers, better-off multi-ethnic areas	4.02	4.00
F Striving	21.53	21.37	13	Older people, less-prosperous areas	3.87	3.85
			14	Council estate residents, better-off homes	10.74	10.66
			15	Council estate residents, high unemployment	2.82	2.79
			16	Council estate residents, greatest hardship	2.27	2.24
			17	People in multi-ethnic, low-income areas	1.83	1.83

Source: CACI, 1998

The role of children in the consumer behaviour process

The influence of children in the family decision-making process has not received the attention from researchers that it deserves. While the parents are responsible initially for a child's consumer behaviour, as the child learns about purchasing and consumption primarily from his or her parents, the child eventually becomes a dominant force in certain purchasing decisions. Families where both parents are working are increasing which means less time is spent with children. In America in the early 1990s 70 per cent of mothers worked full or part-time (Gubar and Berry, 1993) compared to 30 per cent in 1980. Parents may overcome their guilt of not providing enough attention to their children by spending more money on them or giving them extra pocket money. Moreover, children between the ages of six and fourteen are expected to do more around the house than in the past, with many having to cook for themselves on weekdays. This means that children are taking on different roles and becoming more self-reliant.

Children are targeted at an early age by companies so as to build brand loyalty. There are promotions utilising long-term collector schemes, direct contact forms of promotion or membership of clubs. The long-term collector schemes rely on the child saving tokens from packaging to obtain a reward. This may be a reward for a school project – for example to collect tokens in order to obtain books as in the case of a recent Birds Eye promotion involving thousands of schools – or it can be for a personal reward. Many children want instant gratification of their needs and, therefore, scratch card promotions by companies such as Golden Wonder are used to provide an instant reward for a minority of purchasers. The most successful brand building schemes are probably the clubs which banks and building societies have deployed in order to capture the early saver. Clubs such as the 'saver's gang' may provide free gifts, organised outings to zoos and museums, and free personal insurance. Some supermarkets and fast food chains in the USA and Europe have formed clubs which provide children with comic books, coupons for purchasing certain foods, and information packages on environmental and educational issues. Burger King has used to good effect a passport which gives the child certain entitlements to free gifts, magazines and other incentives. Banks realise that it is important to capture the younger banker as they are likely to stay loyal. This has led to a number of schemes including offering incentives to school leavers to open an account. Each of the schemes described have the ability to influence the child at an early age and bias their brand loyalties and prejudices when an adult consumer.

In order to use direct marketing techniques, marketers are faced with several issues. The main issue is to deal with any negative reaction the parents would have. Parents may perceive direct marketing as a means of increasing children's desires, and thus increasing the 'pester' factor in their own homes. In order to eliminate these problems, marketers need to orient their messages to both parents and children. This can be quite a challenge as the message has to reach and influence two separate target groups. The parents will want to have sufficient information on the promotion whereas the child will want to see some fun in the offer, such as humour, visual attraction, excitement and reward. Another possible solution is for the marketer to contact the parents first in order to gain their consent for a further mailing to the child. This sort of approach is often used by the financial service sector.

After discussing various other aspects of family decision making, it is interesting here to conclude with a brief overview of the relative influences of family members. Figure 3.7 provides an account of the individual (adult partners) as opposed to joint decision

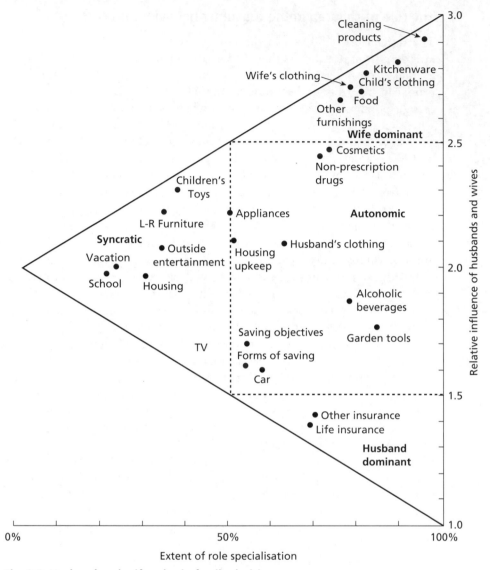

Fig. 3.7 Husband and wife roles in family decisions
Source: Davis and Rigaux, 1974

making which may take place in families. This model is of an average of all findings and it should be noted it will be affected by the number of years of marriage (or relationship), socio-economic background of partners, time available for both parties, etc.

SOCIAL INFLUENCE

The family may introduce political ideas and consumer attitudes to purchasing to the children. However, the reference group of the individual is just as important. Purchases take place on the basis of thinking about the way the purchase may help provide status within the group, how the purchase may need to consider other members and what messages the purchase communicates to those from whom an individual wants recognition and acceptance.

There are four types of reference groups:

- primary reference groups;
- secondary reference groups;
- aspirational groups;
- disassociative groups.

Primary reference groups include the family as well as groups of close friends, co-workers and so on. Secondary reference groups are those where there is formal contact but it is less continuous. This will be based upon membership of clubs, professional associations, religious organisations or a result of the contacts from the area someone lives in, or the occupation they have. There are also aspirational groups to which the purchaser has positive feelings; they would like to be considered a member. Personalities are often used to endorse products as part of the marketing of expensive aspirational products. Finally there are disassociative groups, with which the individual does not want to be associated. For example, if yuppie group association is not valued then the type of products a member of a yuppie group may purchase, such as a Filofax, may be avoided.

Case example – approaches to decisions

According to Carmouche and Kelly (1995), when an individual considers the choice between the alternative fast food outlets of Burger King and McDonald's they will pass through a number of phases. To understand the process we need to:

1 **identify the relevant decision maker**
   In this case it would be the individual involved but if a family, or group of friends, were dining out the complexity of parents and children's wishes would need to be considered.

2 **identify the courses of action available**
   In this case there are only two alternative outlets, but in more complex situations the evoked brands and those considered are important.

3 **identify the relevant uncertainties in the purchase situation**
   Possibly the time available, food preferences, choice of menu, etc. If it is time the three possibilities envisaged could be:

   - there will be no queues and food will be served immediately;
   - there will be long queues and consequently considerable delay in being served;
   - the outlet will be closed.

4 **create a matrix that includes the relevant information**
   This will be based on a set of values related to the three scenarios in relation to the two outlets. This provides for six possible utility values which can then be summed based on the two outlets in order to provide for the subjective utility of each individual. The likelihood of choice can be assessed based upon the calculation which indicates the highest expected value of outcome of utilising either one of the outlets. Of course in reality this iteration is carried out in seconds.

CONCLUSION

In order to satisfy customer needs the retailer must have a thorough understanding of how customers make store choice and purchase decisions. Consumer behaviour provides some valuable insights into the process and, therefore, is useful for retail management decision making. It is important to realise the purchase of products involves motivational, social, psychological and economic factors. In addition there are important stages involved in the purchase process and the type of purchase – as well as the risks of the purchase – which will affect the buying behaviour.

Retail consumers need to be understood on a variety of levels.

- They are problem solvers, deciding on what offer satisfies their needs. All retail activities and promotions should therefore aid the consumer to make a decision.
- Consumers seek to reduce the risk of their purchase. Retailers need to provide information, guarantees, and after-sales services to reduce the perception of risk.
- Consumers will go shopping for a variety of reasons. The complexity of the shopping trip *per se* should be clear to retail staff.
- There are a number of demographic and other changes which are having an impact on the patterns of purchasing and consumption.

EXERCISES

The exercises that follow relate to the contents of this chapter. It is suggested that you work through them before you move on to Chapter 4.

1 Think about the last time you bought an expensive item. Write down why you think you recognised the need to buy the item, what information you looked at, who you talked to about the purchase and why you bought the brand you did. Did you then worry that you may have made a poor purchase decision?

   What links are there between the theory of consumer behaviour discussed in this chapter and your purchase? Are there any other influences you can identify?

2 List the key demographic changes which are occurring throughout Europe. Assess what implications these and the following will have for different types of retailers. Use the grid below as a guide.

Change to birth rates and long-term prediction of fewer younger people	Implications for grocery retailers, DIY retailers, etc.
Smaller families and households	Implications for grocery retailers, DIY retailers, etc.
Other key trends identified	Implications

3 Produce a decision making flow diagram based upon a choice between going to the cinema or hiring a video for the evening. The choice process should include your best friend. What are the key aspects of the decision you would make?

4 Utilising Maslow, list the type of products and brands which will appeal to self-esteem rather than those which will satisfy more basic needs. What can a retailer learn from this?

REFERENCES AND FURTHER READING

Assael, H. (1987) *Consumer Behaviour and Marketing Action*. Boston, MA: Kent.

Ajzen, I. and Fishbein, M. (1980) *Understanding Attitudes and Predicting Social Behaviour*. Englewood Cliffs, NJ: Prentice Hall.

CACI (1998) *Geodemographic Pocketbook*. Henley, Oxfordshire: NTC Publications.

Carmouche, R. and Kelly, N. (1995) *Behavioural Studies in Hospitality Management*. London: Chapman and Hall.

Chisnall, P.M. (1994) *Consumer Behaviour*. Maidenhead: McGraw-Hill.

Davis, H. and Rigaux, B. (1974) 'Perception of marital roles in decision processes', *Journal of Consumer Research*, 1, June, 51–60.

Dellaert, B.G., Arentze, T.A., Bierlaire, M., Borgers, A.W. and Timmermans, H.J.P. (1998) 'Investigating consumers' tendency to combine multiple shopping purposes and destinations', *Journal of Marketing Research*, 35 (2), 177–88.

Engel, J.F., Blackwell, R.D. and Miniard, P. (1986) *Consumer Behavior*. New York: The Dryden Press.

Engel, J.F., Kollat, D.J. and Blackwell, R.D. (1968) *Consumer Behavior*. New York: Holt, Rinehart and Winston.

Fant, D. (1998) 'Understanding customers the key to retail success', *Marketing News*, 32 (4), 7.

Gubar, S. and Berry, J. (1993) *Marketing To and Through Kids*. Maidenhead: McGraw-Hill.

Harverson, P. (1998) 'Sports retailing: relegating less active sectors', *Financial Times*, 17 March.

Hurley, R.F. (1998) 'Customer service behavior in retail settings: A study of the effect of service provider personality', *Journal of the Academy of Marketing Science*, 26 (2), 115–27.

Hollinger, P. (1998) 'Home shopping: homing in on niche markets', *Financial Times*, 17 March.

Howard, J.A. and Sheth, J.N. (1969) *The Theory of Buyer Behavior*. New York: J Wiley & Sons.

Institute of Grocery Distribution (1997) *Grocery Retailing 1997: The Market Review*, July. Watford: IGD Business Publications.

Living in Britain – Results from the 1994 General Household Survey. London: The Stationery Office.

Maslow, A.H. (1943) 'A theory of human motivation', *Psychological Review*, 50, 370–96.

Maslow, A.H. (1954) *Motivation and Personality*. New York: Harper and Row.

Maslow, A.H. (1965) *Eupsychian Management*. Homewood, IL: Irwin.

Maslow, A.H. (1968) *Toward a Psychology of Being*. 2nd edn. New York: Van Nostrand, Reinhold.

Maslow, A.H. (1970) *Motivation and Personality*. 2nd edn. New York: Harper and Row.

Nicosia, F.M. (1966) *Consumer Decision Processes: Marketing and advertising implications*. Englewood Cliffs, NJ: Prentice Hall.

Office for National Statistics (1997) *1994 based National Population Projections Report*. London: The Stationery Office.

Olsen, D. and McCubbin, H. (1983) *Families, What Makes Them Work?*. Beverley Hills, CA: Sage Publications.

Qualls, W. (1987) 'Household decision behaviour: The impact of husbands and wives sex role orientation', *Journal of Consumer Research*, 14 (2), 264–78.

Sheth, J. (1974) 'A theory of family buying decisions' in Sheth, J.N. (ed.) *Models of Buyer Behavior*. New York: Harper and Row.

Snyder, C. and Fromkin, H. (1980) *Uniqueness: the human pursuit of difference*. New York: Plenum Press.

Solomon, M., Bamossy, G. and Askegaard, S. (1999) *Consumer Behaviour – A European Perspective*. Upper Saddle River, NJ: Prentice Hall Europe.

Tauber, E.M. (1972), 'Why do people shop?', *Journal of Marketing*, 36 (4), 46–9.

Tuck, M. (1976) *How Do We Choose?* London: Methuen.

Wells, W. and Gubar, G. (1966) 'Life cycle concepts in marketing research', *Journal of Marketing Research*, November, 355–63.

Williams, T.G. (1982) *Consumer Behaviour, Fundamentals and Strategies*. St. Paul, MN: West Publishing Co.

4 The management of service and quality in retailing

This chapter should enable you to understand and explain:

- the characteristics of the retail and service product;
- the basics of the service encounter;
- some of the ways in which service and quality are managed, monitored and controlled;
- quality both as a concept and within the context of a model.

A great deal of retail management involves taking decisions based upon judgement, information and experience. All areas of retail management should, therefore, be fully informed of the ways in which the quality of the service and product offer are a key to the processes used by customers to judge competing retail services. The strength of demand may be directly related to the way service activities create store or channel selection, loyalty and purchase frequency. In order for retail managers to be better at managing quality they need to start with a knowledge of the specific characteristics of retailing, based upon its tangible and intangible nature. When the retail experience is more tangible it is easier to assess the quality because physical aspects of the store and merchandise can be subjected to examination. However, retail transactions include a service element which is difficult to assess until the sale has taken place. This is especially the case with direct services such as insurance, banking and travel, all of which have risen throughout the final decades of the twentieth century. Therefore, when marketing any one of the retail operations we find in the marketplace, there are a number of tasks and attributes we need to be aware of. The first major factor modern retail managers have to understand is the growing expectation by consumers that they will receive a quality product and service. The management of quality is associated with the need to understand these customer expectations – and to attempt to respond to them – by monitoring and control methods. However, for retailers to be successful at quality management it is necessary that they should also understand the special services marketing characteristics related to retailing.

WHAT CONSTITUTES RETAILING?

We can begin with the separation of the retail offer into two broad areas:

1 Tangible features

Retailing is an amalgamation of goods and services. It is a channel service but may also involve a mix of the physical surroundings, signage, uniforms, changing rooms, displays and other tangible features such as the merchandise. Retailing provides, most of all, the beneficial utility of a place for purchase. It also includes the characteristics of the service component, such as the 'intangible' interaction with sales staff and other retail departments. Other characteristics take into consideration the type and timing of the service delivery, other customers and the nature of a retail sales transaction. These are based upon the ability of retail staff to add extra value to the retail environment through advice on the use of the product, any need for maintenance and care, or, if it is a garment, the type of alterations that can be made to improve its fit and so on.

2 Intangible services

Retailing is also largely intangible and at the extreme matches the main characteristics of pure services with operations such as banking, insurance and investment services.

These broad categories are further explained by comparing 'transaction with' merchandise with 'transaction without' merchandise (*see* relevant sections below).

To understand the nature of retailing from a store environment perspective we need to understand it in relation to its special features. With retailing we are dealing with an amalgam – a mixture – of a good and a service which has specific characteristics. These characteristics set retail marketing apart from some other principles of marketing and the marketplace. As discussed, retailing can be seen to be pure services such as insurance and banking or the amalgam between services and goods which is related to high street shops and merchandise offers.

The blurring of the boundaries between the areas comprising retail is clear when it is considered how many different services could easily be included within retailing: dry cleaners and laundries, photographic studios, hairdressers, shoe repairers, undertakers, health clubs and centres, reprographic shops, public houses, garage services, car hire, cinema, catering outlets, travel agents, banking, insurance, investment. With many of these service-dominant retail businesses there is little or no movement of physical goods through a distribution channel.

THE SERVICE–PRODUCT CONCEPT

An understanding of the complexity of the service–product concept is an essential prerequisite for successful retail marketing. Some important factors and basic differences are identified below.

Transaction with merchandise

In retailing there are three types of services with goods: owned-goods service, rental-goods service, and service with bought goods.

1 **Owned-goods service** would be the traditional outright purchase and ownership of a good from a retailer. The retailer would have performed the service of channel management.

2 **Rental-goods service** would deliver a tangible car or some other good for the personal use of the customer. No ownership exists and the good has to be returned.

3 **Service with bought goods** would be the extra services performed by the retailer. This includes extra services such as delivery, wrapping, providing credit, etc.

Transaction without merchandise

In retailing there is also service without goods: pure services without goods. **Pure services** are provided by a wide range of retailers who are involved in arranging or organising travel, financial transactions and services, or providing personal services such as dry cleaning, a haircut or shoe repairs.

The onus is increasingly being placed on the marketer to develop a deeper understanding of the links which correspond to consumer benefits sought, through to the nature of the service delivery system. A starting point is an examination of the traditional dimensions of the various concepts of service.

THE INTANGIBLE–TANGIBLE PRODUCT CONTINUUM

All products fall on a continuum between pure services and goods, with most products being a combination of the two. A pure service would be consultancy or financial advice, whereas a pure good would be more tangible, such as a can of beans or a bottle of lemonade. Very few products are purely intangible or entirely tangible; services such as retailing, however, tend to be more intangible than manufactured goods. Some products will have more of a service content than others and if they are assessed as being placed to the left of the centre of the continuum they may be termed service products (*see* Fig. 4.1). Retailing falls to the service end of this continuum, despite being associated with the sale of goods. This is due to the nature of transactions involving the interpersonal skills of service providers. The added service element is a core part of the transaction.

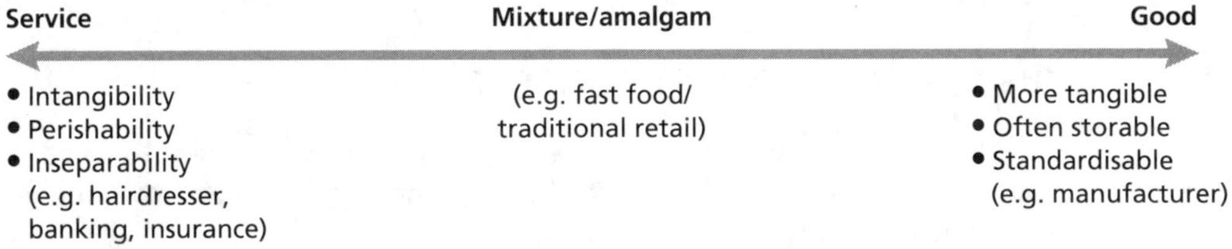

Service	Mixture/amalgam	Good
• Intangibility • Perishability • Inseparability (e.g. hairdresser, banking, insurance)	(e.g. fast food/ traditional retail)	• More tangible • Often storable • Standardisable (e.g. manufacturer)

Fig. 4.1 Service–good/product continuum

Services, such as retailing, can be characterised as having the following attributes (discussed in more detail below):

● intangibility;

● perishability;

● inseparability.

Intangibility

This means that some products cannot be easily stored, evaluated or demonstrated in advance of their purchase. For example, a travel agent cannot allow for the testing or sampling of the tourism product; a bank cannot easily demonstrate its service. On the other hand, a car or a computer game can be tested prior to purchase and clothing may be tried on – but this occurs in a retail environment and not in the home. Mail-order sales or similar methods of selling have to utilise printed literature to communicate the benefits of the product. In addition mail-order sales offer only limited visual clues as to the benefits of the product. Prior to the arrival of the goods the potential customer has to make use of intangible clues. However, the clearest example of retailing related to intangibility is telephone banking, where transactions can be carried out by voice mail and no personal or tangible interface exists. Moreover, the experience of retail purchases is not something that can easily be explained or demonstrated away from the branch, store or mall.

Greater difficulty is faced by the marketers of the more intangible services which make up retailing. Because of fixed time and space constraints, they cannot easily demonstrate the benefits of the retail offer or any merchandise they may be selling. The challenge for the retail service marketer is to overcome intangibility through the use of selling techniques, the physical layout of the store or a depiction – by graphical, video or display means – of the product in use. In addition, the creation of a positive image surrounding the service will enable the consumer to envision the retail experience benefits.

Perishability

This means that unlike goods, the service product cannot be stored for sale on a future occasion. For example, if customers do not enter the store when it is fully staffed sales may not occur, for which the revenue can never be recouped. This perishability factor

---

MINICASE 4.1

Improving service for the consumer

Granada's television rental arm completed the roll-out across the UK of a revamped service that is expected to generate significant cost savings. Roger Mavity, group managing director of the media and leisure group's TV rental business, said the new system of operation had increased the rate of first-time fixes from 75 to 91 per cent after initial trials. The group has torn up the old image of its TV repairman, now equipped with mobile phones. The initial spur was puzzlement that 3 million service calls a year were being made when statistics showed that modern televisions do not often go wrong. A survey threw up a tale of missed appointments, repeat visits and reluctance by staff to concede defeat on repairs in the home. Astra estate cars have been swapped for large Mercedes trucks so that a big stock of televisions can be carried. The working week has been changed from 9a.m.–5p.m. Monday to Friday to 9a.m.–8p.m. Monday to Saturday. The repairmen, who use their mobile phones to check on appointments, have also been trained as salesmen. If a problem cannot be solved in minutes, the customer is either given a replacement set or offered a deal on a better model. The latest action follows the 1997 decision to close 100 shops. Mr Mavity said the cost of revamping the repair service would be almost nothing as the phones and vehicles were leased.

Source: David Blackwell, *Financial Times*, 9 March 1998

leads to the high risk nature of the retail industry. Marketers in the retail industry have to devise complex pricing and promotion policies in an attempt to create demand in 'off season' periods and create greater synchronisation of staffing levels and supply with demand patterns. Weak demand is not the only problem; the industry is also characterised by seasonal demand, such as during the Christmas period, when shoppers are more selective where they shop due to overcrowding and related problems that occur. Stores have a fixed capacity with a maximum upper level demanding constraint. In peak periods retailers often have difficulty in coping with demand; therefore, they offer only full prices or have to resort to queuing systems. In the low periods of demand, however, there is a need for greater marketing activity.

The challenge for marketers arising from perishability problems is to try to smooth out demand curves by careful use of the marketing mix. To achieve this the forecast of demand must be relatively accurate to ensure a productive use of staff.

Inseparability

This means retailing delivers a service which is utilised and produced simultaneously for each customer. Because there is less opportunity to pre-check each sales activity, it may vary in the standard of its service delivery. This is sometimes characterised by theorists as *heterogeneity*. Variance occurs due to the inseparable nature of the retailing product's delivery where the customer is part of the sales process. The simultaneous process of production and consumption may lead to situations where it is difficult to assure the overall satisfaction of consumers. For example, peak loads of demand cannot always be forecast and may create dissatisfaction and secondary problems. There is also a constant threat of problems being caused by one set of customers who may upset another. This provides for the potential for conflict on various levels. Whether it is the young out enjoying themselves, perhaps congregating by the tapes and CDs or in the electrical department by the computer games and annoying older customers, or restaurant users involved in a clash of social values, sets of unacceptable behaviour may be exhibited by various groups. Manufactured goods, on the other hand, are produced in advance of being sent to the warehouse and there is little or no contact with the end consumer.

The service aspects of retail are inseparable – service is intrinsic to retailing. Staff may have personal problems or be feeling ill or tired and this type of problem may affect their level of commitment to giving good service or resolving problems. Because the nature of the retail service product is one of interpersonal relationships, where the performance levels of staff are directly related to the satisfaction experience of the consumer, there is a need for quality assurance mechanisms. Staff are emotional and changeable and if a high content of the sales experience is based upon interpersonal relationships between 'strangers' – as client and a service provider – it is important to ensure standardised service levels are understood and adhered to by everyone. In order to reduce the problems associated with inseparability there is a need to invest in company training programmes.

The problems discussed above make it clear that there is a need to ensure quality is managed, as a basis of planning to achieve competitive advantage. The following section on service and quality classifications will provide insight into the process of service delivery.

A CLASSIFICATION OF SERVICE AND QUALITY

We can classify the different approaches to quality management into two categories: first, the product-attribute approach; second, the consumer-oriented approach (Gilbert and Joshi, 1992). The product-attribute approach is based upon trying to match the product's conformance to standardised requirements which have been set by reference to what company managers think the failure point to be. Product-attribute approaches rely on trying to control the company's output by using an internal standard-setting perspective. This relies on an inward-looking and trading-led management style, rather than a marketing-led approach.

It would seem more appropriate to adopt a consumer-oriented approach which recognises that the holistic process of service delivery has to be controlled by taking into consideration the expectations and attitudes of retail customers. If the starting point for management is the understanding of how quality is judged by customers then the perception processes of this judgement, as to whether a service is good or bad, can be managed. Gronroos is a leading author who has defined this concept.

The Gronroos model of perceived quality management

Gronroos (1982) developed a model, which is a form of gap analysis, to explain what he calls the 'missing service quality concept'. The model (*see* Fig. 4.2) focuses mainly on the construct of image which represents the point at which a gap may occur between expected service and perceived service. Gronroos allows us to be aware of the ways that image is created from the aggregation of different aspects of technical and functional

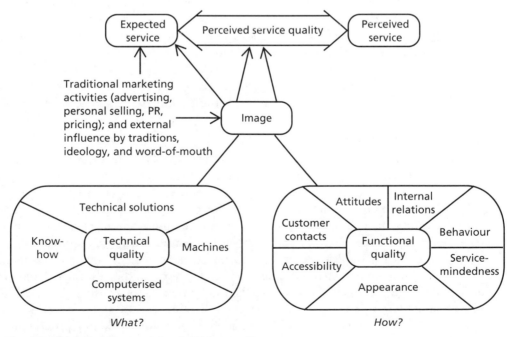

Fig. 4.2 Managing the perceived service quality
Source: Gronroos, 1982

variables. By following his model of different inputs we are alerted to the fact that we should not reduce quality to a simplistic description of itself but that we should try to understand the full range of inputs. This is because to speak simply of quality gives the manager no indication of what aspects of the whole retail experience should be controlled. Gronroos argues the function and range of resources and activities includes what customers are looking for, what they are evaluating, how service quality is perceived, and in what way service quality is influenced. Gronroos defines 'perceived quality' of the service as dependent on two variables: *experienced service* and *perceived service*, which collectively provide the outcome of the evaluation.

Gronroos distinguishes between *technical quality* and *functional quality* as the components of the service image delivery:

1 *technical quality* – refers to what the customer is actually receiving from the service. This is capable of objective measurement, as with tangible goods

2 *functional quality* – refers to how the technical elements of the service are transferred or perceived. We know that a customer in a restaurant will not only evaluate the quality of the food consumed but also the way in which it was delivered (the style, manner and appearance of the staff or the ambience of the place itself). Figure 4.2 shows that the attitudes, behaviour and general service mindedness of personnel can be influenced by management.

The Parasuraman, Zeithaml and Berry model

Parasuraman *et al.* (1985) have also developed a model of service quality which claims that the consumer evaluates the quality of a service experience as the outcome of the difference (gap) between expected and perceived service (*see* Fig. 4.3). The model highlights the main requirements for a service provider delivering the expected service quality. From the model five gaps may be identified that could lead to unsuccessful service delivery. By understanding this model, it is possible to provide greater management control over retail customer service relationships. This should lead to an improved realisation of the key points at which the marketer can influence the satisfactions of the consumer. The marketer is then in a better position to be able to reduce or close the gaps.

Gap 1: Ignorance of the customer's expectations

This is the gap between consumer expectation and management perception. The gap may result from a lack of understanding of what consumers expect from a service. The literature confirms this disparity by revealing that what providers perceive as being important to consumers is often different from what consumers themselves actually expect. The gap may relate to a lack of communication or feedback from customers or an unpreparedness to address important changes which are required.

In the early 1990s, Sears failed to realise that customer buying habits had changed and the company retained its traditional catalogue when the customers had embarked upon different modes of shopping. In the modern marketplace there is a need for responsive and adaptive adjustment to the service provision, based upon feedback from staff at all levels in the company. In addition, good relationship marketing programmes should also help in the reduction of customer and company problems arising from different expectations of what constitutes an 'appropriate' service.

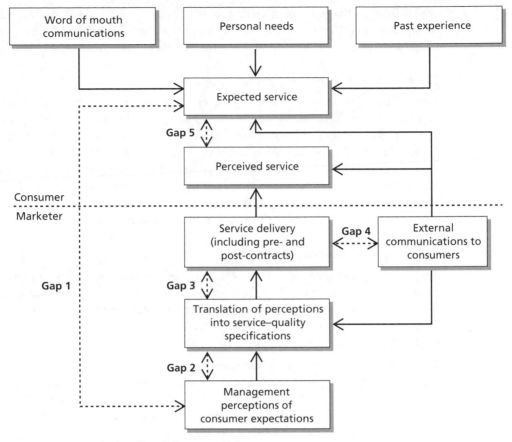

Fig. 4.3 The service quality delivery model

Source: Reprinted with permission from the American Marketing Association from Parasuraman *et al.*, 1985

Gap 2: *Requirement for service design standards*

This is the gap between management perception and service quality specifications. It results when there is a discrepancy between what management perceives to be consumer expectations and the actual service quality specifications established. Management may not set quality standards; the ones they set may not be very clear; or the quality standards set may be clear but unrealistic. Alternatively, although the standards are clear and realistic, management may quite simply not be committed to enforcing them. The need here is to provide service design standards which are supported by everyone and form the yardstick against which all service standards are judged. These standards will then provide the guidelines against which the overall service and retail staff may be evaluated.

Gap 3: *Not delivering to service standards*

This is the gap between service quality specifications and service delivery. Even where guidelines exist for performing a service well, service delivery may not be of the appropriate quality owing to poor employee performance. The employee plays a pivotal role in determining the quality of a service. This is because retail staff and their actions are visible to the customer, and can be assessed and judged on a constant basis. Companies may have service standards but not facilitate the service with adequate technology, the appropriate human resource policies or a positive company culture.

Gap 4: *Inconsistency between performance and promises*

This is the gap between service delivery and external communications. Consumer expectations are affected by the promises made by the service provider's promotional message. Marketers must pay close attention to ensure consistency between the quality image portrayed in promotional activity and the actual quality offered. The problem is any discrepancy between those who describe and promote the service and those who are delivering the service. If a marketing promotion promises a certain offer or service, it has to be available when customers demand it. Marketing has a key role in ensuring that all promotions are coordinated effectively and monitored closely.

Gap 5: *The service shortfalls*

This is the gap between perceived service and delivered service. This gap results when one or more of the other gaps described occurs. If these shortfalls arise, company staff have to ensure they reduce or close the gaps where problems have appeared.

Further factors in service quality delivery

Within the delivery of services consumers will have different levels of tolerance to what may be judged adequate or expected service. This is known as the *zone of tolerance*: customers are willing to accept different levels of service which fall within a zone between the desired and adequate levels of performance. It is important to realise that there are differences between individual customers' perceptions; similarly each customer may have different expectations of one brand in comparison with another. For example, if Marks & Spencer has delivered more consistent service over time than C&A then the expectations for the M&S brand are higher. If Marks & Spencer service were to decline to the level consistently offered by C&A, the customer may be more disappointed by the service received from Marks & Spencer – even though the service standards are similar.

The focus on perceptions and expectations provides a guideline for quality management intervention strategies. To this end, the model proposed by Parasuraman *et al.* has the following two main strengths.

1 The model presents an entirely dyadic view to the marketing task of delivering service quality. The model alerts the marketer to consider the perceptions of both parties (marketers and consumers) in the exchange process.

2 Addressing the gaps in the model can serve as a logical basis for formulating strategies and tactics to ensure a consistent marketing approach to the creation of experiences and expectations.

Providing promotional methods which lead staff to achieve high levels of customer care and service quality is becoming increasingly important. One poster targeted on staff read, 'Good enough is not good enough' which set the standards and aims of the company personnel above the average. This type of inward marketing is used as a means to change the general attitudes of staff toward quality.

A well-positioned service enables the company to:

- differentiate its position so as to distinguish itself from competitors;
- deliver superior service to that accepted as the norm.

This allows the company to plan and build competitive advantage by establishing leadership principles of service standards and delivery. Once the standards are established there should be a policy to communicate and reinforce the service provision philosophy at every possible opportunity: meetings, training and internal marketing programmes, induction programmes and appraisal systems. The human resource function needs to be aware of marketing so as to ensure that the different levels in service delivery process (*see* Fig. 4.4) are always clearly understood and reinforced throughout the company – in its culture and in its reward systems. Without good internal company procedures and relationships it is unlikely that even the most well conceived of quality programmes will be successful.

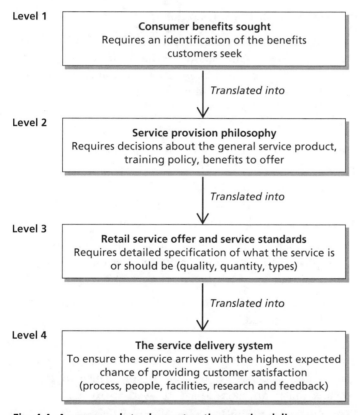

Fig. 4.4 An approach to deconstructing service delivery

IMPLEMENTATION OF SERVICE MANAGEMENT

For the model in Fig. 4.4 to be successful there is a need for the implementation process to consider the following areas vital to success.

1 Leadership and commitment by senior management, with clear goals and a policy on quality being set and communicated to others. There is also the need to release the

appropriate resources to create changes and achieve the required results. Sam Walton, founder of Wal-Mart, adopted the following philosophy to direct his retail staff and gain pre-eminence in the retail marketplace:

- realise that customer service is key;
- design for comfort and convenience;
- provide one-stop shopping;
- customise;
- invert the organisational chart so that the customer is on top and company management is on the bottom;
- empower the sales staff;
- provide servant leadership – Wal-Mart's managers are servants to the needs of their employees and customers;
- recognise that the customer is always right.

2 The focus of all changes and objectives should be defined by the customer. All the definitions of quality delivery and standards have to be delineated in all of the dimensions of the service delivery with reference to customers' needs. These should be incorporated into the training policy and induction programmes.

3 The orientation of the organisation needs to adopt a process and systems approach to match or exceed customer expectations. This relies on a workable quality audit system which applies measurement and inspection to ensure defects are corrected and the system delivers optimum quality results.

4 Human resource management is required to motivate, reward, train and educate staff to understand and deliver the concepts of quality. Teamwork values with champions of quality product delivery are a prerequisite for competitive advantage.

5 Assessment needs to be made of the added value and benefit of any change rather than there being an emphasis on costs and profit implications. That is, the long-term benefits of any change need to be the focus of decision making.

6 A need for quality audits and control to assure the service meets or exceeds customer expectations must be recognised.

An organisation has to create a quality management culture and not just attempt to be the clone of a system learnt elsewhere. This requires honest two-way communication between management and staff which will build confidence in the implementation process. It also means that staff have to be allowed to own up to weaknesses and problems of poor quality in a supportive atmosphere where the company attempts to learn from weaknesses rather than punish them. Such an atmosphere will foster teamwork, confidence and commitment. However, there is also the need for competence to deliver the changes. This may require further training and seminars for staff and follow-up sessions. The recognition that other members of staff should be treated as internal customers will assist the transition to a total quality management (TQM) system. It is obvious that organisations have customers from within as well as from outside them. If employees visualise the relationships between each other based upon supplier and customer links as a quality chain, then the question is always: am I meeting the full requirements of my role? For example, the secretary is a supplier to the boss and needs to provide timely, error-free work in order to assist the boss work as supplier to his or her internal customer, who may be a director. A company, therefore, is a web of internal suppliers and customers. Such chains are easily weakened or broken by faulty equipment or people. The important issue is that an internal quality chain failure will ultimately have some effect on the outside customer.

Minicase 4.2, in discussing process engineering in banking, indicates how the service quality approach can be applied to the retail industry.

MINICASE 4.2

Re-engineering service quality

Lloyds Bank used to send out forms for opening accounts the day after seeing a new customer, but now sends them out at once. In doing so, they have increased the one branch's computer-generated business score from 45% to 90%. The performance is also monitored by 'mystery shoppers' – 'spies' who visit or telephone the bank three times a month to check on quality. This exercise in 'business process re-engineering' has changed operations that account for over two-thirds of the costs at each of the bank's branches and has involved nearly all of its 29,000 employees. Re-engineering involves using technology to reorganise people around 'processes' rather than grouping them in functional fiefdoms, such as 'the marketing department' or 'production'. Pioneered by big manufacturers, such as Ford, the technique has also been embraced by service organisations as diverse as AT&T and the New York Police Department. Lloyds has undergone the most comprehensive re-engineering exercise in commercial banking. Lloyds managers claim that the main reason for turning to re-engineering in September 1992 was to improve the quality of its service in the

face of growing competition from more friendly building societies. Under the bank's old system, staff were given narrow jobs in a rigid hierarchy. Countless people and bits of paper were involved in what, from customers' point of view, was a single process. Under the old system of opening an account, for instance, a piece of paper could spend a month wandering from desk to desk as different staff ordered bank cards, checked credit details and so on. Re-engineered so that one person is responsible for a largely paperless 'quality welcome' process, it now usually takes less than a week.

Five other processes, including 'lending control' and 'periodic payments', were broken down and re-assembled in the same way. In some cases, the results look fairly contrived. For example, customers leaving the bank used to give details of their new bank account to a cashier. Now, 'customer retention' means that a would-be leaver is quizzed, and sometimes persuaded to stay. This sounds like common-sense marketing, but the bank's management insist that re-engineering focused their attention

Source: © *The Economist*, London, 22 July 1995

The findings of research into hotels by Cadotte and Turgeon (1988) led to a simple typology of what may lead to complaints or compliments. This acts as a framework which may inform retail managers of what is required for a desirable service. The research showed that weak performance of the technical service (parking availability, prices, speed of service, credit availability, checkout times) will seriously detract from the customer's evaluation whereas high performance did not enhance the hotel's image. However, the compliments of helpful attitudes and service knowledge of employees, neatness and spaciousness of the building and convenience of location can all lead to high satisfaction if present, while few complain if they are absent or the performance is only indifferent.

		Potential for compliments	
		Low	*High*
Potential for complaints	**High**	Dissatisfiers	Criticals
	Low	Neutrals	Satisfiers

Fig. 4.5 Factors with potential for prompting complaints and compliments

Source: Cadotte and Turgeon, 1988

The potential for compliments and complaints can be illustrated diagrammatically (*see* Fig. 4.5) in terms of four categories: dissatisfiers, satisfiers, criticals and neutrals. These may be described as follows.

1 *Dissatisfiers*. Low performance or an absence of the desired feature is more likely to produce a complaint. Exceeding the threshold performance standard will not, however, generate a compliment. For example, if a customer arrives at an out-of-town retail store and cannot find a place to park they may complain; whereas if a parking space is found, this is what a customer expects and so will not prompt a compliment.

2 *Satisfiers*. Unusual performance beyond expectation will elicit compliments but average performance or even absence of such an aspect of service will not cause dissatisfaction or prompt a complaint. For example, providing large portions in a restaurant.

3 *Criticals*. These are capable of eliciting both negative and positive feelings. The quality of service is important as it ranks high in both compliments and complaints along with employee knowledge of the service.

4 *Neutrals*. There are performance ratings which receive few compliments or complaints and, therefore, are not important to the judgements made by customers regarding standards of service provision.

WHY THERE IS GROWING EMPHASIS ON CONTROL OF QUALITY

Quality has emerged as a major competitive component of company strategies. There are four main reasons which may account for the increasing relevance of quality management.

1 Companies need to find new ways of creating differential advantage by providing better service levels than their competitors. Retail competition has increased because services and goods are available from a wide range of channels and manufacturers are creating technically satisfactory goods which require little after-sales service.

2 The increased level of consumerism and the greater media attention on quality have meant that companies have to be more responsive to quality issues. Consumers are far more aware of their rights and are less likely to suffer quietly from the results of poor quality.

3 There has been a growing sophistication of consumer markets, with the non-price factors of image, retail offer positioning and service delivery processes becoming more important.

4 Technology is one of the new applications to quality enhancement. It can aid service by providing higher levels of convenience; for example, automatic vending or ticketing machines, bar code checkout systems to improve accuracy and speed of transaction, or smart card developments which provide memory of purchases.

It is important for the quality of retailing to be controlled, especially in relation to the process of service delivery. This is because relative quality between service providers or retailers has linkages to market share and profitability. Quality is, therefore, one of the key components that leads to a successful strategy. This is why quality has emerged as a major competitive component of service company strategies. However, when we examine the use of the term 'quality' there appears to be almost a super abundance of its use in relation to the way management operates. Overall, there is a crusade for quality management and improvement within industry worldwide. The campaign for improved quality can be traced to its roots in the manufacturing industries prior to its expansion into the service industry. However, many individuals in industry are still unaware of the theoretical grounding of quality management. Knights and McCabe (1997) have carried out research which illustrates that management often does not understand either the weaknesses or the underlying philosophy of TQM. They argue that management continues to adopt 'inconsistent' approaches, such as concentrating on the control of costs and employees while advocating the importance of the customer and the need for a trust-based culture.

WHAT ARE THE KEY TERMS FOR QUALITY?

Kay (1995) reminds us that the quality of MFI's flatpack furniture was the butt of jokes in the 1980s. However, the senior management at MFI recognise it still has an image problem even though the days of ill-fitting flat-pack furniture are long gone. It is reported that although the jokes are slowly dying, many people remember MFI the way it was and have not been back since. This indicates the importance of a quality image and shows that a poor image is not easily improved. To understand the complexity of quality management there are several key concepts which have to be mastered and these are discussed below.

Quality is the totality of relationships between service providers (functional aspects) and the features of retailing (technical aspects) which are related to the delivery of satisfaction. It is, therefore, important to create systems of *quality control* which are checks and monitoring processes to ensure measurement of service delivery is taking place. To this end *total quality management* (TQM) is a holistic organisational approach which systematically attempts to improve customer satisfaction by focusing on continuous quality improvements without incurring unacceptable cost increases. These improvements are part of an unending quest for excellence in all aspects of quality service delivery. Therefore, TQM has to influence the values and form the mindset of all employees, leading to the creation of an integrated corporate culture because quality is required to be the concern of all employees. The culture should not be based upon a departmental or technical understanding of quality but on a holistic view of quality as a systematic process extending throughout the organisation. From a retail approach perspective, the focus of any change in quality must be based upon external customer expectations and not on internal company ideas.

TQM is managed by *quality assurance* arrangements; that is, a system is instituted to allocate responsibility for planned and systematic activities which will ensure the product will provide the right levels of satisfaction for all concerned. Hart (1988) has postulated that a service guarantee system allows for more quality control and data capture in the organisation. This information on what goes wrong allows for improved service. A good service guarantee is identified as unconditional, easy to understand and communicate, meaningful, and easy to invoke and obtain recompense. It is also recognised that there is a need not to:

- promise something your customers already expect;
- shroud a guarantee in so many conditions that it is meaningless;
- offer guarantees so mild that they are never invoked.

A guarantee can set clear standards and allow company personnel to be clear about what the company stands for. If customers can make complaints without difficulty, the company has the benefit of being able to collect data on common problems which need to be addressed and eradicated. This is because a guarantee system trains the spotlight on why the failure occurred and what needs to be done about it to improve service quality. Moreover, a guarantee adds credibility and weight to the marketing effort of the company. It allows for the emphasis of the guarantee which also provides for a reduction in the perception of risk associated with purchase and may lead to higher levels of customer loyalty.

In order to measure whether the quality delivery complies to the planned delivery of the service a *quality audit* needs to take place to judge the effectiveness of the total service delivery arrangements. For a system to be audited correctly a method of creating unbiased feedback must be found. While a range of aspects of quality can be assessed, a number of categories exist. These may include the following which are based upon various research studies which have attempted to establish categories of service quality determinants.

CHARACTERISTICS OF QUALITY

There are two sets of quality characteristics which are important to a retailer. These are the characteristics related to either merchandise or service categories.

Merchandise (products)

Merchandise categories include the following elements:

- performance based upon their inherent operating characteristics, such as the sound and clarity of a hi-fi system;
- features which add to the basic function of the product;
- reliability of the product not to break down in normal use;
- conformance to standards of safety or operating performance needs;
- durability based upon the length of time a product will last;
- serviceability – relating to the after-sales service and ability to be repaired;
- aesthetics of the look, feel, design, sound and smell of the product;
- image of the brand association, reputation and personality of the product.

Services

Service categories include the following elements.

1 *Tangibles*: what can be experienced from personnel, company literature and signs, and the physical environment of the retail encounters. These include aspects of the store or material the customer can see, touch, use, etc., such as:

- physical facilities;
- appearance of personnel;
- tools or equipment used to provide the service;
- physical representation of the service, e.g. store credit card, fascia design;
- other customers in the service facility.

2 *Reliability* of staff to deliver the expected or promised service dependably and accurately. This involves consistency of performance and dependability. It means the company should perform the service right the first time, and honour its promises. This factor also demands that the company is able to trust employees with the responsibility to deliver service which, consistently and accurately, meets policy standards, including.

- accuracy in charging;
- keeping the correct records;
- performing the service at the designated time – for example, accurate to opening hour promise.

3 *Responsiveness* of staff to help customers and provide timely service. This concerns the willingness or readiness of employees to provide service – to help customers and give timely service, such as:

- mailing a transaction slip immediately;
- calling a customer back quickly after a query;
- giving prompt service (e.g. arranging an appointment).

4 *Competence*: an assurance of employees' ability to convey trust and confidence through company and product knowledge, as well as by the courtesy of their interpersonnel skills:

- knowledge and skill of the contact personnel;
- listening to customer needs and explaining the desired product or service;
- reinforcing the company's reputation;
- personal characteristics of the contact personnel;
- ability to respect confidentiality, and display financial and personal security.

5 *Empathy*: having an understanding of what customers as individual humans require in relation to psychological as well as physical needs. This concerns individualised attention to customers – a caring, individual concern and attention for others and their emotions:

- recognising regular customers;

- learning the customer specific requirements and anticipating their needs;
- being attentive and providing individualised (customised) service;
- ensuring that if there is a problem it is acknowledged, responsibility is taken, and some action is carried out to ensure the service fault is compensated for.

The above points allow a retailer to focus on a systems perspective which identifies the linkage between consumers' needs and service delivery. This highlights the management principles associated with service products. It may also be utilised in the establishment of benchmark points against which the service can be positioned.

The elements which could be assessed in the course of establishing the position of a service could also include: availability of items the customer demands; after-sales service and contact (e.g. Amazon.com has an e-mail system to let customers know when a book has been despatched); the way the telephone orders and queries are handled; the reliability and safety of the items being sold; availability of sales literature and brochures; the number and type of items which can be demonstrated; technical knowledge of staff; the way an employee deals with a complaint; etc.

MINICASE 4.3

Service can include the customer

IKEA of Sweden has managed to be highly successful due to the service role it has developed with its customers. IKEA recognised that customers are happy to be part of the business system by taking on responsibility for the services normally carried out by paid service staff. When customers enter the store they are given a catalogue, tape measure, pen and notepaper. This means they are able to perform the function normally carried out by the salesperson. The new role of some of the staff is to look after customers' children in a supervised child centre, allowing a less stressful decision-making process for the parents. After choice and payment customers can then take the purchase to their car on a cart. If necessary they can hire, or buy, a roof rack for the transport of larger items. Once home the customer assembles the new furnishings with the aid of carefully written instructions. Complete service is not always necessary as sometimes less service is better service. This is especially the case if the customer enjoys more involvement in the manufacture and retail process in order to achieve lower prices. The new role for the customer developed at IKEA provides added personal value and contributes to the overall satisfaction experience.

Source: Based on company information

The following section indicates some of the ways that quality may be assessed. It is important to realise, however, that whatever system is used to audit quality, at the end of the day, that which is not measured cannot be controlled.

QUALITY AUDITING SYSTEMS

There are various methods that may be used to measure and monitor quality. Figure 4.6 lists some methods of internal inspection and of auditing.

Internal inspection	Auditing
• statistical process – control based upon quality failure information and objective measures • visual inspections to check against standards and consistency • management by walking about • quality control group feedback • inspection of competitors' offer and assessment of own company offer	• internal auditors of quality • external bodies • consultants, regular users, non-user surveys and feedback • cross-department audits • mystery shoppers • content analysis of complaint and praise letters and documented problems • Freephone line feedback

Fig. 4.6 Summary of some methods of internal inspection and auditing

Buttle (1994) indicated that following research of loyal Jaeger customers a list of 180 service variables was reduced to 26 key attributes against which mystery shoppers could assess a store's service performance. It is important to note that the final list was based upon *customer preferences* and did not correlate with what Jaeger's own employees had identified as being important. The key items identified by customers were:

• external appearance of the branch;
• merchandise pricing in window display;
• greeting upon entry;
• staff approachability;
• staff availability to help;
• manager availability;
• whether the manager is recognisable;
• the number of customers served simultaneously by one staff member;
• efficiency/promptness of enquiry handling;
• branch stock levels;
• staff awareness of fashion trends;
• speed of stock location;
• staff awareness of advertised lines;
• helpfulness of staff advice;
• honesty of staff advice;
• standard of fitting rooms;
• availability of advertised stock;
• colour/size availability;
• selection within size;
• availability of alterations advice;
• availability of garment reservation;

- eye-catching quality of window displays;
- eye-catching quality of interior displays;
- speed of till transaction;
- comparability of service in other Jaeger branches.

Benchmarking

Another method now widely used for assessment of the service standards of a company is to compare them with those which are deemed to be the best available – the benchmark. Benchmarking is a continuous process of selecting the best practices and services against which to judge. It is based upon the Japanese concept *dantotsu*, meaning 'the best of the best', the underlying philosophy which says if you seek out and match best practice, there is the possibility of the attainment of superiority. By identifying a guideline, benchmarking will allow a company to know what operating standards to apply.

Four types of benchmarking exist:

- *internal* where the best internal company examples are utilised;
- *competitive*, based upon external directly competing retailers and their merchandise;
- *functional*, which measures against the best external market leaders or functional operations;
- *generic*, which is to take measures of the best practices regardless of what sector or industry is represented.

Companies such as American Express may be benchmarked for service standards, Marks and Spencer for specification of product, TGI Friday for service training, etc. For example, American Express has a service tracking report which systematically assesses customer satisfaction and employee performance on a worldwide basis. The report is generated each month based on measurement against 100 service quality factors grouped into the three major service dimensions of responsiveness, timeliness and accuracy. Within the first three years of the adoption of this system American Express improved service delivery by 78 per cent and reduced costs of the average transaction by 21 per cent. Therefore, for a retail operation to try to learn from American Express by benchmarking its service tracking system makes marketing sense.

IS QUALITY A COST OR A LONG-TERM BENEFIT?

It is found that smaller firms embarking upon service quality programmes (SQP) perceive them to be: costly, needing a lot of management time, difficult to measure the intangible benefits, and finally not easy to implement. Given the nature of retailing (people-based with employee performance and interaction being of paramount importance), it is clear that errors are inevitable. In addition to this element of human error is the nature of human response to it. It is estimated that there is a ratio of 4 : 1 where individuals will speak of poor service to good service and therefore pass on more negative than positive aspects of service delivery. The moment of truth – the impact on the bottom line of any organisation – is the judgement of customers on the quality of its service.

Figure 4.7 is based upon the model of Heskett *et al.* (1990) who argue that the linkages of service encounters create a self-reinforcing mechanism. Figure 4.7 indicates the relationship between the customer on the left with the service provider to the right. This overcomes the notion that improvement in quality is associated with increased costs. The model indicates that, in the long term, true quality improvement leads to an improved trading position.

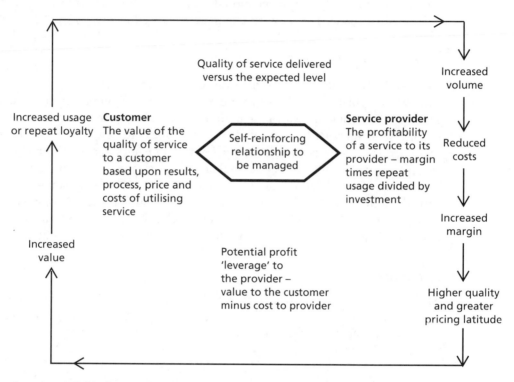

Fig. 4.7 Model indicating quality improvement leads to an improved trading position
Source: Based on Heskett *et al.*, 1990

This proposition, that a continuous improvement in service is not a cost but an investment in a customer who will return more profit in the long term, is becoming more widely supported. The premise is based upon research which indicates that the cost of acquiring a new customer is much higher than that of retaining an existing customer through providing quality service. Such an argument is based upon non-traditional accounting practices which stress satisfied customers will be willing to pay higher prices due to the service quality they have experienced and liked; there is a free advertising benefit due to the positive word of mouth recommendation; and there is a different cost in acquiring new customers as opposed to retaining existing customers over longer time periods. In general, following the ideas of relationship marketing, it is suggested that to keep a customer over the long term provides important savings. On a cost–benefit basis, good service quality is thought to increase revenue and reduce long-run costs.

Service recovery

Given the estimated cost of finding a new customer is five times that of retaining an existing one, there is growing emphasis on customer retention and relationship marketing. Long-term revenue can be enhanced by *service recovery* strategies. Good service recovery procedures allow a customer to refocus on the satisfactions received from the service delivery process rather than to question why corrective action was not taken. A problem tests the system and if a customer complaint is dealt with appropriately the customer is likely to become more loyal.

Individual service recovery strategies are discussed below.

Watching for sign language

Consideration needs to be given to those customers who are reticent or mute when it comes to complaints to be able to break their silence. Companies need the opportunity to prove their commitment to the customer through service quality measures. However, the silent customer who is not satisfied will escape company notice but may tell many of their acquaintances of the problem. Some companies have Freephone numbers for complainants to make a call to complain or adopt employee training to enable staff to test for weak signals of a customer's dissatisfaction. Many companies empower staff to provide immediate remedial action if they suspect poor service. A long wait to be seated in a restaurant, for example, may be acknowledged by a reduction in the bill or free coffee. Others place emphasis on mystery customers or research feedback.

Preplanning

There is a need to analyse the service delivery process so as to anticipate those aspects of service which may exceed the tolerance level of customers. Times of peak demand, or low levels of staffing may affect the judgement of the customer in relation to the overall level of service quality delivery.

Training

As service is an interpersonal performance activity, the provision of communication and customer relation skills training will enhance the ability of staff to deal with the most difficult of situations. Perhaps more important, training will allow staff to feel confident in the service encounter transaction and allow them to deal professionally with all situations. Training has to be allied to labour retention strategies; overall service recovery may suffer if there is too high a proportion of untrained staff or seasonal employees.

Empowerment

A great deal of staff service delivery goes unsupervised. Front line retail staff, therefore, need to react quickly to service problem situations without the input of supervisors. A staff member who provides some extra means of satisfying a customer may stave off a more difficult or serious situation. Empowerment conveys responsibility too – an obligation to act; front line staff are trusted to act, not simply to focus on who is to blame for a poor service encounter. The benefits of empowerment are that decisions are taken more quickly and service recovery occurs on the spot, allowing employees to feel more responsible and in control of the situation. This is likely to motivate the staff more and may affect the whole service encounter due to staff feeling better about themselves as well as the customers.

A summary of the key components of a quality-led approach

1 An unending quest for excellence in all things.

2 A system which offers continuous improvement and reduces failure repetition. A feeling that there is no such thing as an insignificant improvement in quality or service. However, this has to be cost-effective.

3 An orientation which focuses on the customer and stakeholder satisfaction outcomes. The philosophy is always to plan to give the customer a little more than they expect.

4 A feeling of total involvement of all concerned with ownership of the quest. Senior management commitment being particularly important.

5 Regular measurement, monitoring, evaluation and adjustment to changing circumstances.

CONCLUSION

The management of retail cannot be divorced from the management of service and quality. The marketing management of retail cannot ignore the primary characteristics which set retail apart from other products. These are the important aspects of being intangible, perishable and inseparable. Retail, as a specialised service, creates a number of important considerations which need to be fully understood if a retail enterprise or organisation is to be successful. The customer service approach has to support all other functional strategies with the objective of exceeding customer expectations. At the very minimum it has to be able to provide an effortless retail sales purchase experience.

EXERCISES

The exercises in this section relate to the management of service and quality in retailing. It is suggested that you work through them before moving on to Chapter 5.

1 Think of a retail outlet you frequently visit. Assess the quality encounter utilising a checklist of quality attributes drawn from this chapter. How and why does the level of service you experienced differ from any of the material in this chapter?

2 What would be the differences, in service and quality management, if you were the marketing manager of a chain of supermarkets or banks as opposed to the sales and marketing manager of a manufacturer of heavy machinery? What are the implications for the retail industry?

3 Select and visit five similar retail outlets in your local high street. Using the following grid as a guide, assess each store in turn.

External appearance:	Assessment by store:
• paintwork (colours and state of repair) • cleanliness of windows • window display • lighting (list others)	
Internal: • any welcome by staff? • was the body language of staff friendly? • was the layout of the store user helpful? • was the standard (of the fitting room, etc.) acceptable? • did the till transaction look efficient? (list others)	Assessment by store:

Compare your findings with what you believe to be the key requirements of quality management for any high street retailer.

4 Look at the literature dealing with service encounters and think about any dissatisfying and satisfying aspects of service encounters you or your friends have experienced. Based upon these experiences, and the literature, describe the policies you would implement if you were responsible for the service quality management of a retail company.

REFERENCES AND FURTHER READING

Blackwell, D. (1998) 'Companies and finance: Granada's rental revamp', *Financial Times*, 9 March.

Buttle, F. (1994) 'Jaeger ladies', in McGoldrick, P. (ed.) *Cases in Retail Management*. London: Pitman Publishing.

Cadotte, E.R. and Turgeon, N. (1988) 'Key factors in guest satisfaction', *Cornell HRA Quarterly*, February.

Cope, N. (1995) 'Jobs cut in Safeway shake-up', *Independent*, 25 May.

The Economist (1995) 'The black horse goes to the vet: Retail banking – Has Lloyds Bank "re-engineered" itself, or simply cut costs?' *The Economist*, 336, 22 July.

Ernst, Ricardo and Powell, Stephen G. (1998) 'Manufacturer incentives to improve retail service levels', *European Journal of Operational Research*, 104 (3), 437–50.

Fant, D. (1998) 'Understanding customers: the key to retail success', *Marketing News*, 32 (4), 7.

Fitzsimmons, J.A. and Fitzsimmons, M.J. (1994) *Service Management for Competitive Advantage*. Singapore: McGraw-Hill.

Gengler, Charles E., Leszczyc, Peter and Popkowski, T.L. (1997) 'Using customer satisfaction research for relationship marketing: A direct marketing approach', *Journal of Direct Marketing*, 11 (1), 23–9.

Gilbert, D.C., and Joshi, I. (1992) 'Quality management and the tourism and hospitality industry' in Cooper, C. and Lockwood, A. *Progress in Tourism, Recreation and Hospitality Management*. London: Belhaven Press.

Glyn, W.J. and Barnes, J.G. (1996) *Understanding Services Management*. Chichester: Wiley.

Gronroos, C. (1982) *Strategic management and marketing in the service sector*. Helsinki: Swedish School of Economics and Business Administration.

Gwinner, K.P., Gremler, D.D. and Bitner, Mary Jo (1998) 'Relational benefits in services industries: The customer's perspective', *Journal of the Academy of Marketing Science*, 26 (2), 101–14.

Hart, C.W.L. (1988) 'The power of unconditional guarantees', *Harvard Business Review*, July–August, 54–62.

Heskett, J.L., Sasser, W. and Hart, C.W. (1990) *Service Breakthroughs – Changing the Rules of the Game*. New York: The Free Press.

Hoffman, K.D. and Bateson, J.E.G. (1997) *Essentials of Services Marketing*. Fort Worth, FL: Dryden Press.

Hurley, R.F. (1998) 'Customer service behavior in retail settings: A study of the effect of service provider personality', *Journal of the Academy of Marketing Science*, 26 (2), 115–27.

Kay, W. (1995) 'Profile: The self-made man from MFI: John Randall', *Independent on Sunday*, 23 April, 20.

Knights, David and McCabe, D. (1997) '"How would you measure something like that?": Quality in a retail bank', *Journal of Management Studies*, 34 (3), 371–88.

Kotler, P. (1996) *Marketing Management – Analysis, Planning and Control*. 9th edn. Upper Saddle River, NJ: Prentice Hall.

Morrison, L.J., Colman, A.M. and Preston, C.C. (1997) 'Mystery customer research: Cognitive processes affecting accuracy', *Journal of the Market Research Society*, 39 (2), 349–61.

O'Reilly, A. (1984) 'Manufacturers versus retailers: the long-term winners', *Retail and Distribution Management*, 12 (3), 40–1.

Palmer, A. (1994) *Principles of Services Marketing*. Maidenhead: McGraw-Hill.

Parasuraman, A., Zeithaml, V.A. and Berry, L.L. (1985) 'A conceptual model of service quality and its implications for future research', *Journal of Marketing*, 49 (4), 41–50.

Rust, R.T. and Zahorik, A.J. (1993) 'Customer satisfaction, customer retention and market share', *Journal of Retailing*, 69 (2), 193–215.

Stern, B.B. (1997) 'Advertising intimacy: Relationship marketing and the services consumer', *Journal of Advertising*, 26 (4), 7–19.

Zeithaml, V.A. and Bitner, M.J. (1996) *Services Marketing*. Singapore: McGraw-Hill.

5 The retail marketing mix

This chapter should enable you to understand and explain:

- what constitutes the marketing mix;
- the importance of targeting and the marketing mix;
- different methods of pricing, retail product formulation, promotion and distribution;
- the concept and meaning of price sensitivity in retailing;
- approaches to markdown policies;
- logistics management and distribution;
- pressures to increase the four Ps of the mix for services.

When you have finally decided to use a retailer you have probably been influenced by a promotional campaign, have assessed the product offer, considered whether you are willing to pay the price, and finally thought about how easy it would be to buy it. Each of these aspects of purchase is part of the marketing mix, which is carefully planned by marketers in an attempt to convince you to utilise a particular outlet or make a transaction. The four Ps – *product, price, promotion* and the *place* of purchase – are the basic ingredients of the marketing mix. However, these ingredients mask a major role of the retailer which is to select and acquire the goods they plan to sell. There is a need for retailers to devise and implement a well developed merchandise plan in order to be a successful retailer. This will ensure that the proper assortment of goods and services is made available, based upon historical demand patterns and the strategic positioning of the company or store as a brand. When relating back to the marketing mix, the part dealing with merchandise becomes part of the product.

Because merchandising is so important to the success or otherwise of a retailer it is dealt with in a separate chapter (*see* Chapter 6, Merchandise management) although merchandising falls within the category of the product. Merchandising is a key area as traditional retailing is positioned as the final distribution stage in the channel of sales to the consumer. This is not to deny the importance of the rest of the mix. Each of the areas which make up the marketing mix involves a complex set of management decisions which have to be taken into account for the retailer to prosper. This is both for the individual mix strategy and for the combined effect of the whole mix on the target market sub-groups. In fact the mix has to be combined across its different parts so that each aspect of the mix reinforces and reflects the other parts of the mix. This creates a synergy effect, where the whole becomes greater than the sum of the parts. The combined mix has to be positioned so as to create a clear proposition for the customer. As Ries and Trout (1981) commented, 'Positioning is not what you do to a product; positioning is what you do to the mind of the prospect.' This chapter's information will, therefore, provide you with an overview of the most important considerations for planning the marketing mix.

WHAT IS THE MARKETING MIX?

It is customary to accept the classic marketing mix to be made up from the four Ps of product, price, promotion, and place (channel service).

1 The *product* is the totality of the offer which will normally include the services, store layout, merchandise. It will also include the company, and own product, brand name.

2 The *price* is what the customer has to be willing to pay in exchange for the benefits of the product and channel service. The price is related to a perception of value based upon the way the whole of the marketing mix creates an image of the transaction experience.

3 The *promotion* is the means by which the retail offer is communicated to the target groups in order to inform and persuade different segments of the benefits of utilising a specific retailer's outlet or to make a purchase.

4 The *place* is based on the retailer's activities in supplying a channel service. This includes the logistics of inventory management systems.

Kotler *et al.* (1999) indicate that the marketing mix is one of the key concepts in modern marketing theory. The definition of the marketing mix is provided as:

the set of controllable tactical marketing tools that the firm blends to produce the response it wants in the target market.

Figure 5.1 illustrates the approach to the interrelated nature of the marketing mix favoured here. While the four Ps are a traditional way of understanding the key

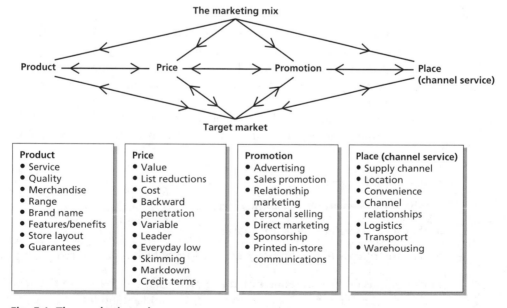

Fig. 5.1 The marketing mix

aspects of marketing which are within the control of the company or managers, there are alternative approaches where authors stress the need for an expansion of these four components. This is an interesting development because the four Ps were provided by McCarthy (1978) as an abridged version of a much wider range of what were termed, 'marketing ingredients'. McCarthy based his four Ps upon a simplified version of a range of twelve marketing ingredients offered much earlier by Borden (1965).

THE MARKETING MIX FOR SERVICES – ARE THE FOUR Ps SUFFICIENT?

The adaptation of the marketing mix by authors such as Booms and Bitner (1981) has been based upon arguments which stress that the 'four Ps' marketing mix is more appropriate to manufacturing than to service companies, such as are found in retailing. For example, Booms and Bitner add the three extra Ps of people, physical evidence and process (*see* Fig. 5.2). Authors such as Booms and Bitner argue that the marketing mix of four Ps is not comprehensive enough. The major difference is argued to be the intangible element of human behaviour, where quality and its control is of paramount importance. We believe that there is enough scope in Fig. 5.1 to incorporate each of the additional areas of Booms and Bitner.

For the present it is believed the four Ps offer an adequate framework into which the differences can be incorporated. The main task of marketers in retail is to understand many of the complexities of the marketing mix contained in this chapter in order to ensure they will be better prepared to plan, control and manage different types of retail operations. Retail managers have to control the aspects of the marketing mix which have most bearing on the demand creation and satisfaction level of consumers. While it is obvious that there are differences between manufactured and service products, the framework of the four Ps is sufficient for retail planning purposes, based on the content of this chapter and the following chapter on merchandise management (*see* Chapter 6). The four mix categories do not presuppose the relegation of service product considerations to secondary importance. On the contrary, the four categories should ensure that within any mix formulation greater emphasis will be placed on the integration of all the different service management considerations.

Whatever approach is taken to the classification of the controllable aspects of marketing there is a need to realise that purchases do not take place unless customers know:

- that an offer exists;

- where it is best to purchase the offer;

- that it offers value and is affordable;

- that the offer is likely to satisfy the need for which it is required.

The essentials of the marketing mix for retail are explained fully in the next four sections of this chapter. First, however, it is important to understand how the target market plays an essential part in the formulation of any retail mix strategy.

Product	Price	Place	Promotion	People	Physical evidence	Process
Range	Level	Location	Advertising	Personnel:	Environment:	Policies
Quality	Discounts:	Accessibility	Personal selling	• Training	• Furnishings	Procedures
Level	• Allowances	Distribution channels	Sales promotion	• Discretion	• Colour	Mechanisation
Brand name	• Commissions	Distribution coverage	Publicity	• Commitment	• Layout	Employee discretion
Service line	Payment terms		Public relations	• Incentives	• Noise level	Customer involvement
Warranty	Customer's			• Appearance	Facilitating goods	Customer direction
After-sales	perceived value			• Interpersonal behaviour	Tangible clues	Flow of activities
service	Quality/price			• Attitudes		
	Differentiation			Other customers:		
				• Behaviour		
				• Degree of involvement		
				• Customer/customer contact		

Fig. 5.2 The marketing mix for services

Source: Reprinted by permission of the American Marketing Association from Booms and Bitner, 1981

TARGET MARKETS

The fundamental starting point for the creation of a successful marketing mix strategy is to ensure that the target market is clearly defined. While the target market is not part of the mix, its role in dictating the different ways the mix is used makes it indistinguishable from the concept, and of paramount importance. In any management decision which is related to the marketing mix, the customer base or target market is always the initial focus of all marketing mix activity. This is because the potential consumer has to remain the focus for all retail decision making. For example, we need to know what minimum and maximum level of price or what retail offer proposition will be acceptable to target consumers.

The retail market is made up of actual and potential consumers. This total available group of consumers will be analysed and a decision made as to which segments or sub-groups will be targeted. The segments would probably have been identified as part of the marketing planning process and would have been specified at the time of the setting of objectives. A clear specification of the target market allows for a number of benefits, including improved levels of understanding of:

- the characteristics and needs of the group targeted;
- the main competitors;
- the changing/developing needs of targeted consumers.

Benefits of targeting

1 A fuller understanding of the unique characteristics and needs of the group to be satisfied is reached. The target market acts as a reference point for retail marketing decisions, especially as to how the marketing mix should be planned. This should lead to greater effectiveness for the mix, which in turn provides for the success of the programme.

2 A better understanding of the main competitors is gained because it is possible to detect those retail companies who have made a similar selection of target markets. If a company does not clarify the markets it wishes to target, it may treat every other company in its sector as an equal competitor. Once main competitors are identified, their marketing efforts can be more closely followed – or benchmarked if appropriate – so as to improve marketing decision making.

3 Improvements can be made in understanding the changes and development in the needs of the target market. Awareness and knowledge of retail demand is heightened due to the scrutiny focused upon the target group's actions and reactions to slightly different forms of the marketing mix.

Target markets may be based upon socio-economic groups, geographic location, age, gender, income levels, shopper type, benefits sought, purchase behaviour and attitudes. The target market acts as the focus for tailoring the mix so that target customers will judge it to be superior to that of the competition. Segmentation and target marketing is central to marketing because different customer groups should dictate the search for the correct marketing mix strategy. (For further discussion, *see* Chapter 7, Methods and approaches to retail marketing planning.)

Retailing in shopping centres may need to target the leisure segment of the market in order to encourage that group to use other retail facilities such as food courts and shops.

Product decisions – the shop as a destination?

Is shopping a leisure activity? Behind that question lies a raging debate over the design and management of shopping centres in which a growing number of real estate professionals are arguing that the two are inextricably linked. 'Shopping is leisure,' says John Milligan, partner in the retail practice at property consultants Jones Lang Wooten. 'If you don't make it a leisure activity, you're dead.' The introduction of a cinema, with its evening operating hours, entices a far wider range of food retailers than may be prepared to occupy a shopping centre and these may be prepared to pay far more for the space. Thus, the addition of a cinema encourages further daytime shopping and the growth of food courts, leading to a virtuous circle resulting in higher revenues for everyone. Mr Ronson (Heron) is

developing retailing/entertainment complexes in Continental Europe. However, he cautions that the retailing element itself must contain a leisure theme. White goods superstores and food supermarkets, he says, will not be a feature. 'We're thinking of music superstores, bookshops, that sort of thing,' he says. 'The shopping centre has to be a destination,' he argues. 'It's a day out.' However, Michael McCarty cautions against a headlong plunge into leisure/retailing development. 'The conventional wisdom is that the entertainment and leisure component can enhance the value of a retail development,' he says. 'But it is not a panacea for a bad centre. It will make a good centre better but it will not make a bad centre survive.'

Source: Norma Cohen, Financial Times, 17 March 1998

Minicase 5.1 introduces the debate as to what product types should be available in a shopping centre, based upon the link between shopping and leisure.

The marketing mix is put together to ensure the highest expected outcome of demand from the customer. Therefore, when the marketing mix is delivered to the target market it has to produce an outcome of higher value than any competing form of retail offer. What we have to consider is that all retail purchases are related to a cost for the consumer. The marketing mix amalgam has to create greater value than the travel costs if a car or transport is used, the time costs which have to be taken from an individual's total time budget for leisure as well as shopping, etc. Figure 5.3 is a simple illustration of the components of a purchase situation, with the customer derived value being an

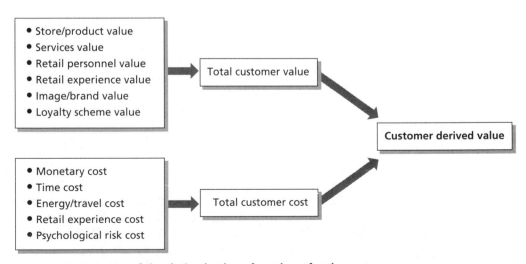

Fig. 5.3 Components of the derived value of purchase for the customer

outcome of a deduction of value from costs. The figure reflects the need to create perceived or actual positive outcomes from any creation of a retail marketing mix strategy. The objective of creating high levels of derived value should be borne in mind when assessing the underlying concepts which follow. Some aspects of value and costs are discussed more fully in Chapter 3 and later in this chapter.

THE PRODUCT

The effectiveness of planning the marketing mix depends as much on the ability to select the right target market as on the skill in devising a retail offer which will generate high levels of satisfaction. *A product is anything that can be offered to a market that may satisfy a need or a want.* This means a combination of goods and services which includes the store, the staff and the merchandise. In retailing the complete retail offer of location, price levels, merchandise, store layout or method of selling, brand name and service provided play a pivotal role in a firm's existence and long-term success or survival. The shopper has to believe that the merchandise, or outlet, offers added value in order for it to be successful. Retailing comprises everything an individual or customer receives – both favourable and unfavourable – as part of the total retail transaction. It should be noted that Chapter 6 is dedicated to a full explanation of the role and functions of merchandise management, which is an important aspect of any discussion of the marketing mix.

A BREAKDOWN OF RETAILING AS A PRODUCT

The formulation of a successful retailing operation involves a combination of:

- service;
- quality;
- merchandise;
- brand name;
- features and benefits.

Service

An agreement to service provision is concerned with creating the level of services to be offered. In a store, how much of the service should the client be expected to perform and how much should be provided by staff? For example, in supermarkets the self-service of food and the customer carrying their own purchased items are now thought of as acceptable – and at times desirable – by clients. The use of automatic teller machines (ATMs) at banks extends the availability of the cash retrieval service (and others) beyond typical bank hours, and also allows customers to estimate roughly how long a transaction will take. There are also systems for self-scanning of goods which cut down on the cost of time.

Quality

A decision regarding quality involves deciding on quality standards and implementing a method of assurance on the performance level of staff and facilities. The management of quality is becoming an increasingly important management function. It is important to create a good quality reputation for the product and service offered as this provides a positive image for the company or organisation and is a major advantage in countering the perception of risk which, for many retail consumers, is high. Retail service providers are more likely to be successful if they can be depended upon to deliver higher quality service levels than their competitors. Success through quality is often seen as, for certain product categories, the outcome of a relationship between a customer's prior expectations of service delivery and the perception of the actual service experience. Quality is also used strategically: as a way of differentiating merchandise and of positioning the offer or retail outlet in an exclusive way. However, an exclusive position does bring with it the added problems of needing to source more widely to continue to find unique merchandise and having to bear additional overhead costs as a consequence of exclusivity.

Merchandise

Retailers need to decide on the merchandise to offer by engaging in the sorting process of assembling a range of goods and services from a variety of suppliers. The depth and width of this range will depend on the specific strategy of each retailer, who must decide how different products will fit into the overall range of products they offer to the marketplace. (Chapter 6 offers a more detailed description of the role of the merchandise manager.) A retailer must also decide on whether to include various brands in the range, and whether the offer of traditional or new products should be included. The range of the offer and how each product matches or complements the chosen positioning of the retailer is an important retail consideration; for example, is the company maintaining an upmarket, mid-market or economy position? The decision regarding the range of products is also important as it affects the need for space for display at the point-of-sale as well as stockholding. The width and depth decisions over the range of merchandise to offer have to be linked to both the expectations and the financial considerations of the consumer target group. Decisions over merchandise have to take into account that a consumer may want to choose to purchase from a range of different types of goods. This could encompass the following categories.

National brands

These are the brands which are heavily promoted by companies, such as Sainsbury, Boots and Kwik Fit, to achieve consumer awareness and preference, e.g. Boots No. 7. (*See* Chapter 9 for a discussion of brand management.) For the retailer the problem in offering such a range is that they have no exclusivity and are open to price competition from those discounting national brands.

Own-label

A retailer can offer the advantage of exclusivity and have more control over the product. They thus need not enter into heavy advertising, which may give the flexibility of being able to offer lower unit prices.

Licensed merchandise

The importance of TV or film characters has led to the addition of images and symbols on a range of merchandise from everyday items to clothing. Disney characters, Bart Simpson, etc. have appealed to the children's market and led to major opportunities for increasing the desirability of different types of merchandise.

Franchised products via concessions in a store

An advantage may be gained through an exclusive deal with a manufacturer (for example, Clinique, Principles, Alexon, etc.).

Brand name

A brand name which is well known and associated with high satisfaction levels imparts an improved image and added value to the product or the store. This can lead to store loyalty or consumers insisting on the product by brand name and being less price sensitive. This brand name may be a national brand or an own-label brand. Brand names can be family brands where each of the company's products adopts the same brand name. Umbrella brands which use a corporate brand symbol are being used to project a consistent image across countries. Nestlé's brand policy, for example, uses umbrella and sub-umbrella branding; corporate branding takes place with Nestlé, Carnation, Maggi, C&B, Chambourcy, Buitoni, Findus, Friskies, Herta and Libby's while sub-branding is used for Nescafe, Nestea, Nestum, Sveltesse and Lean Cuisine. Additionally, individual product brand names such as Nido, Milo, Crunch and KitKat are used, where each product is branded differently. It is argued that it is difficult to create marketing success across a wide range of products due to the problem of providing complex brand values to dissimilar products. However, Marks & Spencer are renowned for having built their success on an umbrella own-brand, St Michael, which is associated with added value but which may be produced by a range of manufacturers in a number of countries.

Some companies opt for individual brand names such as those associated with the Debenham's organisation. The individual brand name approach allows the retailer to search for the most appropriate brand name; its weakness is that the promotional budget for each brand has to be sufficiently large to support that brand. With individual branding, a company is able to position brands and products at the cheaper end of the market without the brand damaging the image of the rest of the company's brands. In addition, if there is bad publicity for one of the company's brands then the other company brands do not necessarily suffer.

With umbrella or family brands there is a spin-off effect for each of the brands from the expenditure on any one brand. Conversely, if one of the family brands attracts poor publicity, because of association there will be damage to the other brands. For family branding, careful attention has to given to the quality control of the products. One other benefit of family branding is that each product brand performance (PBP) can be measured against the overall family brand performance (FBP). That is to say, when FBP is divided by PBP and the quotient shows an increase over time, without good reason, it may mean that the product brand needs modification, revitalisation or a detailed review.

Features and benefits

A product includes everything that the customer receives and this includes the core product which is made up of the delivery of benefits and features. We know that consumers buy products for the benefits they deliver to them as this is the outcome value of the purchase. There are also the different features which are the tangible aspects of the product which help to differentiate it from competitors. Adding in the right features increases the probability that a purchase will occur. Features in a store such as a play area for children, baby change facilities, fast checkouts, free gift wrap service, free delivery, and so on are all added benefits which may be planned into the product offer. Retailers should take the opportunity to consider factors such as fitting rooms, appropriateness of in-store music at mid-week periods as well as weekends when the market profile of their customers may change, gift wrapping service, loyalty programme benefits, etc.

STORE LAYOUT

The store is a product in its own right. The customer's product decisions can be enhanced, or ruined, by the type of planned store layout. Stores should be designed to facilitate the movement of customers, to create a planned store experience and to allow the optimum presentation of merchandise. This also involves the full use of the floor area – to utilising obscure and unproductive areas. The retailer's goal has to be a store layout which reflects the brand position of the store and ensures the most effective use of the space. It also has to be designed on a proactive rather than a passive basis.

Proactive planning is based upon the manipulation of the in-store experience rather accepting a passive, totally random experience for customers. Proactive planning accepts and responds to the data showing that store layout can influence the consumer's shopping behaviour and perceptions. It is well known that the use of different layouts and aisle design will influence the patterns of traffic flow to pass the principal merchandising groups. The correct display of merchandise in a highly frequented area can dramatically increase sales; conversely a poor display will have a negative affect.

Customers have to feel happy and comfortable in an environment if they are to relax and stay for any length of time. Customers are more likely to want to enter and shop in a store when their senses are satisfied by the way the store environment has been planned. The use of space, colour, walls, pillars, floor coverings, lighting, music, scent and so on can be controlled by the retailer. The combination of these physical messages which are planned are known as *atmospherics*. This is reinforced by the type of merchandise offered and the method of its display – down to the style and pose of mannequins. Atmospherics are created by the combination of a whole series of cues and stimulants to produce the desired ambience and emotional response from the group of target customers. The emotional state of the shopper will lead to an increase or decrease in the planned level of purchases. It is essential to know what factors stimulate and please consumers as the result will capture individuals for longer periods in a store and make them more susceptible to merchandise offers.

Therefore, the design of stores has to strive to produce an efficient layout with the qualities of ambience that attract members of the target market. The following list of factors is useful but not exhaustive.

1 Space must be used effectively, with territorial areas planned to break up the store into logical sales sections and functional areas such as changing rooms, restaurants and pay points – effective use of space. The store's layout should be planned for optimum circulation around the store. It should not be forgotten that the entrance to a store, both outside and inside, has to transform the customer's attitude and to create a promise of the experience to come.

2 Layout should be planned to encourage customers to circulate in specific patterns so as to visit as many merchandise areas as possible – *productive layout*. The retail layout logic has to be easily comprehensible so that the potential customer quickly understands and assimilates the route they can negotiate past the merchandise. This is often achieved by the use of different floor coverings or textures which act as clues to the customer. It may also be accomplished through the use of clear and stylish signage.

3 Stimulants to the senses to improve sales must also be planned. Music can be changed to suit the type of shopper in the store such as playing 'younger' background music

just after the schools close. Faster or slower music will affect the speed at which shopping occurs; national music, such as French or German tunes, played in a supermarket will increase the sales of a particular country's wines. Classical music will lead to sales of more expensive wines. Another option available is to vary the tempo of the music, at different times of day or in different areas, to influence the pace of in-store traffic movement. For example, when a higher turnover of customers is required in the restaurant around lunchtime, increasing the tempo of the music will achieve this behavioural effect. Fragrance and scents of perfumes, leatherwear, houseplants and so on may influence customers to purchase. The aroma of fresh bread, pastries, cheese, coffee, chocolate, etc. can stimulate sales and some stores or restaurants extract the aroma, pumping it outside their building to attract the passing public.

4 Lighting is an important mood setter and very useful in the production of a desired ambience. Lighting can be soft, bright or produce colour washes. Merchandise can be highlighted by directional lighting or with the combination of low-voltage and energy-efficient systems. Different types of lighting can be used in combinations to create interesting contrasts throughout a display area. The use of sophisticated lighting systems allows the retailer to adapt the ambience at regular intervals. This can alter perceptions of the size of different areas, complement the merchandise by bringing out its colours and direct the attention of the customer's gaze. One other important aspect of lighting is that in fitting rooms or where there are mirrors to view merchandise the lighting should be flattering.

From a strategic marketing stance it is important that in highly competitive retail sectors the layout of the store is planned in order to reflect the desired market position (*see* the section above on brand positioning). The position has to be planned in conjunction with clear ideas as to how the atmospherics will differentiate the store as a brand from its competitors. Store layout planners must also take into account who the target segments of the market are and what sort of buying experience they may seek from the store.

Aspects of atmospherics and store layout may affect:

- the speed at which consumers move from one point to another in the store;
- the degree of well-being felt by the staff working in the store environment;
- the total sales revenue, sales patterns and type of product sold;
- the image the consumer has of the store and its merchandise.

CONCLUSION

Product planning allows a retail company to understand and pinpoint marketplace opportunities so that the merchandise range can be co-ordinated to ensure that successful products are maintained and undesirable ones deleted. It allows for an understanding of the complexity of the retail product so that aspects of service and quality are considered as part of the overall retail offer. This section is brief as the following chapter is devoted to the important area of merchandise management; Chapter 6 discusses the different approaches to planning and controlling merchandise in terms of the width and depth issues, the assessment of stock levels and issues in buying.

RETAIL PRICING

The pricing policy selected by a retailer will usually be directly related to the resultant level of demand over a period of time and, with the right margins, to the profitability of the enterprise. For the retailer, pricing decisions are critical because without adequate margins the business will not survive for long. As a business, the retailer has to seek cash flow, profitability and growth in order to improve their market position. The importance of selecting the right strategy is growing as battles among retailers to increase market share are fought on the basis of offering quality, selection and availability at competitive prices. To be successful, retailers are having to forge partnerships with manufacturers and introduce technology, in order to gain cost advantage without compromising quality. Given this situation it is not surprising that cost, margin and price comprise the most important element of the marketing mix for most retailers. This is especially the case given the existence of discount store formats, the entrance of continental discounters and cheap sources of supply. Even for others, such as convenience stores, price is important even if it is secondary to the benefits of location and the opening hours for trading. The current situation is that in the competitive retail marketplace, price is a major strategic weapon in the battle with the competition.

UNDERSTANDING PRICE AS A CONCEPT

Price may be usefully described as follows:

> **Price is the monetary value assigned by the seller to something purchased, sold or offered for sale, and on transaction by a buyer, as their willingness to pay for the benefits the product and channel service delivers.**

This definition clearly separates the way the retailer treats pricing – as a cash flow or income generating function – from the view of the customer, who sees price as more than money. The purchase for the customer includes the complexity of emotional and functional benefits derived from the product and the brand. This means that value for the customer is a complex set of perceptions. This is discussed in more detail later in this chapter.

We believe that of all the elements of the marketing mix, good pricing decisions are the hardest to make. This is because prices for retail products and channel services have to take into account the complexity created by seasonality of demand and the inherent perishability of the product due to factors related to fashion or being past the sell-by date. There has also been a major influence on the grocery sector due to the abolition of resale price maintenance (r.p.m.) which has led to the offer of loss leaders and more complex pricing policies in order to achieve optimal overall profit. In conjunction with this, consumers are now pressurising retailers to change their pricing policies to offer greater value for money.

A retailer's pricing policy must be consistent with the overall objectives and reputation of the business. This could be in financial terms such as sales, profits, return on investment, etc. or as pricing's role in the growth and expansion of the business. There may also be broader objectives such as the number of sales periods, total number and range of prices to be made available, and positioning of the store and merchandise in relation to prices. These pricing goals are important as they provide the consumer with an image of the retail outlet based upon its approach to pricing. In addition, pricing has to be integrated with other aspects of the marketing mix and take account of the target market.

According to research carried out by Datamonitor (1996) the pricing initiatives of the major multiples create distinct differences which pass on specific images of the company brand. Asda's catalogue and price promotions have reaffirmed the company's position as the most 'value led' multiple and this leads to long-term loyalty. Tesco's and Safeway's promotions have not only led to loyalty but also created a full-scale customer database. On the other hand, Sainsbury's price promotions are used mainly as an aid to stores facing local competition.

PRICE SENSITIVITY

The understanding of the way different price points affect demand or how demand operates between price points is an important consideration for the setting of retail price policy. Within retailing there are also major differences between market segments, such as youth markets and upper income groups, whose tastes may dramatically change from one period to another. Quite often the relative elasticities of demand for these segments is dissimilar. There is a range of different factors that affect price sensitivity which deserves discussion. First, however, we need to understand the demand curves which illustrate the different market reactions to price change, known as elastic and inelastic demand (*see* Fig. 5.4).

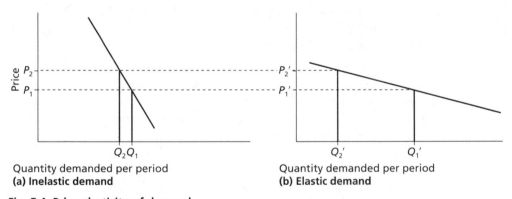

Fig. 5.4 Price elasticity of demand

Elasticity is a key element in the understanding of the demand process. It is defined as the ratio of the percentage response in the quantity sold to a percentage change in price or one of the other marketing mix elements, such as the expenditure on advertising. It therefore measures the sensitivity in quantity demanded to a change in the demand determinant. Mathematically elasticity can be calculated as follows:

$$\text{Elasticity} = \frac{\text{Percentage change in quantity demanded}}{\text{Percentage change in any demand determinant}}$$

For price elasticity the denominator is simply changed to a percentage change in price. The coefficient of price elasticity is nearly always negative because the price and quantity are inversely related. This means that when the price falls, the quantity demanded tends to rise; and when price rises, the demand tends to fall. Thus the retailer would be interested in the size of the coefficient as a coefficient of more than one indicates that demand is elastic (if price rises, demand falls significantly) and less than one that it is inelastic (if price rises, demand falls but only slightly).

From this it follows that the mark-up on highly competitive merchandise tends to be low because the demand for such items is price elastic. In general, retail mark-ups should vary inversely with price elasticity of demand if profits are to be maximised.

Factors affecting price sensitivity

A number of factors will affect the price sensitivity of products. From a marketing viewpoint a deeper understanding of price sensitivity assists with an understanding of the different retail segments and the development of strategic planning. The main factors when considering retail pricing are listed below.

Perceived substitutes effect

Buyers are more sensitive the higher the product's price is in relation to another product or substitute they could purchase. Therefore, the consumer may choose a substitute or forgo the purchase if they believe the overall value is unacceptable. For example, local residents may avoid an area with higher priced shops frequented by tourists who are unaware of the alternatives.

Unique value effect

Buyers are less sensitive to a product's price the more they value any of its attributes that differentiate it from competing products. For example, many customers are loyal to Heinz or Nestlé products because they perceive them to offer superior benefits.

Importance of purchase effect

If the risk of the purchase increases then the price will not be the most important aspect of the purchase. This occurs when the item is an important present or when there is a need to purchase medicines. The greater the importance of the product, the less price sensitive (more inelastic) the purchase will be.

Difficult comparison effect

Buyers are less sensitive to price when they find it more difficult to compare alternatives. This may lead to a demand for the more established brands, or greater store loyalty, in order to reduce the perception of risk.

Price quality effect

A higher price may signal that the product is of superior quality. The result may be less sensitivity to price. This is not a conclusive effect as it applies to some products, while others may generate different reactions. For example, whisky at a higher price may signal improved quality but very few people would think higher priced petrol offered any quality advantage.

Expenditure effect

Buyers become more price sensitive when the expenditure is larger, either in absolute money amounts or as a percentage of their income. This is most prevalent in low income households in which all expenditure is carefully controlled. This effect is also stronger and more likely to occur in times of recession.

Fairness effect

If the buyer believes the price falls outside a band of what would be judged reasonable and fair then they become more price sensitive. With some types of products it is relatively easy to judge the offer of alternative brands and products and therefore easy to switch demand to cheaper alternatives. At certain times alternatives are not easy to find. Consumers will perceive retailers, or the brands they stock, to be 'ripping-off' customers if they exploit situations of shortage by being greedy. For example, street vendors are often seen to be selling drinks or ice creams at highly inflated prices when the temperature is extremely high.

MINICASE 5.2

Reduced prices based upon the 'grey market'

They claim they are waging a war against artificially high prices. But when supermarket chains advertise designer products at reduced prices – against the wishes of the brand's owner – they are sending out subtle messages about their core business. 'The implication is that everything else you buy in the store is sold at competitive prices,' says a supermarket executive, who co-ordinates purchases on the 'grey market', where stores obtain brand-name goods. Food retailers are increasingly waking up to the promotional advantages of using this market. Asda reinforces its low-price image by selling fine fragrances at up to 50 per cent less than department stores and claims to be a leading campaigner for consumer interests as a result. Recently, Tesco said it had gone to 'extreme lengths' to find Ralph Lauren shirts and T-shirts to sell at less than half price. Both stress they cannot promise a consistent supply of such products, since up-market brand owners refuse to distribute to mass-market food retailers. 'It is difficult for a retailer to get a clear idea of how the grey market works,' says a large chain, 'because traders keep their sources close to their chests.' The market's secrecy makes it difficult for anyone to gauge the size of the grey economy. Tesco estimates last year it sold about £20m of grey market products.

Source: Peggy Hollinger, *Financial Times*, 16 May 1998

The choice process of the consumer based upon price is quite a complex matter and each of the effects discussed above may be working in conjunction with each other. While price may be an indicator of quality, the consumer is capable of choosing between several offers. The consumer is able to judge the materials used in the manufacture of the product, the brand name and reputation, and after sales-service guarantees. On the other hand the consumer may be ignorant of such factors and therefore will rely on a trusted retailer or brand.

FURTHER FACTORS INFLUENCING PRICING

Price sensitivity is only one of the factors which a retailer has to consider in its approach to pricing. A retail company in formulating price policy decisions has to consider a range of influences, including the following aspects.

1 The perishable nature of some products, such as high fashion items or those with 'sell by' dates, is influential. Products which cannot be sold on a future occasion lead retailers to engage in various forms of last minute tactical pricing or seasonal sales.

2 The competitive nature of the industry places emphasis on setting prices at competitive levels or retailers could face losing sales.

3 The market is volatile due to:

- short-run fluctuations in international costs;
- the need to stock saleable items;
- problems of supply;
- shrinkage rates;
- the need for an adequate return for each square metre of floor space or page in a catalogue.

This requires sophisticated forward planning.

4 Cost control is an important part of pricing policy. Many retail enterprises have high fixed costs and yet need to set competitive prices. This can make them vulnerable to financial collapse or takeover if costs are not controlled.

5 Seasonal demand leads to peak and low season periods which require demand management pricing to cope with the need to shift old stock or improve cash flow situations.

6 Price is associated with the psychological aspects of both quality and status. It is therefore always important to gauge the way prices or their change will be perceived by different target segments.

7 Intermediaries may influence prices through changes in costs of supply, bank charges and interest rate changes, increases in wages due to national minimum wage rates, etc.

APPROACHES TO PRICING THE RETAIL PRODUCT

Pricing policy has to consider all the potential influences and factors affecting the market and therefore the scope facing the retailer is remarkably wide. The choice made will probably be one, or a combination, of the following. The major difference is between the *cost-oriented* and *demand-oriented* approach to pricing.

Cost-oriented pricing

Cost-oriented pricing is related to the costs a retailer incurs when purchasing a product or service for sale to its customers. Cost-oriented pricing refers to setting prices on the basis of an understanding of costs to the retailer.

Cost-plus pricing

For the cost-plus method this will be in relation to either marginal costs or total costs including overheads.

The approach could be to:

- select the target market;
- determine the cost of the goods in store – storage costs, selling costs, shrinkage estimates, overheads, etc.;
- determine the ceiling price above which the retailer would be offering expensive prices compared with those of competitors;
- apply the mark-up, given the possible range has been identified, in order to achieve profit objectives. There may be some discretion for pricing individual items within a department or section as it is the overall profit which is important. A percentage mark-up is then normally applied to reach the final selling price. This may be expressed as a percentage of cost or of selling price. It should cover operating expenses and provide the desired level of profit. For example, if we assume a retailer purchases a dress at £60 and prices it at £90 then the mark-up on cost (£30/£60) expressed as a percentage is 50 per cent and the mark-up on selling price (£30/£90) is 33.3 per cent. Some minor adjustments may take place, such as bringing the price to £89.95 – fine-tuning the final price for psychological and other reasons.

Knowing the cost breakdown of the product is extremely important and it is essential to have calculated the operating cost of each retail outlet or page in a catalogue. This allows the marketer to know what the net effect of any tactical price reduction will be.

The weakness of cost-oriented pricing as a method is that it does not give adequate consideration to demand for the product, what prices the marketplace will bear, or the different price levels of the competitors.

Rate of return pricing

Another cost-oriented method is that of rate of return pricing which provides the company with an agreed rate of return on its investment. Whereas the cost-plus method concentrates on the costs associated with the running of the business, the rate of return method concentrates on the profits generated in relation to the capital invested. This approach ignores the need to link the pricing policy to the creation of a sales volume which is large enough to cover overheads or to ensure demand will remain consistent over time. Cost-plus or rate of return methods of pricing are not appropriate for those retail products which have to survive in a highly competitive marketplace.

Demand-oriented pricing

Demand-oriented pricing takes into consideration the factors of demand rather than the level of costs when setting price. In times of shortage of products – from candles at the time of power cuts, to vegetables out of season – prices are usually raised to take advantage of higher demand and scarcity of supply.

Discrimination pricing

Discrimination pricing, which is sometimes called *variable* or *flexible pricing*, is often used when products are sold at two or more different prices. Quite often students, the unwaged and older people are charged lower prices than other consumer segments at attractions or events. A garage will offer different prices for servicing company cars as opposed to private cars. A customer known to a retailer may be given a personal discount as part of a flexible approach to pricing based upon a personal relationship with that individual. Discrimination pricing is often time-related, for example cheaper drinks charges in 'happy hour' periods or cheaper meal prices in the early evening prior to the high demand periods. For price discrimination to be successful it is necessary to be able to identify those segments which, without the price differentials, would not purchase the product. To obtain a high flow of business, a DIY retailer will often discount to those customers who offer significant sales demand. This means that small businesses may benefit from volume discount rates and those individual customers building their own extension, for instance, may be offered a special one-off discount rate.

Discrimination may also be based upon increasing the price of products which have higher potential demand. For example, if the product is a fad product (for further explanation *see* Chapter 6) then it is normally in high demand, usually demand so strong that it outstrips supply. Therefore, such products as Rubik's Cubes or Teletubbies dolls could be priced at a higher price based upon an increasing level of demand. Another example of this is exhibited on special celebration dates, such as Mother's Day or Valentine's Day, when the price of flowers or plants is raised.

Backward pricing

This is a market-based method of pricing which focuses on what the consumer is willing to pay. The price is worked backward, as the name suggests. First an acceptable margin is agreed upon. Next the costs are closely monitored so that the price which is deemed to be acceptable is able to be matched. If necessary an adjustment is made to the quality of the product offer or service to meet the cost-led needs of this technique. Retailers selling on a price-led basis often insist that their suppliers meet specified costs, even if this compromises some aspects of the quality.

This approach can be associated with *price lining*. Price lining is a method of simplifying the merchandise comparisons for the customer by establishing a number of lines within price points for each classification. Once the price lines have been determined, the retailers purchase goods which fit into each line. For example, for men's shirts the price lines could be £25, £35 and £45. In order to be a successful trader the monetary difference between the price lines has to be large enough to reflect a value difference for the consumer. Such steps of change in price and value enhance the ability of the salesperson to convince the customer to trade either up or down. The selection of price lines has to be based upon the strength of consumer demand for the bands. The benefit of limiting the number of price lines is that a retailer can achieve broader assortments, which leads to increased sales and fewer markdowns. For example, a retailer which stocks 180 units of an item and has 6 price lines would have an assortment of only 30 units in each line. On the other hand, if the units were divided among only three price lines there would be 60 units in each line. By utilising such an approach a retailer may specialise more easily in relation to lines and so create a more defined store image for its merchandise. The advantages of price lining are:

- sales volume can be increased by the provision of larger assortments at each price line;
- there is greater clarity of price offer for the customers;
- salespeople can offer stepwise change to the customer in order to enable them to convince the customer to trade up or down;
- line concentration allows for improved displays and promotional messages;
- with improved effectiveness of pricing there may be less markdowns;
- the buying process is improved as buyers have to focus on the retail price point and 'buy backwards';
- control may be easier with greater price coordination and fewer pricing variables.

Skimming pricing

Skimming is utilised when there is a shortage of supply of the product or the brand has been associated with added value and, therefore, demand will not be dampened by charging a premium price. Market skimming policies can only occur where there is a healthy potential demand for the product on offer. Top fashion houses dealing in haute couture or cosmetics companies with strong branding utilise this approach.

Leader pricing

Some retail items may be priced very competitively in order to sacrifice profit on those items but to generate more overall demand for other items. These are often known as 'loss leaders' if they are sold below cost but in reality retailers seldom make a cash loss on the items even though they are heavily discounted. The leader items are normally sold near to cost rather than at a loss. However, a supermarket may sell turkeys as loss leaders at Christmas in order to achieve extra sales of other Christmas holiday provisions. The purpose behind the use of leader prices is to increase store visits, purchases and the perception of good value.

The items chosen for inclusion as loss leaders should be widely known and bought on a frequent basis. The objective would be to price the item low enough to attract numerous buyers. In addition, if information is made available as to the value of the offer, the promotion will usually be far more successful. The approach is often employed by supermarkets which feature leader items on a regular basis. As with all forms of price promotion there is an obvious need for retailers to monitor and evaluate their usefulness. In offering lead pricing, the danger is that customers may be selective in what they purchase. If customers are limiting their purchase to the lead item or if that item competes with other items in the store, the price promotion may need to be revised.

Competitive pricing

Competitive pricing is employed to match the market prices of competitive retailers. This is a technique which requires knowledge of actual costs as matching the prices of a more efficient retailer may lead to losses on particular items. It also requires an understanding of the importance of the pricing policies of the competition from a consumer's perspective. Competitive pricing is a reactive rather than proactive form of pricing as a retailer with a strong brand image does not necessarily need to match competitors' offers.

Market penetration

Market penetration pricing is similar to competitive pricing but is adopted when a company or brand wants to establish itself quickly in a market. Prices are set below those of the competition in order to create high initial acceptance for the company's retail offer. A company selling fast moving consumer goods (FMCGs) may use market penetration pricing in the first couple of years and then, when the product becomes established, will slowly increase the prices. In 1996 there was all-out war between the food retailers and major oil companies over the price of petrol, based upon various supermarkets trying to obtain a major market share. It is estimated the petrol price war of 1996 cost Tesco £30 million and 2000 independent companies were forced out of business. According to an article in *SuperMarketing* (1996), at the height of the price war the average gross profits were only 0.03p a litre and these rose to 5.5p a litre when the war subsided in July of the same year. The penetration strategy quickly established a 21.5 per cent share of the petrol market in the UK for the combined supermarkets.

Psychological pricing

This is sometimes referred to as *odd pricing*. Retailers will often price products below a round figure, changing a price from say £10 to £9.95 or £9.99 to foster the perception of the price as being below that at which the customer is willing to buy. Just as £9.95 may appear to be significantly less than £10, so a price of £488 may seem more on a £400 level than a £500 level. However, there is no conclusive evidence that such pricing policies make any significant difference to profits.

Everyday low pricing

A number of retailers now adopt the strategy of everyday low pricing (EDLP). This strategy stresses the use of a pricing policy with the continuity of prices at a level between the normal own store price and the price of the deep discount competitors. The term 'low' does not mean 'lowest'; it simply refers to a price position which is competitive and, therefore, can remain stable. A number of retailers who operate EDLP do not believe in markdown policies and sales but attempt to generate all-year-round demand by setting the prices at the right level. One of the most well known retailers to have adopted this strategy is Toys Я Us. EDLP is a strategy which is open to large operators who have significant economies of scale and buying power.

EDLP can offer a number of benefits, as the following list attests.

1 *Perception of fairness.* Many customers have become increasingly sceptical about the mark-up and mark-down strategies of retailers. There has been a trend by consumers to wait for sale periods or to attempt to get the best bargains by shopping around for promotions. EDLP allows retailers to withdraw from sale period pricing wars and to concentrate on creating a market position that imparts a perception of fairness of pricing.

2 *Reduced advertising.* The stable price policy of EDLPs eliminates the need for communication of sale or special price offers. Instead, the retailer can use the budget to concentrate on improvement of image or the building of relationship marketing schemes.

3 *Improved customer service management.* If the policy is set to banish sale periods then the demand created is less seasonal and volatile, and sales staff are able to spend adequate time in dealing with customers. This will improve the customer's perception of the level of service they receive. The lack of high demand sales periods also has the benefit of allowing staff levels to remain relatively constant.

4 *Reduced stockouts and improved inventory management.* With more even demand for the products it is easier to control the stock situation. EDLP reduces the large variations in demand and, therefore, periods of stockout when customers may feel dissatisfaction with the retailer's service.

5 *Increased profit margins.* If a retailer can impart to the customer an image of fair pricing then, although the prices may be generally lower, the overall effect can be to increase turnover and consequently profitability.

EDLP has some major benefits to recommend it; however, it would not be appropriate for all retailers. Some retailers would find it difficult to maintain low prices for a continuous period due to a lack of economies of scale in buying or due to the competitive nature of their business. Also, retailers selling goods which have a strong fashion content are more likely to want to set initial prices at a high level as this is good business practice. Fashion goods are often priced differently because if a subsequent sale is created for this type of merchandise, it often creates a high level of excitement. The motivation to purchase created from the sale enables the retailer to move a large amount of merchandise in a short period. Therefore, EDLP is not a sensible strategy for some retailers to adopt.

PRICING AND THE RELATIONSHIP TO VALUE

Whatever pricing policy is adopted, a company has to take into consideration the potential consumer's perceptual assessment. In deciding to buy a product a consumer has to be willing to give up something in order to enjoy the satisfactions of the benefits the product will deliver. This concept is more complex than it seems. The majority of consumers are looking for value when they buy a product and value is derived from the functions of quality and price, as well as the added value of the image or brand. This may be expressed as:

$$\text{Value} = \frac{\text{Quality}}{\text{Price}} + \text{Image}$$

If a consumer believes the image and quality of a product is good they will be willing to make greater sacrifices in order to purchase that product. This explains how first class travel continues to be successful on different forms of transport such as trains, aircraft and cruise ships, and why leading brands are able to attract higher prices. The interrelationship between price, quality and value plays a significant role in store patronage and the buying behaviour of customers. Value was grouped into four categories by Zeithaml (1988). These are:

● value as low price;
● value as whatever is wanted from a product;
● value as the quality one gets for the price paid;
● value as what one gets for what one gives.

Zeithaml describes value as a 'trade-off between salient benefit components and sacrifice components'. Benefit components according to Zeithaml include intrinsic attributes, extrinsic attributes, perceived quality and other relevant high abstractions. This means value is a judgement about superiority and benefits delivered. Therefore, having the lowest price is not a sufficient strategy as the best route to retail marketplace success.

If prices change, this can affect the consumers' quality perception. A price reduction may be associated with a belief that the company is in financial trouble, that it will have to cut service and quality, or that prices are falling and if one waits, a price will come down even more. The value of the product is thought to have decreased because quality, by association with the changes, is observed to have fallen by a greater ratio than prices. The following shows the perception that the new value is at only half the level of its former position:

$$\text{Value} = \frac{\text{Quality}}{\text{Price}} \text{ then if } V = \frac{Q/2x}{P/x} \text{ then } 1/2\ V = \frac{Q}{P}$$

The above relationship indicates that the quality of the merchandise or service is perceived to drop by half its former position while price remains the same. With the assumption that this is the same factor of x then value as judged by the consumer drops to half its former value. This indicates the importance of not dealing with price in isolation from other factors.

Alternatively, a price increase may be interpreted as the way the company is going to pay to improve the quality and service of the retail offer. However, some consumers may simply think that the company is being greedy and that quality has not improved. This means the consumer may judge the value to have fallen. The outcome quite often depends on how the retailer explains the increase in price to the consumer.

To ensure the maximum chance of success for the pricing policy adopted there is a need to check each stage of the procedure, as in Fig. 5.5. This figure identifies the important considerations required for the successful evolution of a pricing policy.

Other costs and therefore pricing implications

There are other costs which a retailer needs to bear in mind when attempting to judge how competitive the store product price may be. These can be based upon:

● consumer travel costs such as the need to purchase petrol to travel to a store in a distant or out-of-town location;

● any parking charges related to a shopping visit to town;

● the level of traffic congestion in getting to the store;

● whether there is a free transit scheme to a local store or whether a park and ride scheme is available;

● pricing mix changes which affect price in terms of the provision of loyalty rewards or trading stamps. Any change in these is, in effect, a change in price and cost;

● the need for multi-purpose visits to a store or location.

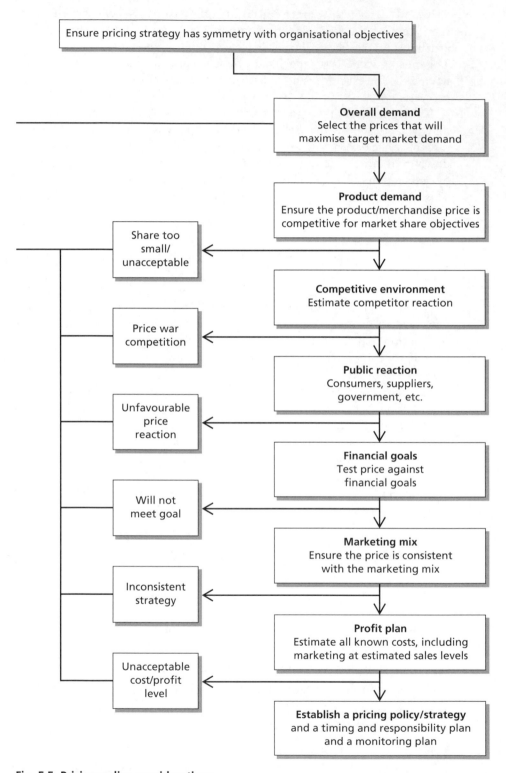

Fig. 5.5 Pricing policy considerations

MARKDOWN POLICY CONSIDERATIONS FOR RETAILERS

Price competition is an important feature of the grocery marketplace. Prior to its merger with Somerfield, Kwik Save sparked off a grocery price war in 1995 when it announced a nationwide promotion cutting up to 15 per cent off the price of one in ten of its top brands (Cope, 1995). While rivals such as Asda dismissed Kwik Save's actions as a 'panic move', others promised to retaliate. Netto, a Danish discount operator, said it would match the prices if any of its lines were directly undercut. Kwik Save had been under pressure in the grocery market where it was caught between the larger superstore operators and the aggressive Continental discounters such as Aldi, Netto and Lidl.

Virtually all retailers will have occasion to utilise price markdowns. It is typical for markdowns to be used as part of a clearance sale in order to provide space for new merchandise. However, while the list below indicates there are a number of reasons to use markdowns, it should be remembered that other elements of the marketing mix can be used to increase sales, or alternatively merchandise may be carried over into the new season. In the use of price to increase demand, markdown reductions of the original price may be necessary due to a number of reasons:

- competitor activity affecting demand;
- inadequate original pricing policy;
- merchandise did not meet consumer needs or preferences;
- economic or seasonal problems;
- overstocking of merchandise or poor stock keeping;
- quality of merchandise inferior due to manufacture or damage;
- problems of seasonality and poor timing of offer;
- merchandise became shop-soiled or damaged on the shop floor;
- need to release the display space for other merchandise;
- the selling space or display of the merchandise had been inadequate or in the wrong location;
- a policy decision taken to develop improved customer goodwill through markdowns;
- an error by the buyer with regard to style, fashions, research of market, etc.;
- an initial markdown being too small to achieve desired sales results;
- sales staff not being briefed properly or encouraged to sell old as well as new lines.

A retailer has to be clear about how any downward adjustment to original prices (markdowns) should be handled. This is important as markdowns are a consistent feature of retail marketing. For example, merchandise which sold originally for £50 may have to be reduced to £35 prior to the generation of adequate sales. In such a case the markdown is 30 per cent (£15/£50). However, some retailers prefer to express the markdown as a percentage of the new selling price. In the case given above this would be 42.9 per cent (£15/£35). Expressing markdowns as a percentage of the new selling price is often adopted as it can be more easily related to the method of accounting for the markdown for an entire department over a period of time.

$$\text{Markdown percentage on net sales} = \frac{\text{Markdown amount}}{\text{Net sales}}$$

For example, if a department achieved net sales of £10 000 after £2000 worth of markdowns, the markdown percentage of net sales would have been 20 per cent.

Most retailers that rely on a high inventory turnover will endeavour to use an early intervention for markdowns. However, there are a number of considerations which need to be addressed when utilising markdowns. There is consideration of the frequency and timing; retailers have to be aware of the negative consequences for exclusivity, image and quality of the type and number of sales or other promotional price reduction events. An early markdown policy may move the bulk of the stock more speedily, limit shop-soiling, and free up space for the new merchandise and enable the remaining stock to be better presented. A late policy may allow more stock to have been sold at a higher profit and could help maintain a more positive image for the retailer. If a markdown is used at a late stage it will necessitate a longer stockholding period, but the price cut should be large enough to ensure the remaining merchandise is moved quickly. Whatever the policy, markdowns should be of a sufficient size to attract those who would have bought the merchandise but rejected it on the basis of price. The size of the markdown is important. A small markdown may be ineffective and a large one may make the customer question the value of the merchandise – it may be felt that the retailer had previously been greedy. A reduction of 20 per cent is sufficient for the customer to notice the difference. Whatever approach is decided upon, a retailer should not allow unauthorised ad hoc reductions to be made. In some situations it may also be beneficial to remove the old prices, to retain the image of the store and to ensure that customers who bought previously are not dissatisfied. In other situations, however, the need to encourage customer perception that the new markdown prices offer a bargain is important.

In September 1996 Tesco launched their 'Unbeatable Value' campaign, during which they offered discounts on 600 products and challenged shoppers to find the same product on sale for less at a competitor's outlet (Atwal, 1996). This competitive pricing strategy was backed up by an extensive internal and external marketing campaign aimed at communicating the offers to their target market. Other retailers who wished to remain competitive had to react to this initiative in order to have a competitive stance. All companies reacted to varying degrees, with the most notable response coming from Sainsbury. The setting of price cannot be solely concerned with the consumer. Care and attention has to be given to appraising the reactions of both the consumer and the competition. Due to the high risk nature of some sectors of the retail industry, a price advantage which takes share from a competitor may often provoke hostile repricing reaction.

In Fig. 5.6, if company A attempts to increase its market share by price cutting it will need to take share from companies B and C (Fig. 5.6(a)). This is a situation in which C and B react by cutting their own prices. The outcome is that the market shares remain similar and may, as in Fig. 5.6(b), lead the market to grow in volume, but perhaps not in overall revenue. The long-term result is that the market remains extremely unstable due to smaller margins being applied. In this situation a company has to ensure it has a high volume of business in order to exceed its breakeven point. Price cutting policies have always been a feature of retail businesses in the UK and this has led to the collapse of many smaller companies which could not compete effectively with companies which had advantages of stronger buying power.

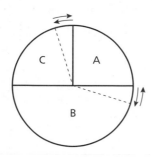

(a) Reactive price cutting, creating medium/long-term stabilisation but with less total revenue

(b) Lower prices increasing market size, but not necessarily to total revenue levels before the price cut

Fig. 5.6 Price cutting considerations

CONCLUSION

Price is a very important element in the marketing mix as it has to be set at the right level to ensure retailers have the capability to generate profits. It also represents an essential ingredient for the customer as price is all about the offer of value and benefits as part of the retail exchange process. It will be found that some retailers utilise EDLP but the majority still use price adjustments in order to create the right levels of demand for the ever changing market conditions of the modern marketplace.

RETAIL PROMOTION

Retailers communicate to their customers on a continuous basis through the store atmosphere, the products and services, promotional literature, advertising and other promotional means. *Retail promotion* is the descriptive term for the mix of communication activities which retail companies carry out in order to influence those publics on whom their sales depend. Retailing promotion will have the main objective of influencing consumer perceptions, attitudes and behaviour in order to increase store loyalty, store visits and product purchase. However, the important groups which need to be influenced are not simply the target market group of current and potential customers. There is a need to influence trade contacts such as agents and suppliers as well as opinion formers such as journalists and writers. Even local, national and international politicians and important professional groups may need to be influenced.

SETTING OBJECTIVES

As there is a range of promotional methods which can be employed by the marketer, it is important to define what the promotion has to achieve. The marketing objectives need to be clearly defined so that the most effective types of promotion can be utilised. Figure 5.7 explains how promotional objectives may be developed.

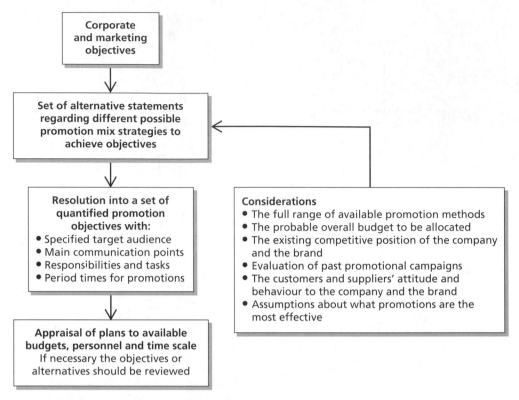

Fig. 5.7 Development of promotional objectives

The promotional objectives should have some precise terms in order to carry out the promotion and then monitor the results – so-called SMART objectives. SMART objectives will provide Specific, Measurable, Actionable, Realistic and Timed results along the following lines.

1 The target audience or market has to be identified (by segment, geographical spread, and for what stores). For example, identifying parents of school age children living in London.

2 The specific product (goods and service) to be promoted has to be identified. For example, identifying children's school-related products for a 'back to school' promotion.

3 Specific goals should be set, perhaps that sales will increase by £x in specific departments or across the store, or that attitudes to the store or brand will become more positive for the 40 plus age group. To continue the back to school example, to target an increase in sales of £15 000 for each London store for children's wear and £12 000 for school-related equipment.

4 The time horizon of when the expected effect will have occurred should be stated. For example, targets should be achieved by September of a specified year.

Taking up the example used in the list above, a SMART objective would therefore be:

> To ensure that the parents of children between the ages of four and sixteen, within seven miles of each London store, are communicated with and receive information on the back to school children's offers. Subsequently, sales for these products will increase by £15 000 for children's wear and £12 000 for school-related equipment by 1 September.

COMMUNICATION EFFECTS

There is always the need to plan to achieve the most effective response from the target market. An important part of the promotional effort is the building of *brand and product awareness*. Sometimes it will take a long time for the consumer to learn about the brand and the type of products which will be on offer. A promotion campaign should aim to provide *knowledge* of the product, to ensure that the consumer will feel favourable toward the product and build up a *preference* for it. Any campaign has to sell the benefits that a customer would be seeking in a credible way so that the potential customer feels *conviction* and is more likely than not to make a purchase.

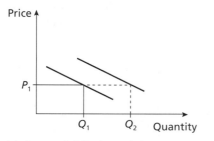

(a) Demand shift through better awareness

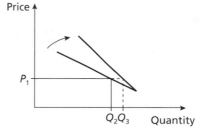

(b) Demand becomes more inelastic due to image improvement

Fig. 5.8 Promotional effect on demand

Figure 5.8 shows how a promotional campaign should aim to create increased demand through awareness and information. It also shows that the development of a positive image for a product creates a more price inelastic demand curve (*see* Fig. 5.4 for an illustration of the basics of elasticity), which means the product is more resilient with regard to price rises and does not have to rely on having low prices. P_1Q_1 is existing demand before a campaign has been developed to create more awareness in the target audience. At P_1Q_2 demand has increased because more people are aware of the company, the product and the benefits it can deliver. At P_1Q_3 the campaign has been planned to improve the image of the company or product so that more status is derived from the transaction process. This changes the shape of the demand curve – it becomes more inelastic.

Advertising and sales promotion are the most widely used forms of promotion. Because of the intrusive characteristic of these forms of promotion most consumers relate ideas of marketing to the use of advertising or sales promotion. The other main forms include public relations and personal selling. Retail promotion can be defined as any communication that informs, influences and prompts the target market about any aspect of the retail sponsor.

123

ADVERTISING

The term advertising includes any paid form of non-personal communication through the media about a product, that has an identified sponsor. The use of payment differentiates advertising from public relations for which no payment is made for the time or space to convey a message. The media may include telephone directories, guides, newspapers, magazines, radio, television, direct mail, Web pages and billboards. It is normally associated with mass communication, where a broad target market is to be contacted.

Advertising is used to achieve a whole range of objectives which may include changing attitudes or building image as well as achieving sales. Advertising is often described as above-the-line promotion with all other forms of promotion being termed below-the-line. The difference between above and below the line is simply academic now as the emphasis is on both areas, for example sales promotion and advertising, working together to achieve the greatest impact.

Moreover, in decisions over communication plans, it is the cost-effectiveness that matters most. The use of different combinations of what has traditionally been known as above and below the line has blurred the meaning of the terms and there are many promotional strategies which can be seen to erase the line or, as it is known, pass 'through the line'. With direct mail being used to build awareness and TV being used to sell products direct to the consumer, there is a great deal more flexibility in the use of different promotional mediums.

Communication theorists have proposed several models to explain the way advertising works and each have some similarity. One model known as the DAGMAR model (Defining Advertising Goals for Measured Advertising Results) describes the sequence of stages through which the prospective customer has to move:

- unawareness;
- awareness;
- comprehension of the offer;
- conviction;
- action.

Through advertising, the retailer will make the potential customer aware of the store and its range of offers. As part of the advertising communication process, information has to be clearly transmitted so it can be decoded and comprehended properly. The process is then to make the offer credible so that the potential customer can be moved to a favourable attitude to the store or product. The act of purchase may then follow.

Advertising has the potential to affect a large number of people simultaneously with a single message. The secondary effect of advertising is personal communications among consumers. This is known as the *two-step flow of communication*. The first step in the process is the communications flow from media to opinion leaders – the individuals whose attitudes, opinions, preferences and actions affect others. The second step is word-of-mouth communications from opinion leaders to others (followers). This communication can occur through personal conversation between friends or with work colleagues based upon communication about the store or its offers. It can also occur through non-verbal communications when someone displays newly bought merchandise in their home or by means of the labels on or in their clothes. One implication of the need to achieve as much benefit as possible from the two-step model is the requirement to reach and influence opinion leaders.

Types of advertising

Product advertising

Product advertising is aimed at enticing people to the store in order to consider specific merchandise. Product advertising will feature the promotion of merchandise that is new, exclusive, and superior in aspects of quality and design as well as creating awareness of complete assortments or special merchandise events. It is aimed at creating awareness of the product, its availability and benefits.

Markdown event advertising

This is used to create some excitement about a special period of lower cost offers for products. It is likely to be more successful if the reduction is believed to be part of a genuine sale of products which in the past had been fairly priced.

Institutional advertising

This type of advertising is used to sell the store or shopping mall as a pleasing place to shop. With the use of institutional advertising, the store attempts to reinforce the image of one or more of the following: a leader in fashion, fair prices, wide merchandise selection, superior service or quality, a leisure experience or somewhere to enjoy visiting. There is now a trend to advertise a shopping centre rather than individual outlets. The communication emphasis is on the available range of shops, ease of parking or other consumer benefits. The frequency of this type of advertising increases at peak demand times such as Christmas.

Co-operative advertising

This is used where manufacturers fund part of a promotion by supplying leaflets or advertising material for use by the store. The store can add its own address to ready prepared printed material and carry out mail drops or other methods of distribution. Alternatively a manufacturer may agree to share equally the costs of an advertising campaign. Manufacturers are keen to have their brands stocked and sold; therefore, they often enter into joint advertising schemes with retailers. Co-operative advertising may involve a combination of one or more retailers in an area as well as the manufacturer. In addition, co-operative promotions may well extend to agreements to provide joint branded window display material and point-of-sale material.

Retail promotion in relation to that of manufacturers

There are differences between retailer and manufacturer advertising strategies. Retail advertising is often based upon short-term objectives with the emphasis on value or price of the products on offer. This is unlike manufacturers' approaches; they often attempt to build favourable attitudes or improve the image of the brand or organisation over an extended period of time. Whereas a manufacturer will need to create awareness of its brand across major market areas, a retailer may have more geographically concentrated target markets. Therefore, a retailer has to take into account local habits, conditions of the marketplace, availability of local media and have a clear idea of the housing areas where potential customers are living.

The expense of some forms of advertising is excessive – for example TV advertising is extremely expensive due to production as well as transmission costs – and therefore only the larger companies or franchisers will use this medium. The alternative use of direct marketing is often a more cost-effective form of promotion for smaller more geographically dispersed retailers.

Push versus pull strategy

The promotional decisions have to consider whether the company chooses a push strategy or a pull strategy or a balance of the two. A push strategy involves 'pushing' the consumer through the channel by directing the marketing activities to promote the store or benefits of the channel (*see* Fig. 5.9(a)). As retailing is a channel service this approach is unlike that of more traditional forms of product marketing as it is the channel service which is promoted. The pull strategy is where marketing promotion activities are targeted to the consumer to induce them to buy the retailer's merchandise or services (*see* Fig. 5.9(b)). Retailers may enter third party agreements for promotion whereby the cost of the promotion is shared between the retailer and the manufacturer to encourage more sales of the manufacturer's product.

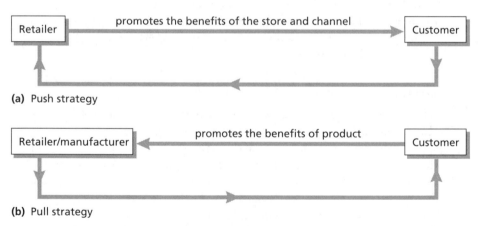

(a) Push strategy

(b) Pull strategy

Fig. 5.9 Push versus pull strategy for a retailer

With the growing use of relationship marketing and the compilation of customer databases, retailers have been concentrating more on push rather than pull strategies. Companies are increasing their efforts to select the most appropriate target groups to direct offers at. This allows marketing programmes to be more finely targeted, with literature for sale periods, special events or offers being tailored to suit the individual customer group.

SALES PROMOTION

Sales promotion involves any paid non-personal marketing communication activity, other than advertising, which offers an incentive to induce a desired result from potential customers, trade intermediaries, or the sales force. This is sometimes referred to by the term *sales incentive*. Sales promotion campaigns will add value to the product because the incentives will generally not accompany the product but will typically be offered as mail drops or as coupons to be cut from newspapers, etc. It is usual for a sales promotion campaign to be used as a temporary offer to the customer in order to stimulate an immediate response. For example, free samples or money-off vouchers and offers are frequently used in sales promotion campaigns for brands or companies which need to improve demand at certain periods. Included in these campaigns are: displays, contests, sweepstakes, coupons, frequent user (loyalty) programmes, prizes, samples, demonstrations, referral gifts and other limited duration selling efforts not included in the other techniques – *see* summary of types of sales promotion below. Most incentives are planned to be offered on a short-term basis only.

Summary of types of sales promotion

Type of sales promotion	Description
Point-of-purchase/ Point-of-sale	Retailer or manufacturer displays for the window, floor and counter to enhance impulse purchase
Contests	Reinforcement of brand or outlet through competitions (skill games providing slogans doing puzzles, etc.) for prizes
Sweepstakes	Similar to contest but winner chosen by chance, by filling in application form, rather than skill
Coupons	Special discounts are advertised with a coupon being cut out and redeemed as part of an at-store purchase. Modern approaches utilise optically read coupon cards at checkout
Frequent shopper	Customers are rewarded by points or stamps for repeat purchase or total amount spent
Prizes	Similar to frequent shopper programmes except retailer offers prizes whereby a piece of a set, such as a glass or part of tea set, is gained on predetermined threshold purchase levels
Demonstrations	Products or services are shown in use or what they can achieve and the benefits they give, for example, demonstration of a foot massager to customers
Referral gifts	Presents or gifts are given to existing customers who introduce new custom. Often used by direct sales retailers such as those selling books or tapes and CDs
2 for price of 1	Extra items of merchandise added to pack free of charge to increase sales
Branded giveaways	Items such as pens, calendars, shopping bags, etc. with the retailer's logo are given to customers
Samples	Free samples of products, tastes, smells given away to customers
Premiums	Merchandise item given free of charge or at substantial reduction for traffic building of increase in store visits or to encourage sales. Self-liquidating premiums are when the customer pays something towards cost
Special events	Fashion shows, autograph sessions with celebrities, art and craft exhibitions, school holiday activities, topical local interest displays. Retail store openings are often linked to a special event

Sales promotion is often used in combination with other promotional tools in order to supplement the overall effort. However, it has to be remembered that it is sometimes difficult to terminate or change special promotions without causing adverse effects. Loyalty programmes are an example of this (*see* following section on relationship marketing). A sales promotion (or series of promotions) also has to take account of the likely effect it may have on the image of the brand or outlet due to the negative perception change which may occur due to association with banal and frivolous promotions.

To evaluate a sales promotion the retailer should consider:

- the cost of the promotion in employee time, as well as for the cost of any merchandise, giveaway items or promotional literature;

- the increase in sales and profit, or improvement in awareness, based upon the campaign;

- whether the campaign had secondary effects of switching demand from other retailer products;

- whether there were any additional sales outside of the promotion, due to customers being attracted to the store.

It is not always easy to isolate the above effects from other factors, but it is always important to make some assessment of the benefit of different types of promotion.

RELATIONSHIP MARKETING – LOYALTY SCHEMES

The retail marketplace is maturing and due to a slow down in growth is becoming more competitive. Against this backdrop, retailers seek different ways of improving sales and profits. In order to address these problems retailers are adopting relationship marketing (RM) schemes based upon loyalty cards which aim to:

- build greater customer loyalty and retention;

- develop methods of creating longer-term relationships;

- Lead ultimately to increased sales and profits.

RM has been defined by Gronroos (1990, 1991, 1994), who has consistently argued for the importance of ensuring that relationships with customers should be continuously developed:

> **Marketing is to establish, maintain and enhance relationships with customers and other partners, at a profit, so that the objectives of the parties involved are met. This is achieved by a mutual exchange and fulfilment of promises.**

Gronroos argues that all marketing strategies lie on a continuum ranging from transactional to relational marketing, where relationship marketing can be judged in terms of measures of *customer retention* rather than market share. Christopher *et al.* (1996) have developed the idea of a ladder whereby relationships develop as part of growing customer loyalty (*see* Fig. 5.10).

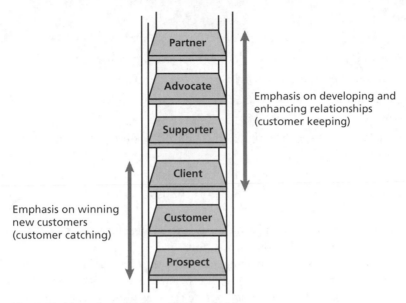

Fig. 5.10 The relationship marketing ladder

Source: Payne *et al.*, 1995. Reproduced with permission

The RM process helps to advance relationships to higher levels until advocate status is achieved. This is where the customer as advocate is not only loyal but also champions the company, the employees and the service to others. RM should not be confused with brand loyalty based upon commitment to the product; RM is a far more complex and wider alliance and association.

The rationale for RM is that it makes business sense to focus on long-term financial benefits which may accrue once a customer has been won for the first time. This is because it has been estimated it is five to ten times more expensive to recruit a new customer than to retain an existing one. This is based upon the estimated cost of prospecting, advertising and selling, commission, product samples, credit checking, administration, and database management. The true value of retaining customers is that it enables the costs of conversion of the prospect to be set against the revenues earned over the longer term. Sales and profits improve in direct proportion to the longer a relationship lasts.

RM requires the effective *acquisition* and *retention* of customers for the building of a more efficient operation and, ultimately, a stronger competitive position. Acquisition is based upon the traditional approach to marketing with the identification of customer needs, development of a retail offer to satisfy those needs, and then the targeting of prospects. The movement from acquisition through to retention is sketched in the following.

Acquisition:

● current methods used to acquire customers from prospects, which then require effective retention. (Customers must be given an incentive to part with their personal information and be recruited to any scheme.)

Retention:

- *identify* more about customer through database analysis;
- *improve* and make the retail outlet/offer/service more attractive;
- *inform* to build customers' knowledge of the company;
- *tempt* customers through special targeted offers to purchase more regularly, try different products, etc.;
- *retain* the customer by developing and delivering different forms of loyalty schemes and rewards;
- higher patronage should provide *increased* customer value to company, which should result in *higher* profits and the ability to make increased *investment* in further acquisition of new members to the scheme.

The foregoing process can be viewed as an increasing outward spiral which places the company in a stronger and stronger position.

Incentivised relationship marketing has become more prominent during the 1990s following the launch of loyalty card schemes. The customer is rewarded for their loyalty through the collection of points which entitle them to money off products, free items and other incentives such as Air Miles or charity donations. It would be useful if we were to define loyalty. Loyalty is

a state of mind which predisposes an individual toward a particular retailer and leads to a higher than normal proportion of expenditure to be devoted to the retailer's offers.

Relationship marketing or loyalty schemes have a number of benefits for the retailer.

1 The retailer can accurately track the purchasing habit of large numbers of loyalty scheme members and this enables the acquisition of important data which can be utilised for planning and promotional purposes.

2 A good scheme will lead to repeat purchases through targeted incentives and benefits to visit the retail outlet and make purchases.

3 The scheme will act as a promotion for new customers and they, in turn, can tell others about their experience.

4 The customer may be willing to pay higher prices if the scheme enhances the purchase experience.

5 Customers will not take as much notice of alternative offers and promotions if they are already linked into a worthwhile loyalty scheme.

The growth of schemes to encourage more loyal customers

Early methods of building loyalty were carried out by small shopkeepers who could get to know their customers personally and reward some of them with special services or attention – and even discounts or gifts at times such as Christmas. As companies began to grow, it became increasingly difficult to identify who the most valuable customers were and to collect and retain accurate information.

In the 1950s the Co-op led the way with cash dividend schemes for the 12 million members who regularly shopped at Co-op stores or benefited from the door-to-door services of the Co-op. Then, in 1963, Tesco introduced Green Shield stamps as an incentive scheme. This led to many of the smaller traders having to follow their lead in order to retain business. More recently, petrol retailers introduced point or reward schemes in order to create more regular custom. However, the recent development of loyalty cards by Tesco is a major departure from any previous marketing promotion scheme operated in the UK. This is because the loyalty card is able to provide instant and accurate feedback information on individual customers and their purchase patterns; this subsequently allows more individualised relationship marketing to take place.

In the UK from 1995 onward the major grocery retailers embarked upon the development of loyalty cards for their retail operations. The schemes are designed to ensure that a customer is retained and remains faithful to a particular retailer. The Tesco scheme was launched in 1995 and quickly built up a customer base of an estimated 9.5 million customers. Wanting to go even further, in 1996 Tesco launched Clubcard Plus which allowed customers to pay a set amount of money into the Clubcard scheme each month by standing order and then the cost of a cardholder's shopping to be deducted automatically from their Clubcard account. Any balance on the account earns interest; credit is extended for larger expenditure in any month with low rates of interest charged. This strategy by Tesco aimed at winning new customers was quickly followed by defensive strategies from other grocery retailers who needed to retain their own existing customers. This situation is very similar to what happened in the airline industry with frequent flyer programmes. These programmes brought major competitive advantage in the early stages of introduction but ended up by providing little advantage to the retailers when all airlines created similar schemes (Gilbert, 1996).

A loyalty scheme will collect information such as name, address including postcode, sex, date of birth, household size, children's dates of birth, ownership of consumer durables, preferred place(s) to carry out shopping, pet ownership, etc. Once this information is collected, the card customer data related to household type and size can be related to the postcode geographic data and then matched to the use of the card – the EPOS sales data. The record of purchase will provide information about time and frequency of visits, expenditure patterns, products and brands purchased as well as the success of any special offers. The combination of this data will allow for: data mining and data extraction for further promotions; improved decision making for new store development; targeted marketing via direct mail to promote sale periods; or to tempt back a 'lapsed' customer by the use of different promotions. Relationship marketing schemes are normally built around communication with members through magazines. With the larger schemes, the membership magazine may be targeted to different groups, such as students, pensioners or other life-cycle groups. This allows a company to target specific segments with information and offers which are attractive to that particular group.

The worry is that a growing number of customers will belong to several card schemes and this will dilute the impact of individual schemes. In 1997 it was estimated there were 55 million active loyalty programme participants in the UK, indicating a crossover between many of the schemes (IGD, 1998). Table 5.1 indicates that 35 per cent of Tesco cardholders will also belong to the Sainsbury Reward Card scheme and that 30 per cent of Sainsbury cardholders belong to a Tesco scheme.

Table 5.1 Multiple use of loyalty cards (November 1997)

Cards held by company name	All (%)	Tesco Clubcard (%)	Sainsbury Reward card (%)	Saveway ABC card (%)	Argos Premier Points (%)
Tesco	31	100	35	34	35
Sainsbury	26	30	100	25	29
Safeway	16	18	15	100	20
Argos	14	16	15	17	100
Boots	12	15	18	17	21
Homebase	10	17	16	15	13
M&S	10	18	19	14	15

Source: Institute of Grocery Distribution, 1998

With the figures in Table 5.1 in mind, we need to ensure we realise that there are different types of shopping occasion. It was found by *Which? Magazine* (Which? Magazine, 1996) that customers are more loyal to those stores where they do most of their shopping and are more likely to embark on secondary 'top up shopping' for daily essentials such as bread or milk. Therefore, the penetration of the market in the use of cards reflects this type of activity. This is because the convenience of the location is a major determinant in the loyalty process not simply the fact that someone has joined a loyalty scheme.

PERSONAL SELLING

Personal selling is an attempt to gain benefit through face-to-face or telephone contact between the seller's representative and those people with whom the seller wants to communicate. This may be based upon sales activity in-store, evening calls to try to sell services or products, or sales calls by paid salespersons either to companies or to private individuals. The importance of personal selling differs among retail businesses on the basis of the type of merchandise offered. A retailer offering low-risk, low-price goods, which are promoted, need only employ sales staff who can complete the transaction and deal with minor enquiries. The typical information required will be the current policy on reductions or special offers, guarantees or possible methods of payment. While the demeanour of the staff in this situation is important, there is little sales negotiation skill required to conclude the transaction. However, it should be noted the trend is toward retailers reducing the number of sales personnel by offering greater self-selection of products in order to save on sales staff costs.

In a store where there are highly priced or more complex items for sale the consumer has to cope with not only finding a salesperson to relate to but also one who has expert information. Such retail sales employees are often viewed as *order takers* but they should be viewed as *order procurers*. This is because for higher risk purchases customers utilise and seek out expert advice and help. Situations where it is important to have trained staff are:

- where the item has to be made to fit the customer's specific requirements, for example a wedding dress or made-to-measure clothes;
- where the product is technically complex and the range is wide, for example a computer or a video camera;

MINICASE 5.3

The expert shop assistant is making a comeback

We modern, independent-minded women who think we know it all have much to answer for. We have made the expert shop assistant not merely redundant but an endangered species. And, when fashion is all about 'pieces' that are lovely in themselves but as difficult to put together as a Chinese puzzle, we are reaping the whirlwind. The decline began some 30 years ago. Women without access to the new boutiques blossoming in city centres bought clothes at department stores or at independent 'madam shops', so-called because, before you had both feet through the door, the assistant was trilling 'Can I help you madam?' Often she couldn't. The cool clothes were all in the boutiques. The madam shops were increasingly left to elderly assistants whose desperation to make a sale led to uncomfortable pressure and purchases later regretted.

After style-awareness exploded in the 1980s, we became confident enough to accept clothes stores that were virtually self-service. The more sophisticated among us believed that the hallmark of a fashion individualist was trawling through lots of sources and coming up with a more chic mix than one so-called expert in one store could produce. How false was our sense of security in our own abilities. It worked well while the neutral suit was king, co-ordinates its consort, and black the only colour that mattered. Any fool could find a trouser suit that flattered, organise a white shirt and T-shirt for formal and laidback occasions, and add the designer pumps and bag which showed you knew the logo to go for. It is much harder in fashion's new climate. The universal and easy way of dressing has been replaced by something infinitely more difficult to achieve – something 'individual'. The high street's much-criticised uniformity has resulted in a stampede to shops promising a look no one else will have. The prototype is Voyage, which has been hyped and vilified in equal proportions and is both very interesting and a touch peculiar. Tatum Mazzilli, daughter of the owners and a stunning advertisement for its eclectic neo-hippy style, justifies its closed-door policy on the grounds that 'everyone who comes in deserves time and attention to make their choice and we cannot help them if we are over-stretched'. In a way, she is right – the choice of colour and styles (there is no black and no two pieces are identical) is so overwhelming that guidance is essential.

Source: Avril Groom, *Financial Times*, 30 May 1998

- when the product is expensive in relation to the individual's income, such as an overseas holiday;
- when flexible pricing is practised and negotiation over price takes place, for example car sales.

The importance of the service aspects of retail were discussed in Chapter 3, with the one-to-one contact of the salesperson being seen as key to the way the retail company is judged. For this reason sales staff have to be carefully selected and then well trained.

The intention of personal selling is to:

- obtain a sale. Often customers enter the retail outlet after acquiring information and the salesperson needs to persuade them to purchase;
- stimulate sales of 'impulse buy' purchases by bringing attention to extra requirements;
- complete a successful transaction with the customer;
- leave the customer satisfied and well informed, no matter whether a transaction has or has not occurred;
- create good customer relations.

The rationale for personal selling, as listed above, means there should never be a role conflict between whether a salesperson should be straightening and folding stock as opposed to engaging any customer entering the department in a conversation. To reduce any conflict felt by the salesperson, the high service retailer should reinforce the message that the customer is always the priority for attention. The overriding values of the retailer – the commitment to excellence in selling – have to be reinforced through compliments, incentives and rewards, and training. This training should include aspects of merchandise manufacture, buying and control as well as selling techniques. A salesperson can only sell convincingly if he/she understands fully the product and its benefits.

Selling is a process of steps whereby the salesperson builds up a personal obligation for the customer to make a purchase. This selling process is a series of moves and countermoves to ensure that the offer is acceptable and should follow seven basic steps (*see* Fig. 5.11).

1	Preparing through skills and knowledge	Feedback and learning from prior listening and training
2	Anticipating and identifying a prospective sale	Feedback and learning from prior listening and understanding customers
3	Method of approaching the potential customer and task	Feedback and learning from prior listening plus asking appropriate questions
4	Presenting the features and benefits	Active selling and listening in order to check on acceptability of offer
5	Dealing with customer concerns	Active listening in order to revise the argument to overcome objections
6	Building obligation and commitment	Active listening in order to ensure the offer is acceptable and the sale can be concluded
7	Establishing affinity and relationship	Reinforcement of the relationship through creating a satisfied customer

Fig. 5.11 The retail selling process

The retail selling process is made up of a number of the steps outlined in Fig. 5.11: preparing, anticipating a prospective sale, approaching, presenting, dealing with concerns, gaining commitment and establishing relationships. All these are linked into the feedback process of active listening and response. This is because the approach allows the salesperson to relate to the individual needs which will be specific to that customer. Most salespeople think their job is to talk rather than to listen, but it is only through listening that a good salesperson can provide the right offer and arguments to achieve the sale. The advantage of personal selling is that a salesperson can adapt the communication of benefits to be gained to the specific needs of the customer. The feedback process of listening to the customer's needs allows the salesperson to be flexible in their approach. This is made easier in a selling situation because the personal contact produces heightened awareness and attention by the customer. However, the sales functions of retailers have to be carefully handled because less skilled staff, who lack empathy, will be judged as being 'pushy'.

A salesperson will use questions to focus both on what the consumer is looking for and on why, when something is offered, they may have objections to it. An *open-ended question* which requires the customer to explain their response in some detail is often preferable to a *closed question* which will require only a yes or no answer. Open questions such as, 'What are you looking for today?' are far better than, 'May I help you?', which can prompt: 'No thank you'. Asking for the reasons for a purchase, or what the feelings and attitudes are to any merchandise shown will allow the salesperson to select an appropriate type of offer.

PUBLIC RELATIONS

Public relations is non-personal communication which changes opinion or achieves coverage in a mass medium, which is not paid for by the source. The coverage could include space given to a press release or favourable editorial comment. Public relations (PR) is important not only in obtaining editorial coverage, but also in suppressing potentially bad coverage. A company which has good links with the media is more likely to have the opportunity to stop or moderate news which could be damaging to the company. Consumer affairs television programmes quite often berate retailers for poor service or dangerous products. More recently, the use of cheap child labour in the production of merchandise for Western markets has become a newsworthy subject. This all requires sensible public relations reaction in order to retain a positive image for the retail company and industry.

The major benefit of PR is that it can promote and enhance a company's image. This is very important for service-based companies which are reliant on a more tangible positive image in order to be successful. PR is a highly credible form of communication as people like to read 'news stories' and will believe them to be less biased than information provided in advertisements. However, editorial decisions over what is communicated will mean control over the message, its timing, placement and coverage is out of a company's hands.

PR activity can either be planned or unplanned. Planned activity means the retailer attempts to retain control over the activity and news release. With unplanned activity, the retailer simply reacts in the most beneficial way to the chance of some publicity or to suppress a negative news item. Planned publicity will involve sending press releases and photographs to the media (trade papers, local and national press, radio and television), organising press conferences for more newsworthy events, sending letters to editors of journals or local newspapers, organising different creative 'stunts' to acquire the right tone of media coverage, and making speeches (or writing articles) on informed retail issues in order to be perceived as a well-informed company. The media are interested in their own circulation, listening and viewing figures and, therefore, to be successful all PR has to be newsworthy and of benefit to media interests. New and unusual information on new products or technology, expansion and development plans, human interest stories about staff and their achievements – all written up and complemented by photographs – may be placed in trade and local press.

OTHER IMPORTANT PROMOTIONAL TOOLS

Within the field of promotion, there is the important area of *visual merchandising*. Advertising may encourage consumers to visit the store but the retailer's display may make the difference between making a sale or not. The use of visual merchandising includes visual materials and window displays used in retail outlets to stimulate sales. Visual merchandising is non-personal in-store presentation and exhibition of merchandise, along with printed forms of communication. The approach is to:

- ensure maximum product exposure;
- provide displays which enhance product appearance and create interest;
- provide sales and product information such as display cards and posters;
- allow for storage and security of stock;
- generate additional sales through impulse purchases or by reminding the consumer of what is on offer based upon a message which is directly related to the product.

If retailers rely on self-service of items then a selection display such as those found in greetings card or music shops is required. Selection displays are generally open to facilitate easy browsing and inspection. Retailers use selection displays to exhibit their everyday assortments of convenience or shopping goods. Effective use of this approach requires a logical grouping of the merchandise by its usage. Ease of selection through uncomplicated, well-organised arrangements will increase sales. There are also special displays which are placed in well-exposed locations to bring some interest to the store. These can offer a dramatic impact by the use of display equipment and merchandise. Point-of-purchase displays are a particular type of special display which will be on the counter, in the store window or other relevant places. The visual display may include banners, counter cards, end-aisle stands, video-screen displays, floor-stand displays and shelf extenders.

There is a growing use of *sponsorship* and *direct marketing* which do not comfortably fit into the other four promotion categories (*see* Fig. 5.12). Sponsorship is the material or financial support of a specific activity, normally but not exclusively sport or the arts, which does not form part of the sponsor company's normal business. As Meenaghan (1998) has pointed out, throughout its relatively brief history commercial sponsorship has changed in many fundamental ways. Most evident has been its development from a small-scale activity to a major global industry. Sponsorship is treated much more seriously today, with sponsors adopting sophisticated planning, selection and evaluation procedures for their sponsorship programmes.

Direct marketing is being used more extensively by a range of direct sell companies as a means of utilising a retailer's loyalty scheme's database address list. The main method is direct mail which is postal communication by an identified sponsor. This is being expanded into database marketing based upon relationship marketing principles and an increasing use of telephone sales campaigns. Direct methods of contacting prospective customers are used to:

- encourage store visits from new customers;
- increase sales when there is a unique or special merchandise offer to be made;
- take full advantage of using the information from one department to cross sell other aspects of the store or its services;
- build loyalty programmes in order to retain customers and increase revenue;
- improve the image and competitive position of the store in relation to the competitors;
- send out special offers for low season or sales periods in order to increase in-store traffic and sales. There is often resistance to too much direct mail as it is often

associated with 'junk mail'. Good direct marketing selects the target carefully and provides the correct offer.

Finally *billboards*, sometimes referred to as *poster sites*, are used as either permanent painted sites or covered in prepared poster advertisements which can be frequently changed. The space is normally available on a rental basis, depending on the site and time of year. The use of this form of promotion can be beneficial if located near to the store, on a transport route which services the store or area or on the vehicles themselves. The costs are relatively low, based upon estimate of numbers of passing observers. However, car drivers, those travelling on public transport and the walking public need to have a short, clear message if the medium is to be successful. It is also important to realise that if the site is not illuminated then in the winter there will be less opportunity to see the message than at other times of the year.

The growth of database marketing/relationship marketing

Against a despairing background of retail product failures and weakening effectiveness of advertising, the attractions of database marketing are immense. Powerful, data-crunching computers with neural-network software (which searches, like the human brain, for patterns in a mass of data), hold out a vision of marketing nirvana: instead of advertising their products indiscriminately to fuzzy segments of the population, marketers can speak directly to individuals. Kraft food's division has tapped in the addresses of 30m customers who have replied to free-sample offers or other promotions. Unilever is centralising the customer data amassed by its British subsidiaries. However, the pioneers of database marketing are financial-services firms and airlines, which tend to know a lot more about their customers. American Express, for example, uses its customer database to tailor offers to small groups of cardholders according to their spending patterns. In Belgium, it is testing a system that combines offers based on tallying cardholders' past spending with postal-code data: if a new restaurant opens, for instance, cardholders who live within walking distance and are known to eat out a lot might receive a special discount.

Database marketing enables firms to keep existing customers over longer periods of time. In highly competitive markets, pushing up the 'lifetime value' of the customers you already have is just as useful as bringing in new ones. Building 'relationships' with old customers is central to marketing's new gospel. Procter & Gamble claims success for its use of databases to market Pampers, a disposable nappy, using such tactics as 'individualised' birthday cards for babies, and reminder letters to move up to the next size. But Dick Johnston, P&G's marketing manager in Britain, points out that this approach is cost-effective only because the product's potential customers are limited by nature to around 3% of the population. Nestlé, is trying similar techniques to push pasta. Its British subsidiary has signed up around 80,000 customers to its Casa Buitoni Club: they get a quarterly newsletter with recipes and competitions for Italian holidays. The firm says members have increased their purchases of Buitoni pasta by 15% since the club was launched in 1993, while the brand's total sales have fallen by 0.5% thanks to increased competition from own-label products.

Database marketing is not risk-free. The pitfalls start with widespread hostility to junk mail, and concerns about privacy; the trick seems to be to use databases to target letters as closely as possible to the known preferences of particular individuals. As a rule of thumb, database marketing makes more sense the higher the price of the product and the more often it is bought. That is a problem for consumer-goods manufacturers, whose products are mostly low-priced. In 1995 a quarter of American consumers have access to frequent-shopping programmes at their local supermarket and in Britain, Tesco became the first supermarket to launch a loyalty card scheme. These schemes can be targeted for different purposes such as to encourage customers to increase their purchases of retailers' own-label products.

Source: © *The Economist*, London, 1 April 1995

CHARACTERISTICS OF PROMOTIONS

Each of the promotional elements discussed above has the capacity to achieve a different promotional objective. While personal selling has high potency for achieving communication objectives only a relatively small number of people can be contacted. Therefore, advertising is a better method of reaching a high number of people at low cost. Public relations is more credible than advertising but there is more control over what is communicated through advertising messages and these messages can be repeated on a regular basis. When it is difficult to raise advertising budgets, public relations is a lower cost alternative but it is difficult to control the timing and consistency of PR coverage. Sales promotions, such as leaflet drops which offer retail price discounts may produce an initial trial for a product – for instance, the purchase of a product which is being launched into the market – but this type of promotion is most suitable if used only for a short-term period.

Each part of the promotions mix has its own strength and weakness. While this may include the factors of cost, ability to target different groups, and control, there are other important considerations. Figure 5.12 indicates the relative strengths of each of the four forms of promotion: advertising, personal selling, PR and sales promotion. They are compared on the basis of the level of awareness of the communication and its comprehension, as well as whether it can build conviction and succeed in creating action.

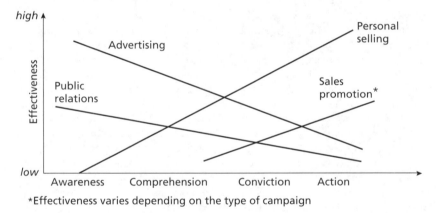

*Effectiveness varies depending on the type of campaign

Fig 5.12 Effectiveness of the four major methods of promotion

CONCLUSION

Retail promotion involves a complex series of communications to inform the target groups of the retailer's store and its offerings so as to increase demand and profits. There are a number of promotional mix tools available to achieve this. They consist primarily of advertising, sales promotion, personal selling and public relations. However, we should not forget the store itself will play a part in this process based upon its atmospherics and visual merchandising. Like other elements in the marketing mix, promotion does not work in isolation. Promotion is often used in conjunction with other constituents of the marketing mix, such as pricing markdowns, to stimulate the demand for products and subsequent store visits. Retail promotion is mostly used to convey the store's current offer – whether it be product, place or price, or a combination of these. However, a consistently good set of promotional campaigns will help establish a store's long-term image.

Each component of the promotion mix has unique advantages and disadvantages. The appropriate choice has to be based on which method is most suited to the marketing objectives at any one time. The largest proportion of a retailer's promotion budget will be allocated to advertising and sales promotion. Advertising is used a means to inform, persuade and remind customers that the retailer's merchandise and service offer is the one best suited to their individual needs. Sales promotion is used as a means to generate short-term increases in sales and, therefore, is an important part of the promotion mix. One other tool is public relations which does not require large budgets to be successful. Public relations allows the use of other media channels such as journalism, radio and television to act as opinion leaders for the personality and image of the retailer's business and product offering.

PLACE–SUPPLY CHAIN MANAGEMENT

The special characteristics of retail businesses and the emergence of major retailers in the marketplace have led to specific forms of distribution or channel service. Prior to consumption, the retail product has to be both available and accessible. This requires a supply chain distribution system. A distribution system is the channel used to bring items to the place of sale, or the means by which a retail supplier gains access to the potential buyers of the product. More recently the efficiencies of supply chain management linked to IT have made major differences to the effectiveness of retailers and their overall profitability. (Read Chapter 10 in order to understand the way IT has changed the whole field of distribution logistics.) With the ever-growing size and dispersal of retail operations, controlling merchandise as part of store operations has been of paramount importance. This goes beyond an administration system; modern supply chain management can achieve competitive advantage through shorter lead times for restocking, reduced inventory size and costs, improved management information and greater overall control.

Retailing cannot be divorced from an understanding of the supply chain as the following retail definition from Davies (1993) indicates:

> **The management of resources to supply the product and service needs of the end-consumer, encompassing the supply chain of any physical products and the exchange processes involved.**

The supply chain includes all the activities and exchanges involved in extracting, processing, manufacturing and distributing goods and services from raw materials through to the end consumer. Supply chain management requires a holistic view of these activities and an innovative approach to their organisation, in order to meet customer needs with the greatest efficiency.

CHANNELS AND CHANNEL FLOWS

There are different supply chain structures based upon *extended*, *limited* and *direct channels*. The discussion of supply chain management here will concentrate on the extended channel of retail distribution as this is the most prevalent. An extended channel (*see* Fig. 5.13) is where the manufacturer, wholesaler and retailer provide a chain of facilitating services in order to sell the right product to the final customer. The limited channel is when a retailer works directly with the producer and, therefore, can eliminate the wholesaler and the extra costs of this part of the chain. The retailers of furniture, white goods, electrical goods, and so on quite often deal direct with the supplier and create limited supply channels. The final alternative is the direct channel. In this case the product is sold direct by either the producer or retailer. By using different direct sales marketing promotions such as direct mailing, Internet services, telephone sales techniques, etc., the channel is kept direct and the extra charges and commissions are thus eliminated. This allows some of the saving to be passed on to the customer who will purchase on the basis of lower price. It is important to realise that whatever part of the chain is eliminated, some of the functions of that link in the chain have to remain. Even if the retailer were to be dispensed with, some of the retail functions have to remain in order to achieve a transaction.

Within any of the different types of channel the flow is not restricted to physical goods alone. Other types of flow of equal importance in ensuring the channel is successful are as follows:

- *physical flow* – the movement of goods and method of transport, from one part of the chain to another;

- *ownership flow* – the transfer of title for ownership/usage from one channel member to another. This is important for legal aspects of delivery, damage and storage by the producer and intermediary as well as for the final customer;

- *service flow* – if services are rendered as part of the process or the end product is a service or mainly service based, it is necessary to ensure all the characteristics of the services are fully understood (*see* Chapter 3);

- *information flow* – there is a need for timely and accurate two-way information between all channel members;

- *payment flow* – there is a necessity for agreed payment transfer terms based upon services rendered or goods delivered;

- *promotion flow* – a flow of communication material needs to be used to influence both trade partners and consumers. The objectives of the promotion will be to produce a positive attitude and image for the retailer.

With the extended channel, the distribution of goods ('inventory') by retailers to consumers is achieved through the movement of goods to and from stockholding points (normally warehouses) and then on to points of purchase (stores). In marketing terminology this part of the marketing mix is referred to as 'place' but the stages involved in this chain may be referred to as 'distribution and warehousing' or, more aptly, as 'logistics' and 'supply chain management'. In the modern competitive marketplace, retailers need to achieve high levels of customer satisfaction and service but at acceptable costs. This has led to the development of increasingly sophisticated distribution systems to ensure optimum service for the supply of goods to the customer. According to Davison (1995), large highly complex and often computerised warehouse facilities may handle several million cases per week (or in excess of £10–15 million worth of stock). Computerised stock management and information systems (for example Tesco's Dallas,

Sainsbury's BRS, Safeway's SM3, etc.) which link retailer communications direct to suppliers have been developed (for example Tradenet) and transportation is subject to computerised control systems (for example 'Paragon'). These comprise sophisticated logistics systems which have become not only a means of managing the supply of goods to the customer but are key strategic tools.

Many retailers benefited from the introduction of new logistics systems in the 1980s through increasing market share or increasing profitability. Companies which have benefited from such policies are generally those which no longer consider distribution and warehousing as purely a support function or an operations' headache. Rather than simply a functional supply line, the use of retail logistics is now a valued management area with its own operational and strategic objectives.

THE SUPPLY CHANNEL

The supply channel is the total process by which products reach the end consumer as goods or services. Figure 5.13 indicates the components of the traditional supply chain channel. Such a chain is an arrangement between paired links, where the emphasis has to be on controlling and managing the relationships in order to move products through the process effectively. This should be based on a marketing and business need for the chain to achieve:

- reduced inventory investment in the chain;
- improved customer service through its effectiveness;
- development of strong links, and hence a strong chain, in order to build competitive advantage; and
- lower unit costs which can be used to price more competitively.

As the whole chain is dependent on the way any two of these parts of the chain interact there is always a question of whether the working relationships will be good and provide the service and economies required. In practice, it is found that the relationships are often ones of rivalry, mistrust and secrecy. None of these is conducive to a retailer being able to provide any added value from the supply chain.

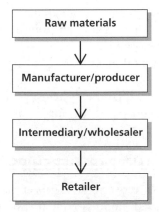

Fig. 5.13 **The traditional supply channel for retail products**

The manufacturer

The manufacturer or supplier processes raw materials into the finished consumable article. Suppliers may specialise in the type of products that they process (for example Birds Eye) or diversify into a wide product range (for example Unilever). Suppliers of leading brands will use a high level of marketing, including sales representatives and advertising campaigns in order to ensure that their products are given maximum public exposure. They may even reduce the cost of their products to encourage retailers to have their products featured in high flow locations within their stores.

The intermediary function

The intermediary, the wholesaler, is in effect a distributor of goods from the manufacturer or supplier to the retailer. Wholesalers have traditionally been responsible for holding large stocks of products, attempting to anticipate demands and seasonal trends, etc. Traditionally the wholesaler has also provided a warehousing function for both the supplier and the retailer. This ensures that the supplier does not end up with stockpiles in the factory and is able to continue or switch production; the retailer has similarly benefited from the use of this intermediary in the supply channel by avoiding the need to hold large quantities of stock. This enables the retailer to free up capital, which would otherwise be tied up in stock, for other purposes.

However, modern multiple store groups and supermarket chains have rendered the use of wholesalers unnecessary in the supply chain by assuming the function of the intermediary. This has a cost saving function. At each stage in the chain of distribution the cost price of a product is added to. This build-up of extra costs may reduce profit margins for the retailer or increase the final selling price to the customer. This is not in harmony with the normal retail objective which is to maximise sales and profitability. Additionally, each extra stage in the supply chain makes it more difficult for the retailer to control the service or the quality of the final product. The more links that are involved in the distribution chain, the less control there may be. This is allied to the risk of conflicts over relationships with each partner attempting to maximise profit.

The larger retailers have, therefore, sought to extend their control over the supply chain and moved away from the use of the intermediary. This has been particularly so in the grocery sector, where currently four grocery chains, Sainsbury, Tesco, Safeway and ASDA, account for a major share of sales in the UK packaged groceries market. The size of market share gives these companies enormous power over suppliers to negotiate discount prices and to absorb the role of the former wholesale intermediary, while ensuring the quality and service of product to the customer.

For such companies the traditional supply chain no longer exists. Multiple retailers – with their clearly defined strategic objectives, extensive national coverage, centralised organisational structures and highly accurate information systems – have created logistics networks which supplant the intermediary's role of supply in filling gaps between production and consumption.

GROWTH OF CHANNEL RELATIONSHIPS AND PARTNERSHIPS

A number of interrelated power relationships characterise the UK grocery sector. These range from mutual dependence to alliances based upon secondary suppliers. The relationships are also affected by the concentration of market share in that suppliers are constrained in who they can deal with as the market is dominated by a limited number of multiple-outlet retailers. The negotiating strength of retailers has increased, and this is even more apparent when own-label products are being offered with gross margins higher than manufacturers' brands. The power that individual retailers now exert is also compounded by the centralisation of decision making, with fewer individuals at head office being involved in deciding the fate of numerous different suppliers. This has meant that store managers have little input to supplier choice and are freer to concentrate on personnel and service quality functions. Such developments have had the effect of fundamentally restructuring the supply chain. This does not apply only to food retailers as the new methods of working have affected all aspects of retail.

Driven by competitive pressure to improve efficiency and to deliver added value for customers, major players in the supply chain have been changing the way that they do business with each other. Retailers and suppliers have started to recognise the degree of mutuality between each of their own objectives. Traditionally supply chain relationships have been adversarial, exhibiting a high degree of conflict; during the 1990s there has been a recognition that there are benefits in closer working relationships. However, there is always a potential problem for the large suppliers, which utilise logistics contractors, utilising their power; this may lead to a situation founded on fear rather than mutual interdependence. Any trading relationship will include a measure of conflict and of co-operation. This can be seen as a continuum extending from a single transaction, with a very minimal requirement for trust between the two parties, to a long-term supply chain 'partnership' with a very high degree of trust, at the other extreme. Conflict imposes additional costs on the trading arrangements. Therefore, the aim is to move along the continuum, reducing the level of conflict and increasing the co-operation so that costs are reduced and quality improves.

In pre-checkout scanning days, the retailer had privileged access to current sales data and would use this as a weapon to counteract suppliers' bargaining strength. We can contrast this with recent trends of using EFTPOS and EDI technology to delegate the entire replenishment administration activity to suppliers. Technology has had a major impact on distribution. Inventory management is now driven by the scanning of merchandise at the checkout. This allows sales for all outlets to be collated and communicated straight through to the supplier, who will be responsible – within agreed parameters – for ensuring that fresh supplies arrive at retailer distribution centres to replenish outlets.

It is important to recognise that transformation to a partnership arrangement represents radical change. The previously prevailing adversarial climate, with its relatively low levels of trust, will remain deep-seated. It is not realistic to expect two organisations previously engaged in a form of opposition to each other suddenly to adopt a spirit of openness, and exhibit faith in each other and the co-operative pursuit of mutual goals. Making such changes requires a fundamental shift in the culture of each organisation. This is not achieved overnight and can be a slow process, fraught with difficulties.

Leading proponents of supply chain partnerships have been vocal in their support. There has been little public expression questioning the value of these trading arrangements. The existence of a partnership does not change the fact that some large retailers tend to be dominant in their respective sectors and are not afraid to exert their power over the supply chain. In these cases, if the retailer wants a 'partnership', then a smaller supplier is unlikely to object. The very term 'partnership' conveys a message of mutual objectives, trust and co-operation. Whether the benefits of this strategy accrue on an equally mutual basis has yet to be proven.

DISTRIBUTION LOGISTICS AND STOCK CONTROL

The customer's central expectation of retail service delivery is one of availability. No amount of service enhancement or added incentives will effectively make up for an empty shelf. As a customer, the ultimate measure of a retail service is whether the goods or services are available as required. Modern retailing is underpinned by a complex infrastructure that seeks to meet this central customer expectation. All of this has its cost and, therefore, from a management perspective it will be vital to deliver the retail service in an efficient manner. This is becoming increasingly important as profit growth cannot be easily achieved when sales growth is not high; such extra profit has to be gained from improvements in productivity. The achievement of productivity gains is available from a retail logistics system infrastructure which consists of several elements, as is discussed in the sections that follow.

RETAIL LOGISTICS

The word logistics is derived from the French word '*loger*' which means to quarter and supply troops. Logistics has developed from the systematic planning required when large numbers of troops and their equipment move, to that of the moving of large amounts of goods. Retail logistics is the organised process of managing the flow of merchandise from the source of supply to the customer – from the producer/manufacturer, wholesaler/intermediary through to the warehouse, transport to the retail units until the merchandise is sold and delivered to the customer. Retail logistics systems incorporate the following functions:

- the physical movement of goods;
- the holding of these goods in stockholding points;
- the holding of goods in quantities required to meet demand from the end consumer;
- the management and administration of the process which, in modern complex distribution systems, is a function in its own right.

All of this is based upon the aspects of:

- transport;
- storage;
- inventory.

Christopher (1992) defined logistics:

Logistics is the process of strategically managing the procurement, movement and storage of materials, parts and finished inventory through the organisation and its marketing channels in such a way that current and future profitability are maximised through the cost effective fulfilment of orders.

Gattorna and Walters (1997) have added elements of information flow to this understanding but we believe the infrastructure elements supporting availability for a customer can be more easily identified as warehousing, transport, inventory and administration. The cost structure of each will be considered next, but at this stage it is important to recognise the interrelationships that exist between the elements. A holistic perspective is essential if management is to identify the optimal organisation and realise the greatest efficiency for the system as a whole. A ruthless pursuit of cost savings within one element is flawed if the result is simply to push a cost burden onto another.

A similarly holistic view is required of the supply chain in a vertical sense. Porter's value chain analysis (1985) recognises that as well as seeking to improve the internal linkages between the activities of the retailer, it will be important to acknowledge the fit with the wider value adding system. Retailer activity should strive to add value for the customer. This will not be realised if in seeking to pursue efficiency in the supply chain element under the direct control of the retailer, costs are simply pushed onto suppliers. The cost will remain in the system and will ultimately be borne by the customer. Managing retail logistics requires a vision of the supply chain 'big picture'. How could activities be organised or reorganised to take cost out of the supply chain completely and deliver better value for customers at the same time? Such an approach may see retailers taking on an additional cost burden to facilitate a saving for suppliers and, ultimately, a net saving for the customer. Here, there is a congruence in the objectives of retailers and suppliers. The recent shift towards supply chain partnerships is logical as it is driven in part by the need to exploit the potential for taking cost out of the supply chain completely.

This holistic approach to retail logistics can be illustrated by the trend in the 1980s and 1990s toward centralised distribution. Depending on volumes, retailers have increasingly created central or regional distribution centres: a major investment in property, plant and equipment with associated overheads. Suppliers making individual direct deliveries to retail outlets may then be replaced by suppliers delivering to the retailer distribution centres by the truckload. The centre then breaks the bulk to create store orders, which are then transported on the retailer's own vehicle fleet. Lead times are reduced and so are the levels of stock held at retail outlets. There are major cost savings and improved supply chain efficiency delivers added value for the customer in the shape of the most recent product being available. Centralising retail distribution represents a very significant redistribution of costs across logistics elements and between supply chain organisations, with substantial net benefit. The store staff are more aware of deliveries, stock is less of a problem and stock space is kept to a minimum.

RETAIL LOGISTICS – THE COST STRUCTURE

Many retailers pursue distribution strategies which explicitly or implicitly acknowledge the importance of the Total Distribution Concept (TDC) which is based on the work of West (1989). In so doing they are taking a holistic approach, strategically and operationally integrating the functions listed below. The TDC encourages everyone in the company to think in terms of all components of distribution from the moment of manufacture to when, in the case of the retailer, goods are sold through the checkout – as an integrated linear model.

Total distribution costs (TDC) = TC + FC + CC + IC + HC + PC + MC

where: TC = transport costs
                 FC = facilities costs
                 CC = communications costs
                 IC   = inventory costs
                 HC = handling costs
                 PC = packaging costs
                 MC = management costs

Fig. 5.14 Total distribution costs for the supply chain

Source: West, A. 1989. *Managing Distribution and Change.* Copyright John Wiley & Sons Limited. Reproduced with permission.

For example, when we think of some of the costs of inventory (*see* section below), we should be aware that all of the total distribution costs (*see* Fig. 5.14) must be considered in relation to each other. This will often involve various trade-offs, for instance between service levels and quality, or between margins and investment in systems. As such, optimising a logistics system is a difficult and demanding task as each component of the system is affected by the level of investment the company is able to make in it. TDC allows retailers to extend their control over the costs as well as supply of goods to the consumer. This requires an understanding of the interaction of all parts of the logistics process. These costs are discussed in the following sections.

Transport

Transport cost structures include substantial fixed cost elements, but perhaps include greater scope to adapt capacity to match volume. Centralising retail distribution has had the benefit of dramatically decreasing the number of journeys made with less than full loads, thereby improving efficiency. The use of composite distribution facilities, where the same vehicle handles merchandise categories requiring different storage regimes, has meant more frequent full-load deliveries to stores. Computer software now supports route planning, using iterative programmes to identify the optimal schedules for each day's deliveries and thereby achieving lower costs. In addition, retailers make use of back haul, where the trucks make collections from suppliers rather than return empty to the distribution centre.

Facilities cost – warehousing

As already identified, retail logistics can be reduced to the areas of warehousing, transport, inventory and administration, each with its associated cost structure. Facilities costs are taken as the capital and running costs associated with providing warehousing infrastructure and internal systems to store and pick stock. Warehousing has a high fixed cost element. The lack of flexibility makes the initial decision to create warehouse capacity crucial. Spare capacity represents wasted resource and short-term measures to cope with insufficient capacity will be expensive. Once created, the ability of the business to match warehousing facilities to fluctuating demand will be strictly limited. This is further accentuated if there is to be capital investment in automated merchandise handling equipment.

A regional distribution centre (RDC) is usually located in a low-cost area. Such a centre can handle a volume in excess of a million cases of product a week as recent advances in information systems have had a huge impact on the efficiency of the operation. It is the application of technologies such as electronic data interchange (EDI) that have facilitated a reduction of stockholding at both store and distribution centre level. The extent of channelling of supplies through RDCs may be gauged by the examination of UK grocery retailers (*see* Table 5.2). Retailers such as Asda have moved from channelling 10 per cent of their supplies through RDCs in 1986 to over 80 per cent now. Similarly, the competitive change in Tesco's position may be gauged from its major increase in usage of RDCs.

Table 5.2 Changes in UK grocery retailers usage of RDCs, 1986–96

Retailer	1986	1993	1996
(Argyll) Safeway	40–80	95	95
ASDA	10	78	84
Co-op Retail	40–60	95	95
Co-op Wholesale	40–60	93	93
Wm Low	50	94	–
Morrisons	50	90	90
J Sainsbury	80	95	95
Tesco	40–60	95	95
Waitrose	80	90	90
Average	61	92	93

Source: Institute of Grocery Distribution, 1997

Within an RDC, communication between the Warehouse Management System (WMS) and each operative is by radio link, drastically reducing the amount of travel within the centre. The WMS tracks the throughput of merchandise and the activity of each operative. This can allow for individual piece-rates which replace team-based bonuses. The wage bill is a major element within the cost structure of an efficient distribution centre. Hence, with the need to match the labour resource with the volume throughput, 'annualised hours' contracts are now commonplace. This is not always a straightforward task as warehouse staff are often unionised and the union holds power. Developments have to be carefully negotiated and this has led to local agreements, often producing localised differences in working practices and sometimes less efficiency.

The costs of inventory

The first thing to note is that with steadily increasing sophistication in many product categories – and this is particularly the case in retailing – the costs of holding inventory have increased. This, coupled to the increasing concentration in retailing, means that the end consumer currently expects a wider range of products in smaller quantities. Irrespective of the type of inventory system used by the retailer, and regardless of set service levels, attitudes to distribution, etc. there will be costs incurred as a result of the maintenance and replenishment of inventory.

Maintaining inventory is an investment which ties up large amounts of capital. This has obvious cost implications for (retail) companies, regardless of their size. In accounting terms, the retailer must invest in a certain level of the stock asset in order to service the needs of customers. Greater investment should ensure higher levels of availability and satisfied customers; insufficient investment runs the risk of poor availability and, by implication, customer dissatisfaction.

It is clear that opportunity costs exist in the capital costs of inventory; the capital tied up in inventory could be available for investment elsewhere within the company or outside the company. For these reasons, systems have become based upon demand pull rather than supply push, as demand pull allows for restocking to occur in relation to customer demand. One method of achieving this is through just-in-time (JIT) deliveries. (JIT is discussed in more detail below as part of corporate replenishment systems.)

As previously noted, carrying stock involves a level of risk, which represents additional cost to the business. Some of the costs associated with stock cannot be eliminated by systems such as JIT. There are costs which occur as a result of damage, pilferage, wastage, maladministration, etc. (that is, shrinkage) or markdown action occurring as a result of inappropriate inventory holding. Markdowns, particularly in fashion related sectors, can account for a sizeable portion of turnover. It is clear that 'risk costs' represent a significant cost of inventory holding.

Administration costs

Communications costs (*see* Fig. 5.14) are, largely, the administrative costs associated with order processing and electronic data interchange (EDI). Inventory costs include the direct capital costs of buying stock, the opportunity costs of carrying inventory by having capital tied-up in stock which could be otherwise invested in the company, insurance charges and, in some countries, a tax on stockholdings. Handling costs (*see* Fig. 5.14) may include the 'risk' costs of damage and spoilage that may be caused through the movement of stock through warehouse and transportation systems. Every time an item is moved or stored, a potential for damage, pilferage or deterioration exists. Packaging costs (*see* Fig. 5.14) will be incurred by the retailer through the use of pallet boards on which deliveries may be shipped and the use of shrink-wrap or cling wrap film to secure pallets and roll-cages during transit. Management costs (*see* Fig. 5.14) refer to those costs which are incurred as a direct result of control systems and mechanisms which are built into the retailer's logistics systems such as security systems, temperature monitoring computer systems, etc.

Stock management costs, which are essentially the costs of controlling inventory, are not easy to isolate. It may be relatively easy to identify the fixed investment cost of installing an EPOS, or a Computerised Shelf Management (CSM) system of inventory control but it is quite another matter to isolate the stock management costs. It is widely believed that computerised inventory management systems have improved efficiency but it seems equally likely that such systems have increased stock management costs in achieving that goal. When one thinks of the plethora of expert support staff, the costs associated with electronic transmission of data, the greater level of control (and therefore more time required) afforded to management, etc. it is difficult to argue otherwise. Administration costs will occur for every part of the inventory, whether one of the top selling 20 per cent or the remaining 80 per cent of products stocked (the Pareto principle); all inventory has to be tracked and controlled in terms of receipt, location and despatch for example.

Much of recent innovation in retail logistics has been in pursuit of reducing levels of stockholding in the supply chain. Retailers of highly perishable products have perhaps most to gain from such developments and have led the way. Retail distribution centres have been used for bulk storage of product. This has relieved individual stores of the need to carry stock and, in efficiency terms, has represented an improvement on previous direct delivery arrangements. However, the technology now facilitates the 'stockless' distribution centre. Via EPOS and EDI, suppliers can arrive at the centre with supplies exactly tailored to immediate store requirements. The stock is then 'cross-docked' for shipment to outlets on the same day. Using this just-in-time (JIT) strategy there is no need for bulk storage or double handling at the centre. Figures from IGD (1997) indicate that up to 98 per cent of the UK grocery multiples have committed themselves to EPOS and EDI implementation.

MINICASE 5.5

Example of computer applications to Wal-Mart's distribution logistics

The late Sam Walton's entrepreneurship is a key reason for Wal-Mart's success – his strategy of avoiding competition by putting larger discount stores into small towns which everybody else was ignoring; his insistence on saturating one area with stores before moving on to the next; his drive to keep costs down and sell at 'everyday low prices'; and his policy of 'empowering' staff while keeping trade unions out. Wal-Mart was not the first to harness computers to retailing but it went further than others by installing an integrated computer system network.

That the greatest innovator in recent retailing history should emerge from the backwoods of Arkansas is perhaps less surprising than it might seem. Many of Wal-Mart's strategies were born of necessity. Its very obscurity prompted disdain from suppliers. 'Sometimes it was difficult getting the bigger companies – the Procter & Gambles, Eastman Kodaks, whoever – to call on us at all, and when they did they would dictate to us how much they would sell us and at what price', Walton said later. This forced him to set up his own distribution system. In 1969, with just 32 stores, he built his first warehouse so he could buy goods in volume.

In the past each store manager would order goods to replace those sold, relying on suppliers to deliver them direct to the shop – a hit-and-miss system that took up potential selling space for storage and often left shops out of stock. As Wal-Mart developed its distribution centres in the 1970s, it introduced two innovations. The first was 'cross-docking': goods were centrally ordered, delivered to one side of the distribution centre, and then transferred to the other side for delivery to an individual shop, along with other goods that shop had ordered. This meant that one full lorry would make frequent trips to each store, instead of several half-empty ones visiting less often. To make this system work well, the firm had to keep track of thousands of cases and packages, making sure they were delivered to the right shop at the right time. That was where computers came in. By the early 1980s Wal-Mart had not only set up computer links between each store and the distribution warehouses; through a system called EDI (electronic data interchange), it also hooked up with the computers of the firm's main suppliers. The distribution centres themselves were equipped with miles of laser-guided conveyor belts that could read the bar codes on incoming cases and direct them to the right truck for their onward journey. The final step was to buy a satellite to transmit the firm's enormous data load. The whole system, covering all the firm's warehouses, cost at least $700m, but it quickly paid for itself. The first benefit was just-in-time replenishment across hundreds of stores. This has since been refined further, using computer modelling programmes to allow the firm to anticipate sales patterns. The second benefit was cost. Wal-Mart's distribution costs in 1992 were under 3% of sales, compared with 4.5–5% for the firm's competitors – a saving of close to $750m in that year alone. In 1987 real advantage occurred when Procter & Gamble proposed setting up a 'partnership' that involved not just data-sharing through EDI but joint management of the whole relationship between the two companies. P&G uses this to tailor production to Wal-Mart's demand.

Source: Reid. © *The Economist*, London, 4 March 1995

Outsourcing

It is common practice for retailers to contract out some or all of the distribution activity. A strategic argument for this would be to allow management to focus on those parts of the business where the retailer adds value for the customer – that is, their core competence. It is potentially more flexible and spreads risk. From a financial viewpoint, the contractor should enjoy economies of scale that may be enjoyed by both parties and passed on to the consumer. From the retailer's perspective it represents a form of off-balance sheet financing, with the contractor obliged to invest in assets that are effectively dedicated to the retailer's business. Many such contractors' vans carry the logo of the retailer but remain the contractor's property.

COMPUTERISED REPLENISHMENT SYSTEMS (CRS)

The benefits of the new distribution systems are numerous and extend well beyond inventory control and replenishment. The systems are becoming increasingly important in the competitive environment of multiple retailing. J Sainsbury, Tesco and Safeway have almost 100 per cent of stores with EPOS scanning. In the variety chainstores, BHS has been on full EPOS for several years, their EPOS system being directly linked to their replenishment through central distribution centres at Atherstone and Dundee. Marks and Spencer also have full EPOS and have implemented a computerised inventory system, ASR (Automatic Stock Replenishment), from an initial investment of £78 million in 1988/89.

The perceived benefits of these systems for inventory are shared and are simple: a reduction of stockholding through more accurate ordering and replenishment (which in turn gives better product availability to the customer and thus maximises sales). There is also the benefit of far more accurate sales data on which improved decision making can take place. It can be readily seen that EPOS may serve replenishment. By accurate data capture obtained via EPOS, forecasting (for example, on the basis of experimental smoothing) future merchandise requirements and inventory control is facilitated. This enables both more accurate and economical buying. It also affords greater control of stockholding through greater inventory control, by the removal of the human error associated with other forms of stock control.

CORPORATE REPLENISHMENT POLICIES

Corporate retail planning often involves formalised logistics policies related to distribution networks, warehouse systems, information systems, and replenishment systems. These policies allow the head office (HO) of a retail organisation to be responsive to operational needs, which include general as well as local patterns of demand, and new market opportunities. Companies that have built into their corporate strategies the logistics of distribution have created dramatic improvements in their return on investment whether that investment be fixed (warehousing vehicles or other equipment) or current (inventory, accounts due and cash). Corporate replenishment (CR) has thus become an integral part of the corporate strategy and is instrumental in enabling the achievement of financial and strategic objectives.

Corporate replenishment policy is a broad policy based upon the organisation's replenishment ethos related to a system approach. There are two types of stock control systems: the push strategy, where quantities of stock are pushed into stores in anticipation of demand; and the pull strategy, where merchandise is pulled through the supply chain to replenish sales at stores, and a minimum stockholding is planned to be retained in the store. Systems have been developed in the 1990s to encompass quick response or Just-In-Time (JIT) methods, where the pull strategy becomes the leading method to link inventory to actual customer demand. The channel then becomes a continuous replenishment system triggered by accurate electronic information from the use of EPOS and EDI. As such, JIT systems allow for restocking to occur in relation to customer demand. JIT is a philosophy as much as a technique, it is based on the premise that no products should be made or moved until there is a 'downstream' requirement for them based upon feedback from the supply chain. Within retailing, the fundamentals of JIT are often known as 'quick response' (QR). The logic is that demand is captured as close to the final customer as possible, allowing a logistics response to be made as a direct result. Quick response will thus include the manufacturer in a vertically integrated supply chain so that all means of JIT are triggered based upon changes in consumer demand patterns. Quick response is a series of technologies which comprise the electronic scanning of product codes, the application of EDI, and the identification and tracking of goods in the supply chain. The main users of QR are the grocery multiples but other companies such as Benetton and Arcadia (formerly The Burton Group) developed the systems at an early stage (Dapiran, 1992).

Advantages of corporate replenishment (CR)

There are four different beneficiaries of corporate replenishment systems:

1 the customer;
2 store management;
3 the company;
4 suppliers.

The advantages for each of these groups are discussed below.

Customer

The customer is able to receive an improved level of service as the goods are available at the point of sale, where and when the customer needs them. When items are advertised they are in stock and this adds to customer goodwill as stock is assured through the system. Stores can, and do, order promotional lines in some manual ordering systems. However, across a chain of stores it is unlikely that all relevant managers will order sufficient stock levels – or indeed place orders at all – to meet the promotion, product introduction or range change needs, at the right time. Also, in emergencies, substitute products and so on can be sourced more effectively in advanced CR systems.

Through economies of scale and inventory savings made by being able to carry less 'safety stock' the retailer can pass on savings to the customer. The retailer is, through feedback from sales systems and the resultant flow of accurate sales information, able to forecast bulk buying requirements more accurately. This allows the retailer to obtain greater discounts from suppliers, so making savings which can be passed on to the customer.

Store management

Store management, through corporate replenishment, may be relieved of the time-consuming task of stock checking and ordering if the CR is well designed. Under automatic stock replenishment through EPOS and central distribution, store management may be completely freed from stock and ordering worries. This means they have more time to manage resources and implement company policies. Under highly computerised goods receipt systems other duties, associated with shrinkage and delivery security, may also change significantly.

It is believed that automated systems will mean managers will not worry about stock situations. This is possible but it must be realised that a basic function of store managers is to ensure stock counting is accurately recorded, whether they or a Head Office buyer is responsible for ordering stock. In EPOS replenishment, stockouts occur for a variety of reasons: unpredictable shifts in demand; product unavailability; poor data capture control; loss of information or computer failure; etc. In such a situation it is incumbent upon store managers to ensure that major stockouts are communicated as soon as possible to the Head Office buyer or allocator so that remedial action may be taken. EPOS merely removes the task of physically ordering stock; it does not remove the manager's responsibility to ensure that maximum customer service, through product availability, is achieved. To achieve this, accurate information input by stores on stockholding is vital. Even with EPOS systems information can be corrupted by poor data capture, by incorrect codes being entered at the checkouts, or by staff coding articles or merchandise incorrectly.

Company

The company benefits from maximising service and minimising costs. The central control of inventory replenishment can be managed to keep the amount of stock to an acceptable level. CR avoids dead stock being built up through discontinuity of buying or ordering by store-based management. The main benefit is that reduced stockholding figures prevent capital from being tied up; it may be freed for the expansion and development of the business.

Because of the ability to control stockholding, previously used warehousing and store space is no longer required for that purpose. This enables retailers to maximise store shop floor selling space. In a self-service environment you cannot sell stock that is in the warehouse. In conjunction with central warehousing, economies of scale can be made through composite transport systems. Whether it is an agency or own-transport network, corporate replenishment enables improved utilisation of the transport fleets and improvements in service.

Given the constraints of supplier fed deliveries, marketing may also benefit from corporate replenishment. It can be assumed that stock will be allocated and received into stores to coincide with advertising, other promotional activities and videos, coupons, competitions etc. Advertising products which are not available in stores is a major fault – a possibility that can occur in any type of replenishment system. CR ensures that it is not left to department managers, some of whom will – due to other pressures – be unable to meet the requirements of the promotional activity.

Supplier

It is far easier for a supplier to cope with one order for upwards of 300 stores than for each store independently to place orders. Consequently, the supplier can deliver economically the quantity required in good time. Similarly, it is much more desirable to organise this through central distribution warehousing (CDW). Phoning, faxing or using traditional forms of placing orders is time consuming and often inaccurate. To deal with one electronic system of ordering is desirable to the supplier as well as to the retailer. However, orders may also be placed by the buyers – professionals who are specialists in their field, knowing the merchandise and seasonal trends. Therefore, from the supplier's point of view, it is preferable not to deal with store-based management who have numerous responsibilities to perform and ordering is only one of a list of urgent priorities.

INTERNET AND DIRECT DISTRIBUTION SYSTEMS

In addition to more traditional methods of channel management, there has been a change of distribution strategy to increase sales through direct channels. Large retailers now offer many of their products on-line through the Internet. While this is an important trend, retailer's long-term strategies are still hard to discern. In 1995 J Sainsbury, the supermarket group, announced it was offering wine on the Internet; anyone with a computer, a modem and a subscription to an Internet service provider could choose wine on-line, though they had to confirm the order and pay for it by telephone (*see* Chapter 10 on IT and retail for further discussion of the possibilities of the Internet).

CompuServe, the US-owned on-line information system, announced its UK Shopping Centre in 1995. Subscribers who paid about £7 a month could buy books from WH Smith, CDs from Virgin and cameras from Dixons. Because CompuServe is considered more secure than the Internet, the retailers ask customers to enter credit card numbers directly into their computers. The results of the early schemes have been commented on as positive. WH Smith, Sainsbury's and Tesco reported the service to have been effective. The question underlying any change in channel level is why anyone would need a superstore if manufacturers started selling their well known brands on-line. This would mean that large food retailers may treat on-line shopping as both a threat as well as an opportunity.

Logistical problems will also have to be overcome. These will not be on the hi-tech ordering side as the problems of security for customer and retailer have been largely overcome through sophisticated encryption systems; and devices such as an 'intelligent agent' that will search out the best value on the Internet have also been developed. Ordering will soon be possible via a number of media – the Internet, private on-line services, interactive television and even special in-home devices. It is the routine business of delivering goods which could prove to be a problem. For example, big retailers are used to shifting pallets of products by lorry, and the packing and delivering of single items quickly is much more difficult and expensive. Therefore, any need for home deliveries may lead the retailers to make alliances with parcel companies, the Post Office, or even local dairies. It may also cause retailers to consider pricing levels. Early adopters may well be prepared to pay a little more for a home delivery service, recognising the additional value of the saving in time.

Distribution based on travel retail

In an increasingly competitive world it has been necessary for most companies to consider different forms of distribution. The ability for companies to sell direct – either from their place of location or through direct marketing methods – currently exists. Some stores combine direct marketing, by use of advertisements, catalogues, telephone sales or electronic mediums, with their retail outlets. The structure of distribution channels in tourism is illustrated in Fig. 5.15.

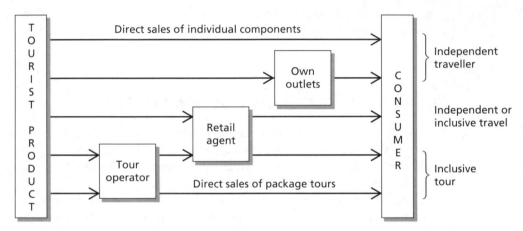

Fig. 5.15 Structure of distribution channels in tourism

In the UK there is the opportunity to have access to a wide network of around 7000 travel agency distribution outlets. These agents charge commission on the sales they make and they need to hold a stock of the companies' brochures or sales literature. The travel retail agent sells a product that is both intangible and perishable and this is very different from some of the more traditional types of retail. The bookings made for travel abroad, from the UK, are mostly organised through either high street travel agents for holidays or by specialist business travel agents for business travel. The UK has a different pattern of purchase from that of the rest of Europe where most bookings are made direct rather than through agents. In many European countries, twice as many bookings are made direct than in the UK.

To date there has been a lack of conversion of the British holidaymaker to buying direct. There is little doubt that for many, the convenience of using an agent is an important element in the buying process. This is because a travel agent may offer greater opportunities for one-stop shopping, allowing the parallel purchase of insurance, car hire, rail travel to the airport, traveller's cheques, and so on. The travel agent offers a number of benefits which may have led to the reason more travellers have not booked direct (Gilbert, 1990). *See* the following summary of possible reasons for customers to continue to use travel agents.

The use of more direct systems of booking are expected to make inroads into traditional forms of distribution but, given the example of the failure of any major

Possible reasons for the use of retail travel agents and lack of direct channels

Easy accessibility:
- to a range and choice of brochures;
- to product components of visas, traveller's cheques, insurance, etc.;
- to booking points in every main town and city;
- to an alternative agent as well as products and brands.

Convenience:
- for obtaining information and advice;
- for making the purchase and payment for the holiday;
- for making complaints and being represented if things go wrong.

Habit:
- people can get into a pattern of behaviour which becomes habit forming. Only a major campaign by direct mail operators could change this habit.

Security/risk:
- consumers feel more secure when dealing with a reputable operator or agent. Those who buy from the Association of British Travel Agents (ABTA) feel they obtain ABTA protection and that products which are offered have been vetted.

Environment/atmosphere:
- travel agents offer an environment which is part of the holiday experience. The travel agency environment is the perfect setting for personal selling methods which are a powerful means to generate bookings.

Economic:
- because travel agents compete on price or added value, and tour operators have the smallest of margins, there is little difference in the price between travel agents and direct sell.

expansion of direct sales for holidays, it is debatable whether direct selling will prove to be successful in the short term. However, for the business traveller, access by means of the Internet is predicted to alter purchasing habits.

CONCLUSION

Following on from the previous marketing sections you should now be aware that marketing mix decisions have to be linked to achieving the objectives of the company or organisation and should be coupled to acceptability throughout the company. While marketing departments often lead in setting the marketing mix strategy they should not ignore input from others, nor should they fail to check with others that the strategy will be workable from an operational standpoint.

The marketing mix offers the range and spread of alternative strategies by which a retail marketer can influence demand. For any retail marketer, while the available range is very similar the choice is not. The process of mix formulation and balancing is quite often unique to each organisation because the way the mix is combined allows the company to provide the augmented product with which it will compete with others.

In the competitive retail marketplace, a business can be successful only if its complete marketing mix offer matches what the consumer wants. To be truly successful, the offer has to be as good as – but preferably better than – that of the competition. The marketing mix is planned and coordinated by marketers, so the onus is on them to control the inputs in such a way that the overall effect maximises the demand and satisfaction of the consumer. For a company to be successful with its marketing mix, it has to develop a differential advantage which will distinguish the company's offer from that of the competition. Only when a company has built an advantage will it find that store visits increase and profits rise. The advantage may be based upon value for money, product service and quality, overall image or distribution logistics.

EXERCISES

The exercises in this section relate to the issues discussed in this chapter. It is suggested that you work through them before moving on to Chapter 6.

1 Take one component of the four Ps and look at it in relation to what a retail company of your choice does. Now compare it to its competitive rivals and decide on areas in which improvement could be made.

2 Visit at least two large department stores and note the way the marketing mix has been formulated. Do you think the marketing mix is well integrated? For example, does the retail environment match the product offer and range, the types of promotion, and pricing policy?

3 Examine the pricing strategies of different retailers. Make a list of branded and own-brand products which you can compare, using the following grid as a guide.

Visit and make notes at:	How were price and offers displayed?
• Tesco • Sainsbury • Boots • convenience store • others (list)	
Note prices of similar brands/own brands, by retailer of: • shampoos/toiletries • over-the-counter medicines • branded perfumes • health products	**What is your assessment of the different pricing policies by company?**

4 Visit a store when it has embarked upon markdowns. Try to assess the level and effectiveness of the different methods and, from discussions with staff, assess the reasons for the markdown policy.

5 Explain what is meant by a sales promotion. Either collect five examples of different retail sales promotions to discuss and/or describe what types of sales promotion would encourage you to buy, and why.

REFERENCES AND FURTHER READING

Alba, J., Lynch, J., Weitz, B. and Janiszewski, C. (1998) 'Interactive home shopping: consumer, retailer, and manufacturer incentives to participate in electronic marketplaces', *Journal of Marketing*, 61 (3), 38–53.

Allaway, A., Mason, J.B. and Brown, G. (1987) 'An optimal decision support model for department-level promotion mix planning', *Journal of Retailing*, 63, Fall, 215–42.

Atwal, K. (1996) 'Sainsbury's cuts prices to counter Tesco scheme', *Marketing Week*, 13 September, 6.

Bell, D.R. and Lattin, J.M. (1998) 'Shopping behavior and consumer preference for store price format: why "large basket" shoppers prefer EDLP', *Marketing Science*, 17 (1), 66–88.

Bell, J., Gilbert, D.C. and Lockwood, A. (1997) 'Service quality in food retailing operations: a critical incident analysis', *The International Review of Retail Distribution and Consumer Research*, 7 (4), 405–23.

Betts, E. and McGoldrick, P.J. (1995) 'The strategy of the retail sale, typology, review and synthesis', *The International Review of Retail, Distribution and Consumer Research*, 5 (3), July, 303–32.

Blois, K.J. (1994) 'Discounts in business marketing management', *Industrial Marketing Management*, 23, 84.

Booms, B.H. and Bitner, M.J. (1981) 'Marketing strategies and organization structures for service firms', in Donnelly, J. and George W.R. (eds) *Marketing of Services*. Chicago, IL: American Marketing Association.

Borden, N.H. (1965) 'The concept of the marketing mix', in Schwartz, G. (ed.) *Science in Marketing*. Chichester: J. Wiley and Sons.

Bowden, D. (1995) 'Problems with delivery delay on-line shopping', *Independent on Sunday*, 4 June, 4.

Bowlby, S. and Foord, J. (1995) 'Relational contracting between UK retailers and manufacturers', *International Review of Retailing Distribution and Consumer Research*, 5 (3), 333–60.

Branigan, L. (1998) 'The Internet: the emerging premier direct marketing channel', *Direct Marketing*, 61 (1), 46–8.

Britt, S.H. (1975) 'How Weber's Law can be applied to marketing', *Business Horizons*, February, 21–9.

Carlson, P.G. (1983) 'Fashion retailing: the sensitivity of rate of sale to markdown', *Journal of Retailing*, 59 Spring, 67–78.

Christopher, M. (1992) *Logistics*. London: Chapman Hall.

Christopher, M. (1997) *Marketing Logistics*. Oxford: Butterworth Heinemann.

Christopher, M., Payne, A. and Ballantyne, D. (1996) *Relationship Marketing*. Oxford: Butterworth Heinemann.

Cohen, N. (1998) 'Leisure: the shop as a destination', *Financial Times*, 17 March.

Cooper, J., Browne, M. and Peters, M. (1994), *European Logistics: Markets, management and strategy*. Oxford: Blackwell.

Comer, J.M., Mehta, R. and Holmes, T.L. (1998) 'Information technology: retail users versus nonusers', *Journal of Interactive Marketing*, 12 (2), 49–62.

Cope, N. (1995) 'Kwik Save starts price war', *Independent*, 3 May, 34.

Corliss, L.G. (1995) 'Differential responses to retail sales promotion among African-American and Anglo-American consumers', *Journal of Retailing*, 71 (1), Spring, 83–92.

Cox, A. and Cox, D. (1990) 'Competing on price: the role of retail price advertisements in shaping store price image', *Journal of Retailing*, 66 (4), Winter, 428–45.

Dapiran, P. (1992) 'Benetton – global logistics in action', *International Journal of Physical Distribution and Logistics Management*, 23 (4), 7–11.

Datamonitor (1996) *Loyalty Discount Schemes*. Report. July.

Davies, G. (1993) 'Is retailing what the dictionaries say it is?', *International Journal of Retail and Distribution Management*, 21 (2), 3–7.

Davison, J. (1995) *Lecture Notes on Distribution Management*. Guildford: University of Surrey.

Dawes, J. (1998) 'Winning new customers in financial services: using relationship marketing and information technology in consumer financial services', *European Management Journal*, 16 (2), 249.

Delbridge, R. and Oliver, N. (1991) 'Just in time or just the same', *International Journal of Retail and Distribution Management*, 19 (2), 20.

Dickenson, P.R. and Sawyer, A. (1990), 'The price knowledge and search of supermarket shoppers', *Journal of Marketing*, 54, July, 42–53.

East, R., Harris, P. and Willson, G. (1995) 'Loyalty to supermarkets', *The International Review of Retail Distribution and Consumer Research*, 5 (1), 99–109.

The Economist (1995) 'How to turn junk mail into a goldmine – or perhaps not', *The Economist*, 335, 1 April.

Fernie, J. (1995) 'International comparisons of supply chain management in grocery retailing', *The Service Industries Journal*, 5 (4), 135–47.

Fernie, J. (1997) 'Retail change and retail logistics in the UK, past trends and future prospects', *The Service Industries Journal*, 17 (3), 383–96.

Fernie, J. and Sparks, L. (1997) *Logistics and Retail Management*. London: Kogan Page.

Fiorito, S., May, E. and Straughn, K. (1995) 'Quick response in retailing: components and implementation', *International Journal of Retail and Distribution Management*, 23 (5), 12–21.

Gattorna, J.L. and Walters, D.W. (1996) *Managing the Supply Chain – A Strategic Perspective*. Basingstoke: Macmillan.

Gengler, C.E., Leszczyc, P. and Popkowski, T. (1997) 'Using customer satisfaction research for relationship marketing: a direct marketing approach', *Journal of Direct Marketing*, 11 (1), 23–9.

Gattorna, J. and Walters, D. (1996) *Managing the Supply Chain – A Strategic Perspective*. Basingstoke: Macmillan.

Gilbert, D.C. (1990) 'European product purchase methods and systems', *Service Industries Journal*, 10 (4), 664–79.

Gilbert, D.C. (1996) 'Relationship marketing and airline loyalty schemes', *Tourism Management*, 17 (8), 575–82.

Gilligan, C. and Sutton, C. (1987) 'Strategic planning in grocery and DIY retailing', in Johnson, G. (ed.) *Business Strategy and Retailing*. Chichester: John Wiley.

Gronroos, C. (1990) 'Relationship approach to the marketing function in service contexts: the marketing and organization behavior interface', *Journal of Business Research*, 20 (1), 3–12.

Gronroos, C. (1991) 'The marketing strategy continuum: towards a marketing concept for the 1990s', *Management Decision*, 29 (1), 7–13.

Gronroos, C. (1992) 'Facing the challenge of service competition: the economies of services', in Kunst, P. and Lemmik, J. (eds) *Quality Management in Services*. Maastricht: Van Gorcum.

Gronroos, C. (1994) 'Toward a relationship marketing paradigm', *Journal of Marketing Management*, 10, 347–60.

Groom, A. (1998) 'Fashion: the expert shop assistant is making a comeback. Everyone interested in modern style should rejoice', *Financial Times*, 30 May.

Hollinger, P. (1998) 'When prices are not black and white: food retailers are increasingly waking up to the promotional advantages offered by the "grey market" ', *Financial Times*, 16 May.

Institute of Grocery Distribution (1997) *Trends in Grocery Retailing – the market review*. Institute of Grocery Distribution, Watford: IGD Business Publications.

Institute of Grocery Distribution (1998) *Grocery Market Bulletin*. Institute of Grocery Distribution, Watford: IGD Business Publications.

Kalwani, M.V. and Chi, K.Y (1992) 'Consumer price and promotion expectations', *Journal of Marketing Research*, 29 (1), 90–100.

Kiran, W.K. and Kumar, V. (1995) 'The effect of brand characteristics and retailer policies on response to retail price promotions: implications for retailers', *Journal of Retailing*, 71 (3), Fall, 249–78.

Kotler, P., Armstrong, G., Saunders, J. and Wong, V, (1999) *Principles of Marketing*. 2nd European edn. Hemel Hempstead: Prentice Hall.

Kumar, V. and Pereira, A. (1997) 'Assessing the competitive impact of type, timing, frequency, and magnitude of retail promotions', *Journal of Business Research*, 40 (1), 1–13.

Lam, S., Vandenbosch, M. and Pearce, M. (1998) 'Retail sales force scheduling based on store traffic forecasting', *Journal of Retailing*, 74 (1), 61–88.

Levy, M. and Howard, D.J. (1988) 'An experimental approach to planning the duration and size of markdowns', *International Journal of Retailing*, 3 (2), 48–58.

Manning, K.C., Bearden, W.O. and Rose, R.L. (1998) 'Development of a theory of retailer response to manufacturers' everyday low cost programs', *Journal of Retailing*, 74 (1), 107–37.

McCarthy, E.J. (1978) *Basic Marketing: a managerial approach*. 6th edn. Homewood, IL: Richard D. Irwin.

Meenaghan, T. (1998) 'Current developments and future directions in sponsorship', *International Journal of Advertising*, 17 (1), 3–28.

Mulhern, F.J. (1997) 'Retail marketing: from distribution to integration', *International Journal of Research in Marketing*, 14 (2), 103–24.

Nagle, T.T. and Holden, R.K. (1995) *The Strategy and Tactics of Pricing*. Englewood Cliffs, NJ: Prentice Hall.

Ogbonna, E. and Wilkinson, B. (1996) 'Inter-organizational power relations in the UK grocery industry: contradictions and developments', *International Review of Retailing Distribution and Consumer Research*, 6 (4), 395–414.

Ortmeyer, G., Quelch, J.A. and Salmon, W. (1991) 'Restoring creditability to retail pricing', *Sloan Management Review*, 33 (2), 55–6.

Payne, A., Christopher, M., Clark, M. and Peck, H. (1995) *Relationship Marketing for Competitive Advantage*. Oxford: Butterworth-Heinemann.

Porter, M.E. (1985) *Competitive Advantage*. New York: The Free Press.

Powell, T.C. and Dent-Micallef, A. (1997) 'Information technology as competitive advantage: the role of human, business, and technology resources', *Strategic Management Journal*, 18 (5), 375–405.

Reid, M. (1995) 'Survey of retailing (2): stores of value – computers are no longer enough. To stay ahead, retailers must use them to innovate', *The Economist*, 334, 4 March.

Rhodes, E. and Carter, R. (1998) 'Electronic commerce technologies and changing product distribution', *International Journal of Technology Management*, 15 (1, 2), 31–48.

Ries, A. and Trout, J. (1981) *Positioning the Battle for Your Mind*. London: McGraw-Hill.

Rogers, D. (1998) 'Barclays offers on-screen links', *Marketing*, 21 May, 2.

Rogers, D., Daugherty, P.J. and Stank, T.P. (1992) 'Enhancing service responsiveness: the strategic potential of EDI', *International Journal of Physical Distribution and Logistics Management*, 22 (8), 15–20.

Schary, P.B. and Coakley, J. (1991) 'Logistics organization and the information system', *International Journal of Logistics Management*, 2 (2), 22–9.

Schindler, R. (1991) 'Symbolic meanings of a price ending', *Advances in Consumer Research*, 794–801.

Sheombar, H.S. (1992) 'EDI-induced redesign of co-ordination in logistics', *International Journal of Physical Distribution and Logistics Management*, 22 (8), 4–14.

Smith, D. and Sparks, L. (1993) 'The transformation of physical distribution in retailing: the example of Tesco plc.', *International Review of Retailing Distribution and Consumer Research*, 3 (1), 35–64.

Stern, B.B. (1997) 'Advertising intimacy: relationship marketing and the services consumer', *Journal of Advertising*, 26 (4), 7–19.

SuperMarketing, Anon., (1996) 'Relief as petrol war cools', *SuperMarketing*, 11 October, 14.

Walmsley, A. (1998) 'New media choice: The Gap web site', *Marketing*, 19 February, 15.

West, A. (1989) *Managing Distribution and Change*. London: John Wiley and Sons.

Which? Magazine (1996) 'Food for Thought', *Which? Magazine*, March, 8–12.

Zeithaml, V.A. (1988) 'Consumer perceptions of price, quality, and value: a means–end model and synthesis of evidence', *Journal of Marketing*, 52, July, 2–22.

6 Merchandise management

This chapter should enable you to understand and explain:

- the definition and role of the *retail* merchandiser;
- the development of a merchandise plan;
- what is involved in range planning;
- inventory turnover control.

The development and implementation of a merchandise plan is one of the most important phases in any retail strategy. This is because the primary objective of any retail organisation is to ensure the sale of its merchandise. In order to be successful, retailers must make competent decisions over what is to be bought, in what quantities and at what time. The overall choice of merchandise also presents a clear message to consumers about the type of company they are purchasing from. As such, the selection and presentation of merchandise enables a key source of difference to exist which will allow one store to differentiate itself from another. There is an old adage which states 'goods well bought are half sold'. While true, this masks the fact that merchandise has to reflect the different market segment needs and wants and there is a requirement for a sophisticated approach.

WHAT IS MERCHANDISE MANAGEMENT?

Merchandise management focuses on the planning and controlling of the retailer's inventories. The role has to balance the financial requirements of the company with a strategy for merchandise purchasing. We believe the complex role of merchandise management can be defined as the:

> **planning and implementation of the acquisition, handling and monitoring of merchandise categories for an identified retail organisation.**

The definition stresses a number of key points. As merchandise has to be acquired for future purchase opportunities, forward planning is needed in relation to changing consumption tastes and demand. There is a need for acquisition from either wholesalers or manufacturers and for the merchandise to be handled in an appropriate way to ensure it is able to be sold in perfect condition. As the financial aspects of buying merchandise can be treated as an investment decision, there is the final aspect of monitoring all aspects of the process to ensure adequate returns are achieved.

The complexity of modern retail operations often requires the grouping of the buying process into an individual *category*. This is normally structured to ensure that the buyer can understand different market segments such as those defined by age (infants, children's, youth, etc.) or by gender. In general a category is an assortment of items that the customer would perceive as being substitutes for each other. For example, a customer may substitute a pair of trousers for jeans but not for a swimsuit. This approach enables a customer led focus on the assortment profile and the issues of the width and depth, quality and cost to price implications. Category management, working with key brands is a feature of modern retailing. Cobb (1997) explains that at the point of purchase, the shop-in-shop concept, traditionally utilised to promote a single manufacturer or brand, has been developed to improve category differentiation in the grocery multiples. A prime example is at Sainsbury's where Cadbury, in partnership with the supermarket, developed a novelty confectionery section in a Treasure Island children's area. Other developments are the retailer's link with Duracell, to create a battery centre area. As brand leader, Duracell commissioned NDI Display to work with the store group to create a specialist merchandising system.

The phases in developing a merchandise plan are listed in Fig. 6.1. In all marketing led approaches the consumer will ultimately dictate the strategy options. In Fig. 6.1 there is no exception. (*See* Chapter 7 on marketing planning in order to understand the full complexities of a planning approach.) The customer will have expectations of an assortment profile with issues of choice (width and depth), sizes, quality, exclusivity, availability and cost (as indicated in points 1 and 2 in Fig. 6.1). The consequence of understanding the expectations is for these to be translated into a particular structure for the buying organisation (as indicated by point 3 in Fig. 6.1). If exclusivity is required, then there is a consequent requirement for selective sourcing. If quality is important, a

1 Marketing considerations	Store and image, trading format, environment, retail proposition, fashion trends, customer base, potential buyers
2 Merchandise strategy options	Availability based upon assortment profile and issues of choice (width and depth), quality, exclusivity, seasonality of range, estimated cost, promotional agreement
3 Type of customer base	Items purchased, range purchased, length of season, average transaction value for different lines, frequency of visits and purchases
4 Financial considerations	Profitability and sales performance projections, stock investment and stock return, type of contract and payment terms, corporate objectives and pricing
5 Merchandise assortment search	Ensuring merchandise meets criteria of: required range, comparison, cost, price range offer, brand policy, availability, delivery, stockholding needs, financial returns

Fig. 6.1 Merchandise plan considerations

great deal of quality control is necessary as part of the buying procedure. Whatever the approach decided upon, buyers will be expected to source only after extensive research and searching out all the alternatives. The next consideration is a financial one (point 4 in Fig. 6.1): having to meet company profit and market requirements before the merchandise stock is acquired (point 5 in Fig. 6.1). Some of the important merchandise decisions related to this plan are discussed below.

Availability is an important concept. The availability is based upon the need to ensure the level of stock required meets the demand from the consumer. However, the higher the level of stockholding, the higher the level of costs. The importance of wanting to derive the availability measure is based upon knowing what orders will be satisfied over a specified timespan. This is typically a percentage – say 90 per cent of orders will be satisfied. The notion of availability introduces a need to manage the reorder/ replenishment cycles on an efficient basis. Of course high levels of stockholding will require working capital to be tied up. On the other hand improved stockholding may increase sales due to the rapid flow of merchandise. The balance between these two factors need to be carefully assessed. In current businesses information systems have had a considerable impact on the whole area of availability. (This is discussed in Chapters 5 and 10.)

The availability performance is linked to *inventory turnover*, which can also be described as merchandise stockturn. The inventory turnover concept allows us to work out how long inventory is on hand prior to it being sold. Goods with a high turnover will need to be planned differently from those with a low turnover. Retailers can call upon different ways to measure this:

$$\frac{\text{Net sales}}{\text{Average inventory at retail store}}$$

$$\frac{\text{Cost of merchandise sold}}{\text{Average inventory at cost}}$$

$$\frac{\text{Units sold}}{\text{Average units in inventory}}$$

The inventory turnover concept allows a store to operate at a more optimal level. As an indicator of the differences which can exist, the National Retail Federation of America (1991) found that the annual inventory turnover level of large department stores varied from 1.5 for home furnishings to 1.7 for footwear and leisure and home electronics, 2.3 for cosmetics and drugs, 2.9 for female apparel and infants and children's clothing and accessories.

METHODS OF PLANNING AND CALCULATING INVENTORY LEVELS

Basic stock method of planning inventory

The merchandiser may have to plan to have a basic level of stock based upon the basic stock method (BSM) when it is agreed there should be a particular level of inventory available at all times. The inventory with BSM will meet sales expectations and also allow for a margin of error. This approach is based on ensuring stock levels are not depleted and customers dissatisfied. It is especially important if sales are higher than expected or if there could be any problem with the shipment and delivery of stocks. However, this method is better suited to a low turnover or when sales may be erratic. It has the advantage that stock can be added to over time rather than all of it being purchased in advance, but this method does not take into consideration stockholding costs.

The level of the beginning of month stock (BOM) for a retailer can be calculated by taking the figures for a season (say 6 months in this case) and working out the BOM as the planned monthly sales plus the basic stock. If this were based upon an inventory turnover of 2 and total sales of £600 000 then the calculations would be made as follows.

Note: Calculations are for a season.

Beginning of month stock (BOM) = Planned monthly sales + Basic stock

where

$$\text{(a) Average stock for season} = \frac{\text{Total planned sales for season}}{\text{Estimated inventory turnover}}$$

and

$$\text{(b) Average monthly sales} = \frac{\text{Total planned sales for season}}{\text{Number of months}}$$

and

$$\text{Basic stock} = \text{(a)} - \text{(b)}$$

which is:
$$\text{(a)} = £600\,000 \div 2 \text{ or } £300\,000$$
$$\text{(b)} = £600\,000 \div 6 \text{ or } £100\,000$$

From this we are able to provide the basic stock calculation as:

$$£300\,000 - £100\,000 \text{ which is } £200\,000$$

The final average basic stock requirement for the season is:

$$£100\,000 + £200\,000 = £300\,000$$

This means the retailer may require the following inventory:

Beginning of month @ retail	*Basic stock + planned monthly sales*
March =	£200 000 + £80 000 = £280 000
April =	£200 000 + £110 000 = £310 000
May =	£200 000 + £105 000 = £305 000
June =	£200 000 + £110 000 = £310 000
July =	£200 000 + £100 000 = £300 000
August =	£200 000 + £95 000 = £295 000

Percentage variation method

An alternative method for determining planned stock levels, especially when turnover is higher than six or more annually, is the percentage variation method (PVM). The method is recommended when stock is quite stable since it results in planned monthly inventories that are closer to the monthly average than other techniques. If the retailer faces fluctuations in sales but does not want to ensure a given level of inventory is available at all times then this approach would be acceptable. The technique assumes the monthly percentage fluctuations from average stock should be half as great as the percentage fluctuations in monthly sales from average sales. This would be calculated as follows.

$$\text{Beginning of month planned inventory level} = \text{Planned average monthly stock for season} \times \frac{1}{2}\left[1+\left(\frac{\text{Estimated monthly sales}}{\text{Estimated average monthly sales}}\right)\right]$$

Since the PVM utilises the same basic components as the previous example we can utilise the same data:

Beginning of month @ retail	Average stock for season + planned monthly sales ÷ average monthly sales
March =	£300 000 × 1/2[1+ (£80 000/100,000)] = £270 000
April =	£300 000 × 1/2[1+ (£110 000/100 000)] = £315 000
May =	£300 000 × 1/2[1+ (£105 000/100 000)] = £307 500
June =	£300 000 × 1/2[1+ (£110 000/100 000)] = £315 000
July =	£300 000 × 1/2[1+ (£100 000/100 000)] = £300 000
August =	£300 000 × 1/2[1+ (£95 000/100 000)] = £292 500

The PVM is a better choice when the annual turnover rate is greater than 6 as the results will fluctuate less. Below 6 the BSM method of calculation would be preferred.

Weeks' supply method

The weeks' supply method (WSM) for planning inventory involves forecasting average sales on a weekly rather than monthly basis. The WSM formula assumes the inventory carried is in direct proportion to sales. It is utilised by retailers which need to plan on a weekly basis, such as supermarkets where sales do not fluctuate by significant amounts. The calculation is based upon a predetermined number of weeks' supply which has to be linked to the stock turnover rate desired. In WSM there is a proportional link between the value of the stock and the forecast of sales. Thus, if forecasted sales double then inventory value will triple. In order to understand WSM the following example can be considered:

BOM stock = Average weekly sales × Number of weeks to be stocked

where

$$\text{Average weekly sales} = \frac{\text{Estimated total sales for the period}}{\text{Stock turnover rate for the period}}$$

and

$$\text{Number of weeks to be stocked} = \frac{\text{Number of weeks in the period}}{\text{Stock turnover rate for period}}$$

$$\text{Number of weeks to be stocked} = \frac{26}{2} = 13$$

$$\text{Average weekly sales} = \frac{£600\,000}{26} = £23\,076.9$$

$$\text{BOM stock} = £23\,077 \times 13 = £300\,000$$

With the number of weeks supply to be stocked at 13 weeks based upon the average weekly sales of £23 076.9 stocks may need to be checked on a regular basis to ensure there is no danger of stockouts or a build-up of stock which will increase holding costs. It would therefore be clear that this method requires both stable sales and turnover for it to prove beneficial.

Stock-to-sales method

One other method that can be employed is known as the stock-to-sales method. It is beneficial to utilise such an approach if a retailer wants to maintain a specified ratio of goods on hand to sales. The retailer has to use a beginning of the month stock-to-sales ratio. This ratio informs the retailer as to the amount of inventory required in order to sustain that month's estimated sales. A ratio of two, for example, would require a retailer to have twice that month's expected sales available in inventory at the beginning of the month. The method is not difficult to calculate. Stock-to-sales ratios can be calculated from a retailer's own historical results or from external sources as long as these are reliable.

All the preceding methods of estimating inventory requirements need to be understood in conjunction with a number of other factors. These are the level of shrinkage, markdowns and employee discounts as these will affect both the financial and availability aspects of the business. These reductions will cause the retail value of the inventory to be lower than it was at the beginning and, therefore, the estimates should be included in the merchandise budget. *Shrinkage* is the difference between the amount of merchandise which is reported on the inventory stock system and what is available for sale or on the shelves. The difference in value could be due to any one of a number of actions: due to shoplifting, employee theft, vendor overbilling, distributor theft, paper work errors, and breakage and spoilage. The effect of shrinkage is that the total retail value of the merchandise is reduced. The level of shrinkage may alter by merchandise type or by department and therefore adjustments cannot be made without some detailed understanding of the business. *Markdowns* are a lowering of the prices of the merchandise so that the reduction (markdown) acts as a promotion: for special sales periods or for moving sluggish lines, because of damage or soiling of merchandise, due to end of range offers, or because of greater price competition from competitors or manufacturers who may have made adjustments to their prices. *Employee discounts* are part of planned reductions and offer value to the employee in working at the store. However, these sales should be recorded so that all such discounts are accountable.

MERCHANDISER SKILLS AND PROFILE

The role of merchandiser is pivotal between the pursuit of the strategic objectives of the retailer and operational activity. The merchandiser is responsible for planning and controlling stock ranges and replenishment. Successful execution of the role will require close liaison with, and support for, the retail buyer. Also required is a holistic view of the supply chain and regular interaction with central functions such as management accounting and distribution, through to those operating at store level.

The effective merchandiser will therefore need to be an effective communicator with appropriate interpersonal skills. The nature of the job will specifically require advanced numerical capability supported by PC literacy, notably in the use of spreadsheets and databases. Due to the complexity of merchandise management it follows that the post would also require administrative competence. There are a number of key areas to control which relate to the need for attention to detail in order to ensure the plan is always aligned to operational objectives (*see* Fig. 6.1 and boxes summarising requirements in the text that follows).

Developing the first stage of the merchandise plan

It requires:

- understanding the target market groups;
- agreeing regional and branch sales forecasts;
- collecting information on competitors and any new branch plans;
- taking into consideration branding and corporate policy;
- agreeing merchandise budget;
- liaison and initial discussion with buyer(s).

While a brief outline of the function of the merchandiser has been given, it should be noted that the parameters of the job vary widely between retailers. The key common element is the support role to the buyer. It follows that an effective working relationship with the buyer will be vital if the trading objectives are to be delivered on the shop floor. Beyond that, the extent to which the merchandiser is expected to be a reactive number-cruncher or a proactive trader, actively seeking and exploiting opportunities, will vary.

The role of the merchandiser is driven ultimately by the budgeting process. Budgeting seeks to quantify in financial terms the objectives of the retailer for a defined period of time. Once this financial plan or master budget has been devised, it can then be used to monitor the performance of the business. Retailers need to buy merchandise that can be set at an acceptable market price and also provide a planned gross margin. There are two values as part of this process: the retail value of sales and the cost value based upon the purchase cost of the merchandise. The merchandiser has an important role to play in both planning and controlling retail activity. In the early stages it will be necessary to analyse market research information and sales trends in order to produce agreed forecasts which can be incorporated into the master budget.

Planning sourcing and buying

The world of retailing is getting smaller every day and the global consumer is getting more demanding. To understand these dynamics, one must first understand the forces driving this change. Retailers are having to adapt to the growing expectations among consumers for round the clock service and for more personalised product offerings. There are also price cutting pressures. Retailers view low price as a differentiator to achieve competitive advantage.

Many retailers are also reorganising the way they operate, often around principles of category management, which seeks to exploit benefits from closer relationships between suppliers and retailers, takes a multi-disciplinary approach to products. Inevitably this means the introduction of increasingly complex processes, but they must be easier to manage and control. This contradiction is apparent in the challenges facing each component in the traditional retail supply chain.

- Product development and sourcing: regional consumer preferences must be identified and products developed or sourced to satisfy these unique needs.

- Supplier management: this historically difficult relationship becomes even more complex, as language, cultural, and commercial impediments are introduced.

- Buying: negotiating prices based on the true profit contribution is made more difficult by currency fluctuations, extended transportation channels, and commercial practices unique to each culture.

- Merchandising: retailers must create the right mix of product to appeal to local needs, and still have rapid response processes in place when the mix must be changed or replenished.

- Distribution: this must be more diverse, with typically longer channels to move product from source to consumer. It also needs to accommodate market-specific packaging and environmental needs.

- Retail operations: again, there is a need to tailor product presentation and service offerings to each specific market.

Who is doing this well today? A few retailers stand out, due to their ability to capitalise on these four competencies. Marks & Spencer, the UK's largest clothing retailer ... Its success has been built on the back of a mature and controlled supply chain, centred on a vertically-integrated supplier group. WalMart, a US retailer, has moved its price/value competitive advantage overseas. This price advantage is obtained through a remarkably efficient supply chain process, seamlessly integrated with major suppliers. The Gap, the US retailer of casual clothing, maintains strict control over its supply chain, with its employees overseeing every step. Even in contract plants, Gap exercises control, thus ensuring that its customer receives consistent quality, at the best price, coupled with service that complements the brand's image.

Source: John Karonis, *Financial Times*, 17 March 1998

The merchandise budget becomes a tool for the financial planning and control of the investment the retailer has had to make in the inventory acquired. The master merchandise budget will be required to offer: a gross sales projection, stock level requirements, retail reduction estimates and expected profit margins. Following this, a large part of the merchandiser's function is the disaggregation of this figure into merchandise plans which are going to meet the projected sales. The resultant process has three dimensions: the merchandise range itself, the profile of stores in the group, and variations in sales demand over time.

Variations in demand over time

The merchandiser, as part of the above planning approach, needs to contend with the extent to which demand for product lines fluctuates. This was touched upon earlier in this chapter with the discussion of availability and inventory turnover. There are lines which exhibit remarkably constant levels of turnover, all year around. In such cases, the planning is comparatively straightforward. A good match between the retailer's facility to meet demand and actual turnover will meet customer expectations with the minimum of wasted resources. However, many merchandise categories will exhibit a degree of seasonality.

The merchandiser has to have intimate knowledge of customers and the type of demand for the product being sold. The variations on the category lifestyle whereby some products will sustain demand for longer periods is an important aspect in deciding upon the merchandise plan (*see* Fig. 6.2). For example a *fad product* will generate a high level of sales due to a large segment of the population requesting the item. However, the demand will only last for a short time and perhaps not even for the whole season. Hula hoops, yo-yos, Rubik's cubes, Teletubbies and Batman toys are all examples of this phenomenon. Given that a high number of fad items can be sold in a short time they can, or need to, be sold at substantial mark-ups due to their price insensitive nature and suppliers' price increases based on their decisions to 'cash in' while the fad lasts. Fads are difficult to predict and demand often places a great deal of pressure on distribution chains as demand will always outstrip supply. The only way to deal with a fad is to recognise the signs of its importance as early as possible.

	Fad	Fashion	Staple	Seasonal
Sales over several seasons	No	Yes	Yes	Yes
Sales of a specific style over many seasons	No	No	Yes	Yes
Sales difficult to forecast one season to the next	Yes	Yes	No	Sometimes
Demand curve over time				

Fig. 6.2 Merchandise category life-cycle analysis

The *fashion product* demand cycle will last for several seasons although sales may vary from season to season. The demand depends on the type of customer and the product categories. Men's suits will have a different demand curve to that of teenage clothing. *Staple merchandise* will provide continuous demand over an extended life span. Most food products and household cleaning items are examples of staple products. *Seasonal merchandise* will be characterised by fluctuations in demand according to the time of year. In addition, both the fashion and staple merchandise categories will normally have seasonal variations of demand based upon the season and the weather. The merchandise manager will find the staple category to be the easiest to manage because it offers a reliably repeatable sales history on which to base predictions of planned stock. The inventory system for fads and fashion merchandise requires much more careful appraisal.

RANGE PLANNING

A retailer's stock range can be described in terms of its *width* and *depth*, with the extent of each determined by company policy. This is sometimes termed the *assortment*.

The width will relate to the number of categories that are found in the merchandise line and different generic classes of product or merchandise carried. A wide and narrow stock assortment is normally where there is little choice in brands, styles, etc. within an individual range. Stockturn could be higher for a broad merchandise assortment, but margins will be slim in order to encourage custom.

The depth relates to the sizes, styles, colours, and prices within a particular generic class of product. There are specialist shops, such as the niche boutiques, which offer a lot of depth but with a narrow product range. We could also compare the typical UK grocery superstore carrying upwards of 20 000 individual lines, with the more restricted 600–1000 lines of the Continental 'hard' discounter. The retail offer of each business is substantially different, with the respective stock ranges of each being an integral part of their strategy. The superstore is seeking to charge a premium price for added value as perceived by the customer. It is important to disguise the premium, and the leading operators are skilled at promoting a limited part of their ranges on a price basis to create this effect. The profitability comes from offering a very extensive range of lines, some with comparatively slow rates of stockturn, at healthy profit margins. The number of different lines a retailer stocks in store is often referred to as the *variety* of the merchandise mix. Obviously department stores will have many more lines and variety than a store such as Bally or Clarks selling quality footwear. The extent of the range is a key part of the customer's perception of added value. In the case of the hard discounter, the offer is extremely competitively priced – the key concern of the target customer. Profitability stems from achieving a very high rate of stockturn, and by maintaining management emphasis on keeping costs to a minimum. Product line proliferation would be the undoing of this discount strategy, as it is not what target customers expect and would impact on stockturn and costs.

In extreme cases, such as toys and lingerie, most of the annual turnover is concentrated in a very few weeks of the year. This represents a significant challenge to the merchandiser in range planning. Treading a course between meeting customer expectations and not wasting resources will not be easy. Stock needs building against an anticipated rise in demand. This will have implications for supply chain management. Distribution networks have limits in terms of capacity. Peak trading will place massive physical demands on the warehousing and transport system and on store staff handling the merchandise.

There are other examples of the central role that range planning plays in retail strategy. Of particular interest is the attempt by some multiple chains to become 'category killers'; that is to meet all customer needs within a particular category of merchandise. The 'category killer' is normally a large store that concentrates on one category, thus making it possible for it to carry both a broad assortment and deep selection of merchandise, coupled with low price and moderate service. A good example of this is the US retail brand, Toys Я Us.

> ## Developing the range planning and merchandise allocation plan
>
> It requires:
>
> - understanding the selection process of consumers;
> - deciding upon core and seasonal merchandise;
> - agreeing the range – e.g. style, size and colour mix – depth and width;
> - taking into consideration the sales to stock level targets and calculating the optimum level of stock by utilising one of the stock inventory planning methods;
> - relating the range plans to individual stores and possible promotional plans;
> - briefing the buyer(s) on agreed source.

The range will need to take into consideration the space constraints imposed upon the merchandise manager. If breadth and depth are important then this requires both stock space as well as display space to separate merchandise. There is also a need to ensure that any move into providing more depth does not affect turnover. To provide more depth the retailer will have to stock more variations of the product for smaller retail segments; this may mean turnover could deteriorate and stock levels would be difficult to control.

Any decision over the range and amount of inventory to stock has to be followed up by the determination of the source. In agreeing the source there should be some consideration of: previous sales performance, acceptability of the design or brand name, manufacturing and product quality, reliability of delivery and service, assurance of ability to provide further stock if required, and cost of items. With some high fashion lines, the buyer may want to know who is being supplied and may even specify that the contract will deny their competitors the purchase of a similar range.

In summary, range planning needs to be customer driven. The merchandiser needs to identify which product attributes are most important to the customer and plan accordingly. In underperforming retailers, problems are often most apparent in their ranges as a direct consequence of losing touch with their customer.

The types of depth and width assortment profiles of *narrow and deep*, *square*, and *broad and shallow* are more easily understood using a graphic illustration; *see* Fig. 6.3. The main factors which need attention when planning width and depth of assortment are those of estimated sales and profit performance.

Many merchandise lines will be far more successful if given adequate promotional support. Merchandisers will attempt to evaluate the significance of the offer of different types of assistance with the promotion of different items. This can assume many different forms including advertising allowances, co-operative advertising, free display materials, in-store demonstrations or videos, consumer sales inducements – such as special offers, coupon redemptions, free samples, and contests. Also any major advertising carried out by the manufacturer to support the brand, or product, will be an important consideration.

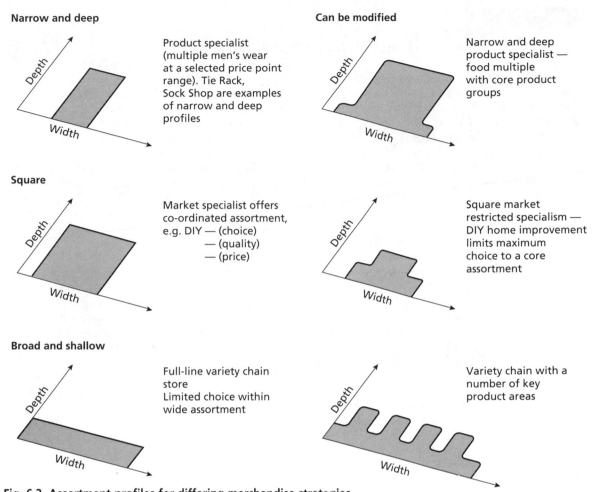

Narrow and deep

Product specialist (multiple men's wear at a selected price point range). Tie Rack, Sock Shop are examples of narrow and deep profiles

Can be modified

Narrow and deep product specialist — food multiple with core product groups

Square

Market specialist offers co-ordinated assortment, e.g. DIY — (choice)
— (quality)
— (price)

Square market restricted specialism — DIY home improvement limits maximum choice to a core assortment

Broad and shallow

Full-line variety chain store
Limited choice within wide assortment

Variety chain with a number of key product areas

Fig. 6.3 Assortment profiles for differing merchandise strategies
Source: Cook and Walters, 1991

Store grading

Taking a very simplistic approach, store grading can be related to the gross sales forecast. The gross sales projection for the company needs disaggregating across the portfolio of stores. Each store will therefore have its own budgeted gross sales figure. Part of the merchandiser's job will be to see that the merchandise plan for the store will meet the projected target. Rather than produce a unique plan for each store, it is common practice to grade the stores. As shelf or display space is the key yet limited selling medium, this grading is normally conducted on the basis of floor sales area. However, it should be recognised that this must inevitably be a crude device as, depending on the location, there will be smaller stores capable of achieving much higher than average sales densities and larger units with the reverse characteristic. An extreme example of this would be the Marks & Spencer store at Marble Arch or Timberland in Bond Street (both London), where the sales density achieved is uniquely high.

Store grading can be a major source of controversy between store operations management and central merchandise functions. From the perspective of store management, crude grading may be perceived as yet another example of how Head

IT and merchandise management

For today's retailers, 'integration' is the name of the game when it comes to software and IT. Not only do they want a transparent data flow from the buyer's laptop and digital camera to the 'planogram' store layouts downloaded to branches, but a seamless supply chain as well, with product and demand data from raw materials' supplier to end-consumer, all regarded as part of the total 'enterprise'.

In Holland, the food division of the Vendex group – owners of Vroom & Dreesman – has thrown out merchandise management applications from Retek and Armature to embrace the SAP message in a Fl 50m investment. C&A, the fashion and clothing retailer, is also opting for the single message with installation of Comshare's Arthur Enterprise Suite at its two European buying offices and all its stores in ten countries. Even companies such as Armature which had tended to focus on supply chain offerings, are now extending their appeal with a central 'library' of application tools to allow retailers to develop a more fully integrated solution.

'We operate in a highly competitive marketplace', says Wim van Dierman, financial director of the Dutch grocery chain, Sperwer. 'Our market is extremely fragmented and we're introducing Armature's software to ensure we sharpen our competitive edge. By integrating supply chain information and purchasing behaviour at store level, we will be able to improve customer service.' That is, of course, the key: as retailers move from a product-led to a consumer driven market, they increasingly need to integrate information about consumer buying patterns with product data.

Category management – a technique for managing groups of related products as a whole – is also taking centre stage. 'The category is becoming a profit centre,' says Mr Nivoix, 'and it is consumer-focused rather than seen in the old terms of "vendor managed inventory".' Best Buy – a leading US electronic goods retailer – is currently evaluating its approach to many new products. 'They are asking: "Do we sell digital cameras, or do we sell tools to help the consumer have fun with digitisation?",' he adds. 'If the answer is "tools to have fun", then they need to bundle together the cameras, computers, and software to provide a total offer. That approach is creating totally new segmented category groups and putting considerable strains on existing retail supply systems which are still largely product and volume-led.'

Source: Penelope Ody, *Financial Times*, 3 June 1998

Office is out of touch with what is happening at the 'sharp end'. This illustrates the need for effective liaison between stores and the central buying function. This liaison will be an important part of the merchandiser's remit. It will involve making sure that all relevant local characteristics are accommodated in the merchandise planning, while realising the efficiency benefits that accrue from store grading.

Developing the control mechanisms of the merchandise plan

It requires:

- an understanding of comparative frequency of store visits, based upon the browsing of, or items purchased by, the target market groups;
- forecasting sales of range items and profitability;
- monitoring stock levels and availability of new stocks and replenishment levels;
- assessing value of merchandise through shrinkage, markdowns, employee reductions;
- liaising with the buyer(s) to discuss the performance figures;
- expanding or reducing merchandise categories, based upon sales performance.

MERCHANDISE ASSORTMENT AND SUPPORT

Having devised the range plan to take account of the nature of the merchandise, the spread of stores in the company portfolio and the variations in demand over time, the role then becomes one of monitoring actual sales performance against the budget. The merchandiser needs to be proactive in seeking out opportunities to maintain and improve the rate of stockturn. This requires sophisticated analysis of merchandise category performance. If demand exceeds the projected figures, there is the prospect of missed opportunities and disappointed customers. Early warning of this situation may allow some degree of remedial action but, depending on the category, this may be limited. At the very least, the higher than anticipated sales volume will give the buyer greater freedom to increase supply, and, if necessary, from different sources.

The lower than anticipated sales volume of the under-performing category will raise the prospect of markdowns. The merchandiser has a key part to play in the markdown decision-making process. In purely financial terms, retail profitability stems from both the gross margins realised on each product line and from the frequency with which the business is able to turn the product line over, that is the rate of stockturn. Therefore, in marking-down a product line by reducing its selling price, the retailer is accepting a lower gross margin in return for an anticipated increase in the rate of stockturn. The key point is to recognise that gross margin is only realised when the stock is turned over or sold.

All retailers have to execute markdowns. The merchandiser's skill and expertise is to know when and by how much to mark down in order to achieve the desired effect. Again, this requires careful monitoring of performance and a proactive rather than reactive approach. Given the direct financial implications, strict controls are vital. The markdown policy of the retailer will seek to support positioning strategy. Customer perceptions of reduced merchandise are a key consideration and the public profile of the 'bargain-bin' cannot be allowed to compromise image. So the merchandiser has to strike the balance between stimulating stockturn with price reductions, and not undermining the perception of added value that the retailer has to preserve in order to command its 'full' price on the remainder of the stock range.

NEGOTIATING THE PURCHASE

When all the different aspects of the merchandise have been assessed and the source, through evaluation, has been evaluated and carefully chosen, the retailer has to negotiate the purchase and its terms. This can be carried out through *centralised buying* where coordination takes place to achieve scale of purchase discounts based upon full-time buying specialist inputs. However, centralised buying can lack the flexibility of responding to local market needs or ensuring good communication takes place between the buyers and the store units. *Decentralised buying* may take place at the local level based upon geographic market needs. There has to be some control with this approach as it can lead to inconsistency of the store offer and a loss of economies of scale for purchasing. Some retailers structure the buying function with *specialist buyers* in one or a few merchandise lines and also *generalist buyers* who can buy across a number of lines which need less specialist knowledge. The specialists can become experts in the merchandise areas related to their field and so identify the best suppliers as sources for the company's product offer. The control of quality, cost and delivery are necessary starting points for any discussions.

A new or different type of order will require a *negotiated contract* specifying all aspects of the purchase. Alternatively where regular orders are already agreed and reorder needs to take place, there will be a *uniform contract* with the standard pre-agreed conditions forming the basis of the agreement. However, the purchase terms should be stipulated whatever the type of contract. These should involve clear documentation of aspects such as: delivery date; quantity to be purchased; method of delivery or storage, and who should bear the related charges; price and payment terms including any discount for level of order or returns allowed by the retailer; advertising or merchandising support from the supplier; the stage in the process as to the title and ownership responsibility; and so on.

CONCLUSION

Merchandise management requires a systematic approach as well as adherence to the concept of marketing. The marketplace is uncompromising when merchandise selection does not reflect consumer tastes and trends. In addition, a company has to ensure that the optimal level of stock is held to improve cash flow and profitability. Merchandise management has to be underpinned by a merchandise plan to ensure the chances of success are maximised. This should be related to: marketing considerations; merchandise strategy options; type of customer base; financial considerations; and merchandise assortment search. The role of merchandiser is central to the pursuit of the strategic objectives of the retailer, and the operational activity surrounding planning and controlling stock ranges and replenishment. Finally, no plan will be able to succeed unless the negotiating and contracting skills of those involved ensure that quality, delivery and cost are acceptable to the consumer.

EXERCISES

The exercises in this section relate to merchandise management. It is advised that you work through them before moving on to Chapter 7.

1 If you had to plan the merchandise stock changes for a food retailer during the Christmas period what would you recommend? What considerations did you make in coming to your conclusions?

2 What checklist of questions would you ask the merchandise manager, to help you make your selections, if you had just been appointed to act as the buyer for children's wear for a leading department store?

3 Discuss the implications of width and depth considerations for a specialist outlet such as a leading women's fashion boutique and compare these to a leading DIY home improvement retailer.

4 You are asked to draw up a list of requirements for the selection of a merchandise manager. With the information in this chapter and from other sources what would you recommend? Use the following grid as a guide.

type of personality management skills intellectual ability experience others (list)	**Recommended characteristics:**

Now identify and discuss a priority list of characteristics you would recommend, including the reasons for inclusion on your list.

REFERENCES AND FURTHER READING

Boyle, K.B. (1987) *Direct Product Profit – A Primer*. Food Marketing Institute Research Dept., USA.

Branigan, L. (1998) 'The Internet: the emerging premier direct marketing channel', *Direct Marketing*, 61 (1), 46–8.

Cash, R.P., Wingate, J.W. and Friedlander, J.S. (1995) *Management of Retail Buying*. London: John Wiley.

Christopher, M. (1992) *Logistics and Supply Chain Management – Strategies for Reducing Costs and Improving Services*. London: Pitman Publishing.

Cobb, R. (1997) 'Space exploration', *Marketing*, 17 July, 29–32.

Cook, D. and Walters, D. (1991) *Retail Marketing: theory and practice*. Englewood Cliffs, NJ: Prentice Hall.

Corstjens, J. and Corstjens, M. (1995) *Store Wars*. Chichester: J. Wiley.

Cox, R. and Brittain, P. (1993) *Retail Management*. London: Pitman.

Davies, G. (1993) *Trade Marketing Strategy*. London: Paul Chapman.

Harris, D. and Walters, D. (1992) *Retail Operations Management – A Strategic Approach*. Englewood Cliffs, NJ: Prentice Hall.

Hill, T. (1991) *Production Operations Management Text and Cases*. 2nd edn. Englewood Cliffs, NJ: Prentice Hall.

Johnson, M. and Pinnington, D. (1998) 'Supporting the category management challenge: how research can contribute', *Journal of the Market Research Society*, 40 (1), 33–54.

Karonis, J. (1998) 'The supply chain: small needs, big solutions', *Financial Times*, 17 March.

Lewison, D, (1994) *Retailing*. 5th edn. New York: MacMillan College Publishing Company.

Lucas, G., Bush, R. and Gresham, L. (1994) *Retailing*. Boston, MA: Houghton Mifflin Co.

MacDonald, M. and Tideman, C. (1993) *Retail Marketing Plans*. Oxford: Butterworth-Heinemann.

Martin, C. and Parfett, M.C. (1992) *What Is EDI: A guide to electronic data interchange*. 2nd edn. Oxford: Butterworth.

Mulhern, F.J. (1997) 'Retail marketing: from distribution to integration', *International Journal of Research in Marketing*, 14 (2), 103–24.

National Retail Federation of America (1991) *Merchandising and Operating Results of Department and Speciality Stores in 1990*. New York: Financial Executives Division, National Retail Federation of America.

Ody, P. (1998) 'A transformation in retailing: information technology is helping to transform retailers', *Financial Times*, 3 June.

Porter, M. (1985) *Competitive Advantage – Creating and Sustaining Superior Performance*. New York, London: The Free Press.

Risch, E.H. (1991) *Retail Merchandising*. New York: Macmillan.

Rogers, D. (1998) 'Barclays offers on-screen links', *Marketing*, 21 May, 2.

Senn, J.A. (1995) *Information Technology in Business*. Englewood Cliffs, NJ: Prentice Hall.

Shipp, R.D. (1985) *Retail Merchandising*. 2nd edn. Boston, MA: Houghton Mifflin Co.

Smith-Bohlinger, M. (1993) *Merchandise Buying*. Needham Heights, MA: Allyn & Bacon.

7 Methods and approaches to retail marketing planning

This chapter should enable you to understand and explain:

- the reason why retail companies should adopt planning;
- problems which may occur due to a lack of planning;
- the purpose of a marketing plan;
- the structure of a marketing plan including SWOT, PEST analysis, segmentation and strategic decisions over competitive positioning;
- the need to create ownership of plans through involvement of staff.

The pace of change is unrestrained and nowhere is it more unrestrained than in retail. In the past 30 years we have witnessed a dramatic increase in competition in the marketplace. Within this turbulent arena some retailers manage to stand out from the 'crowd' due to their ability to create successful marketing changes through well-devised plans. All planning options have to be considered within the light of their feasibility and acceptability in the marketplace. This is not to say that planning is not part of our everyday experiences; planning is simply part of daily existence whether it be for social or business purposes. We all have to plan to some extent in order to be successful in life. Very few Olympic medallists could be successful without a planned programme of training and events leading up to their Olympic finals and achievements. Whether it is for examinations, sports events, going on holiday or organising a party, the use of planning leads to a greater certainty that the event will be a success. Without the right approach, and a sensible plan, alternative courses of action will have seldom been considered and, consequently, there is the likelihood that an individual, company or organisation will not function as well as might be expected. Knee and Walters (1985) have referred to the way retail management is alleged to have a propensity for 'the butterfly' spirit and approach to problem solving rather than adopting a clearly defined approach. If a retail company is to remain competitive, continual improvement in systems of planning and increasingly sophisticated approaches to strategic planning are necessary.

Planning is the most important activity of marketing management. Retailers need to plan for merchandise, inventory control, logistics development, pricing, promotional campaigns, store location and layout, positioning of the business, branding, growth and development of the business – and other functional activities. The plan, which needs to ensure that the previous areas are considered, should provide a common structure and act as a focus for all of the company's management activities. It is, therefore, essential for us to understand marketing planning in its context as a key function of management.

Planning in retailing is based upon a number of approaches. Retail planning often occurs in cycles due to the seasonality of much of retail activity. Any marketing plan is normally related to activities which will look ahead to a horizon of one to five years, whereas long-range plans deal with time spans over five years. There are also strategic plans which are concerned more with external environmental influences, and opportunities, and less with the detail of functional company marketing activities. Strategic plans are normally either medium or long term and marketing plans typically cover the short or medium term. The purpose of creating different types of retail plans are to improve the overall business both currently and for the future, and to ensure that customers continue to be satisfied with the retail experience and offer.

The retail industry provides for a combination of different products and services – from the small local convenience store to the larger high street chains, major food retailers, banks or building societies. It can include the fast food outlet and the petrol forecourt. The concept of change and survival are as important to small businesses as to larger organisations such as Marks & Spencer or Sears. That change will occur, and with increasing speed, is the most predictable aspect of contemporary business life. It would therefore seem sensible to try to become familiar with the underlying trends and forces of change which impinge upon retail business activities. This enables the management of change towards desired objectives rather than the organisation being driven blindly before the tide of market forces. We only have to remember retail problems such as the demise of Athena and Rumbelows to realise the importance of clear planning.

The long-term survival of any company is dependent on how well the business relates to its environment. In spite of its dominant market share, Sears' British Shoe Corporation failed to understand the changes which were taking place in shoe buying behaviour. The company introduced clementary notions of market segmentation that failed to address the substantial problems it was facing due to increasing competition in that market. All retailers have to devise forward plans of where a company, an outlet or product would be best placed for the future. The plan therefore needs to specify the changes that have to be made, needs to allow for the exploitation of any short-term advantages, and has to demonstrate the application of analysis and reason as part of the planning procedure. The Sears Group in the UK demonstrated a lack of consistent focus in the moves it made. It entered and withdrew from the menswear market, became market leader in sports goods with the Olympus chain, and then divested this business and other parts of the organisation when problems arose in the retail marketplace.

PROBLEMS THAT MAY ARISE IF RETAIL PLANNING IS IGNORED

A range of problems may be faced if retail planning is ignored. For example, this could involve a variety of difficulties and/or missed opportunities:

● failure to take advantage of potential retail growth markets and new marketing opportunities – such as the Internet and the expansion of the financial services market;

- lack of maintenance of demand from a spread of markets and erosion of market share due to the actions of competitors – such as competition for supermarket chains from the deep discounters such as Aldi, Lidl and Netto;

- customers' expectations are not met and service delivery weakens – as almost occurred at Granada Rentals;

- increasing demand problems in low demand periods – such as when the economy is weak and levels of confidence are low when consumers spend less;

- low level of awareness of the competition's strategies whereby there is no strategic response;

- poor image associated with the shop/group name or brand – for example, when the Forte Group was unaware of the intentions of Granada, which eventually took over the hotel group. Companies such as MFI and Ratners suffered this problem;

- lack of support for co-operative marketing initiatives;

- decline in quality levels below acceptable limits;

- difficulty in convincing suppliers of the strengths of the company;

- disillusionment and lack of motivation of employees.

As can be seen from the above, there are many potential problems which face retail organisations when there is a lack of planning. This happened to Arcadia, the former Burton Group, the UK's largest menswear retailer, which had dated outlets and a poor image in the 1970s and 1980s. The problem was that the company misjudged the declining market for men's suits and the emergence of a demand for a wider product range of leisurewear, jeans and other forms of casual clothing. A major change of direction needed to be planned in order to modernise the stores, improve the merchandise, promote the changes and identify with the changing market needs.

While planning cannot guarantee success, it can make the organisation less vulnerable to market forces. Day-to-day problems can be more easily avoided if more attention is given to planning activities, especially in relation to cash flow, fixed cost and expansion plans. It has been argued that much of retail management has been reactive, opportunistic and dedicated to crisis firefighting than to long-term analysis and planning. Retail companies need to plan to have world-class service or at least distinctive competence in order to be successful. This means that, through sensible planning, companies will attempt to associate their brands or company name with service excellence in order to establish a reputation for meeting or exceeding customer expectations. The methods of service delivery have to be planned to achieve superior systems and support the nature of the business.

Companies which rely on ad hoc initiatives or fail to manage their future will find that their future has been managed for them. Even though the jewellers Ratners suffered major problems due to bad publicity and over-expansion, no company can ignore the significance of the way this retailer grew through its planned pricing policy. Ratners are a lesson that retailers need to ensure that high margin products should be bought at the appropriate cost and sold at competitive prices. Each company will adopt a different approach to the task of planning, based upon the way senior executives see the purpose of marketing plans. The values of any company may be said to fall somewhere along a continuum which runs from a simple *wait and see*, through a more rigorous *prepare and predict* stance to companies at the opposite end of the continuum who want to *make it happen*. A company will benefit more from a future that is made to happen because the clear direction provides fewer surprises for the workforce and places less pressure on other company resources. At present, great importance is placed on building brand strength and, if appropriate, own brands. This is because of the realisation that retail brand strength can allow a company to be more successful in new ventures such as loyalty schemes or financial services. The German men's clothing company, Hugo Boss, has managed to develop a strong emotive brand based upon a systematic approach to research, development and promotion. Brands that are strong are said to be elastic and can have a spin-off effect on new products or services. This is important for retailers who wish to expand.

The plan has to be formulated in relation to those forces which impinge on the likelihood of success. Prime among such forces is competition. The plan cannot exist in isolation of other factors. As Porter has argued (1980), it is easy to view the competition too narrowly and too pessimistically. Porter views intense competition as natural, with the state of competition depending on the relationship between five basic forces (*see* Fig. 7.1). Porter argues that it is the collective strength of these forces that determines the ultimate profit potential of any industry. The model has become widely known as the 'five forces' model of competition.

Fig. 7.1 Five forces governing competition in an industry

The focus of rivalry among existing competitors are (1) the outcome of rivalry; (2) the bargaining power of suppliers; (3) the bargaining power of buyers; (4) the threat of new entrants; and (5) the threat of substitute products or services. Each of these forces, in turn, can be broken down into its constituent elements. The following discussion of these forces helps with our understanding of the retail industry and clarifies the considerations we must take into account.

1 Rivalry among existing competitors

Factors which might affect the nature of competitiveness or 'the jockeying for position' by the use of tactics in the industry include the following:

- the degree of concentration in the industry, and the number and relative size of the competitors;
- if industry growth is slow there will be fights for market share;
- the extent and nature of product differentiation;
- when fixed costs are high or the product perishable;
- capacity in relation to demand and characteristics of demand;
- high exit barriers will keep companies competing even though they may be earning low or negative returns.

2 Bargaining power of buyers

The bargaining power of the buyers (that is, demand for the products or services whether it is the retail company acting as buyer from suppliers or whether it is the retail customer) is related to the following features:

- the degree of concentration relating to the relative importance of levels of demand on the customer side by comparison with that of the competing suppliers;
- the relative significance of the produce or service to customers in terms of quality, expenditure and service;
- relative ease and cost of changing to new suppliers (switching costs);
- the amount of information possessed by buyers;
- the ability of buyers to integrate backwards;
- profit levels of buyers;
- the extent to which buyers want differentiated products.

3 Bargaining power of suppliers

Factors relevant to the supply side of the industry will be similar to those mentioned on the customer side of the industry and, thus, include:

- the structure of the supplier side relative to the producer industry;
- the degree of produce differentiation/substitutability;
- the potential for forward integration;
- the relative importance of the industry demand to suppliers;
- the feasibility and cost of producers switching suppliers.

4 Threat of new entrants

The ease, or difficulty, with which new producers may enter the industry affects the degree to which the structure of the industry can change due to the extra competition and the desire to gain market share. The seriousness of the threat is dependent on the type of barriers to entry and on the way existing competitors will react:

- the extent to which there are economies of scale;
- the amount of capital required to capture customer loyalty and create brand identification;
- the capital required for inventories and absorbing start-up costs;
- existing companies may have experienced learning curve benefits which lower costs;
- the level of customer switching costs;
- the existence of government regulation and legal limitations and barriers.

5 Threat of substitutes

- the availability of substitutes and willingness of buyers to purchase substitute products which have the same functional capability;
- the impact on profits of close substitutes;
- the impact of the comparative price and quality of substitutes.

The above approach to industry analysis can allow a retailer to understand the pressures on the industry and the likely effect on the prospects for short- and longer-term success. More specifically, a retailer is able to take into consideration its true competitive position with regard to its opponents and can identify the possible strengths and weaknesses due to the current state of rivalry in the industry. It may then proceed to consider what level of importance should be attached to the marketing planning process in order to provide a competitive advantage and a position from which to achieve its financial objectives.

THE PURPOSE OF A MARKETING PLAN

It should now be clear that planning is an important activity for any company. We now need to reinforce the essential points which bring value to a company. Some reasons for planning follow:

- To provide *clear direction* to the overall retailing operation based upon a systematic, written approach to planning and action. The planning system allows direction by virtue of requiring a written mission statement and a set of objectives to be established, which can be transmitted to the workforce. This provides clear leadership principles and allows the workforce to know how their own efforts are essential to the achievement of desired results.
- To *coordinate the resources* of the company. This eliminates confusion and misunderstanding so that there is maximum co-operation. Tasks and responsibilities may be set which clarify the direction and objectives of the company. To ensure there is a united effort, recommendations have to be presented in such a way that they can be fully understood at all company levels. The plan then acts as a master guide which will underpin all endeavours and decision making. The plan should lead to greater employee cohesion and make everyone feel part of a team in which each individual believes they can make a valuable contribution.
- To *set targets* against which progress can be measured. Quantified targets for quantity of merchandise sold or revenue generated provide the focus for individual,

departmental or company performance. Some companies will set targets at achievable levels whereas others will set targets at a higher than expected level in order to stretch employees to gain better results.

- To *minimise risk through analysis* of the internal and external environment. The planning procedure allows managers to identify areas of strength and weakness so that the first can be exploited and the second surmounted. In addition, threats and opportunities can be assessed.

- To *assess targeting* by examining the various ways of targeting different retail market segments. This allows for different marketing mix strategies to be appraised prior to their implementation.

- To *provide a record* of the company's marketing policies and plans. This allows managers to check on what has been attempted in the past and to evaluate the effectiveness of previous programmes. It also provides continuity and a source of reference for new managers joining the company.

- To *focus on longer-term action* in relation to business objectives so that the company plans to be in the best current position to achieve its future aims. This allows management to develop continuity of thought and action from one year to the next.

Given that you have understood the previous information in this book, it will be accepted that company objectives should be based upon relevant market-centred opportunities. It is the responsibility of retail marketers to identify these opportunities and to have devised a system of planning which may lead to their exploitation.

MINICASE 7.1

Supermarkets have identified an opportunity of offering banking services

The chief executive of Sainsbury's Bank was told recently that he had personally changed the face of UK banking. That view came from someone who ought to know: a senior executive of a traditional clearing bank. The five big supermarkets are pushing rapidly into financial services. J. Sainsbury has teamed with Bank of Scotland and Tesco with the Royal Bank of Scotland. Abbey National, Lloyds TSB and Midland are opening outlets respectively in Safeway, Asda and Morrison stores. Tesco and Sainsbury, the leaders, have more than 1m deposit account holders between them, and total deposits exceeding £2bn. Sainsbury has taken £1.5bn of deposits in a year, beating Barclays, where personal balances grew £1.2bn. Sainsbury is doing sufficiently well to be talking of profits next

year, earlier than analysts had expected. Strong brands, large customer bases and low costs have given supermarkets their opportunity. Low overheads have allowed them to offer more attractive interest rates than most bank or building societies. Supermarkets are targeting financial services to find new profit streams to offset the maturity of the UK grocery market. Similar motives underpinned their expansion into petrol retailing where they have nearly one-third of the market. Such diversification, while not precluding overseas expansion, is less risky given the poor record of UK retailers abroad. Supermarkets are also exploiting the banks' poor reputation for customer service.

Source: Christopher Brown-Humes, *Financial Times*, 16 May 1998

REASONS FOR POOR PLANNING EXPERIENCES

The standard approach to planning can be found in most textbooks to follow a series of simple steps. However, the true art of planning is to understand both the human aspects and procedural necessities of planning. A poor planning experience may be a function of one or a combination of the following issues or problems.

1 One major problem which is difficult to resolve is if there is weak support for the plan from senior people and the chief executive. Any planning requires senior management support if it is to be treated seriously by employees.

2 The system of planning which is adopted may not suit the company. There is often the separation of different planning functions from each other which leads to a lack of integration. Therefore, the system often has to be designed to match the company and to achieve harmony between groups.

3 The planning system is often blamed when the weakness is actually poor planning and management. Sometimes there is confusion over data or planning terms. The requirement is for a plan to be compiled which clarifies times and responsibilities for different actions and meetings.

4 Unexpected environmental changes may create adverse effects on the company's performance. Planning is then often blamed for not having incorporated such a scenario. Plans need to be flexible and updated when necessary.

5 The values of the management team will imply different acceptance levels of the plan and, ultimately, its success or failure. There is often hostility toward plans because of the feeling of a lack of involvement in the planning process. This often occurs when the planning is left solely to a planner or it becomes an annual ritual.

6 Problems occur when there is an over-abundance of information which has to be filtered for its relevance. Too much detail in the early stages can produce what is often referred to as 'paralysis analysis'. There is a need to decide what is important and what is not.

It is distressing that companies which have recognised the need for a more structured approach to planning, and have subsequently adopted formalised procedures found in the literature, seldom enjoy the advantages that are claimed for organisations which embark on planning. In fact it is often planning itself which is brought into disrepute when it fails to bring about the desired changes within a company. The problems faced in marketing planning have led to a growing body of literature which indicates companies should do what they are good at, rather than embark upon higher level planning exercises. This could be a retrograde step because companies should attempt to take the most logical direction and not be hampered by internal failings of the human resource aspects of implementation, lack of planning expertise, or disregard of the involvement of others in the planning process. The argument put forward here is that an understanding of the social aspects of the company is a prerequisite for successful planning.

It is necessary for those involved in planning to recognise the need for involvement of all departments in the company in the formulation of the plan. This will ensure various personnel are more likely to be motivated toward its successful implementation. Such motivation is vital to success, quite apart from the valuable knowledge and expertise which key personnel bring to marketing plan formulation. The reality of this is that most accomplishments, in service industries, are made through people. The control of schedules, budgets, monitoring performance or corrective decisions can only take place with the involvement of people. Each employee who has responsibility requires clear objectives against which to judge whether tactical action needs to be carried out.

It is important to ensure that plans are not prepared within the vacuum of one department or by a marketing team who believe they are an elite. Well-structured management meetings may offer a setting where deliberation, responsibility and authority are shared and taken by all. This precludes dogmatic assertions about the particular methods of preparing and organising marketing planning.

The marketing planning system offers a structured and market-led approach to organising and coordinating the efforts and activities of those involved in deciding on the future of an organisation. However, there is no one 'right' system for any particular company as companies differ in size and diversity of operations, as may the values of senior management, and the expertise of those involved in the planning exercise.

THE STRUCTURE OF THE MARKETING PLAN

The construction of the marketing plan is characterised by a range of headings which have been developed by different theorists. Some authors offer a list of sections with the first headed SWOT issues or situational analysis, the second headed statement of objectives and goals or setting objectives, the third is strategy or marketing programming, and the last is monitoring or control. We prefer to use different stages which are more easily understood by managers and students.

The stages are:

1 What is it we want?

2 Where are we now?

3 Where do we want to go?

4 How do we get there?

5 Where did we get to?

These stages are represented in the model in Fig. 7.2. For an understanding of the model it is important to realise that the system is not always linear, as would appear from the seemingly hierarchical stages. Quite often the process needs to involve an interplay between the various stages, with the flexibility to move backwards as well as forwards in an interactive process. We should also understand that refinements of the plan take place as understanding of the interconnections improves. We should not presume that anything close to perfection will apply until a number of drafts have been completed.

The approach to retail marketing planning is described in the following six main sections:

1 the corporate mission and goals;

2 external and internal audit;

3 business situation analysis;

4 creating the objectives;

5 providing an effective marketing mix strategy;

6 monitoring the plan.

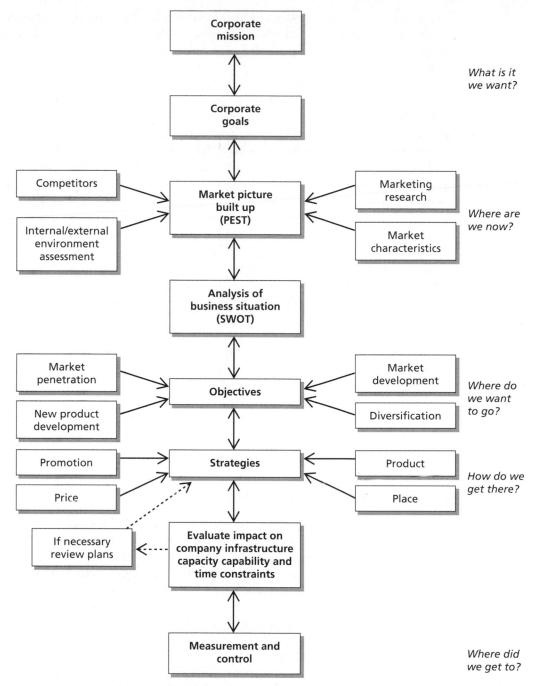

Fig. 7.2 A model of a marketing plan

THE CORPORATE MISSION AND GOALS

It is important to understand what is expected of the plan from the long-term goals set at corporate level. A clear mission statement enables the retailer to concentrate on core business objectives and what it wants to accomplish.

The mission statement is a confirmation of what business the company is in from a consumer viewpoint and also acts as a guide for employees to know what the purpose of the company is. For example, the statement could stress: 'serving customers better than the competition and supporting the local community and employee needs through excellence in retailing'. The mission statement then represents the overriding goal of the company or organisation. It is a statement of what the company wants to accomplish within chosen markets for the stakeholder groups it will serve. The mission statement is a clear expression of what the company or organisation will attempt to achieve from the other inputs in the marketing plan.

The goals of a mission statement may be based upon the values and objectives of the key shareholders, board directors or senior managers. In some situations, goals are set only after the establishment and evaluation of the marketing programmes. This is a parochial, programme-led method of planning where management does not attempt to meet higher level corporate goals within the planning process because managers are more prepared to settle for what they believe will work rather than what should be made to work. A decision to agree easier targets may mean that a company, or organisation, will not investigate as broad a range of alternatives, objectives and strategies as their competitors who may be driven to ensure leadership and competitive supremacy.

Whatever approach is taken, the most effective form of planning has to create a balance between setting corporate direction and ensuring employee commitment to that direction by the process of their involvement (*see* Fig. 7.6). If goals are dictated to employees by a 'top-down' approach there is very little sense of ownership of the plan which can lead to a corresponding lack of motivation. As will be realised from Fig. 7.6 there can be a balanced approach through the combination of bottom-up and top-down processes.

EXTERNAL AND INTERNAL AUDIT

An external and internal audit is carried out as part of the broader process of market analysis to determine the opportunities existing in the retail marketplace. It is necessary to gather enough relevant information about the external and internal company environment to be able to construct a business and market picture of current and future pressure and trends. One important part of marketing planning is knowing what to analyse. Executives have to be careful that they do not have too limited a focus in terms of the environment. Checklists of necessary information is one way to stop companies scanning the environment based upon what they intend to do, rather than in relation to what they could or should do.

The information collected should at the very least, form the basis of a PEST investigation. *PEST analysis* is an examination of the Political, Economic, Social and Technological changes which may affect the company and the plan. The information gathering utilising PEST is part of an internal and external audit which could involve the business/economic environment and the market environment – discussed in more detail below.

Business/economic environment

Political: taxation, duty, regulation, policies, local authorities, statutory holidays, Sunday trading, opening times, planning permission for buildings

Economic: inflation, unemployment, fuel costs, exchange rates, average salaries, market environment (*see* market environment list below)

Social: demographics, holiday/leisure time entitlement, values (consumerism), lifestyle, male/female role changes, delay of first child, education, workforce changes

Technology: innovations, new retailing systems, home technology, electronic fund transfer, Internet, distribution systems, stock handling mechanisms and control

Market environment

This is an expansion of the economic category above.

Total market: size, growth, trends, value, industry structure, barriers to entry, extent of under or over capacity of supply, marketing methods

Companies in the market: level of investment, takeovers, alliances, promotion expenditures, redundancies, profits, expansion plans, trading formats

Product development: trends, new product types, service enhancements

Price: levels, range, terms, practices

Distribution: patterns, trade structure, policies

Promotion: expenditure, types, communication messages

The information listed above should be gathered on the basis of how it affects the company and service. For example, it will be found that shops in single-site positions are disappearing and that location in areas where the fascia brands will have pulling power is becoming more important. The task is then to analyse and ascertain the way forward. Identification of objectives may be intuitive and based upon a good idea, or systematic thorough researched evidence, or based upon trial and error from what has been learnt from past events.

BUSINESS SITUATION ANALYSIS

Once sufficient internal and external information has been collected it is necessary to carry out an analysis of the business situation, to identify the major

● Strengths
● Weaknesses
● Opportunities
● Threats

facing the company. This is the so-called *SWOT analysis*. There is also the need to check these against information provided from *PEST* analysis.

The systematic analysis carried out at this stage provides for the formulation of a number of assumptions about the past performance, future conditions, product opportunities, resources, and service priorities which all lead to the possibility of a range of strategic options for an organisation within the retail industry. The analysis may utilise a number of approaches related to life-cycle assessment or portfolio analysis. These are discussed later and describe how to form a clearer understanding of the current position of the retail business which will lead to guidance in the selection of specific objectives and strategies.

The research feedback, from the earlier phase of planning activity, should have highlighted customer satisfaction or dissatisfaction with the current retail offers and services. It will have also highlighted what it is that the competition is doing well, and may indicate the existence of market gaps. For a store, decisions may need to be taken about the merchandise. This may include the width of assortment (number of different product categories carried) and the depth of assortment (the variety of products carried in a specific category). Scanning what is happening in foreign markets will sensitise the planners to what may become new trends or ideas in the home market. The point is that the overall analysis should be far-reaching to ensure that the best possible company options are assessed.

SWOT analysis

A framework of information should be created which is divided into the categories of strengths, weaknesses, opportunities and threats facing the company (SWOT). This will allow further assessment of the information collected and form the basis of a summary of all the main issues which will have been examined. Each of the SWOT points could be fed into the objectives of the plan. For example, if it were found that a weakness existed in the attitude of the target market to the brand or in the lack of knowledge the target market had of the organisation, this could become part of the plan as a promotional objective. The example of a SWOT matrix in Fig. 7.3 is for a hypothetical bank which operates traditional branch retailing.

Strengths	Weaknesses
• financial position • reputation • branch network • technology • employees well qualified	• poor branch service • opening hours restricted • high overheads due to high street locations • no parking
Opportunities	**Threats**
• expansion of investment and financial services • create young investors • develop relationship marketing scheme • expand services for retirees	• the development of tele-banking • encroachment by building societies and grocery retailers • international expansion of banking

Fig. 7.3 Example of a SWOT Matrix

The SWOT analysis may lead to short-term operational imperatives. For example, a SWOT analysis could be a guide for a merchandiser as to how the existing product lines will need to be extended or deleted. It could act as a guide to the buyers to achieve certain price, quality and specification objectives for the retail brand, or even indicate to display people that the different window and in-store promotions need to be more consistent by season across all outlets.

Assessment of the retail operation has to take place in relation to the position of the company in its life-cycle stage (*see* Chapter 1 for a further discussion of this concept). The following life-cycle (Fig. 7.4) and matrix (Table 7.1) provides our approach to the current retail situation and the strategies which may be appropriate at any one stage of the life-cycle based upon a consideration of the competitive position of retail companies. As an example, the life-cycle for retail can be generalised for different types of business, as illustrated in Fig. 7.4 for the UK.

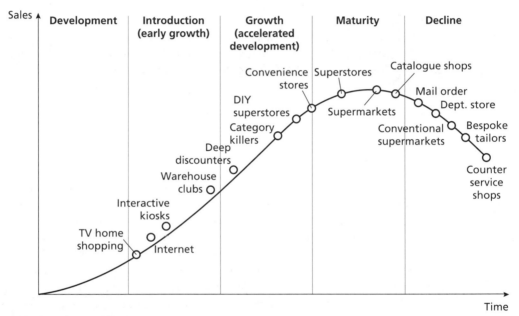

Fig. 7.4 UK retail life cycle

Once the position of an individual business (or its category type) is clear, then the strength or weakness of that retailer's position will dictate the most logical objectives and consequently points to the possible strategies which could be chosen. This is made clear in Table 7.1.

Portfolio analysis

A portfolio approach allows for the analysis of an organisation's current position in relation to the marketplace, its own companies or products. A commonly used technique for consideration of the growth and share of an organisation is the Boston Consulting

Table 7.1 Management of life-cycle position based upon market strength/weakness

Stages/competitive position	Birth	Growth	Maturity	Decline
Dominant	Fast business growth expected due to competitive strength and focus	Defend position and build in strategy of cost leadership and technological superiority	Aggressively defend position and renew efforts of leadership strategies and taking share	Continue to defend position Find way to relaunch retail concept
Favourable	Need to develop strengths of differentiation, cost control, and focus	Need to improve total business to ensure growth within the industry sector	Ensure focus and marketing is maximising returns by attacking leaders' weaknesses Control costs	Plan turnaround Retrench Divest
Weak	Improve to ensure growth will occur Find niche	Require a major turnaround or new focus of the business	Start to harvest returns or plan improvements Take quiet route	Harvest Withdraw

Group Matrix (BCG). Portfolio analysis has been described as a family of techniques with BCG as the most famous (Abell and Hammond, 1979). This is even more true two decades on with the BCG approach being used by a large number of planners in different marketing settings. This approach allows an organisation to classify the position of each of its retail strategic business units (SBUs) on one axis in terms of their market share relative to competitors and on the opposite axis to position annual industry growth. By creating a measurement based upon the scales of each of these axes, a spatial plot is derived which by the use of the creation of quadrants places each plot in a specific category. As part of the analysis, a company may identify which SBUs are dominant when compared to competitors, and whether the areas in which the company operates are growing, stable or declining. The two-by-two matrix describes four types of position as: star, question mark, cash cow, and dog (*see* Fig. 7.5).

Stars

These are SBUs or products with a high market share in a fast growing market and, importantly, offering good prospects for growth. As such, the objective would be for an investment in any SBU or product to fall into this quadrant. The objective is to build on the strength of the position and/or to hold on to it in the face of any competition. If the organisation has a balanced portfolio, the transferring of money from a cash cow (*see* Fig. 7.5 below) SBU could be contemplated if this would create higher returns in the long run.

Question marks

These are SBUs or products where there is some question about their position. Spatially there is the potential for high market growth, but there is also low market share. The objectives would be to investigate further the possibility of any future movement, in the market or from the competition, creating a new position of either a star or a dog. If the question mark has the possibility of becoming a star, and if the organisation has a cash cow then money should be transferred to build the question mark position with the objective of creating a star. Alternatively a poor outcome for the analysis may mean the objective has to be one of becoming a niche retailer – or even divestment. If the unit of consideration were merchandise and certain items fell into this area, there may need to be an expansion of shelf space for the merchandise and the use of in-store promotion.

Cash cow

This categtory is where the SBU or product is enjoying the benefit of a high market share but in a low or zero growth market. The objective would be to exploit the strong, positive cash flow situation but not to devote any investment into the SBU or product apart from to ensure its maintenance. The objective is normally to hold the position and harvest money so that it can be used to grow other parts of the business.

Dogs

These are SBUs or products with a low market share and static or no market growth. The inference is that any future earnings are bound to be low and little or no profit will be made. The objective would be either to create a niche area for activity or to withdraw from this area of business by selling out or planning closure. If the unit of consideration were merchandise and certain items fell into this area, there would be a case for reducing or removing the area of shelf space for the merchandise.

Each of these spatial areas allows an identification of what strategies may be most appropriate. This allows objectives to be decided upon which are in the long-term interests of the organisation as a whole, so that a balanced approach is taken which considers all aspects of an operation.

The assumption is that the higher the market share of any strategic business unit the better its long-term marketplace position, because of the probability of economies of scale, lower costs and higher profitability. In Fig. 7.5 the vertical axis identifies the annual growth rate percentage of the operating market for the SBUs, companies or products being assessed. It does not normally exceed a growth rate of 12 per cent but it depends on the market being analysed. The logic of its inclusion is related to the notion that any organisation in a situation where there is high market growth will have derived benefit from the situation of buoyant development in the marketplace. However, for a retailer, the costs of operation may not decline because of this situation as some merchandise, for stores in a star position, may require prime store sites in order to achieve the optimum level of sales.

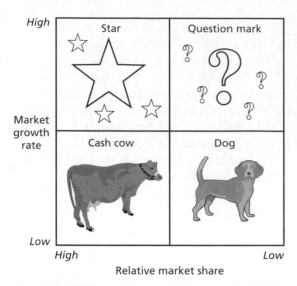

Fig. 7.5 Market growth – market share portfolio analysis matrix

Relative market share is the horizontal axis and is used because of its ability to provide the unit of measurement as an indicator of the ability to generate cash based upon the relative position to the market leader. The measure of market share is expressed as a comparison to that of the largest competitor. This is important because it reflects market share relative to the leader and shows the degree of power the market leader has over others in the market. For example, if company 'A' had 25 per cent share of the market and its competitor 'B' also had 25 per cent, there is little advantage. However, the market situation is dramatically different and more favourable to 'A' if it is the market leader with a 25 per cent share and its closest competitor has a 12.5 per cent market share. The horizontal axis provides a relative ratio to the market leader and, therefore, the example given would create a 1:1 ratio in the first example and 2:1 in the second. These ratios are plotted on the horizontal axis against the market leader's share to reflect the individual positions of dominance for different units of measurement. The axis can be divided on any scale which makes sense for the market being considered but should enable the relative positions, across the range of the axis, to be plotted. As there is the use of a market leader share figure, the left-hand end of the scale will be no larger than 1 as no other SBU, product or company can exceed the size of the leader's share.

A certain amount of caution has to be applied to the indiscriminate use of portfolio analysis. At the outset it should be realised that portfolio analysis has more dimensions than simply market and market growth. In fact, one of the difficulties is to decide upon the scales for the axes. Once these are agreed, it may be difficult to obtain competitive data. With a BCG approach the spatial positioning outcome of any analysis is not necessarily related to profitability, as a high market share could be based upon low profitability if prices are lower than the competition or vice versa. In addition, a higher market share for a retailer or a product may reflect a disproportionate amount of promotional expenditure which in turn could be creating unacceptable cost implications. There are conceptual and practical problems in defining both products and markets when using the matrix. While telephone banking for a bank may be a star, the main business for the bank could be suffering due to the impact of building society and grocery retail activity. Finally, a market which is growing may not be a good environmental fit, or suit the business strengths of the SBU or company. None of these weaknesses indicates there is a major problem with the BCG matrix or its principles, simply that it has to be utilised with some degree of caution.

The human resources considerations for successful planning

The involvement of different departments will help reduce resistance to future changes or tasks. Continuous concern about the human aspects of planning can provide a greater possibility of the plan's success. The planner or planning team should be aware that they are only a technical service to a wider team. However, care must be taken not to make the system too open as to be in danger of creating anarchy. On the other hand, the system should not be too closed, as this leads to bureaucracy and apathy.

Good planning is a combination of qualitative and quantitative factors based upon creative as well as analytical and logical thinking. As Albert Einstein once remarked, 'When I examined myself, and my methods of thought, I came to the conclusion that the gift of fantasy has meant more to me than my talent for absorbing positive knowledge'. Creative thinkers bring specific benefits to the planning process. They enable:

- challenges to norms and assumptions and the ability to question what others automatically accept as true;
- the focus on chance and the unexpected rather than safe answers;
- a group to develop new ways of altering familiar ideas into unconventional approaches and so provide new ideas and means of thinking of situations;
- individuals to make associations and so combine seemingly unrelated events, topics and ideas;
- retail product, service and promotion ideas to be updated and revised;
- planners to keep the planning function from being too boring by bringing humanistic values to the whole process.

One vital behavioural consideration of any plan, which affects all aspects of the company, is that it should not clash with the company culture. Such a clash may be overcome by ensuring that staff values are incorporated into various stages of the planning cycle and the planning method. The involvement of the full range of staff leads to a situation where the company culture values of staff are reflected in the 'bottom-up' comments. This helps to ensure that the plan is created as part of a process which makes it compatible with the company culture.

As you are now aware, we stress that companies have to plan for the involvement level of staff as well as for the market. Figure 7.6 provides one approach to dealing with marketing planning involvement levels.

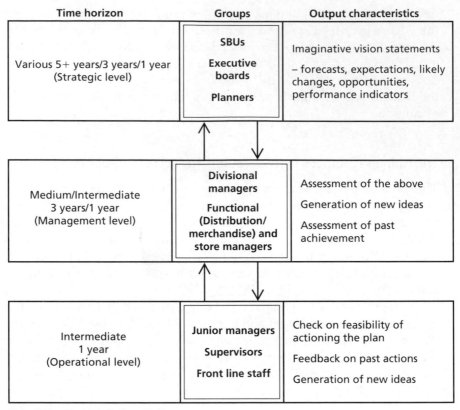

Time horizon	Groups	Output characteristics
Various 5+ years/3 years/1 year (Strategic level)	**SBUs** **Executive boards** **Planners**	Imaginative vision statements – forecasts, expectations, likely changes, opportunities, performance indicators
Medium/Intermediate 3 years/1 year (Management level)	**Divisional managers** **Functional (Distribution/ merchandise) and store managers**	Assessment of the above Generation of new ideas Assessment of past achievement
Intermediate 1 year (Operational level)	**Junior managers** **Supervisors** **Front line staff**	Check on feasibility of actioning the plan Feedback on past actions Generation of new ideas

Note: SBU = Strategic Business Unit

Fig. 7.6 Involvement levels for marketing planning

One other important aspect of influence when including a cross-section of people in planning, is their capability to hinder or help the plan. Within any company or organisation, a manager's competence to plan will reflect the level of activity, the degree of preoccupation with other business, career goals, and their experience and ability to think conceptually and analytically. These attributes are linked to other managers' values and the cultural climate within the company, which may be more or less responsive to change and adaptation, and the willingness to adhere to and use the planning system.

A plan when completed should be read and understood by as many people as possible throughout the company. This is often not possible due to lack of time among busy executives and the complexity of the plan. To overcome the problem, all plans require the addition of a good executive summary – written in clear, concise language – which will ensure that the most salient points and important themes are communicated. The summary should be cogent and logical and should concentrate on objectives, main target markets, opportunities and threats, key strategies and timings.

MINICASE 7.2

The reasons for the success of 7-Eleven Japanese convenience stores

In an age of discounting, competition on price is not an issue for the Japanese convenience stores. In fact, their prices are about 10 per cent more expensive than those of the supermarkets. But the amount of cash involved on each visit is so small that consumers seem to lose their price-sensitivity. The average convenience store spend is about ¥500 ($3.90) – literally small change – while the slump in retail sales has been severest in big-ticket items such as cars and white goods. Customers are drawn to convenience stores by their immediate need for lunch or a new toothbrush.

Another factor in the stores' success is their ability to adapt instantly to changing customer needs, because of their small store sizes and limited product ranges. Hard times mean shoppers are more choosy, and getting the right products on the shelves at the right time is essential.

Most convenience stores are doing better than might be expected from the state of the economy, but according to Toshiko Binder, retail analyst at HSBC James Capel Securities, one stands out from the rest. It is also the company which pioneered the convenience store concept in Japan, translating it successfully from its US origins: 7-Eleven Japan. Since its first store opened in Tokyo 25 years ago, the company has not only outgrown its Japanese parent, the Ito-Yokado supermarket chain, but together with Ito-Yokado now owns a majority stake in Southland Corporation, the US company from which it originally licensed the 7-Eleven name. 7-Eleven Japan is the country's largest retailer and third largest in the world, and ranks 12th in the FT500 list of Japanese companies, according to market capitalisation. With 7,300 stores, the company has the largest network in Japan.

Ms Binder at HSBC James Capel says the computerised distribution system is the big difference between 7-Eleven and its competitors. 'With the system they have established, whatever time you go, the shelves are never empty. If people come in at 4am and the stores don't have what they want, that will have a big impact on what people think of the store.' Distribution hubs divide products into four categories, depending on temperature, and deliver them on rotas ranging from three times a day for the core fast-food products, to once a week for canned foods. This cuts the number of separate deliveries to each store from about 70 to 10 a day, timed to bring in supplies of fast-moving chilled foods just before peak demand periods. The combination of the advanced computer system with central distribution hubs has so far proved unbeatable. Orders for fast foods can be placed in the morning – with an eye to the day's weather – and are delivered the same day.

The product range can also change rapidly with immediate feedback on which items are selling well, and to which customers. 7-Eleven has also led the way in offering other services, such as photo-copying and bill payment facilities.

Source: Bethan Hutton, *Financial Times,* 17 March 1998

CREATING THE OBJECTIVES

This stage involves communicating the company's objectives, which are a combination of what is expected of the company by its shareholders or directors, and an evaluation of the options emerging out of the first three steps. For a small company, the objectives are often less ambitious than for larger concerns, but in terms of achieving market success, no less important.

If at the earlier stage of analysis it was found that waiting times in the shop were affecting frequency of visits in a negative way, then the retailer has to have the following objectives:

- improve the retail operation's service levels;
- enhance the waiting time experience;
- inform customers as to the likely time they will have to wait;
- apologise and give a reason for the delay;
- ensure the customers can judge the progress of their turn in being served.

These objectives will be translated into tactics or operational changes but, as a starting point, it is necessary to know what the main objectives are. At a later stage, changes could be made similar to those at Disney where those queuing for rides can watch TV, listen to music, are organised so that they can see people moving and are given approximate waiting times. In busy booking offices or shops, customers can take a numbered ticket that will guarantee their place in the queue without anyone else pushing in.

The objectives should emerge as the most logical course of action the company ought to embark upon, given the analysis which has occurred in the preceding stages of the plan. We have to ensure that the objectives include not only sales volume and financial objectives, but also broader marketing objectives. Objectives should also include the expected market share achievements because the performance of the company may only reach realistic levels if certain budgets are made available.

At this stage of planning it is possible to circulate the assumptions and forecasts to different stores, functional units and company divisions. These should be offered as a range of alternatives. For example, if you have assumed the market will grow at X per cent and this will create £Y with a specific strategy, then it is also wise to create alternative scenarios. You should estimate sales at lower and higher rates than expected, so that the potential impact on profits can be assessed. For example, a rate of growth of X + 2% (where X is the expected demand) may create a profit of $1.3 \times £Y$, or alternatively X − 2% may give $0.5 \times £Y$. Managers may need to involve their team in discussions about the relevance of the material created from the previous environmental scanning stage to ensure agreement to expected demand level.

One danger in planning is that large companies often only set financial objectives. For example, in terms of growth rate in earnings per share, return on equity or investment and so on, and ignore or forget to set marketing objectives such as the selection of specific segments as target markets and the improvement of merchandise selection, brand image or consumer awareness. Retailers have to establish and maintain a distinctive image in their chosen markets. This image is created only if objectives are set which recognise the need for appropriate physical and attitudinal attributes. These goals need to be related to retail design, ambience, the location decisions based upon surrounding area, and the impact of the retail window area and front of building. The use of promotional techniques and customer service strategies all enhance the position and image of a retail company.

Objectives are often complex. For example, an objective may be to *increase sales revenue*, which could be achieved in a number of ways, such as:

- through increasing average transaction values;
- converting browsing visits to purchase behaviour;
- increasing the frequency of customer visits;
- improving merchandise selection or placing merchandise in proximity to corresponding mix and match items;
- increasing hours of trading, such as Sunday opening.

Another example could be an objective *to create improved productivity*. This could be achievable in various ways:

● through increasing sales and contribution per retail employee;

● introducing technology to provide efficiencies;

● increasing throughput of distribution facilities;

● redesigning the store layout to improve customer flow;

● improved stock control.

Retail companies involve many labour intensive operations and will often set objectives of reducing costs through greater use of technology or systems design. MFI, the furniture retailer, attempted to increase operating efficiencies and sales productivity. There was an investment in systems in order to reduce staff numbers, to improve stock control and merchandise and warehouse space. In addition, store layouts were improved and visual merchandising introduced. The initial changes allowed the company to improve substantially on its previously weak sales and profit results.

In the current marketplace, retailing technology is advancing swiftly with inventory control, automated checkout facilities, vending machines, etc. Any change due to technology innovation has to be carried out with due concern for the marketing implications of that improvement. Any reduction in personal service may be interpreted as a decline in the standards of service. Therefore, objectives need to be a balance between the aspirational and the realistic, so that the company attempts to improve its market position within acceptable risk limits.

Growth objectives

The alternative objective inputs, as shown on the marketing plan schema in Fig. 7.2, are based upon the possibility of the selection of growth strategies, borrowed from the work of Ansoff (1988), whereby a company is attempting to expand by adopting a specific strategy from those of *penetration*, *market development*, *product development* and *diversification*. Companies may want to attack the market share of others by *penetrating* the market to increase their own share of that market. This takes place within the company's current markets and normally involves a more aggressive use of the marketing mix. The company may attempt to increase existing customer usage rates or attract competitors' customers. For example, Visa used promotion in an attempt to get their cardholders to use their card while on holiday and to use it in preference to those of competitors. Some of the current large DIY outlets started as home improvement specialists with initial links to paint and wallpaper stores. These companies realised the growth potential of the whole DIY marketplace and wanted to take market share from their competitors. To back up the setting of the objective of market penetration, there should be some evidence from the analysis that there is buoyancy and growth in the marketplace. Sales can be increased by reaching non-users of the outlet or service, attracting competitors' customers and raising the frequency of store visit of existing customers.

Larger organisations or companies will try to increase sales through *market development* by attempting to sell current products in new markets. As an objective, this is often linked to those retailers which are located on a local or regional basis and want

197

to widen their market by geographical expansion. Companies may develop their markets by expanding internationally, as did the IKEA group, for instance. Market development may also involve the addition of new locations, such as McDonald's outlet openings to compete at airports, at tourist attractions, and even within office buildings. Market development is related to the objective of a retailer wanting to widen its market, attract new market segments or to convince the customer that the business has been repositioned and offers new benefits.

Rapid market development may be achieved through franchising. Franchising is the method by which a company (the franchisee who owns the right to a brand name) will sell, for a fee or a royalty, access to the company's supply of merchandise and the right to trade under the company's name to a franchisor. There will also be a transfer of know-how to those individuals who are deemed suitable to run a franchised operation. The most famous franchises in the UK are Benetton, The Body Shop and Tie Rack. There are advantages to the franchisees as promotion is carried out on a national basis, the niche market is already established through clear marketing strategies, and supply chains are highly developed.

Company objectives may also include *product development* or *diversification*. Product development is a sensible objective for retailers which have strong brands and a good market presence. One of the reasons own-brands have been successful is related to the market presence of those companies which have introduced the concept. Companies often develop new ideas for retailing which need to be planned as new product development. An example of new product retail development is the advent of factory outlet shopping centres. This type of outlet started as an American concept and was developed during the 1990s in the UK. Factory outlets should not be confused with discount centres. They are groups of shops, normally away from town centres, specialising in the selling of seconds or end-of-line goods, usually under a named manufacturer rather than the retailer.

Diversification is an objective linked to a desire not to want to become dependent on one type of retail business. Diversification has occurred where retailers have created mail order operations and vice versa. We have also seen the diversification of retailers such as Virgin into the airline business or Marks & Spencer into food; the diversification into food set a positioning for the M&S business which differentiated it from all other supermarkets rather than M&S appearing to move into line with them. The company planned and implemented a high quality and value added range of premium priced food products targeted at affluent consumers.

Growth, as an objective, can also be achieved through *integrative growth*, which is based upon the three areas of backward, forward and horizontal integration within the supply chain. An objective to increase sales by incorporating one or more levels of the supply chain into the business would be based upon integrative growth. If this were based upon *backward integration*, company changes would need to involve taking ownership or control of the supply aspects of the supply chain (for example, a retailer acquiring a wholesaler or manufacturer). In the case of *horizontal integration*, the retailer would seek ownership or control of competitors at the same level within the marketing channel; mergers, acquisitions and takeovers are the logical outcome of this objective. *Forward integration* is often the objective of manufacturers who want to gain greater control of their distribution through the development or acquisition of retail businesses. For example, British Airways, American Express and the tour operator,

Thomson with the Lunn Poly brand, have opened a number of travel shops to ensure they can have some presence – and control of sales – in the high street.

Competitive advantage

When retail companies decide upon strategies which may lead them towards market success they need to consider generic routes to competitive advantage. Porter (1980) describes the three generic strategies of *cost leadership* (a company that seeks, finds and exploits all sources of cost advantage – providing for a standard, no frills package); *differentiation* (a company seeks something distinctive to set it apart from others that can bring in good profit returns – typically having attributes that are different to the competition); and a *focus* strategy (a company selects a segment of the market and targets that to the extent of excluding other segments).

Cost leadership

Using Porter's terminology, the discounters – such as Aldi and Lidl from Germany, and Netto from Denmark – entered the UK market in the late 1980s and early 1990s with a cost leadership strategy. The only way for them to prosper was through the achievement of competitive advantage by sustaining lower prices than the competition. This placed a great deal of emphasis on their being able to reduce and control the costs of their operations. Cost leadership can be adopted by low cost retail operations which are aiming to penetrate the market and exploit experience curve effects. The low cost supermarkets and discount warehouses have taken this approach. Low priced retailers need to plan to:

- choose to locate outlets on smaller sites that are less expensive than their competitors;
- provide an outlet design which has no lavish facilities and where stock can be moved straight into the sales area, on pallets, with boxes that can be opened when they are needed;
- streamline all systems and employ a minimum number of staff. However, the staff may be paid more to ensure that multi-skilling and productivity gains are achieved;
- keep stockholding to a minimum;
- develop many outlets to achieve economics of scale.

Cost leadership normally requires economies of scale and the ability to control costs better than the competitors. Cost leadership would not be a viable strategy for a small retail operation such as a hairdresser because local competitors could probably offer a similar range of prices. Smaller companies can grow on the basis of cost leadership if they identify segments which offer lower costs. For example, in insurance and banking there are low cost clients who seldom complain, take up less time for any transaction, and are willing to communicate by letter or phone. Such an approach will eliminate many of the costs associated with the running of a traditional retail business. An example is the Abbey National attempting to attract savers to its postal service saving account by offering competitive interest rates. By creating this service, Abbey National can gain the advantage of lowering costs and freeing up its branches to deal with other types of transaction.

Differentiation

Differentiation, as a generic strategy, involves a company developing a product or service that is unique or superior in some way. Retailers that achieve differentiation through quality are often able to charge higher than average prices. As indicated earlier, one major success story is that of Marks & Spencer. In the early 1990s Marks & Spencer were achieving a 40 per cent share of total sales for their range of quality food products. This diversification occurred with a service design back-up to ensure that their food arrived in the freshest of conditions and was then stored at optimal temperatures. This reinforced the commitment to differentiate on quality which is the hallmark of the positioning of their overall retail offer.

A bank could differentiate itself on the basis of its service by offering to pay for the installation of modems and terminals in the homes of its most important customers to enable them to have instant access to their accounts and investments.

Focus

There is often a need to ensure that a business has a clear focus because that is precisely the way a customer needs to have the offer positioned in their mind. Focus, in relation to the retailer, allows the retail offer to be more precisely defined in terms of price, quality and range. This will enable a retailer to be single-minded in creating a highly focused retail mix offer. The success of Mothercare in the early stages was that they built a reputation on the positioning slogan, 'Everything for the mother-to-be and children under 5' and then put together a product range and marketing policy which reflected this. When Mothercare attempted to extend the range to teenagers, it transpired that the baby shop image had been such a strong focus that the younger consumer resisted the change.

As indicated, with a focus approach companies concentrate their efforts on specific segments of the market. This may be because they have insufficient resources to concentrate on a broader market base. Tie Rack, Knickerbox, Accessorize and Sock Shop are examples of such a strategy. However, this does not preclude Tie Rack having a small part of its stock as socks. This can also be a dangerous position. Sock Shop made the mistake of underestimating both the strength of the competition from companies such as Marks & Spencer and the limited size of the market for socks. Although the niche approach has its attractions in terms of being able to concentrate on a focused offer, there is always danger inherent in such a singular and exposed position. This is because if success occurs there is a risk of being attacked by stronger companies and not being able to find alternative competencies in order to survive a strong marketing assault.

Each of the above ways of gaining advantage can be successful, but companies have to be clear about their strategy or they will become 'stuck in the middle' and fail to achieve any advantage. This is because customers will not have a good reason to utilise a particular retailer who is either unfocused, offers no cost advantage or has an undifferentiated store or service image.

There are a number of operational areas where retailers should plan to create sustainable competitive advantage. An adaptation of the article by Knee and Walters (1989) provides the following ways that advantage can be gained:

● strong customer loyalty;
● good location;

- supplier partner relationships;

- technological superiority;

- low cost efficiencies.

In addition, we should also add a further point – higher quality staff, as they are an asset which can provide advantage. The retail business is based around the performance of staff as part of interpersonal relationships. Over 90 per cent of Waterstones' staff are graduates; given the nature of the business, this is an ideal fit both for giving informed advice and the ability to delegate management functions and buying decisions. (The importance of a service culture within retailing was dealt with extensively in Chapter 4.) Companies are attempting to meet the challenges to improve operations and some, such as Marks & Spencer, have built competitive advantage over many years through the relationships they build with their suppliers. Another area mentioned above is the use of information technology (IT). In the retail industry, IT is in widespread use as its application to merchandise control allows for the more efficient use of retail space, improved inventory control and the collection of detailed customer information. The advantages are to be gained by those companies who have developed their systems to create greater efficiencies and customer satisfaction than their competitors.

Location advantage is very important for both large and small companies. The Savile Row tailors gain a great deal of advantage from their location; it provides a focus for their exclusive services, provides synergy of image, and signals the quality and price positioning of the outlets.

Market segmentation

One important part of the analysis stage of marketing planning is the selection of the most desirable target markets. Arising from the SWOT analysis will be the objective to target specific sub-markets – also known as segments. The target market will consist of a group of customers sharing some similar characteristics towards which the retailer will direct its products and services.

Market segmentation is based upon the breaking down of a large heterogeneous market into smaller subdivisions in which there is some similarity of character. In practice, there is always the problem of identifying a large enough group of customers with clearly differentiated needs so that a retailer can position its outlets and offer to that group. Retailing, by its nature, includes a whole range and type of different customers. Even some of the niche retailers, such as new entrants, The Perfume Shop and Games Workshop, or more traditional companies seeking a revival such as Sock Shop, appeal to a cross-section of the public who have very little in common. The determination of the retailer's choice of segments to target relies on the company resources, the nature of rivalry and competition, and the volatility or stability of the marketplace.

We believe that market segmentation, in the context of retailing, can be defined as:

the process of dividing the total retail market into subsets, whereby the potential segments have characteristics in common which lead to similar demand needs for a type of store format, product and service.

201

Pills and pens: Boots and WH Smith

Retailing is a battle between specialists and generalists. Two British high-street favourites must pick a side in order to thrive.

No British town feels complete without a branch of Boots the Chemists, Britain's biggest pharmacist and largest seller of cosmetics, and an outpost of WH Smith, Britain's largest newsagent and bookseller. On the face of it, these two chains have an iron grip on two large areas of retailing. Boots has one-third of the £8 billion British market for health and beauty products, more than four times that of its nearest rival. WH Smith controls 32% of newspaper distribution and 42.5% of the magazines sold in Britain. But both are caught in a pincer movement as rival retailers become simultaneously more diversified and more specialised. On one flank, supermarkets have branched out from groceries into their own brands of shampoo and toothpaste, as well as newspapers, magazines and books. On the other, more specialised retailers are advancing. Boots has had, for example, to devise its own range of 'natural' creams and soaps to fight off the predations of The Body Shop, which sells cosmetics made from plants. Meanwhile each of the departments of WH Smith's stores is under attack from toyshops, bookshops, music shops, stationers and other specialists. The two companies look broadly similar. Each has a core retail division that accounts for the bulk of turnover. Similar organisations and similar problems have not yet produced similar reactions, however. Boots, which sagged towards mushy general retailing through the

1970s and early 1980s, pulled itself together and is now seeing the rewards in steady growth. Its return to shareholders in the past five years, of 106%, is comparable to that of Marks & Spencer, one of Britain's strongest retailers, and three times that of Sainsbury and Tesco, big supermarkets. WH Smith has dallied longer and has a hazier future. It could do worse than study Boots.

Boots's response to the pincer movement is to retreat into specialism. In its 1,260 Boots the Chemists shops, the health-care and beauty business accounted for 75% of turnover in 1996, up from 63% in 1990. Another 10% is baby products, which also benefit from the image of a trustworthy medical authority that Boots gains from its role as Britain's largest dispenser of prescription drugs. As Stephen Russell, managing director of Boots the Chemists, points out, this authority places the firm in a position to take advantage of growing consumer interest in 'wellbeing': looking good and feeling good as well as being free of sniffs and snuffles. One route to expansion is to increase the number of shops. Boots has opened about 160 new shops in the past four years, and plans another 80. It has started to expand overseas too, although opportunities in much of Europe are limited by rules forbidding multiple pharmacy ownership.

Source: © The Economist, London, 19 April 1997

It would follow that retailers should be concerned with the examination of the marketplace to identify those groups which can be differentiated on the basis of shopping habits, desired shopping experience, and demand patterns and needs. The general trends in society have led to a number of changes which create viable opportunities for retailers. Changes in disposable income for the younger groups in society led to the emergence of the opportunity for positioning of brands such as Miss Selfridge, River Island, Top Shop, and Top Man. In addition, the accent on healthy living has given rise to specialist shops such as Holland & Barrett. The retailer has to decide upon the coverage of the target market. This can be any one of a selection from a broad *mass market*, a selective *market segment* strategy, or aiming at two or more *multiple segments*.

Retail outlets selling general products, such as supermarkets and chemists, will target the broader mass market. This is because their trading success lies in offering a wide range of popular items at value-for-money prices. By contrast, a specialist retailer can attempt to identify a new segment, or adopt an upmarket or downmarket position. Anita Roddick is the classic example of someone who identified a gap in the market – one which she successfully exploited with The Body Shop range of natural products merchandise. In the 1980s George Davis successfully used lifestyle and age segmentation for the Next group of outlets. The product was then chosen to reflect the individual's status, lifestyle, gender and age, with a higher quality standard to the clothes which was reinforced by above average prices. Following the success of positioning stores to target specific groups, a number of retailers decided to adopt segmentation strategies based upon different aspects of lifestyle. There were several successful approaches at this time, including those of Habitat, Harrods, Laura Ashley and, more recently, IKEA. A current lifestyle change is toward being healthier. The medical profession and a number of magazines and newspapers have helped to change attitudes to both leisure pursuits and eating habits. These trends will, in turn, have repercussions on fashion and merchandise selection as well as be an opportunity for new product development. For example, Boots having specialist boutiques for health care.

Department stores are likely to judge multiple segments to be a viable business alternative. This is because they supply distinct groups of customers for whom they choose to provide specific goods and services. Department stores are often subdivided within the store, thus creating different shopping experiences for different segments. However, they will design a restaurant to cater for the needs of all the targeted groups.

The identification and selection of segments will require judgement based on the analysis of different data. The main method of segmentation is to select a segment (target market) with the best potential from a range of criteria. Then the objective is to create product benefits, features and promotional messages which will appeal to the needs of the selected segment(s). A number of characteristics are examined when deciding upon target groups. For example, Kmart in the USA describes its target market as middle-class (ABC1), value-conscious consumers. It is geographically located in mid-range shopping centres and offers both national and Kmart brands for sale. On a geographic basis, retailers in America will plan significant variations in the product mix due to geographical segment differences, e.g. between West Coast and East Coast consumers. The size, type and tastes of the population within any geographic area may be different from other areas and, therefore, require a different marketing mix. (*See* Chapter 3 on consumer behaviour in retail for further discussion of some of the segmentation characteristics profiled in Table 7.2 and the following text.)

The approach illustrated in Fig. 7.7 utilises the list of segmentation characteristics given in Table 7.2 and disaggregates the detail in steps 1 and 2 so that all possibilities can be considered. In step 3 the information is analysed, then aggregated and assessed. The retailer will then make a decision in step 4 based upon the consideration of a combination of factors, including the segment's potential sales volume and profits, the retail competition of those companies currently selling to the segments, as well as the company's abilities and objectives. Therefore, the retailer attempts to assess the needs of different sub-groups to see if it can offer now, or in the future, a form of distribution service which will prove successful.

In order for segmentation to be successful, intellectual rigour must be applied to the segmentation procedure. When a target group is identified it is prudent to use a checklist, such as the one presented on page 205, to ensure that the segment offers a viable opportunity for the company.

Table 7.2 Some general characteristics of segmentation variables

Characteristic	Typical classification
Geographic	Region of world, country, area of country – North, Midlands, South, Coastal, County, TV areas Urban, suburban, rural areas, city, town, postcode or type of house
Demographic	By age group, family life-cycle, ethnic group Socio-economic classification of household based upon A, B, C1, C2, D, E classifications
Psychographic	Lifestyle Personality type – introvert, extrovert, high/low ego drive, independent, group worker
Usership	Non-user, current user, past user, potential user, heavy user, medium user, light user, merchandise preferences
Kind of shopping occasion	Store type, regular, special occasion Convenience, speciality, comparison shopping, place of shopping
Attitudes	Toward product area, toward brand Toward usership and use situations
Benefits sought	Utility, convenience, luxury, economy, etc.

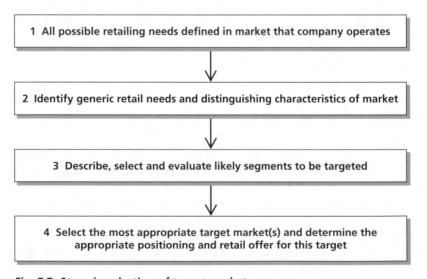

Fig. 7.7 Steps in selection of target market

Segmentation checklist

- *Is the segment identifiable and measurable?* There is the need to identify different types of retail consumers and how different types of marketing mix activity will affect sub-groups. If any changes occur, such as an expansion into loyalty schemes, will the potential market segments (there are several being targeted – *see* Chapter 5) be measurable in the locality of a store?

- *Is the segment accessible?* The segment requires that individual buyers may easily visit the store or be contacted through promotional messages. Also, with new forms of retailing utilising electronic means of transaction, accessibility of segments is a key consideration.

- *Is the segment substantial?* The segment must be large enough to provide a viable level of business and profit. The Body Shop started in the area of Brighton and its success in targeting a particular lifestyle group was substantial enough to support expansion throughout the country.

- *Is the segment sustainable?* The choice of segment has to take into account whether the demand will last. Fashion and 'lifestyle' market segments are prone to change and demise.

- *Is the segment actionable?* Are there any impediments in putting together a local or national marketing mix so that the target market can be reached with a specific retail offer, positioning and message which fits with the plans of the company? A retail group may want to target a segment in order to offer a specific range with acceptable width and depth at acceptable cost, but the reaction of the segment – especially on a local store basis – should dictate the final offer.

- *Is the segment defendable?* Can the target market be defended against competitor activity if the competitors also target the same group? In a small catchment area will increased retail rivalry cause any viability problems for the retailer?

The approach to segmentation selection is as wide as marketers make it. There is no single way which will prove successful. For example, the general list of segmentation variables above does not include retailers segmenting by size (Evans, High and Mighty, Long Tall Sally). Even when a segment has been identified, customers' needs and attitudes are multifaceted and, as such, they move from one segment to another as part of their shopping behaviour. For example, a consumer may buy groceries in a low cost outlet yet go to an Armani store for their clothing.

Positioning

As part of the segmentation analysis, sub-groups will emerge as the ideal customers to market to. Because of the potential of these segments they will form the target groups for the business. The target groups will need to be satisfied with the retail offer. Thus there has to be a clear understanding by consumers of where the company wants its business to be positioned. Positioning is a marketing term which is used to describe the process of establishing and maintaining a distinctive place for a business in its marketplace.

There has to be a compatibility between the product offer and the segment being targeted. Marks & Spencer achieved this with the successful launch of food as well as home furnishings. However, if M&S had launched a cheaper range of furniture – similar to that of the MFI position – they would have confused their customers and compromised their existing position as a service and quality oriented retailer. The successful strategy of MFI in selling cheap furniture is not a strategy M&S would want to adopt because it would not fit with the existing spatial positioning of its current retail offer. The selection in terms of position is based upon how the retailer wants to be perceived by its target group of customers in terms of any one of the factors which it decides is of importance. Any positioning has to take into consideration the three generic strategies of Porter (1980) which are to decide upon only one approach, be it cost leadership, differentiation or focus. A company has to be clear about where it needs and wants to be positioned in the marketplace. One way of ensuring this is to create a perceptual map which reflects the current marketplace. This is one of the customary ways a planner would plot the company's retail business in relation to the competitors. The plots would be based upon customers' and employees' perceptions of where a particular store would be located on the perceptual map. This approach could be used to identify gaps in the market based upon customer desires or lack of competition in certain market positions. The identification of gaps in the marketplace may offer opportunities for new retail formats or product development. There is a wide range of polar opposites which could be utilised for the ends of the continuums such as: high to low value for money; traditional to modern; wide range to narrow range of merchandise; etc. The most simple positioning can be achieved through spatially plotting price and service levels, as illustrated in Fig. 7.8.

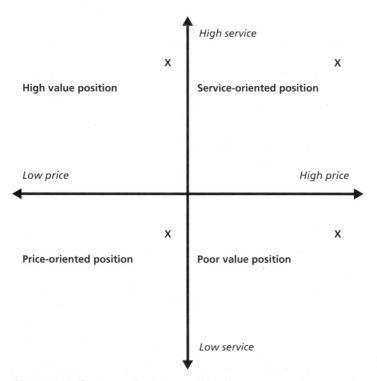

Fig. 7.8 Retail price and service positioning map

High value – low price and high service position

If a retail business is to provide a high service and low price there is a need to examine the business very closely. This is because the cost of delivering a high service has to be recouped and relatively low prices do not usually allow sufficient margins to achieve this. More recently, changes in retail have opened up opportunities for retailers to fill this position. The new retail format of the 'category killer' has allowed this position to be filled due to the ability of retailers to buy in bulk, therefore ensuring merchandise costs are low. Such a format also allows the category specialist to sell in high quantity, thereby achieving high enough revenue to make the operation viable. The use of electronic systems for sales is another area where costs can be controlled more easily and after-sales service levels may therefore be planned to be high.

Service-oriented – high price and high service position

This position is based on providing a very high level of service and charging the customer higher than average prices. In order to be successful within this spatial position, there has to be a segment of the market willing to pay higher prices for the benefit of receiving superior levels of quality and service. The concern of managing this position is whether the higher prices offer perceived value or not. Many companies will attempt to ensure that prices are competitive and this may mean a slide of position toward a more central area, nearer to where the axes cross. This more central position provides little differentiation and can cause problems, as it is open to attack from the other quadrants. Positioning as a strategy has to be clear to both the consumer and the retailer's employees.

Price-oriented – low price and low service position

The low price and low service position is based upon a no-frills retail operation which leads on price as the means to generate sales. Such a position fits with the theory regarding the wheel of retailing, which was covered in Chapter 1 of this book. The example given was that new forms of retailing enter the market as low cost, no frills, low margin operations. However, unlike the development process associated with the theory whereby retailers attempt to move upmarket, the modern low price retailer understands the strength in occupying this position. The deep discounters develop their strategies to ensure that they will remain securely situated in the low price and low service position over the long term. This is a highly competitive position to occupy as competitive buying, cost control, management systems and lean organisation structure all need to be constantly monitored to ensure a sound basis for long-term survival. Such efficiency is not necessarily based upon minimal investment. A high initial investment in technology is required to ensure that just-in-time inventory and management systems are available and utilised. A price-led position can only be achieved if the retailer is relentless in driving down costs, with the clear goal of increasing margins while retaining low price levels and market share.

Poor value – high price and low service position

The least viable position to occupy is one where a high price is charged for a low level of service. This position will only be filled when a retailer can survive due to a lack of competition for a particular good or service. For example, some rural grocery shops are run by older people who give poor service because they have lost interest in the business. However, they have higher costs due to small orders to their suppliers which are passed on as higher prices to customers. The shop is caught in a spiral of decline, with the more mobile people shopping elsewhere while the old and less mobile groups will continue to have to pay the higher prices.

In summary, the use of market positioning is to ensure that the target customers have a clear reason to use a company's shops rather than those of the competitors. The positioning creates a retail offer which is relevant and of value to the different segments, but it is one that needs to be communicated to those segments through promotional campaigns and store design so that the position is both reinforced and clearly recognised. Finally, a strong position in the minds of the customers creates marketing advantage because it clarifies the reason someone frequents the company's stores – and it may be one that competitors will find difficult to copy.

PROVIDING AN EFFECTIVE MARKETING MIX STRATEGY

The success of the marketing plan relies on creating the right marketing mix strategies for achieving the objectives. (*See* Chapter 5 for a clear explanation of the different aspects of the marketing mix.) The use of the marketing mix of price, product, promotion and place – with its special emphasis for retail – involves balancing the marketing mix to achieve the highest expected probability of meeting the plan's objectives. However, mix strategies have to be checked to ensure they are acceptable. This is because they also involve uncontrollable factors such as the reaction of competitors, or changes that may occur in a market due to shifts in fashion or effects due to changes in the economy.

If it is found that there are no problems with the objectives and the plan is to be adopted, there has to be some assessment of whether the objectives can be achieved within specific time constraints. Competitors may be able to react more quickly or the company may find it too difficult to change in a short period of time. The ability to change is often related to the availability of resources. It is necessary to question whether the resources available are sufficient to achieve the objectives (in terms of budgets, personnel, technology, existing outlets, service improvements, brand building). If, after evaluation, it is decided the strategy is unacceptable there is a need to review and revise the plan's objectives.

Agreeing the marketing mix strategy has to be linked to laying down task-related programmes which will allocate budgets and create responsibilities and timings for the plan's implementation. There is an important need to link planning with budgeting and monitoring, which will allow for the adoption and execution of an effective marketing mix strategy to achieve the objectives of the plan. The control and managing of budgets and planned performance are dealt with in the next section, Monitoring the plan.

MONITORING THE PLAN

A business needs a mechanism to monitor the achievements of the marketing plan so that actions can be taken either to get the plan back on course or to take advantage of new opportunities. As such, there is a need for the provision of assessment, as well as measurement methods which will monitor progress towards the achievement of the overall objectives of the plan. Retail businesses are characterised by their diversity and wide range of goods with differing qualities and attributes. However, all managers are required to make appropriate decisions on the basis of sales and performance and deviations from the initial objectives and targets. Managers need to decide if these fluctuations are either acceptable or unacceptable, based upon the effect of over or underperformance on overall company performance. Effective monitoring of performance will allow for the review and amendment of the plan on a continuous basis, to facilitate decisions, such, the introduction of tactical action if sales are behind target. Effective control hinges on the quantity, quality and timeliness of the information made available. The information has to flow on a regular basis to decision makers in a form that enables ease of understanding and the carrying out of effective reaction.

The retail industry has invested in integrated systems, such as EPOS and EDI, which provide for a continuous flow of financial and stock/sales pattern data. This has allowed for the modelling of different performance indicators. These may include forecasts of likely demand factors or purchase levels, as well as assessment of the effectiveness of regional or national sales promotion, price changes and store campaigns. Sales measurements are the basic measure of evaluation based upon sales transactions. With this information a company can analyse sales in terms of cash volume by period or market share, or by location or allocated space. Retail companies regularly use cash volume sales as the figures allow a common denominator of sales, costs and profits. However, changes in retail prices, either up or down, will affect sales figures and may not reflect the actual sales position. Total sales figures are more useful if broken down by size and place of geographic unit, salesperson, product code, price including any discount, customer type and time of the transaction. It is also beneficial to have details of the timing and type of any promotion which may have affected demand. Figure 7.9 indicates the measures that are often utilised to assess previous retail decisions.

Output measures	Input measures	Productivity (output/input)
Net sales Net profits Performance in sales and profits Cost of labour	Square metres of retail space Number of employees Promotional expenditures Number of customer transactions Linear shelf space area	Sales per square metre Sales per employee Return on asset Asset turnover Wage cost per customer Average profit per customer Sales per linear shelf space area
Merchandise net sales Merchandise gross margin Performance in merchandise sales	Inventory levels over time Markdowns Cost of merchandise Advertising costs	Gross margin return on investment (GMRI) Inventory turnover Advertising and markdown as a percentage of sales

Fig. 7.9 Retail performance measurement indicators

It is also necessary to monitor 'softer' aspects of the business, such as brand awareness and customer satisfaction. If these weaken, attention should be paid; they are usually early signals of future problems related to the financial performance. An example of how the monitoring of retail products may lead to important change is to be found in the video games market. The video games market was flooded with too many games titles by Nintendo, Atari and Sega. Consumers became confused and disappointed by the numerous lookalike products having similar names. By monitoring customer reaction, companies such as Nintendo were able to withdraw from the market a high percentage of their games to allow space for new product introductions. This allowed the games market to recover after the fad period of the 1980s.

CONCLUSION

The marketing plan is a structured guide to action. It acts as a systematic discipline for data collection, objective setting and logical analysis of the most appropriate direction for the organisation, retail unit, or its merchandise to develop. If a marketing plan is to be accepted by all concerned, then the compilation of the plan has to involve all levels of personnel. This is because marketing plans require company-wide commitment if they are to be successful. The plan has to reflect the dynamic nature of the marketplace and, as such, the plan needs to be thought of as a loose-leaf binder rather than as a tablet of stone. This means the plan acts as a working document which should be updated to take into account opportunities or problem situations. Finally, any worthwhile plan will contain the expected results for the business based upon different periods of operation. Planning functions have to include the means by which the business will measure its performance in a quantifiable manner that is timely, relevant and accurate. This will allow the plan to achieve its objectives and enable management to function more effectively in its decision-making activities.

EXERCISES

The exercises in this section relate to the contents of this chapter. It is advised that you work through them before moving on to Chapter 8.

1 Read the newspapers from the past four weeks (*Financial Times*, trade papers, *The Economist*, etc.). Write down the changes that large retail companies are making and also what may be happening, by application of a marketplace PEST analysis. Try to relate your findings to what is contained in the approaches to the compilation of a marketing plan as outlined in this chapter. You should also try to identify the link there may be between the theory and the practice of the changes taking place.

2 Think about your own experience in doing things you initially did not want to do. Why did you subsequently agree to do them? How do you think the plans in a retail company could be adopted more effectively throughout the company utilising the ideas in this chapter, further reading and from your own experiences?

3 Identify the different market segments and their reasons for the use of a post office, building society and a bank. Is there anything you may have learnt from this exercise which may assist the bank to change to attract new segments? What would be the outcomes of any repositioning the bank may adopt?

4 List some of the retail changes that have taken place in recent years. How can a medium sized retailer develop an improved competitive position through the use of a planning approach? Use the following grid as a guide.

List competitive changes, for example:	What would you need to know about your competitors and the marketplace in order to develop an improvement in competitive position?
<ul><li>greater use of loyalty schemes</li><li>more direct channel operations</li><li>differentiation through improved service</li><li>more women working</li><li>development of the Internet</li><li>others (list)</li></ul>	

REFERENCES AND FURTHER READING

Abell, D.F. (1982) 'Metamorphosis in Market Planning' in Cox, K.K. and McGinnis, V.J. (eds) *Strategic Market Decisions*. Englewood Cliffs, NJ: Prentice Hall.

Abell, D.F. and Hammond, J.S. (1979) *Strategic Market Planning Problems and Analytical Approaches*. Englewood Cliffs, NJ: Prentice Hall.

Ansoff, H.I. (1988) *The New Corporate Strategy*. New York: John Wiley and Sons.

Brown-Humes, C. (1998) 'Banking in the aisles: supermarkets are shaking up the cosy world of high-street financial services', *Financial Times*, 16 May.

Collins, A. (1992) *Competitive Retail Marketing*. Maidenhead: McGraw-Hill.

Davies, G.J. and Brooks, J.M. (1989) *Positioning Strategy in Retailing*. London: Paul Chapman.

The Economist (1997) 'Pills and pens: Boots and WH Smith – retailing is a battle between specialists and generalists. Two British high-street favourites must pick a side in order to thrive', *The Economist*, 19 April.

Hooley, G.J., Saunders, J.A. and Piercy, N.F. (1998) *Marketing Strategy and Competitive Positioning*. Hemel Hempstead: Prentice Hall.

Hutton, B. (1998) '7-Eleven sets store by computer links: systems allowing rapid replenishment of stock have helped retailer outgrow its parent', *Financial Times*, 17 March.

Jaworski, B.J., Stathakopoulis, Vlasis and Shanker Krishnan, H. (1993) 'Control combinations in marketing: conceptual framework and empirical evidence', *Journal of Marketing*, 57 (1), 57–69.

Knee, D. and Walters, D. (1985) *Strategy in Retailing: Theory and application*. Oxford: Philip Allan.

Knee, D. and Walters, D. (1989) 'Competitive strategies in retailing', *Journal of Long Range Planning*, 22, Dec., 27–34.

Kotler, P., Armstrong, G., Saunders, J. and Wong, V. (1999) *Principles of Marketing*. 2nd European edn. Englewood Cliffs, NJ: Prentice Hall.

McDonald, M. and Tideman, C. (1996) *Retail Marketing Plans: How to prepare them: How to use them*. Oxford: Butterworth-Heinemann.

Palmer, A. (1994) *Principles of Services Marketing*. Maidenhead: McGraw-Hill.

Porter, M.E. (1980) *Competitive Strategy: Techniques for analysing industries and competitors*. New York: Free Press.

Quinn, J.B., Mintzberg, H. and James, R.M. (1988) *The Strategy Process – Concepts, Contexts and Cases*. Englewood Cliffs, NJ: Prentice Hall.

Walters, D. (1994) *Retailing Management: Analysis planning and control*. London: Macmillan.

8 Retail location strategies and decisions

The chapter should enable you to understand and explain:

- the importance of retail location decision making;
- the different types of retail trading areas;
- theories which explain the historical patterns of retail location;
- a range of analytical techniques for assessing the suitability of a retail location;
- different approaches to property development.

It is often said that within the retailing industry that only three things matter: location, location and location. The logic of this is that if the right site is acquired, success should be a simple matter of opening for business. It is not that straightforward; selection of merchandise, sound pricing policy, layout and presentation, as well as other retail marketing factors are also required as prerequisites for success. For example, the customer service policies may be the reason a customer will return again and again. However, the selection of the location site is of key importance and this requires a systematic approach to the acceptance or rejection of certain areas in favour of others. This is because of several issues:

1 *consumer choice*: the location is often the most important consumer behaviour consideration in a customer's decision of where to shop;

2 the need for *competitive advantage*: the decision over where to develop a retail outlet will be of strategic importance because retailers can gain long-term competitive advantage if they develop in the best location;

3 *consideration of trends*: any decision on location has to consider the recent social and structural changes – greater use of the motor car, the importance of out-of-town shopping centres, regional shopping areas, the growth of multiple retailers, the power of retailer brands, and so on;

4 *high investment*: development of a retail site is accompanied by high investment and rental costs and long lead times, which require decisions regarding long-term financial implications;

5 *property asset*: it is important to select carefully as the final property assets of a company can be valued as high as their annual turnover;

6 *declining number of sites*: there are a restricted number of new sites for development and within Government policy guidelines, less opportunity to obtain planning permission easily.

The dimensions of location decision making are extensive. Locational decisions engage the different disciplines of strategic marketing, the geography of retailing, town planning, operations research, consumer behaviour, and economics. If a company has a weak approach to location analysis it may not just be a financial dilemma but could threaten the long-term progress of the retailer. As pressures mount on the availability of sites and the propensity of local authorities to allow development, retail companies have to become better at both the politics and the technical aspects of planning. The obtaining of planning permission is being severely restricted in the UK. The planning policy guidelines issued by the government (PPG6; DoE, 1996) has the objectives of:

1 sustaining and enhancing the vitality and viability of town centres;

2 focusing retail development in locations where the proximity of business facilitates competition from which all consumers are able to benefit and maximising the opportunity to use means of transport other than a car;

3 maintaining an efficient, competitive and innovative retail sector; and

4 ensuring the availability of a wide range of shops, employment, services and facilities to which people have easy access by a choice of means of transport.

The above guidelines are to be utilised on a regional planning basis, with local considerations taken into account. However, developers and local authorities have to prove they have thoroughly investigated all central sites prior to the contemplation of a greenfield site.

In the light of the increased market or political pressure and the resultant government guidelines, Tesco has started to develop smaller stores (*see* Table 8.1). This is also a strategic move to combat the growth of Marks & Spencer and other stores which are successful in town centre locations. This strategy of different sized stores, developed in different locations, also has the advantage that each format is serving a different consumer demand. While the out-of-town, or edge-of-town superstores offer one-stop shopping services for weekly outings, the smaller in-town stores offer top up shopping facilities. In this way, they are complementary formats within Tesco's

Table 8.1 Tesco Group, UK store development programme (total stores built)

Store format and size	1991	1992	1993	1994	1995	1996
Superstore (26 500+ sq. ft)	17	20	20	14	12	8
Compact store (< 25 500 sq. ft)	3	4	4	9	15	14
Metro store (c. 10 000 sq. ft)	–	–	1	3	6	2
Express store (c. 1 500 sq. ft petrol station site)	–	–	–	–	2	10

Source: Tesco Group Annual Reports

213

portfolio. Even if allowed by the authorities, the development of a new superstore often has a negative impact on other stores owned by the company that are operating in the wider area.

Retailers are in business to ensure the long-term goals of providing a maximisation of profit in order to give an acceptable return to the investors. Long-term strategies have to take into consideration a number of alternatives. Retail location requires sophisticated analysis. Once the strategic direction is clear, retailers can increase the size of existing premises, refurbish, reformat premises, build new stores in- or out-of-town, internationalise or acquire other companies, etc. Figure 8.1 gives a strategic overview of the most important choices available.

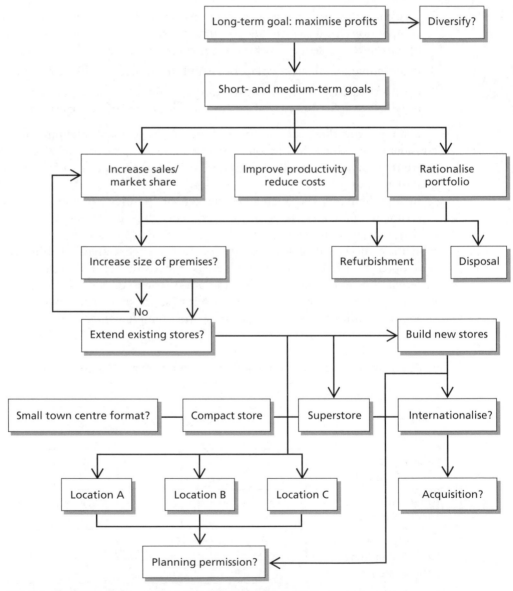

Fig. 8.1 Strategic choice and location decision alternatives

GEOGRAPHIC LOCATION DECISIONS

How then can a retailer find an optimum location? In the past many location decisions would have been made on the basis of intuition or, more likely, the availability of a particular property or 'going concern'. Planning today requires some idea of population shifts, consumer mobility and increases in discretionary income as each will affect shopping habits. With the application of technology a number of developments have taken place. Technology can aid in location decision making; analytical techniques such as SLAM (store location model) allow the assessment, profiling and comparison of market opportunities; the screening of potential sites; the definition of catchment areas; and modelling of the possible impact of competitor strategies (Simkin, 1989, 1990). Clark (1993) has attempted to outline the future usage of geographical information systems with the prediction that they will be integrated more with financial and strategic planning.

A starting point for the understanding of location decisions is based upon the *location area*. There are zones or locations which attract higher levels of custom than others. The location decision may take into consideration the broader considerations of the *region*, which would involve a large section of the country, county or the *market area*; this would be a geographic sector containing zones, of which one would be the *primary trading zone* (*see* Fig. 8.2) which provides the major customer base for a retail outlet.

Regions may contain many specific types of consumers due to average incomes, density of population, climate, geography, and type of economic development – for example, rural or industrial. From a strategic planning perspective, some retailers concentrate on dominating or being successful in regional markets prior to any expansion. Decisions regarding regional markets are based upon the strategic posture of a company; whether it wants to achieve dominance and leadership in the region or whether it wants to be a follower or market niche retailer. The typical assessment of regional markets is based upon the use of secondary information sources because other, more sophisticated, approaches are very expensive.

Market area is a geographic area that will contain the potential customers of a specific retailer or shopping area. This is based upon three zones which take the retail outlet or shopping centre as the epicentre from which bands emanate, based upon access, distance and travelling time. While these may be treated as concentric rings (*see* Fig. 8.2), due to the effect of different road routes and local geography the pattern is somewhat less regular. The zone pattern will also be affected by the location of the competition as well as ease of final accessibility and parking in the primary zone. The market area is made up of the following three zones.

1 *Primary trading zone* where the majority of customers will be based (60–65 per cent or higher if it is a local retail outlet such as a video rental or convenience store).

2 *Secondary zone* which can be any distance from two to seven miles, or under 20 minutes drive time, from the outlet.

3 *Fringe* or *tertiary zone* which will include those who occasionally shop as an alternative to local shopping. This zone depends on the type and size of outlet, and the alternative size and experience to be enjoyed in other market areas. Typically, this zone can extend as far as fifty miles when there is a lack of acceptable alternatives.

Figure 8.2 describes the market area breakdown for a store. The store could be located in any one of a number of sites across a wide area. If we look at this more

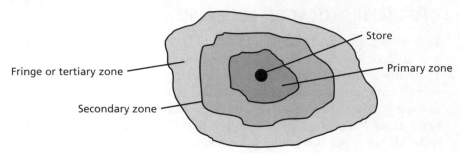

Fig. 8.2 Market area zones

carefully, and examine the use of land in a city, there will be different pressures which will lead more of the major retailers to locate in the central district area than on its outskirts. Figure 8.3 indicates how the city could be divided. As will be discussed later, retail development in different areas will occur due to the benefit of mutual physical location, specialisation of district, rent effects, and problems of loading and unloading. The physical, social and business elements of the city will determine and support a specific type of retailing development. This will lead to specialised land use patterns emerging as retailers, developers and other land users compete for sites which will be the most favourable for them. The result of competitive bidding is a land use pattern which will form the spatial patterns most capable of supporting an urban environment. A group of spatial models are provided in Fig. 8.3 which offer a basic way to describe the distribution of land for different business and social uses.

Concentric zone approaches stress that a city will develop by forming different concentric urban zones focused around a central business district. Growth occurs as each zone expands out into the next zone. This approach recognises that as the residential areas move further out from the centre some of the existing shopping facilities, near the business centre, are liable to be replaced by new retail facilities in the outlying areas.

Sector approaches place the stress on understanding residential areas but take into consideration the importance of commercial areas in relation to residential development. The approach utilises a wedge pattern of development which occurs in relation to major transportation routes and through the creation of sector rent patterns. The model is dynamic. High grade rent, residential areas, are believed to move away from the city and to pull the city in the direction of that movement. In this movement, the stronger and more sophisticated retailers are most likely to follow the high rent areas and move from the business area of the city.

Multiple nuclei is an approach which accepts that different types of activity will tend to group together: shopping centres, business districts, residential areas, and so on. The nuclei effect is created by:

● the mutual need for close proximity of different activities;

● the need for accessibility of shopping;

● the different abilities to afford higher rents;

● any significant physical aspects of the land – such as steep hills or rivers affecting spatial development.

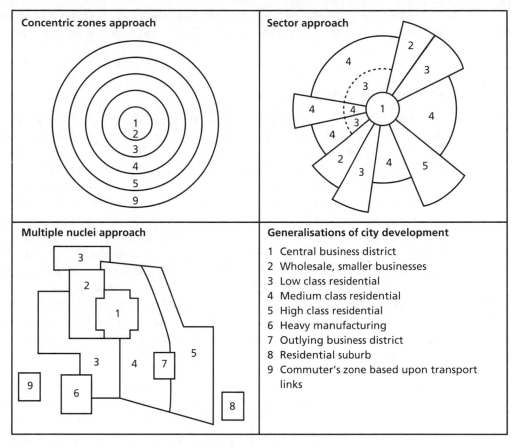

Fig. 8.3 The nature of spatial development in cities

No urban area will conform exactly to any of the above approaches, but in total they help us to understand the development of different districts – some of which will be developed for retailing activities. The underlying ideas derived from above approaches can be developed in greater detail by reference to the spatial distribution theories discussed in the next section.

EXPLANATIONS FOR THE SPATIAL DISTRIBUTION OF RETAIL ACTIVITIES

The spatial distribution of different retail activities have been evaluated as to their locational pattern, size and function of shopping centres and districts, the agglomeration of similar retail outlets and retail intra-spatial arrangements.

Emerging from this approach, it is clear that there are three main spatial patterns which describe most cases of retail location. These are:

- central place theory;
- bid rent theory ;
- the principle of minimum differentiation.

Each of these theories may be found to have specific limitations but, in combination, they help to explain the existence of specific variations of hierarchical patterns to retail location.

Central place theory

Central place theory attempts to explain the existence of city and town shopping districts or regional shopping centres, based upon a description of their size, retail function and relative positions to one another. The central place theory proposes a hierarchy of retail centres. A large retail centre that offers a variety of different retail functions is surrounded further out by smaller centres with less choice and specialist retailers, which in turn are surrounded by smaller centres comprising basic goods retailers. The central place theory is based upon the premise that as distance to a retail centre increases, demand for a product will decrease due to the increased cost of transport. Eventually the demand will drop to zero as this is the cut-off point past which consumers will not travel further to obtain the product. This distance is often termed the *market area* or *range* of a good. Concurrent with this, a retailer will not trade if the level of demand is too low. This level is known as the *threshold* and its level will differ according to the product offered. *High threshold* products are relatively expensive and infrequently purchased, for example, jewellery and furniture. *Low threshold* products are relatively inexpensive and purchased on a regular basis – for example, groceries.

If the market range of a good exceeds the threshold then it can be made available by retailers at a profit. This is because enough potential consumers exist who are willing to travel to acquire the product or product range. Thus, it is predicted there will be many retailers of *low order* goods which are based upon low threshold and low range criteria. This means there is a local demand for frequently purchased, inexpensive goods because consumers are not willing to travel very far to obtain them. At the same time there will be only a small number of retailers offering *high order* goods which are based upon high threshold and high range criteria. The demand for high order goods is based upon infrequently purchased and expensive items, for which the consumer will travel longer distances in order to assess and make a purchase.

As a way of generalising the reasons for the spatial pattern of existing retail sites, the central place theory helps our understanding of the different shopping districts to be found in developed countries. However, the basis of the theory requires a similar pattern of retail outlets equidistant from their counterparts. However, this approach does not account for the agglomeration of retail outlets where centres exist based upon a high number of similar retailers. For example, within two district centres there may be an agglomeration of footwear and fashion retailers in each of the high streets. Additionally, one centre may have developed an agglomeration of electrical retailers while the other has developed a specialisation in antique retailers. The overall functional composition of the two areas may be considered to differ and, therefore, this contradicts the underlying premise of central place theory. The theory is a useful tool to apply in order to generalise about the existence of shopping areas and the hierarchical distribution of retail outlets but, in order to explain some spatial patterns, more detailed analysis is often required. For example, consumer changes may be affecting the patterns – as shown in Table 8.2.

Table 8.2 Consumer changes which may affect the basic assumptions behind central place theory

Central place assumptions of consumer	Modern retail consumer
• Trips are regular to purchase small amounts, especially those with product perishability • Purchase response is based upon price and product range • Trips are home location based and often single-purpose trips to the nearest shopping district where goods are available • The shopping visit decision is based upon the necessity of the trip • The consumer treats each shopping area as a similar experience, i.e. all retailers are assumed to adopt a uniform retail strategy	• The use of large refrigerators and freezers allows less frequent purchases from superstores or retail centres • Non-price factors are increasingly a more important determinant of the purchase decision • Improved road systems, increased number of cars and drivers per family allows multi-purpose trips and greater distances to be covered • There has been an increase in leisure shopping • Retail innovation has taken place, with themed and purpose-built facilities creating retail experiences which appeal to different types of consumers

Bid rent theory

Bid rent theory attempts to explain the internal spatial organisation of planned and unplanned shopping districts. The theory assumes that retailers would always prefer to locate in the central city or town centre, but this in turn increases the rents and costs of these locations. Because of the increased costs, only some types of retailers are able to afford such prime sites and so different types of retailers will be found further out from central locations (*see* Fig. 8.4). Central place theory, as discussed above, describes the hierarchy of retail centres but bid rent theory assumes that the spatial composition of retail outlets is based upon the economics of land value theory. In reality, the use of land is based upon a whole range of different factors, including land-use planning regulations, individual choice and decision making, and perhaps even chance. Bid rent theory is based upon the premise that all economic activities aim to be located in the city centre as it is the most accessible location.

The theory assumes that different types of land use are segregated by the amount of rent that a prospective tenant can pay and that competition ensures that, in the long-run, all sites are occupied by a retail activity capable of paying the highest possible rent; as such, it is argued, the land is employed to its maximum utility. The important premise is that land use is based upon access, because consumers will seek out the most accessible location. As with other neoclassical economic approaches to location, it is grounded on the assumption that an inelastic supply of land exists and therefore land does not become readily available as the demand for it increases, or vice versa. It also assumes the existence of uniformly priced travel which will be as easy to make in any direction, and that land can be acquired through an open and fair competitive bidding process where the highest bidder will acquire a site. Under these circumstances the price a bidder is likely to pay will depend on the use which will be made of the site. For example, a commercial user will earn more from the land and therefore pay a higher price than an

219

industrial user, and an industrial user will in turn pay more than a residential user. This assumes that a plot of land can be equally used for each of the above purposes. In essence that is seldom the case.

In a centre city location there is normally a better transport service and network than at outlying areas. The highest market potential, and optimum access for both consumers and the labour market even though city centre congestion may cause secondary problems. Generally, the more central the location the more desirable the plot, and consequently the higher will be the price as different users will compete to purchase the land. As the economic activity that can gain most utility from that site will be able and willing to pay the highest price, it follows that the land will naturally attract that form of activity. The result is that bands of activity will occur in concentric patterns emanating from the city centre (see Fig. 8.2) as the different forms of economic activity 'naturally' segregate themselves from each other.

Retailers require access to consumers more than any other land use function and this will lead to retailers being prepared to pay very high rents for city centre locations. The bid rent demand from retailers falls away quite sharply as the distance from the city centre increases. This is because the potential in outer city areas is non-existent or too low for major retailers. In contrast, the demand curves for commercial and residential use are more elastic since there is a willingness to accept poorer access in return for lower cost which produces a shallower demand curve. The two-dimensional Fig. 8.2 can be associated with the three bands illustrated in Fig. 8.4: $0-D_1$, commercial use, D_1-D_2 industrial use, and D_2 and beyond for residential use, where each activity will produce a concentric pattern at varying distances from the city centre.

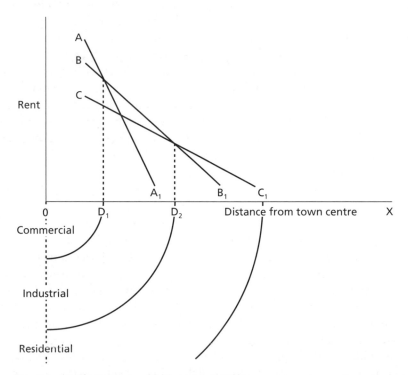

Fig. 8.4 An illustration of bid rent principles
Source: Brown, 1992, p. 54

220

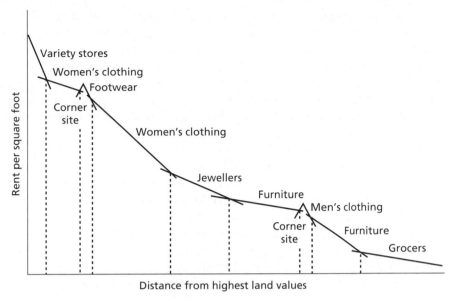

Fig. 8.5 Intra-centre adaptation of bid rent theory
Source: Scott, 1970

Figure 8.5 indicates how the retail sector will be further segmented into different demand schedules, with some types of retail activity being more willing to bid higher rents in order to obtain a central location. Department and speciality stores selling women's clothing, for example, are likely to attach far greater importance to having a central location than would a convenience store or grocery retailer.

Figure 8.5 indicates how the gradient for some retailers is steeper than for others; for example, variety stores as opposed to furniture retailers. This reflects the relative importance attached to a central location by specific types of retailer. The difference in rents paid per square foot is because retailers understand their own marketplace needs and are unwilling to pay prices beyond the attractiveness of the site to their potential customers. Empirical evidence supports the general assumptions associated with bid rent theory, but land may also be affected by planning restrictions on types of use and the type of buildings constructed. On the whole the principles of the theory are a useful way to understand the historical spatial location of different types of business emanating from a city centre.

The principle of minimum differentiation

The principle of minimum differentiation describes the intra-centre agglomeration of similar retail outlets. It is found that many retailers choose to locate near similar types of retail activity in order jointly to attract a higher flow of customers. In addition, some retailers will aim to locate near complementary rather than similar retail functions, in order to maximise the demand from potential customers. Bid rent theory is based upon the assumption that all economic activities aim to be located in the city centre because the centre is the most accessible location. This assumption does not explain why some retailers seek sites that are near to their competitors, or stores providing a similar product offer, rather than choosing to be sited in the city centre. This means proximity to complementary activities is sometimes more important than the benefits of general access. As Richardson (1978) pointed out, the 'agglomeration of retailers may be more attributable to "*economics of concentration*" rather than "*economics of centralisation*" '.

The principle of minimum differentiation has been developed from the work of Hotelling (1929). The assumption behind the theory is that only two firms will be considered although in reality there will normally be more than two. These two firms are located on a linear market line and both are considered to have the ultimate aim of seeking to maximise profits. It is also assumed that transport costs are constant, based upon the distance travelled, and that demand is stable. Potential consumers are assumed to be evenly distributed over the linear market. Therefore, stability exists as no marketing or other influences are brought to bear on the situation. The consumers are considered to be rational and utility maximising, which means they are going to choose the nearest retailer in order to save on transport costs.

The principle of minimum differentiation suggests that a retailer would be able to maximise profits by locating or relocating closer to a competitor in order to gain a larger market area. However, after the relocation the competitor losing out on market share may then move or leapfrog in order to gain a larger market area share; *see* Fig. 8.6 which illustrates the dynamics of the repositioning. Figure 8.6 indicates the movement of the stalls of two ice cream vendors on a beach. Starting initially at opposite ends of the beach, vendor A realises that an advantage can be gained by moving nearer to vendor B as the bulk of the market will be captured by those walking from areas of the beach from X. However, vendor B can retaliate by leapfrogging vendor A to gain the main part of the market and leave A the smaller market share up to Y. Finally A responds by leapfrogging B and assuming a position where a stalemate equilibrium occurs such that both vendors are competing in locations adjacent to each other and with equal shares of the business from the beach.

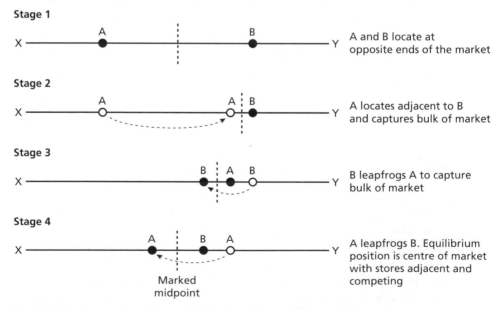

Fig. 8.6 The dynamics of the principle of minimum differentiation
Source: Hotelling (1929), in Brown (1992), p. 68

The long-term outcome of the dynamics of the principle of minimum differentiation is that there is a tendency for some retailers selling similar categories of merchandise – for example, motor car dealers – to cluster together in a pattern of agglomeration. The same phenomenon has been identified for compatible but contrasting retailers such as restaurants and cinemas or grocers and florists.

The evidence of agglomeration patterns suggests that there is a relationship to the type of retailing function. For example, it is much more likely that high order retailers (*see* the discussion on central place theory above) will cluster rather than low order retailers; while boutiques, jewellery or antique shops are often found together in an area or street, lower order outlets such as supermarkets or superstores attempt to be as far from each other as possible. Additionally, there are complementary activity clusters where theatres or cinemas will be positioned near to restaurants, or an accessories outlet near to a fashion retailer.

LOCATION SITE AND TYPES OF RETAIL DEVELOPMENT

The types of location are associated with different types of site selection. A number of different permutations exist but a retailer may decide to locate in one of three typical types of site:

- a solitary site;
- an unplanned shopping area site;
- a planned shopping district/centre.

Each of these site selections are associated with specific strengths and weaknesses. The following is only indicative of what a site may provide; there is a range of complex and different factors which will need to be assessed.

The solitary site may be a single free-standing retail outlet isolated from other retailers and positioned on a road or street. Its strengths are the lack of competition, low rental costs, lower operating costs which can be passed on to the customer, higher impact of presence given traffic visibility is not a problem, and probable ease of parking. For some larger companies a free-standing site offers the benefit of lower cost, provision of a larger display area and a store layout to suit their own specification. It should be noted that free-standing stores, as part of their strategy of differentiation, emphasise location. This is because consumers tend to go to the nearest grocery store; this is in direct contrast to complementary retailers, such as fashion retailers, who agglomerate together to achieve a critical mass to create an attraction to consumers. The site's weaknesses will be the difficulty in attracting initial/new customers, as a single outlet may not have a great deal of gravitational pull. Promotional costs may therefore be higher and there is no shared benefit of security, grounds maintenance or environment improvement. The solitary site is often operated by convenience stores, garages, fast food restaurants or discount warehouses as other types of business find it hard to attract and retain a large enough customer base.

The unplanned shopping area site may be a retail location with two or more outlets in close proximity to each other. Unplanned retailing, as the term implies, has evolved in a gradual or piecemeal pattern. Buildings may have been converted to retail use and the ownership of unplanned retail centres is frequently fragmented among a number of companies or owners. The majority of central shopping areas in cities or towns and small shopping areas are unplanned. Increasingly though they will include planned areas, especially in edge-of-town or out-of-town developments. Normally, a number of retailers will coexist, with perhaps an oversupply of some business types and a shortage of others. No quotas will exist as to number and types of retail businesses. The strengths will be the variety of retail choice in a single area, the ability to compare price, higher levels of pedestrian traffic, probable access to public transportation, and convenience of saving time by utilising different stores. The weaknesses will be the problems of: traffic congestion and parking, organising deliveries, high rents and taxes, poor condition of some of the properties in older city centres and, if travel is expensive to the centre and parking difficult, problems of recruiting and retaining staff.

The planned shopping area site may be a retail location which has been architecturally planned to provide a unified theme for a number of outlets. The planned retail area is a deliberately developed site with complementary retail outlets. Planned shopping sites are developed as an amalgam of different retailers to reflect the market catchment area. The plan is often based upon having some large, key brand stores and a number of smaller retailers adding diversity and interest. Normally a centre will be developed and operated as a single unit, with adequate parking facilities and a balance between the types of stores represented in the centre. The retailers will be allowed to rent space on the basis of being able to complement other centre retail businesses and on the grounds of the quality and type of goods, or services, offered. The strengths will be the balance and comprehensiveness of the retail offers, the freedom for individuals to shop in comfort and satisfy all their needs in the single centre, creation of a single unified image and sense of place, an ability to funnel consumers into a zoned location, the ability to increase security and reduce theft – this all fits in with the growing popularity of malls and shopping centres which have no vehicular traffic and are all-weather or temperature controlled environments. Generally, planned centres tend to be marketed and managed holistically. The weaknesses will be the inflexibility stipulated in the rental agreement such as opening hours; rents may be higher than in other locations; there are often restrictions as to the type of goods which may be sold by the different stores; the smaller stores may not be as successful as the more established ones; and some centres are ageing and are in need of upgrading. The retail park and shopping mall as planned shopping areas are discussed below in more detail.

The retail park

A retail park normally is developed on the outskirts or at an out-of-town site and consists of a purpose-built cluster of free-standing stores with parking facilities. These are usually a minimum of three warehouse type stores based in a retail park of at least 50 000 square feet and built and let as a retail entity. Retail parks were initially developed in the early 1980s and later were developed alongside leisure facilities such as bowling alleys or cinemas. The retail park is different from the shopping mall in that the mall is a single building and marketed as an individual place. The mall often contains small retail outlets but a retail park has retail units that are at least 10 000 square feet.

MINICASE 8.1

The importance of the right anchor store for the development of a shopping mall

No matter which innovative sales angle developers dangle in front of shoppers, a centre cannot attract a critical mass of shoppers without a significant purveyor of a critical mass of goods. And that means finding the right 'anchor' – the mass retailer with the single largest floorspace in the centre – to draw in the right mix of shoppers. So who, then, is the ideal anchor?

In the UK, there is growing consensus that food retailing and shopping malls – at least larger ones – do not mix. Capital Shopping Centres, owner of some of the UK's leading centres, recently announced plans to move Asda, the food retailer that is one of the anchors of its landmark MetroCentre in Gateshead in the north-east of England, to a new site and replace it with Debenhams, a department store. 'At the MetroCentre, we found that the footfall into the Red Quadrant (where Asda is located) from that entrance was not as high as from other entrances', says Douglas Leslie, chief executive of Capital Shopping Centres. 'People were entering through Asda but they were going right back out again. 'It is highly debatable whether food shopping ever had any synergy with comparison shopping.' David Robinoff, managing director at Eastdil Realty Co in New York, says: people who have stocked up on perishable goods do not want to lock them in their cars for a few hours while they take in

the other sights at the mall. Moreover, food and clothing shopping trips are really about different things. According to research by Healey & Baker, it is typical to find supermarkets as anchors in many European countries, including Belgium, Denmark, Germany and Portugal. France shows a preference for a so-called hypermarket anchor. Yvonne Court, retailing specialist at Healey & Baker, says restricted shopping hours in some European states may be part of the explanation. Also, the degree to which supermarkets are desirable anchors may depend on the degree of retailing sophistication of the population generally, says Jonathan Tinker, of Chelverton Properties which specialises in European retail and leisure parks. 'The richer economies anywhere will have less focus on basic goods relative to overall consumption,' he notes. In Poland, where the average annual per capita income is $3,000, a higher percentage of expenditure goes on food than on anything else. But in Germany, with income of $22,000, shopping patterns differ. Thus, understanding the nature of shopping depends on the socio-economic context in which it occurs. In developing economies, it is a necessary chore and in wealthier ones, a leisure activity. And in the most well-off, it is an art form.

Source: Norma Cohen, *Financial Times,* 9 January 1998

The shopping mall

A shopping mall contains a high number of retail outlets in a large building of at least 100 000 square feet in size. The mall normally forms a covered building with open pedestrian walkways which are lined with shops linking the main retailers' sites. If the mall is more than one floor high then the major 'anchor' stores may extend to each of the floors. The mall development may be free-standing or within an existing shopping area. This is because some malls have been built as an infill, as part of an unplanned town centre, whereas others are located on greenfield sites. The property developer's aim is to create a modern themed entity with a balance of types of store. A shopping mall normally contains one or more major branded stores plus several smaller enterprises. They are different from retail parks as the range of store offers is much wider and often includes luxury and leisure items as well as clothing, footwear and other typical central location merchandise. There are a number of examples of shopping malls, ranging from small district size centres to regional malls such as the MetroCentre near Gateshead or Meadowhall in Sheffield in the UK. Regional malls are at least 300 000 square feet in size and often include leisure functions such as cinemas, food courts, ice rinks and restaurants.

A shopping mall is strongly marketed as a unified shopping destination with one name and logo. The success of a mall, however, is quite often dependent on the range and quality of the shops it can attract. The mall is more likely to want to attract non-discount retailers. Table 8.3 explains the differences which often exist between a discount operation and that of a department store.

Table 8.3 Retail strategy differences between a discount store and traditional department store

Discount clothing store strategy	Department store strategy
1 Low cost rental location – which may reflect in a lower level of passing potential consumer traffic or a less prosperous area	**1** More expensive rental location in an established shopping centre which has a high level of pull on potential consumer traffic
2 Simple fixtures and fittings, cheap floor covering, few displays, single fitting room	**2** Elegant fixtures and fittings, carpeted flooring, individual fitting rooms, an abundance of window and interior displays
3 Promotional strategy is based upon price leadership	**3** Promotional strategy is based upon developing brand image, offering quality brands, achieving a positive image and providing superior service
4 Little flexibility in service (few, if any, alterations, phone orders, gift wrapping, credit, etc.)	**4** Flexibility in service (will alter, arrange home delivery, have relationship marketing or loyalty schemes)
5 Reliance on self-service, basic displays, most merchandise being visible and in crowded conditions	**5** Thorough sales assistance, depth and breadth of stock, attractive display of merchandise
6 May stock limited lines and cheap discounted brands	**6** Full selection of branded products and reluctance to have discounted items
7 Continual use of low price offers	**7** Sales limited to specific end-of-season clearances or special occasions
8 No changing rooms	**8** Changing rooms

Two types of retailing in location decisions

Based upon the preceding theories, there are two basic types of retailing which need to be explained: proximity and destination retailing. The nature of any regional development will affect the nature of the sites available for retailers. Each area can be generalised to identify the type of retailing which may be successful. Therefore, two broad types of retailing development may be considered in the location decision: proximity retailing and destination retailing.

Proximity retailing is development-led by locating where the consumer is to ensure high levels of convenience – in the workplace, related to the patterns of movement, near the home or at home. Specific examples include petrol stations, chemists, small convenience stores, newsagents, video outlets, fast-food outlets, mail order and teleshopping. A retail outlet wishing to be successful in this category has to identify sites with maximum passing traffic and visibility, and ensure that the retail offer matches the needs and characteristics of people working or living in the immediate vicinity. Proximity retailing is often associated with convenience or staple goods which are purchased on a frequent or routine basis.

Destination retailing is based on drawing consumers to travel to a store: brand leaders, the major multiple grocers, large outlets for DIY, toys, clothing, as well as the large 'discount' retailers are included in the category of retailers using this type of location. Relatively mobile, car-owning consumers are more likely to be attracted by this type of retailing. Destination retailing is often associated with speciality goods which are characterised by unique attributes that will attract specific segments. For these goods, purchase behaviour is often associated with higher involvement as part of the buying process and more pre-purchase planning than for other types of goods. A recent trend has been the movement of electrical, carpet and furniture stores away from existing centres to fringe and out-of-town locations, usually grouping together in retail parks. The marketing strategy for this trend is often based upon the proposition of providing products which offer good value for money.

LOCATIONAL TECHNIQUES

The use of different forms of analysis is essential to the selection of an appropriate retail location. The appropriateness is based upon the characteristics of the retailer's business and this means different types of analysis will need to be undertaken according to the type and range of products being sold, where the business would ideally be based, and the ideal catchment population.

Factors in the location decision

In order to determine possible catchment areas, to forecast sales and to calculate likely demand and profitability, a substantial number of factors may need to be investigated. Chu *et al.* (1998) have argued that within any discussion on spatial economics and location decisions it is assumed that the firm in question can choose only one store site. This may be restrictive, as spatial decisions may be far more complicated based upon geographic distribution of competitors and competitive prices. The list in Table 8.4 is not exhaustive but serves as an example. All sites need to be examined on a preliminary basis prior to the more detailed location analysis. Road and traffic systems, parking facilities, competitors and pedestrian flows may be easily assessed; some of the other items listed in Table 8.4 need more detailed analysis.

Table 8.4 Sample of location factors

Customers – potential/actual	Accessibility	Competition	Costs
• Numbers by demographics	• Site visibility	• Amount and level	• Building costs
• Income/employment by occupation, industry, trends	• Pedestrian flows	• Type and numbers	• Rent costs
• Spending patterns	• Barriers such as railway tracks, rivers	• Saturation index	• Rates payable
• Population growth, density and trends	• Type of location zone	• Proximity of key competitors, traders, brand leaders – for example, Marks & Spencer	• Delivery costs
• Lifestyles	• Road conditions and network		• Insurance costs
• Car ownership	• Parking		• Labour rates
	• Public transport		

Location assessment techniques

Techniques for assessing a location for a retail outlet range from the simple to the sophisticated. An obvious method, which is the simplest way of assessing a site's viability, is to count the flow of people during five-minute periods at the busiest times of the week. Based upon a crude 'rule of thumb', if it were a site where on average 100 people passed within five minutes then that could be equated to expenditure per person based upon a money weighting, of say £150 each, which would represent a potential of £15 000 a week. Two hundred people would represent £30 000. Obviously there are certain variables which also need to be assessed to ensure the viability, such as being in a central place location among shops with a high customer utilisation. Eppli (1998), in a study of consumer shopping behaviour, revealed that the effects of location, comparison shopping, and department store image are a composite when estimating both shopping centre patronage and retail sales.

The most logical step would be to use a checklist of factors similar to those in Table 8.4. Factors relevant to a potential site could be identified and then allocated a score on a scale of 1 to 10 (1 = poor, 10 = excellent). The final score would act as a management decision input when considering whether or not to proceed in one area as opposed to another. While a small retailer without large resources may adopt such an approach, the location of a superstore would need a more sophisticated approach. This is because of the size of the investment involved, the complexity of the operation and the profit required to secure a return on any investment. Destination retailing, as previously described, requires a much more detailed assessment as part of the location determination process.

CATCHMENT AREA ANALYSIS

Catchment area analysis together with the analogue method (a comparison of similar stores in the group) serves as a useful basis for forecasting sales of a proposed superstore. A superstore wanting to locate to a new site may turn to catchment area analysis. The basic framework is shown in Table 8.5.

Table 8.5 Framework for catchment area analysis

(1) Travel time (minutes)	(2) Population	(3) Weekly potential sales	(4) Competition (total square footage)	(5) Square footage pe head	(6) Forecast sales
0 to under 10 10 to under 20 20 to under 30 30 to under 40 40 to 60					

The columns of Table 8.5 require some explanation.

- Column 1: although expressed in time bands, it could equally be stated in terms of distance. However, distance does not take local road conditions into consideration.
- Column 2 could be broken down into socio-economic groups, age bands, car ownership, etc. It could also be based upon percentage of working population.
- Column 3 would initially be calculated by multiplying per capita expenditure on merchandise lines/goods by the population figure. More detailed analysis would determine per capita expenditure in different consumer categories multiplied by the number of such consumers in the various time bands. The superstore, for example, may be looking to attract the higher socio-economic groups or may be surrounded by specific household types.
- Columns 4 and 5 enable an assessment to be carried out into the potential market for a new store on the basis of existing provision.
- Column 6: by utilising the data from a number of similar stores in the group (analogue method) a realistic forecast can be made. The forecast will indicate the levels of penetration in each of the travel bands, adjusted to take the effect of competition into account. Ultimately, the decision as to whether or not development proceeds will depend on the sales and profit requirements of both retailers and property developers.

Computerised databases are an aid to store location catchment area decisions

In order to evaluate the trade area for a store with some accuracy, a range of different computerised mapping techniques is available. Trade area mapping may be provided by software such as SYMAP, GIS (Geographic Information Systems) or Pinpoint analysis. These systems can assess the geographical and demographic attractiveness of a site with much more accuracy than other methods. Retailers have often been slow to use spatial decision software in order to improve decisions regarding the retail location and operation. The larger multiples, especially food multiples, use GIS because it can give competitive advantage over smaller retailers.

Gravitational model

The use of models is another way to assess the feasibility of a location decision. With the gravitational model, the selection of a primary trading location is based upon the idea that consumers are attracted towards one location as opposed to another due to its draw or pull effect. One of the original exponents of the 'pulling effect' of a location was W.J. Reilly, who published his law of retail gravitation in 1929. The law set out to allow a point of indifference to be established between two cities or communities so that the catchment area could be determined. The point of indifference is the geographic breaking point between two communities, that is, the point where consumers would be indifferent to shopping at either location. This aids one of the crucial tasks in retail location, which is the necessity to delineate the catchment area or geographical area from which a retailer draws custom. According to Reilly, more consumers will be attracted to the larger city or community to shop due to the greater amount of store facilities and choice which would make any extra travelling time worthwhile. Reilly's law may be expressed as:

$$D_{AB} = \frac{d}{1 + \sqrt{\dfrac{P_B}{P_A}}}$$

where D_{AB} is the limit of city A's catchment area measured in miles along the road to city B, d is the distance in miles along a major roadway between A and B, P_A is the population of city A and P_B is the population of city B.

Based on this formula, a city with a population of 450 000 (A) would draw people from three times the distance that a city with a population of 50 000 (B) could manage. If the cities are 20 miles apart, the catchment area for city A extends to 15 miles and for city B, 5 miles (see Fig. 8.7).

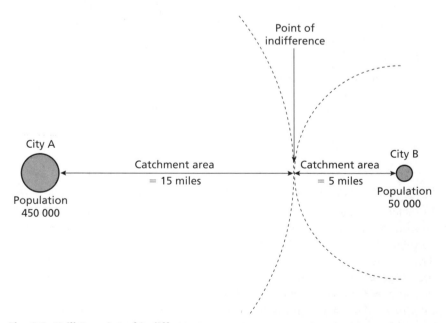

Fig. 8.7 Reilly's point of indifference

However, Reilly's law rests on three major assumptions:

- the two competing areas are equally accessible from a major road;
- retailers in either of the two areas offer no additional competitive advantage and are equally effective;
- the areas are similar and that no bias will occur due to differences in ethnic, civic and general architecture, facilities or parking restrictions.

Consequently, the law has its limitations. Not only is the focus on distance rather than travel times, but also actual distance may not correspond with the consumer's *perception* of distance – for example, a store that offers limited merchandise, parking problems and few services may be at a greater perceived distance from one with an attractive, pleasant environment. Alternatively, consumers may be willing to travel further due to ease of parking or to visit a particular store, etc.

However, despite the above weaknesses, Reilly's law still represents an important contribution to our assessment of retail location as it formalises the interrelationships between competing retail trading areas. In particular, it includes some of the basics of location:

- *spatial convenience* – the increase in travel time and distance to any destination to utilise a store or market centre will restrict and limit the potential size of the market;
- *range* – this is the maximum distance that customers are willing to travel to a shopping destination;
- *threshold* – this refers to the smallest market size needed to support a certain type of store or shopping centre.

REGRESSION ANALYSIS

The large stores may also utilise regression analysis in order to forecast sales. As seen previously, existing stores similar to the proposed new store are used to estimate an equation relating variations in sales to a set of variables, for example population, competition store size, and so on. A hypothetical example will illustrate the procedure.

$$Y = a + b_1x_1 - b_2x_2$$

where
- Y = retail sales
- x_1 = population (within 20 minutes' drive time)
- x_2 = competition (floor space of all stores over 20 000 ft^2 within 20 minutes' drive time)
- b_1, b_2 = regression coefficients
- a = intercept value

Twenty-five observations from analogous stores give us the following regression equation:

$$Y = 200\ 000 + 0.74x_1 - 1.35x_2$$

The overall explanatory power of the regression equation above is known as the coefficient of determination, R^2, which for this equation is 0.83. (The figure of 0.83 is, in turn, the squared value of the correlation coefficient, r, which in this example would be 0.91. Therefore $0.91^2 = 0.83$.)

What does $R^2 = 0.83$ mean? An R^2 of 0.83 means that 83 per cent of the differences in sales among the 25 analogous stores can be explained by variations in population and competition. Only 17 per cent is left unexplained (owing to some other factors, for example income levels, promotional expenditure, product range).

For the regression coefficients: b_1 is equal to 0.74, which means that for a 1 per cent increase in the population, sales will increase by 0.74. On the other hand, a b_2 of -1.35 means that a 1 per cent increase in competitor's floorspace, sales will decrease by 1.35 per cent. Using the area's population and competition figures, a proposed new superstore can use the above equation to estimate sales.

Whereas superstores consider travel times and distance proximity, retailers study geo-demographic profiles for an understanding of catchment areas. More specifically, proximity retailers wish to know the types of people in the immediate vicinity of the proposed site, as it is from here that the vast proportion of its business will come. Geo-demographic systems like ACORN or MOSAIC (*see* Chapter 3 for further explanation), along with TGI information on consumption, can provide detailed information on the catchment area, for example type of housing, consumer characteristics, consumption patterns, suggestions on product ranges, etc. Statistical data and databases can show the influence and distribution of, say, ACORN types within a city, town or village. Further analysis enables an estimate of market size and sales potential.

Index of retail saturation

The level of competition between stores will affect the retail opportunity in an area. Therefore, the competitive structure of a catchment area needs to be studied in order to assess a location accurately. Put simply, a catchment area can be under-stored, over-stored, or saturated. An under-stored area has too few stores selling specific goods or services to satisfy the needs of its population. An over-stored area has a superfluous number of stores and some retailers may not be able to earn an adequate profit. A saturated area has just enough retail facilities to satisfy the needs of its population.

To assess the above, a general ratio model has been developed to measure store saturation in a specific area based upon an index of retail saturation (IRS). The calculation can be made as follows:

$$IRS_i = \frac{C_i \times RE_i}{RF_i}$$

where IRS_i = index of retail saturation for area i (where i = local market area)

C_i = number of customers in area i for the product/service category

RE_i = retail expenditures per customer in area i for the product/service category

RF_i = total retail square footage in area i allocated to the product/service category

Consider the following example of food store saturation in a catchment area. There are 15 000 consumers in the area and they spend, on average, £20 per week in food stores. (Figures for different per capita expenditure on retail products are available from the Family Expenditure Survey.) There are three stores serving the market with a total of 30 000 square feet. Hence:

$$IRS = \frac{15\ 000 \times \pounds20}{30\ 000} = \pounds10$$

The revenue of £10 per square foot of selling area measured against the revenue per square foot necessary to break even provides the measure of saturation.

The use of the IRS can also be illustrated by an analysis of three catchment areas under consideration by a shoe retailer. The company has predetermined that its sales must be at least £160 per square foot of store space to be profitable. The catchment area chosen will be the one that yields the best index of retail store saturation. In this case, the retailer selects catchment area 1 which has an index of saturation of £180 (*see* Table 8.6).

Table 8.6 An example of the use of the index of retail saturation

	Catchment area		
	1	*2*	*3*
Number of customers buying annually	60 000	30 000	10 000
Average annual purchases per customer	£60	£75	£100
Total square footage (including the proposed store)	20 000	15 000	75 000
Index of retail saturation (including the proposed store)	180	150	133
Index of retail saturation (excluding the proposed store)	240	225	400

When calculating the index, the retailer has to remember to include the proposed store. If the store is not included, the relative value of each calculation may be distorted. If the proposed store is excluded in Table 8.6, for instance, area 3 has the best level of sales per square foot (£400). However, this area is not desirable after the prospective store is added to the computation. It should be noted that sales per square foot decline most when new outlets are added to a small area. The retailer should also examine the impact of its business and whether a new store will expand the total market or not. The information in Table 8.6 assumes that sales will remain the same. In the food retailing industry it has been claimed that there should be approximately one square foot of retail space for each head of population living in a catchment area. So 80 000 people should be matched by 80 000 square feet of retail space. However, the complexity of any retail sales situation quite often means that such rules of thumb are too crude an approach.

It should be noted that a market may be saturated in some sectors, for example grocery and superstores, and yet very much underdeveloped in others such as footwear retailing. Each retail organisation must analyse the situation as it affects its business.

RETAIL PROPERTY DEVELOPMENT

Retail property development can be considered as the change of use of a piece of land in order to develop it for retail use. This may be based upon the refurbishment of existing buildings from what used to be a warehouse or factory into retail units. The general definition relating to transforming a plot of land from one state to another is based upon the premise that if there is a higher demand for retail sites in an area and a decrease in the need for industrial sites then it will be inevitable that suitable sites for retailing will be developed. The other type of development is the planned development of new centres in out-of-town locations or the development of retail parks. The latter type of retail property development has been a more recent phenomenon but the overriding motivation for all development is the financial return on any project and the commercial value of the new property.

Retail property development is also reliant on:

- local factors of supply and demand;
- appropriateness of the available site(s) for different types of retailer,
- the experience and preferences of the developer and local planning officers;
- the minimum amount of land required to provide different scales of development and change;
- the costs of the development;
- the time factors in the completion of the development;
- the level of financial risk in undertaking the development.

MINICASE 8.2

Difficulty in developing new sites

'The three most important issues in retailing are location, location, location,' said Sir Charles Clore, the 1950s entrepreneur and founder of retail conglomerate, Sears. The sentiment remains as true today as ever, and is even more important as retailers begin to move beyond their home boundaries. 'The most difficult nut to crack in expanding abroad is finding the right property,' says one retailer. But even once the location has been pinpointed, retailers with global ambitions are faced with widely differing regulations governing their rights and obligations as tenants. Typical lease lengths vary from as low as three years in many eastern European countries to 25 years in Britain, where they can be reviewed every five years, but only upwards.

Extra property costs such as value-added tax are equally variable, from 25 per cent of annual net rent in Sweden to as low as 5 per cent in the Czech Republic. Jones Lang Wootton, the property consultant, argues many of the opportunities for retailers to expand in north-western Europe have already faded due to saturation of the market. However, proposals to increase the membership of the European Union from 15 to 20 countries could result in 'enormous benefits. Current barriers and tariffs hindering expansion would be removed'.

Source: Peggy Hollinger, *Financial Times*, 7 March 1998

THE LEASING OF A RETAIL OUTLET

Once a specific site has been agreed upon a retailer needs to assess the contract or lease offered. There are different types of leases and a variety of terms which may be applied. On the whole it is more usual for a retailer to lease a store site than enter into a loan or mortgage in order to purchase the property. This provides for a more flexible response by the retailer and the ability to free the capital for alternative projects. In addition, it will be found that shopping malls and similar purpose-developed locations are only available as part of a leasing agreement. There are straight leases, percentage leases or net leases.

Straight lease. With a straight lease a retailer will pay an agreed fixed amount per month or quarter over the life of the lease. With a straight lease, both the landlord and the retailer know in advance what payments are expected over the life of the lease. One modification of the straight lease is the *graduated lease* where the amount due increases by a fixed amount after specified periods of time. This may be based upon inflationary clauses using government figures as to how much the lease may increase each year or there may be some pre-agreed increase.

Percentage lease. The percentage lease is based upon an agreement made on the principle of the rent being linked to the percentage of sales. Given leases can run from five to twenty years, there is some protection for the retailer if the rent can fluctuate on the basis of inflation and sales results. In America, this is a very popular form of leasing, accepted as a fair way to set rent as the local and national economy would force rents down if there were a general decline in sales demand – or vice versa. This approach is often combined with an accepted minimum or maximum increase so as to incentivise the retailer and also protect the landlord. The scheme may also be based upon a sliding scale of change in rent whereby a retailer may pay 4 per cent on the first £250 000 of sales and 3 per cent on the next £150 000, etc. This will offer a further reward to those retailers who can improve the achievement of their operation.

The above leases may be based upon *maintenance recoupment* where a landlord will have the right to increase the rent if it can be shown that the property insurance, taxes or utility bills have increased beyond a specified agreed level. The above may also be allied to a *net lease*. With a net lease the retailer is responsible for all maintenance and utility charges; the property owner, therefore, can base the rent on a more stable set of circumstances.

A lease is a formal contract and therefore agreement has to take place regarding the conditions and terms by the lessor (property owner) and lessee (the party signing the lease). A lease may be negotiated to achieve the best conditions for each participant; the outcome, however, is often based upon the relative power of each party and their knowledge of what can be added to the agreement as specific clauses. These clauses may include the following.

A *prohibited use clause* is used in order to limit the landlord from leasing to tenants who may affect the image of the business or building(s) or restrict the demand for the retailer's goods, due to alternative business which may affect the use of parking space and not increase the retailer's sales. For example, certain types of leisure facilities such as a fitness club or day centre may reduce the number of shoppers. There may also be a wish for the list of prohibited businesses to include sex shops, bars, pool halls or other establishments which may affect the overall image of the area.

An *exclusive use clause* will prohibit the landlord from leasing to retailers who will then become direct competitors. For example, if the retail outlet is a video hire business the clause may limit the landlord from renting to another similar business unit; it may also restrict other outlets – such as a convenience store – from hiring out videos from their store. Alternatively a retailer may wish to protect their business on the basis of the continued trading of strongly branded retailers within the area. The exclusive use clause may therefore ensure that the agreement is reliant on key, named retailers remaining in the area.

The lease may also need to include clauses to restrict a landlord from placing any objects or kiosks in a position which may affect the sight line to the store or its visibility to passing potential customers. With the development of stand-alone automatic teller machines, public Internet machines and advances in technology there is the possible threat of land being rented for the establishment of an obstacle which may affect the original lessee's business.

CONCLUSION

The decision regarding where to locate a store is critical to the future performance of that outlet and the retailer's prosperity. This is compounded by the fact that all location plans are important on the basis of the resources required to develop a new store, and the time this takes. Any decision over a retail site requires an appraisal of the potential site area based upon a number of analytical techniques. The retailer's task is to identify the size and profile of the potential market of consumers, assess the different potential sites of an area and then utilise methods of screening the alternatives so that the chosen site offers the best likelihood of maximising the store's retail profitability. This process has to be one of matching the site to the type of business represented by that retailer. It also has to be carried out in a timely manner to ensure there is the maximisation of profits for the retailer.

EXERCISES

The exercises in this section relate to retail location strategies and decisions. It is advised that you work through them before moving on to Chapter 9.

1 What are the major consumer and business influences which have produced the current location patterns of retail outlets in developed economies?

2 Given the recent trends in retail shopping and customer behaviour, what changes may occur in the location of retail outlets in large city centres?

3 Do you believe that some aspects of location analysis techniques are better than others? If so, what are the techniques you would employ and which key aspects would you want to assess prior to location decisions being made? What were the reasons for your choice?

4 In your opinion, what are the most important aspects of location decision-making? Use the following grid as a guide.

Location analysis factors	Comment on the importance of these from a marketing viewpoint
• proximity of competitors • type of housing and lifestyle of households • development costs • in town, edge of town, out of town location • others (list)	

Now comment on how you think location analysis will change over the next 20 years to encourage increased purchases?

REFERENCES AND FURTHER READING

Bennison, D., Clarke, I. and Pal, J. Jan. (1995) 'Location decision making in retailing: an exploratory framework for analysis', *The International Review of Retail Distribution and Consumer Research*, 5 (1), 1–20.

Brown, S. (1992) *Retail Location: A micro-scale perspective*. Aldershot: Avebury.

Brown, S. (1993) 'Retail location theory: evolution and evaluation', *The International Review of Retail Distribution and Consumer Research*, 3 (2), 185–229.

Chu, C.Y.C. and Lu, Huei-chung (1998) 'The multi-store location and pricing decisions of a spatial monopoly', *Regional Science and Urban Economics*, 28 (3), 255–81.

Clark, M. (1993) 'Mapping out retail direction', *International Journal of Retail and Distribution Management*, 21 (2), 36–8.

Clarkson, R.M., Clarke-Hill, C.M. and Robinson, T. (1996) 'UK supermarket location assessment', *The International Journal of Retail and Distribution Management*, 24 (6), 22–3.

Coates, D., Doherty, N., French, A. and Kirkup, M. (1995) 'Neural networks for store performance forecasting: an empirical comparison with regression techniques', *International Review of Retail Distribution and Consumer Research*, 5 (4), 415–32.

Cohen, N. (1998) 'Property market: an anchor in the centre', *Financial Times*, 9 January.

Department of the Environment (1996) *Town Centres and Retail Developments, Planning Policy Guidance*. (Note 6.) London: HMSO.

Drezner, Zvi, Wesolowsky, G.O. and Drezner, T. (1998) 'On the logit approach to competitive facility location', *Journal of Regional Science*, 38 (2), 313–27.

Eppli, M.J. (1998) 'Value allocation in regional shopping centers', *Appraisal Journal*, 66 (2), 198–206.

Guy, C.M. (1984) 'The urban pattern of retailing within the UK' in Davies, R.L. and Rogers, D.S. (eds) *Store Location and Store Assessment Research*. Chichester: John Wiley.

Guy, C.M. (1994) *The Retail Development Process: Location, property and planning*. London: Routledge.

Hallsworth, A.G., Jones, K.G. and Muncaster, R. (1995) 'The planning implications of new retail format introductions in Canada and Britain', *Services Industries Journal*, 15 (4), 148–63.

Hollinger, P. (1998) 'Finding a location is only the first step to expansion', *Financial Times*, 7 March.

Hotelling, H. (1929) 'Stability in competition', *Economic Journal*, 39, March, 41–57.

Jones, K. and Simmons, J. (1990) *The Retail Environment*. London: Routledge.

McGoldrick, P.J. (1994) *Cases in Retail Management*. London: Pitman.

Reilly, W.J. (1929) 'Method for the study of retail relationships', *Research Monograph No 4*, Austin, TX: University of Texas Bulletin No 2944.

Richardson, H.W. (1978) *Urban Economics*. Hinsdale: Dryden Press.

Scott, P. (1970) *Geography and Retailing*. London: Hutchinson.

Simkin, L.P. (1989) 'SLAM: Store Location Assessment Model – theory and practice', *International Journal of Management Science*, 17 (1), 53–8.

Simkin, L.P, (1990) 'Evaluating a store location', *International Journal of Retail and Distribution Management*, 18 (4), 33–8.

Smith, C.A. and Webb, J.R (1997) 'Using GIS to improve estimates of future retail space demand', *Appraisal Journal*, 65 (4), 337–41.

9 The management of a retail brand

This chapter should enable you to understand and explain:

- what a brand is;
- the positioning and differentiation of a brand;
- the role and purpose of branding;
- the importance of own-label brands;
- strategies of brand extension.

In the modern competitive retail marketplace, growth markets are increasingly scarce and consumers are sovereign in dictating what shape the market will be. The consumer is faced with an increasing array of essential, as well as non-essential retail products over which to exercise the power of choice and dictate trends. Improvements and investment in stores or retailing operations are not enough. Returns can be made only if the customer decides to purchase, and purchase again, as part of a relationship with the store and the brand. Simply put, retailers and suppliers of products or services need people to seek out and buy their retail offer. One current marketing method of achieving such a goal is the strategy of *brand building*. This can be adopted by a chain of retail outlets or by a producer of branded merchandise. A successful brand strategy will both aid and convince consumers in the decision-making process to select out certain companies and merchandise. To build a retail brand requires more than trading ability; it requires that the company institutionalise marketing as the means to manage the long-term development of brand values.

The benefit of developing a strong brand is that consumers are often prepared to pay a price premium for added values perceived to be provided by buying well-marketed brands. The price premium, also known as *brand equity*, is the price customers are prepared to pay above the commodity value of a product or service. This being the case, well respected stores or brands – if well positioned and managed – can give a better return on floor space or investment. Brands with a strong personality are attractive to companies who own them and predator companies wishing to buy into their potency. A successful brand is a flag bearer as it provides visible signals of positional strength in the marketplace. In this way successful brands provide their parent companies with a competitive advantage. In the UK, Boots the Chemist, the Early Learning Centre and Marks & Spencer are examples of strong brands which communicate a clear position for both merchandise and service. A secondary consideration is that strong domestic retail brands provide a good base on which to build an international or global presence. Therefore, brand management may become more important for those companies which want to escape the competitive domestic market and attempt international growth. There are few truly global retail brands. The retail financial services market has American Express, VISA, MasterCard and Diners Club. There are some large banks which have followed their domestic business, and private customers overseas, to business centres, tourist destinations or expatriate communities. However, the growth of non-branch banking could lead to far faster global competition due to the low cost operations of direct services and the economies of scale to be found in international expansion.

Companies produce strategies based upon long-term commitment to brand building as a way out of the heavy reliance on offering low prices as the primary reason for consumer choice. However, the long-term success of a particular brand is based not on the number of customers who purchase it once, but on the number who become repeat purchasers. They become *brand loyal* or *store loyal*. The concept of selling a product to as many people as possible at least once may have been relevant in a growth market, but when a market matures companies need to realise that it is of paramount importance to maintain loyal customers as well as search for new customers. For consumers, the familiar associations and standard guarantees embodied in brand offers reduce the perceived purchase risks often associated with high involvement, intangible retail products.

Branding became more important in the 1990s due to the relentless evolution of the marketplace from an environment where satisfaction of basic needs has given way to the need to have brands which engender positive associations. We live in a world where symbolic meaning linked to brand use provides status and social significance for the consumer of that brand. Historically fashion brands have held great significance in retailing. These include such brands as Yves Saint Laurent, Chanel, Christian Dior and Jean Paul Gautier from France; Giorgio Armani, Gianni Versace and Emanuel Ungaro from Italy; Issey Miyake and Kenzo from the Far East; Ralph Lauren, Calvin Klein and Donna Karan from the USA. These fashion brands are all names which have a strong international reputation. Branding is a powerful phenomenon in that it is one of the most successful ways of satisfying customer recognition needs. To understand the phenomenon we need to know specifically the intrinsic properties that constitute a brand.

DEFINITION OF A BRAND

Kotler (1997) defines a brand as:

> a name, term, sign, symbol or design or a combination of them, intended to identify the goods or services of one seller or group of sellers and to differentiate them from those of competitors.

This describes a brand as a purely functional means of distinguishing a retail offer and would have been apt in the early days of branding, but by the 1990s other aspects had been introduced and extensively discussed.

In total abandonment of the focus on aspects of product, Kapferer (1992) produces the more esoteric statement:

> A brand is not a product. It is the product's essence, its meaning and its direction, and it defines its identity in time and space.

An individual's awareness of the world is made up of experiences, learning, emotions and perceptions – or, more accurately, the cognitive evaluation of such experiences, learning, emotions and perceptions. Such awareness may be described as knowledge producing a specific image of the world. This image will obviously affect an individual's preference and motivation towards products, as it will provide a 'pull' effect resulting in different demand schedules. The success of a brand is, therefore, not just what the company puts into the brand but is based upon what the customer associates with the brand – the added value it provides for them. To examine branding from the viewpoint of consumer behaviour, the starting point is to comprehend the way a customer perceives and classifies brands and then how companies can build positive images to reinforce that perception.

The process of brand management has to distinguish a brand from a commodity. The latter is typically characterised by the lack of a perceived differentiation by customers between competing offerings. This being the case, the purchase decision for a commodity is usually taken on the basis of price or availability and not on the brand. Store loyal and brand loyal customers choose on the basis that the shopping experience is 'more than the sum of its component parts'. In other words, the successful brand has *added value* over its commodity content.

Aaker and Biel (1993) give the following definition:

A brand is basically a name that refers to the product of a particular manufacture in a particular product category. A brand includes tangible or intrinsic qualities, such as appearance, performance data, package, and the guarantees or warranties that are attached to it. Perhaps more importantly, a brand involves aspects that the consumer attributes to it, beyond its tangible features. These aspects may include attitudes towards the company that produces the product or towards the brand itself, beliefs about the brand in relationship to self and others, and so on.

They further stress that their definition applies not only to consumer products, but to people (for example, politicians, pop stars, and so on), places, ships, companies and services. This at first seems to be comprehensive. However, brands have to be clearly positioned so as to give distinct signals and demarcations from their rivals. This requires a clear distinction encompassing the need to provide focus and personality for the brand. The need to understand this argument introduces two further aspects – *positioning* and *personality*, which will be discussed below.

THE ROLE OF THE BRAND

Before discussing what brand management involves, we will examine why it is considered a pertinent marketing tool for retail companies in the current developed and highly competitive markets. As the marketplace becomes mature, there is a need to rise above the mass and confusion of competing offers. The brand, if managed properly, confers individuality – something different among the crowd. In a mature market, companies experience slow growth and declining returns. Each company will, therefore, attempt to defend its market share, encourage consumers' purchase loyalty and profitably differentiate their outlets and offer. We believe a brand provides an icon or symbol which helps to identify the promise of a particular retail offer or service and helps to distinguish it from competing offers.

Successful retail outlet brand building enables organisations to:

1 build stable, long-term demand based upon increasing store brand name strength;
2 build and hold better margins than stores which have weak or unsuccessful brand names;
3 differentiate themselves through creating associations that can endure over long periods of time;
4 add values that entice customers to visit and buy;
5 act as a signal to the customer implying trust in the fulfilment of service expectations;
6 promote customer loyalty and launch relationship marketing schemes for their retail offers/services;
7 protect themselves against the growing competition of alternative intermediaries and to gain leverage in the distribution channel;
8 protect themselves against aggressive competitors by strengthening barriers to entry;
9 transform themselves into companies that are attractive to work for and to deal with;
10 negotiate with suppliers from a position of improved strength.

The latter are the potential results of successful retail outlet brand building, but all involve substantial initial, and ongoing, investments to ensure there are long-term returns. Furthermore, brand building needs to be a comprehensive exercise which covers every aspect of the company and every point of contact with the consumer. This puts brand building under severe pressure in modern markets where short-term profits are more commonly the measures of success.

A company may introduce a brand and keep it exclusively for itself, or it can either franchise a brand or manufacture a brand of another company under licence. Franchising is being used extensively by companies in order to expand the brand as quickly as possible in a domestic or global marketplace. With franchising, the company owning the brand will allow others to utilise the brand but with certain preconditions attached. These may be related to an obligation to purchase goods exclusively from the franchiser or to pay a certain percentage of the turnover as part of a royalty payment. The consumer is offered the benefit of the consistency and recognised standards of quality which have been built up in conjunction with the brand. This has led to a number of successful retail operations such as Pizza Hut, Caffé Uno, McDonald's, KFC and Hilton International.

BRAND LOYALTY

Some consumers use the same retail outlet or purchase the same brand of product on most occasions or on a regular basis. This buyer characteristic is known as *store* or *brand loyalty*. In particular, brand or store loyalty will mean that a person will:

- feel positively disposed to the brand, based upon *brand attitude*;
- utilise the store more than other stores or buy the brand more frequently. This will be based upon *store* or *brand preference*;
- continue to utilise the store or brand over time. This is the *brand allegiance*.

This is not to say there is just one type of loyalty; loyalty may be expressed for one or more brands. If we assume that there are five brands, or five properties of brands, that the consumer can choose from – A, B, C, D and E – then we can further segment the demand, based upon brand loyalty, as follows.

1 *Hard core loyals*. These consumers buy one brand all the time and demonstrate strong allegiance. They would therefore on five occasions buy AAAAA, because they have undivided loyalty to the brand.

2 *Soft core loyals*. These consumers will be loyal to two or three brands. Thus a buying pattern of ABABA represents a consumer whose loyalties are divided between two competing brands.

3 *Shifting loyals*. This type of consumer shifts their loyalty from one brand to another. The buying pattern AACCC suggests a consumer whose loyalty has shifted from one brand 'A' to brand 'C'.

4 *Switchers*. These consumers show no loyalty to any one brand. The pattern ABCDE suggests a switcher who is prone to buy when there is deal being given (price offers, sales, extra benefits). They may equally be a variety shopper and wants something different each time they purchase.

Brand loyalty can be explained in a number of ways: habit; maximisation of value over price; a cost may be involved in switching brand; the availability of substitutes; perceived risk of alternatives is high; past satisfaction with the brand; the frequency of usage; influence of the media; the awareness of the alternatives; and so on. For obvious reasons, the loyal customer is of key importance to the retail industry, especially those loyal customers who are high spenders or provide long-term patronage. Loyalty schemes are being introduced in an attempt to retain customers over longer periods of time (*see* Chapter 5 for a full discussion of this). Such schemes are often based upon database programmes which provide benefits such as for those with loyalty shopping cards whose expenditure and frequency of purchase can be assessed. The database can identify individuals' birthdays, when a person is 21 for example, or it can identify lapsed customers to whom a special offer can be made. In addition, the information can be used to understand the patterns of preference and demand at different periods so as to convert soft core loyals and other customers, into hard core loyals.

POSITIONING OF A BRAND

The positioning of a brand places it in its competitive context. It may be determined on the basis of product usage, for instance Müller yoghurt may be positioned as a substitute for dairy cream or as a child's pudding, alongside ice cream. Alternatively, a brand's position may be determined on the basis of price. For instance, top designer branded clothes have a high upper market position which will attract customers who want exclusivity and a positioning which is associated with other luxury items. Benetton's bold and distinctive colours, Laura Ashley's English country patterns and The Gap's understated American casual wear all provide for brand differentiation.

Registering a clear brand positioning is becoming increasingly difficult because competitors proliferate, media costs escalate, and shelf space becomes more difficult to negotiate as retailers exert more influence over manufacturers' brand strategies.

Theorists maintain that focusing on brand positioning is essential for a brand to survive. They express their lack of faith in the intellectual ability of brand managers to assess fully the competition and in the intellectual ability of the consumers similarly to assess the range of brands available to them. The brand managers, who regularly take a sounding of consumer opinion, are the most likely to maintain a brand's positioning successfully. Once the target has been clearly identified, attention needs to be lavished on planning the brand. Furthermore, a brand which is not differentiated from others in its sub-group of brands risks having no distinguishing characteristics and a weak brand position:

Brand differentiation × Brand segmentation = Brand position

Branding places a premium on achieving appropriate positioning. A brand may be made distinctive by its positioning relative to the competition, the main objective is to develop sustainable competitive advantage. As such, a key task for the strategist is to identify those bases which offer the most potential for defensible positioning. In marketing, choosing segments and positioning strategies are inseparable. While segmentation identifies homogeneous groups of potential customers, positioning needs to take into account how customers perceive the competing retail store brands, merchandise offers or services. Both segmentation and positioning research are, therefore, ways of focusing on how customers in a market can be identified and grouped, and then how those customers (segments) perceive the variety of retailers or brands in the marketplace. The furniture maker MFI adopted the strategy of repositioning its retail offer in the late 1980s by the acquisition and use of the Schreiber brand name so that it could sell its higher priced kitchen and bedroom furniture more easily. This complemented its other brands such as its self-assembly Hygena brand, Pronto its low price point products, and Greaves and Thomas and Ashton Dean for upholstery products. The brand segmentation benefits of Schreiber allowed MFI to attract older ABC1 customers and to produce differentiation based upon style and quality. The new brand position can be created by deliberate strategic repositioning.

The use of positioning in marketing shifts the emphasis away from the tangible changes a retailer makes towards the mental perception of the prospective customer. It emphasises the share of mind and judgement of mind based upon brand identity. This is what Ries and Trout (1981) referred to as the 'battle for your mind'. Positioning is the clearest way to establish a distinct place in the minds of the consumer and counteract the proclamations and calls for attention by the competitors.

The market is the ultimate judge of any organisation's work and, although customer perception can be irrational and ill-informed, the way a consumer perceives the brand and the image of the brand is a powerful influence on the way the retail marketplace reacts to different initiatives and changes. In the fluidity of retail market conditions, the more powerful brands will be successful. The challenge, therefore, for any organisation is to position its offer in a way which will be most appealing to the target audience. Market position can also be affected by pricing, distribution and, of course, the product itself.

A firm can position a product to compete head on with another brand. Like for like positioning is relevant if the product's characteristics are at least equal to competitive brands and if the product is priced lower; it may be appropriate, even when the price is higher, if the product's performance characteristics are superior. Conversely, a product may be positioned to avoid competition. This may be the best approach when the product's performance characteristics are not significantly different from those of competing brands, or when that brand has unique characteristics that are important to some buyers. For example, Aldi sells many items which are sold at Tesco but at deeply discounted prices.

Brand strategy is essentially about two variables: the exact composition of the offer made to the market and the part(s) of the market to which the offer is made (that is, brand differentiation and brand segmentation), either of which may provide a competitive advantage. Within this approach brand positioning provides the vehicle to integrate the marketing mix and create overall consumer perception. The Argyll Group decided in the early 1990s to build their business around the positioning of three store brands: Safeway, Presto and Lo-Cost. Safeway was the leading brand, bringing in about 85 per cent of Argyll's profits, and therefore this brand was retained as the major flagship. This use of different brands was in direct opposition to the brand strategies of most of their competitors. The larger stores with the Presto brand were progressively refurbished and rebranded as Safeway stores and this allowed the Presto brand to be related to medium-sized units of around 5000 sq. ft. The Lo-Cost brand was positioned as a discount brand and was made up of the smallest units – around 3000 sq. ft. The positioning of the brands allowed the Safeway brand to compete head-to-head with Sainsbury and, due to the brand rationalisation, it provided a clear positioning statement for its customers.

It can be seen that the positioning process is to make the offer into a clearly defined brand. Ideally the strategist should consider whether the position is:

- apparent to consumers and offers real added value to them;
- built upon real brand strengths which reflect performance potential;
- clearly differentiated from competitor brand positions but not too narrow;
- capable of being understood and communicated to all stakeholder groups;
- able to be achieved, and then defended if attacked by competitors (British Home Stores were unable to position their brand as the first choice for dressing the modern woman and family due to the strength of the Marks & Spencer brand).

The risks of poor positioning

A poorly positioned brand with a fuzzy position or not offering a clear proposition, is likely to be eclipsed or weakened by a stronger competitor. Weak positioning can occur if a retailer consistently cuts a brand's price. The Ratner stratagem of bringing in foreign stock which was cheaper but not hallmarked was at first successful. However, the overstretching of the business in takeovers to expand the brand and then a widely reported statement by Ratner himself that his products were 'crap' led to the demise of the group. Ratner had to leave the company and the brand name was subsequently changed to Signet. In effect, Ratner management had repositioned the brand without thinking beyond the 'price' effect to the 'brand' effect. This led to the alienation of the company's target market.

There are other undesirable consequences of not having the right positioning strategy for a product or service in the marketplace. Among the most common in retail trade are:

- the retail organisation (or its own-label products) may find itself in a position where it cannot escape from direct competition from stronger competitors;

- the retailer may find itself in a position which is weak as demand may be falling and others have left that position knowing there is little customer demand there;
- the retailer's position, or that of its own-label products, is so confusing that nobody knows what its distinctive competence or personality really is;
- the retailer has no apparent position in the marketplace because there is little awareness of the brand or its personality.

PERSONALITY OF A BRAND

As markets have become more competitive and products have only marginal differences in their physical formulation, it becomes more important to create distinction by adding relevant psychological values through advertising, packaging and other aspects of the marketing mix. It is interesting to examine the trend in advertising expenditure for retailers (see Table 9.1). This shows a willingness by major retailers to release large promotional budgets to support their brands. Some of this can be seen to have commenced only in the late 1990s or to have doubled in the case of Boots the Chemist since 1992 to over £37 million, representing a major share of all expenditure shown.

Hankinson and Cowking (1993) define the brand personality as being a unique mix of functional attributes and symbolic values. Functional values are extrinsic, tangible product properties such as 'hardwearing' or 'easy to use'; whereas symbolic values describe intrinsic, intangible properties such as 'friendliness' or 'fun'.

Ultimately, each company needs to find ways of encouraging consumers to build a relationship with a brand for it to have any strength or staying power. This is why *brand*

MINICASE 9.1

Attempt by manufacturers to protect brand positioning

Tesco, the UK's biggest supermarket chain and one of its most respected retailers, was accused of selling counterfeit goods by Tommy Hilfiger, the trendy US fashion label, in what is believed to be the first legal action of its kind in the UK. The US group has issued a writ claiming damages and demanding that Tesco reveal its sources for the £3.5m worth of Hilfiger caps, T-shirts, jackets and other products it began selling at cut prices over Easter. Hilfiger said it had examined the items and believed certain products were not genuine.

'Tommy Hilfiger is a globally respected brand and we owe it to all our consumers that wherever they buy our merchandise they can be sure it is genuine,' said Fred Gehring, Tommy Hilfiger Europe's chief executive. The problem has occurred because most upmarket fragrance and fashion groups refuse to supply UK sources – the 'grey market'. Last year Tesco sold £100m of these products. Until now,

brand owners have tried to block food retailers from selling their products on grounds such as trademark infringement. None has publicly called the grey market products counterfeit. Other supermarket chains said the Hilfiger case would make retailers more cautious. 'Authenticity is a concern,' said one large supermarket chain which has sold grey market products for several years. 'There has been an explosion of people saying they can get you whatever you want at whatever price you want. If you do not know your supplier you are relying very much on what they tell you.' Asda, which sells about £10m worth of grey market perfume a year, said it sourced its products through one trusted supplier. Others said the case illustrated the laxity of procedures necessary to ensure the authenticity of products. A retailer legally only needs a signed assurance from its supplier that the goods are not illegitimately sourced.

Source: Peggy Hollinger, *Financial Times*, 29 May 1998

personality is important and has consequently developed as a term. Well-positioned brands are more effective problem solvers, due to marketing techniques which mould their image into a 'brand personality' that can be understood and accepted.

A strong brand personality is an effective added value at the augmented stage and is reflected in the way consumers describe a brand. The extent to which people perceive

Table 9.1 Advertising expenditure of selected retailers, 1992–98 (£000s)

	1992	1993	1994	1995	1996	1997	1998
Booksellers							
Books Etc.	–	–	–	–	158	169	189
Dillons	577	591	1 900	617	220	173	176
Waterstone's	506	–	–	848	1 150	1 431	2 249
Chemists							
Boots the Chemist	18 816	23 040	26 596	34 850	40 083	38 684	37 660
Superdrug	5 216	6 330	8 141	7 209	6 532	3 117	4 746
Unichem	–	260	1 015	613	514	293	236
Opticians							
20/20 Vision	–	–	530	879	1 155	1 020	1 056
Boots Opticians	1 547	2 937	4 354	2 320	4 885	5 560	6 071
Dollond & Aitchison	2 467	2 310	2 979	4 508	5 658	5 409	4 784
Optical Express	–	–	–	–	676	1 359	2 065
Specsavers	2 198	2 200	5 276	8 588	11 873	15 589	18 286
Vision Express	3 172	4 173	5 250	6 445	6 559	7 881	7 784
Sports shops							
Allsports	–	486	522	930	1 327	1 347	1 068
American Golf Discount	–	206	369	426	453	495	546
Blacks Leisure (First Sport)	–	170	227	193	–	592	735
JD Sport	–	–	–	–	368	263	444
JJB Sports	–	236	534	1 078	1 087	1 380	2 008
Sports Division	710	–	464	1 138	954	3 648	4 050
Toy shops							
Early Learning Centre	–	487	180	751	666	1 085	1 068
Toymaster	360	245	445	766	824	622	619
Toys Я Us	2 939	3 257	3 988	4 592	5 158	5 450	5 571
Jewellery							
Asprey	1 406	996	579	633	2 798	1 387	1 991
Goldsmiths Group	–	–	1 183	1 241	1 509	1 492	1 428
Signet	384	1 302	952	3 160	3 096	1 837	1 856
Photographic stores							
Jessops	685	766	670	450	298	633	605
Tecno	259	–	180	256	313	512	595
Total of above	41 242	49 992	66 334	82 491	98 314	101 428	107 886

Source: ACNielson-MEAL, 1998

and identify brands in different ways is illustrated in the Saatchi and Saatchi Compton Worldwide 1984 Annual Report. This report stated that, 'When probed deeply, consumers described the products they call brands in terms that we would normally expect to be used to describe people. They talk about a brand's persona, its image and its reputation, and it is this "aura" or "ethos" that characterises a brand.' The personality then stands for the *essence* of the corporate or product brand. This essence or personality is the succinct cue that a consumer will use to judge the brand.

CONSUMERS' CONCEPT OF 'SELF-IMAGE'

When consumers choose between brands they rationally consider practical issues about a brand's functional capabilities. At the same time they evaluate different brands' personalities, forming a view which fits the image with which they wish to be associated. When two competing brands are perceived as being equal in terms of their physical capabilities, the brand that comes closest to enhancing the consumer's self-concept will be chosen. Consumers look to brands not only for what they can do, but also to help say something about themselves to their peer groups. Rolex watches are not worn simply for their functional excellence, but also to say something about who the owner is. According to de Chernatony and McDonald (1998), the symbolic nature of brands increases the attraction for consumers as they:

- help set social scenes and enable people to mix with each other more easily;
- enable consumers to convey messages about themselves;
- provide a basis for better understanding of the way people act;
- help consumers to say something to themselves.

In effect, consumers are transmitting subtle messages to others by purchasing and displaying the use of particular brands in the hope that their reference groups decode the messages in a positive and acceptable way. This can be related to the sportswear market in the UK where shoppers identify with the leisure associations of different brands. According to Neely (1997), brand loyalty for sportswear is high in the UK, especially for the upmarket brands which confer a certain cachet. Consumers hold a view of themselves – what is called their 'self-image' – and buy brands which conform to that image. Consumers may be said to admit brands and their 'personalities' into their social circle, in much the same way as consumers enjoy having like-minded people around them. When friends or colleagues admire someone's newly bought brand, that person feels pleased that the brand reinforces his or her self-image and will continue to use the brand. The situation in which consumers find themselves will dictate, to some extent, the type of image that they wish to project. Through anticipating and subsequently evaluating the people that they will meet at a particular event, consumers then seek brands to reflect the situational self-image that they wish to display.

BRAND PROPOSITION

The term 'proposition' is used for a set of statements which summarise the combination of positioning and personality. The proposition allows the brand to emerge from the fuzziness of the competition. However, the secret of success is to have a simple proposition which consumers understand; brand propositions which are complicated or inconsistent will simply confuse consumers.

As part of this concept, two non-functional aspects of brands have been highlighted and are discussed below: *brand image* and *brand identity*.

Brand image

Brands are commonly regarded by consumers as possessing human-like characteristics. These characteristics are projected on them by consumers who experience the brands not only as functional products or services, but also as bundles of associations. Consumers 'see', 'hear', 'smell', 'taste' and 'get gut feelings' about different brands. This profile or 'essence' is called 'brand image'. It represents the consumer counterpart perception of brand personality which, as has been discussed, has to be endowed by the brand marketer. It is important to understand that when a brand image is developed consumers do not judge the image in relation only to other stores, they also adopt best-in-class processes. This means that if other service providers outside of retail – such as British Airways or Marriott Hotels – provide world class standards these can be benchmarked as the best-in-class expectation for the way stores should deal with their customers.

Brand identity

Brand identity is the central concept in promoting a brand. Identity comprises durability, coherence and realism, embodying the personality of the brand. It sends out signals which the consumer decodes and interprets in terms of image. Identity is the solid enduring concept of the brand and is not subject to the idealism, fickleness or opportunism of brand image. A graphic description used is that of the *brand fingerprint*, the unique identity for the company's offering. The power and recognition of brands has become so powerful for some brands that in certain circumstances the brand logo – even without the name – will suffice to provide a clear brand identity. Nike, for example, can rely on its 'swoosh' logo to promote its products. In the UK at least 80 per cent of consumers associate the swoosh with Nike – which is higher than for the recognition of the 'golden arches' as standing for McDonald's (Snowden, 1997).

Figure 9.1 shows the relationship between identity and image.

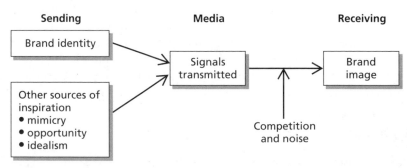

Fig. 9.1 Identity and image
Source: Kapferer, 1992

BRAND NAME

A name also cannot make or break a retailer or company. What matters is how well a retailer's stores, merchandise or services meet its customers' needs. However, a brand name is imbued with associations which conjure up an overall brand image. The choice of a name is only one part of the overall company strategy which has to be backed up by a sophisticated and cohesive branding programme. Consumers normally seek to process only a few rich pieces of information as quickly as possible. Labelling presents shorthand pieces of this information which can highlight key points and facilitate brand choice. A good brand name can communicate a brand's promise and potential. Brand names thus facilitate the consumer purchase decision by acting as a useful and convenient shorthand device. There are instances where there are a number of sub-brands which also act in this shorthand way to confer association with the brand. For example, Big Mac is a coded way of linking a sub-brand to the McDonald's master brand name or Miss Selfridge to that of Selfridges.

Consumers have restrictive cognitive capacities which are protected from information overload by perceptual selectivity. This channels consumers' attention on those attributes considered to be important. To process the minimum of information, consumers develop ways of coping with the extensive – even excessive – information available. It is widely accepted that consumers have a preference for using a brand name above all other informational cues in order to make a decision. There is a school of thought which views the consumer as an efficient information searcher and processor, relying on a brand name as an informational memory device. Through the use of the brand name, the consumer is able to recall numerous attributes, for example quality, availability, guarantee, advertising support, and so on. This emphasises how vital it is for marketing managers to communicate associations for the brand and affect the emotional memory in the consumer's mind in order to form the brand entity successfully. The retailer's name alone, no matter how apt, is not going to ensure a company's success unless there is a well-coordinated marketing and communications programme to build the brand around the name.

BRAND AWARENESS

> People will often buy a familiar brand because they are comfortable with things familiar. There may be an assumption that the brand that is familiar is probably reliable, in business to stay, and of reasonable quality. A recognised brand will thus often be selected in preference to an unknown brand. The awareness factor is particularly important in contexts in which the brand must first enter the evoked set – it must be one of the brands that are evaluated. An unknown brand usually has little chance (Aaker, 1991, p. 19).

Creating awareness of a brand is one of the biggest challenges for marketers; to put their product in a customer's 'evoked set' of brand options. In Fig. 9.2 a customer's evoked set is shown by 'top of the mind' recall; this is the optimal awareness of a brand. This pyramid is only representative as there are no established scales or measurements connected with it, but it does serve as a conceptual framework.

Marketing strategy should take the 'evoked set' into consideration because the actual choices of individual customers depend crucially upon which brands are considered and evaluated by consumers and which are not. According to research it is found that consumers generally carry only a limited number of brands in their 'evoked set' – often no more than three to five brands.

Fig. 9.2 The awareness pyramid

Source: Aaker, 1991, p. 62. Adapted with the permission of the Free Press, a Division of Simon & Schuster, Inc. from *Managing Brand Equity: Capitalizing on the Value of a Brand Name* by David A. Aaker, Copyright © 1991 by David A. Aaker.

Consumers do not necessarily select brands only from their 'evoked set' nor is their selection process logical, but if buyers recall a company's brand first the likelihood of them purchasing it increases. This concept accounts for the enormous amounts of money companies spend in buying out a well-branded competitor, to erase the visibility and reinforcement of alternative brands in the marketplace.

Advertising is often aimed at facilitating the growth of brand awareness. Furthermore, it can develop an image and manipulate consumers' perception, which is fundamental to building values over and above the price–value relationship. Brand advertising communicates the consumer-oriented benefits of owning, displaying or consuming a brand, which increases confidence in the selection process. The process is enhanced by the shopper being provided with bags carrying the store logo. However, the problem facing the marketer is that consumers are selective in their search for brand information and may distort some of the information to ensure it matches their existing beliefs. All brand promotional activity must, therefore, be regularly scrutinised, to gauge the extent to which consumers 'correctly' interpret the desired message.

Good brand advertising ensures that the perceived brand image is not product-based but overrides it in its influence on the target market's mental processes. Brand advertising can also aid repeat purchase and brand loyalty. Advertising's major role is to reinforce and protect brands which, in turn, reinforce and hold market share. The promotion branding role is very much about reinforcing core values and keeping the brand uppermost in the choice process.

MANAGING BRANDS OVER THEIR LIFE CYCLES

Life-cycle theorists believe that a brand is launched, wins market share, enjoys a period of maturity and then declines. These theorists are wrong in so far as they predict an inevitable decline of a brand. The product life cycle refers to the product not the brand. There is no reason why a brand cannot adapt to new technologies and move from mature into relaunch or new growth markets. Therefore, a brand which has been managed properly can extend the timeframe associated with the product life cycle. We may find that well-managed brands are evidence that some brands have longevity. The leading brands are constantly fine-tuned to keep them updated, making it possible for them to survive more than one generation.

Compared to the literature on how to manage a product or service over its life cycle, there is relatively little written about how to manage a brand's image over time. Brands which successfully stand the test of time build up a considerable amount of goodwill with their consumers, so much so that when sales start to fall it should not be automatically assumed that they are in a terminal state and investment must be cut. It is less expensive to revitalise an established brand than it is to develop and launch a new brand consumers are less familiar with. Some brand owners become complacent about their brands, almost preferring to ignore the threat of competitors until it becomes too late. Having lost contact with their consumers, they respond to competitive threats in a less effective manner, for example through pricing.

If a brand is to survive, within the notion of product life cycle, it must first be recognised as symbolising lasting values. An example is Gillette. Its core value in its 90 years of existence had been performance in shaving – it had become a symbol of manhood. In the 1980s disposable razors entered the market, offering convenience and cheapness. Gillette responded according to classical product marketing and introduced its own disposable razor. As a result, the Gillette brand name became subsidiary to the product name and the traditional values attached to the brand were being lost. In order to restore its position, Gillette stopped advertising disposables and emphasised systems. Its successful slogan 'The best a man can get' was an expression of what the Gillette brand had always stood for. To manage a brand properly there is a need to ensure the marketing effort does not endanger the brand's development.

Sales promotion tactics which may endanger brand building

1 While brand-building activities such as advertisements are very much individual creations, sales promotions are easily replicated by competing firms.

2 Strategic activities can be thought of as building up brand loyalty. Sales promotions may be viewed as the reverse: helping to break down competitors' brand loyalty.

3 Sales promotions often cause a Catch-22 situation, in which competitors must retaliate or suffer losses. When a promotions/price-cutting cycle begins it is most difficult to stop; both the customer and the trade become used to it and begin planning their purchases around the promotion cycle – they perceive it as part of the standard product, price or terms of trade. Kotler suggests that 'probably there is risk in putting a well-known brand on promotion more than 30% of the time' (Kotler, 1997). That is why Marks & Spencer almost never have a sale and Harrods only has one a year. They are protecting the brand name and its position.

4 An emphasis on price as a retail strategy can put pressure on organisations to reduce the quality, features and services offered. In extreme situations, a retailer or the merchandise may revert to the status of a commodity as brand added values decline in importance. One danger is that sales promotions can seem even more attractive for their short-term impact, though consumers can quickly become bored with one particular promotion.

5 Sustained sales promotions also cause serious erosion of profitability, which highlights the need to limit them. They can also engender a degree of boredom and acceptability which undermines the impact of the sales promotion effort.

6 Poorly presented sales promotion campaigns may create negative images for the brand. Though sales promotions are not the only brand debilitating device, it remains one of the most visible and often used.

Decisions over branding are strategic issues. The most astute tactical decisions will only build real brand strength if a strategic view underlies all activity. A brand needs to evolve slowly and yet there is the responsibility to consider every response to uncoordinated short-term stimuli. A tactical brand strategy has to be associated with the outcome and impact on the brand. Companies which employ 'brand managers' to cover an individual product line very often have a high turnover in personnel. This may be dangerous as too many changes in advertising strategy or programmes, or in decisions on brand extension, promotion or discounts, confuses distributors as well as consumers. It is significant that brands which have maintained a continuous, consistent message are those belonging to businesses with clear strategies and sustained consistency of brand management. Decisions by these brand managers should have led to successful brands.

SUCCESSFUL BRANDS

Chernatony and McDonald (1998) describe the necessary attributes of a successful brand:

> **A successful brand is an identifiable product, service person or place augmented in such a way that the buyer, or user, perceives relevant, unique added values which match their needs most closely. Its success results from being able to sustain these added values against competitors.**

Successful brands therefore are required to have unique added values. Examples of added value are:

- rituals (Moët et Chandon champagne at celebrations);
- symbols (Perrier as a statement about a sophisticated consumer);
- heritage of good (Kelloggs as a reflection of time-honoured family values);
- aloofness (Carlsberg's time spent brewing and storing);
- belonging (Carling Black Label as one of the crowd);
- legend (Sandeman, St Michael);
- quality and trust (M&S);
- exclusivity (Gucci, Harrods).

To succeed, brand marketers have to ensure that their current added values are appropriate to the preferences of their intended consumers.

Kapferer (1992) introduces the pyramidal model of a brand as a means of successfully managing a brand through time (*see* Fig. 9.3). At the top of the pyramid is the brand's 'core value', its 'essence' or 'kernel'; in the middle are the styles and codes – a brand's specific means of conveying a message in words and images; the lower level represents the brand's communication themes – its current advertising position.

The art of managing a brand over time depends on brand managers being totally aware of what their brand's kernel is and realising that this must not be changed. At the same time, they must beware of two extremes: an 'excess of democracy' – relying too much on the consumer to dictate how the brand should evolve; and 'excess of code' – fear of changing the brand. Kentucky Fried Chicken has faced increased competition during the 1990s from newly launched, chicken fast food outlets as well as from McDonald's and Burger King who have introduced chicken products following the BSE

Permanence

Core values, sources of inspiration or
continuity and identity of the brand

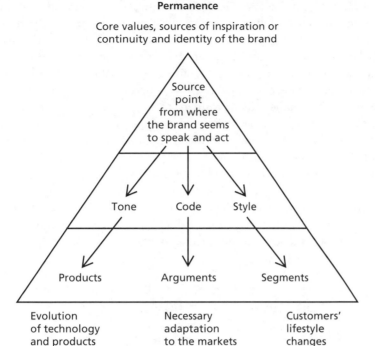

Fig. 9.3 **The pyramidal model of a brand**

Source: Kapferer, 1992

scare. It has also had to contend with the growing problem of fried food being perceived as less healthy. The dilemma was solved by evolving the brand to KFC in order to be able to stand out from the new competition and introducing grilled, baked and rotisserie-cooked chicken.

BRAND UPDATING

Kapferer (1992) maintains that a brand is updated not, as many think, by communication but through its products and meaningful actions. For instance, technical progress alerts the public to a brand's revival and intentions.

Branded products with long histories, for example Kelloggs' various cereals, have been forced subtly to adjust their offerings to keep them relevant to the changing market conditions. For some companies this has been little more than adjusting packaging to update the product; for others it has meant putting the brand's core values in a different context. For example, Lucozade used to promote their drink as providing energy for the sick. When social trends indicated a shift towards a more active population in the early 1980s, Lucozade adapted successfully by presenting the brand as a source of energy for highly active people.

However, updating can have its dangers. It must be undertaken in line with customer expectations. Coca-Cola's move into the caffeine-free Coca-Cola Light was one which achieved consumers' acceptance because the product was essentially unchanged, but the creation of New Coca-Cola, an attempt to introduce a totally new taste, was at odds with the original brand's identity and it had to be dropped.

Some of the largest brand owners have been complacent about their brands in the past, appearing to ignore the changing surrounding environment and the threat of their competitors until it was almost too late. The notion of brand revival was then introduced. Babycham, for example, suffered from its lack of acknowledgement of different social situations and changing consumers. In 1993 the brand was forced to 'grow up' as it entered the decline stage in the product life cycle. Gaymers launched the Babycham revival. The name has remained the same but the product has been reformulated; the packaging has been changed and the well-known fawn logo revised. Brand line extensions have also been introduced to suit different consumer tastes – Xtra Dry Babycham, for example.

Ideally a product should not be allowed to get so close to terminal decline and it must be recognised that initial market research for a brand, however thorough, has limitations in that it only investigates attitudes, beliefs and social norms at that one specific point in time. However successful a brand is, its managers have to be constantly vigilant about potential rivals and their tactics, and need to adapt strategy accordingly.

MINICASE 9.2

Own-label retail branding

A third prong of retailer power, after bigger shops and computerised control of distribution, is own label (known as private label in America). As margins drop and competition intensifies, retailers are becoming ever more aware that selling goods under their own brand-name has two important advantages. The first is that own brands provide fatter margins. The cost of goods typically makes up 70–85% of a retailer's total costs: anything it can shave off that cost must be good business. The second benefit is that own-label goods strengthen a retailer's image with its customers. Since shops the world over increasingly look the same, exclusive products can make a helpful difference. Own label is most developed in Britain where Marks and Spencer is unique among large international retailers in selling only own-label goods – and in food retailing. It accounts for close to 60% of sales at Sainsbury supermarket chain. Own label has helped British food retailers to achieve profit margins averaging 8% of sales which is high by international standards: a typical figure in France and the United States is 1–2%. Britain's lead in own-label goods goes back a long way. Retail co-operative societies pioneered own label during the 19th century. Around the turn of the century Sainsbury began setting up its own farms and food-processing plants to ensure quality and value for its customers as well as higher profits. Weak trade-mark legislation has allowed British supermarkets to sell close copies of manufacturers' brands. In a relatively small, cohesive market food retailing soon became concentrated in a few large hands.

But own label is no longer just a British phenomenon. Across Europe, its share of food retailers' sales is rising steadily. This trend has further to go: for example, Promotes, a large French food retailer, plans to boost its own-label sales from 17% to 26% of its total turnover in the next two years. And supermarkets' own-label products are now challenging some of the world's most powerful brands. In America, private label was long regarded as a cheap and nasty generic substitute for the real thing, rolled out by retailers during recessions and discarded once the economy picked up again. But no longer is that so. Private-label goods' share of total supermarket sales of packaged groceries increased to 19.7% by volume in 1993, from 15.3% in 1988, according to IRI, a market research firm. Just as importantly, the growth came from premium private label – goods that compete in quality with manufacturers' top brands; the share of cheap generics is tiny and declining. Several American supermarket chains have decided to increase or upgrade their private-label programmes, and some of the industry's largest firms are making the fastest progress. Mark Husson, of JP Morgan Securities, a stockbroker, reckons that by the end of the decade private label will account for 27% of American supermarket sales.

Source: Reid. © *The Economist*, London, 4 March 1995

Pricing and brands

In 1993 Philip Morris cut the price of the company's flagship brand of cigarettes, Marlboro, by as much as 25 per cent, to stem the loss of sales and market share to lower priced rivals. City analysts criticised the move as 'killing the brand'. Although the brand dropped in value by £2.4 billion, the real issue in this case was not what it cost, but what it would have cost the company if they had done nothing. Higher price is associated with higher quality and some brands are positioned to be expensive. During the 1980s, price was considered a purely tactical marketing tool. Since 1981, premium lager brand Stella Artois has used the promotional line: 'reassuringly expensive' in its advertising. The phrase explains to the consumer the reason for the brand's high price is the quality of the ingredients.

A more common approach to using price to defend the brand is illustrated in the battle that has been raging between different UK newspapers. Both *The Times* and the *Daily Telegraph* have used price as a short-term weapon to defend market share. However, once a company has decided to embark on the road of using price as a tactical weapon, the process of increasing price is made all the more difficult. In most cases, taking the price war option signifies that the company has failed to build a sustainable competitive edge and price disparities only serve to devalue the brand.

Deciding whether or not to choose price as a marketing tool will depend on the role of the brand within the company's portfolio. For example, it would not be an option for Coca-Cola to introduce price as a weapon against rival colas. The one big advantage that they have is that of image, and their pricing points reflect part of that perception. To destroy that position could lead to commercial and strategic suicide. Richard Branson's Virgin Group attacked the giant cola manufacturers in 1994. The Virgin Cola Brand was launched in November 1994 mainly through Tesco, Iceland and the Thresher chain, with an estimated market share of about 10 per cent (Fagan, 1995). This indicates the strength of the existing Virgin brand in the launch of a new product.

COUNTERFEIT OR COPYCAT BRANDS

Counterfeit trade marks are especially dangerous to brands which rely upon a high price to give them a superior image to the consumer. Cheap imitations lead to proliferation and hence dilute the brand image. Manufacturers are quick to use legislative action wherever possible so as to kill off such imitations. A more generalised threat has been 'copycat' brands which, until recently, have been difficult to fight on legal grounds. These are brands which so closely copy the packaging of an established brand that the consumer is seduced into choosing them, either because they think they are the original brands or because the copy's price is lower and it is assumed represents better value than the original.

However, the Trade Marks Act 1994 gives some protection to the initial brand. Any sign can be registered as a trade mark if it can be represented graphically, and an important new facility is the registration of the shape of goods or their packaging, for example the distinctive prismatic shape of Toblerone or the classic Coca-Cola bottle. The new Act greatly strengthens a trade mark owner's rights. Previously, if a very similar trade mark were used it had to be proved that the public would be confused between the two marks. This is no longer the case. Secondly, a trade mark can be infringed verbally, not just in printed or other physical form. Thirdly, where a trade mark is registered for particular goods or services, and has acquired a strong reputation, the owner of the trade mark can, in some circumstances, prevent it from being used with other goods or services. Finally, action can be taken against a person who applies a trade mark to labelling, packaging or business documents when they ought to know that the use of the trade mark is unauthorised. However, trade mark owners must proceed cautiously before making an allegation since any person who is threatened by court proceedings for registered trade mark infringement without justification is able to seek compensation from the trade mark owner.

OWN BRANDS

On an international basis own-brand retail power is most developed in the UK where Boots, M&S and the supermarkets have led the way. Own brands are the names given to consumer products produced by, or on behalf of, distributors and sold under the distributor's own name or trademark through the distributor's own outlet. The development of own brands has reinforced the position of large-scale concentrated retailers due to the extra control they gain over the value chain. Own brands, sometimes referred to as own-label brands (but this has restricted meaning related simply to groceries), evolved initially as a cheap and inferior alternative to manufacturers' brands. The Co-operative movement in the 1870s initiated the first own-brand products. As time passed own brands grew to replace generic brands, which were commodity foods or household lines which were sold in basic packaging. In the 1970s generic brands were perceived to be similar to own brands and this aided their initial launch. By the late 1980s, own brands had replaced the generic brands which had taken up shelf space and brought in lower margins. With the expansion in the number of supermarkets, own brands became more prolific. This occurred at a time when there was little differentiation in the marketplace and there were a number of similar products. In addition the economic conditions in the late 1980s made consumers more price conscious, while at the same time own brands were improved in relation to their quality and packaging to such an extent that they became brands in their own right. By the 1990s, own brands in Tesco and Sainsbury accounted for over 50 per cent of all sales. The own-brand concept is thus a broader concept than that of manufacturer brands as it embraces both the store proposition and that of individual product lines. It should be remembered that Marks & Spencer's St Michael's clothing, as a brand, had for decades been 100 per cent of all sales. If a retailer such as Marks & Spencer can inspire confidence in a brand as an own-label brand then the company has a distinct advantage in also being able to raise prices. The company is considered to be Britain's largest own-brand retailer but has no manufacturing capacity within its direct span of control. This type of own-label strategy is not easy to achieve and has required Marks & Spencer to have complete domination over its suppliers. The St Michael label was backed by stringent buying and manufacturing specifications. More recently Northern Foods is the supplier for St Michael foods, operating what is termed a mixed brand policy in producing own labels and a number of well-known brands.

The development of own brands may have certain advantages, some of which are listed below.

1 The exclusivity of a good quality own brand, at the right price, can boost store patronage. There is, therefore, the benefit of improved store loyalty due to consumers seeking out a popular own brand.

2 Goods carrying an own label cannot be directly compared on price or attributes in other retail outlets. The result is that own label does not need to be repriced as often as some other lines.

3 If the own brand is well received, the store image is enhanced. In fact, the two reinforce each other as there is a circular reinforcement effect of one on the other.

4 A range of own-brand products which offers advantages over the competition will attract higher levels of custom and lead to the purchase from a wider range of the store's products. This will consequently lead to higher profits through increased sales and the ability to achieve high margins.

5 Own-label products are free from the restrictions which relate to methods of display, promotion or pricing which often apply to manufacturers' brands.

6 Supermarket own brands can become powerful enough for the company to place pressure on some of the major branded manufacturers to make concessions to avoid their brands being delisted.

7 Own brands can be used as a coordinated range or positioned to fill gaps left by the competition. There is also the opportunity to create an own brand which is positioned to appeal to the specific tastes of a store's customers.

8 Launch and distribution costs for new products are far lower than those of conventional manufacturers. The shorter, cheaper route allows for less risk and opens up the market to innovation.

One way that retailers have tried to achieve the advantage of the image of well-known brands is by use of copycat packaging, but the recent Trade Mark Act (as discussed above) will seriously inhibit this and we may see a decline in proliferation of own brands which are hardly distinguishable in packaging and design from their national brand counterparts. Products which are largely image based, such as Coca-Cola, are protected from the threat of price cutting rivals by the consumers' desire to support the status brand. The retailer danger is that consumers will buy rivals' products unknowingly, if they are lookalikes, and that the 'in' brand will shift from being theirs to that of a newer younger rival, for example Virgin.

On the other hand, manufacturers such as Mars are being forced into own-label ventures due to the problems which may face their business if they decide not to co-operate with the larger retailers. However, the own-label phenomenon is probably a serious threat – not only to the survival of a particular brand, but also to the very concept of branding. Manufacturers invest heavily in Research and Development before launching a brand, and the price has to reflect this. If own labels can step in and capitalise on this investment, it is impossible for the initial brand to survive unless the manufacturer can convince the consumer that the price premium is worth paying. This is becoming increasingly difficult as the public acquire a more sophisticated approach to purchasing. The more functional the product, the more threatened it is. For example, BP tried to counteract the price cutting of the new entrant rivals – the multiples – by claiming that BP's petrol contained engine cleaning detergents, but consumers did not acknowledge this product differentiation as important. Within a product category all brands may be perceived as similar and, in this case, all petrol is apparently regarded as essentially the same.

MINICASE 9.3

Problems for own label?

The rapid growth of own-label supermarket goods is over, according to a report published by Corporate Intelligence on Retailing. The £25bn market is still likely to grow from 45 per cent of supermarket sales to 50 per cent over the next five years, but own-label will no longer enjoy the steady growth it once had. The report says own-label may gain ground in some areas where it is under-represented, such as cereals and petfood, and through the fast-growing chilled foods sector. But 'in many areas its share will show little change or may even fall'. Although own-label has been highly profitable for retailers because of the high margins it offers, non-food goods offer potentially higher returns, says the report. Some retailers are reducing the overall number of grocery lines to provide more space for higher margin non-food items. These developments favour retailers with large stores and an established non-foods business, such as Asda and Tesco, says CIR. However, retailers such as J Sainsbury, which is strongly committed to food and own-label goods, face difficult decisions. Of the grocery superstore chains, Sainsbury has the highest proportion of own-label, accounting for 56 per cent of total sales. Own-label makes up 45 per cent of sales at Tesco and Safeway and 37 per cent at Asda. Own-label's position in the mainstream of the market has enabled retailers to exploit the potential of sub-brands. Some retailers have introduced own-label premium and budget brands.

Source: Scheherazade Daneshkhu, *Financial Times*, 2 February 1998

CORPORATE BRANDING

There is a school of thought that believes that brand building will increasingly mean developing the whole company as the brand. The service industries, which include retail, are ideally placed to produce this change because it is difficult for them to sustain a differentiated, competitive product advantage over their competitors. Thus, it will become increasingly important to position organisations as 'brands' in the minds of actual and potential consumers.

According to King (1991), increasingly the company brand will become the main discriminator. That is, consumers' choice of what they buy will depend rather less on an evaluation of the functional benefits to them of a product or service and rather more on their assessment of the people in the company behind it, their skills, attitudes, behaviour, design, style, language, greenism, altruism, modes of communication, speed of response, and so on – the whole company culture could be said to reflect this.

The communication of a company brand is necessarily targeted at a wider variety of 'audiences' rather than simply consumers. Relevant audiences include shareholders, suppliers, government agencies, banks, employees and potential employees, as well as immediate customers. In short, all the company's shareholders. For Hankinson and Cowking (1993) these audiences should understand:

- what the company is;
- what the company does;
- how the company does it.

From a company's point of view, de Chernatony and McDonald (1998) state:

> a characteristic of successful brands is the way that their position has been precisely defined and communicated internally. Everyone working on a particular brand is regularly reminded of the brand's positioning and an integrated, committed approach is adopted, ensuring that the correct balance of resources is consistently applied.

In essence, brand building involves designing and controlling all aspects of a company which may require new initiatives and activities outside of the traditional skills of the marketing department and the agencies that it engages. This is an all-pervasive approach requiring constant and convincing communication with several audiences offering positive images of product or company values, styles and behaviour.

TYPES OF BRAND EXTENSION

A brand can be stretched in the process of product development, by introducing minor product variations (line extension), as in the extension of the Coca-Cola line to include Diet Coke. A report of leading consumer product companies in 1993 found that 75 per cent of new product introductions were line extensions. Another example of the way extension is used is exhibited by the introduction of flanker brands to monopolise shelf space in retail outlets, for example Cherry Coke, Cadbury's Twirl and Procter & Gamble's different washing powder brands. Completely new products can be introduced. A brand may also be stretched in the process of market development, when the original brand (and product) is launched into segments of the existing market and then into new markets (brand leverage) – as in the extension of Yamaha from motorbikes to musical instruments. The Tesco supermarket chain extended its brand to petrol retailing and gained very good publicity for the brand due to low pricing policies and a campaign supporting unleaded petrol.

In many cases, the stretching is a combination of both factors. For example, take the case of Dunhill, where the original brand product (cigarettes) was simultaneously extended into a new segment (pipes), a related product category (lighters), and over time into totally new product sectors (clothing, accessories and cosmetics).

After studying a sample of 276 brand extensions over a long period, Tauber concluded that there are seven types of leverage, which he illustrated graphically (*see* Fig. 9.4).

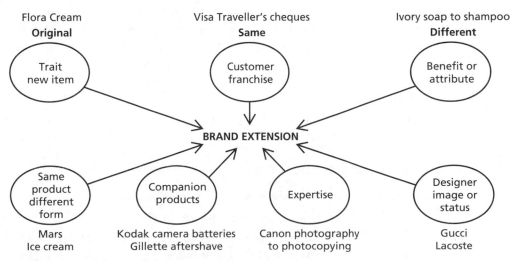

Fig. 9.4 Leverage alternatives for brand extensions
Source: Tauber, 1988

259

Advantages of brand extension

- When market entry barriers are high or rising, brand extension is a means by which a company can achieve growth by capitalising on its existing brand assets.
- It gives ready-made and lower-cost access to an existing distribution and retail operation. For example, traditional menswear brands such as Diesel, Paul Smith and Ted Baker have all incorporated womenswear into their ranges.
- There may be economies in promotion and advertising, since there is no need to build public awareness of the name.
- The use of an existing brand name gives own products or new businesses an instant position and reputation. The customer has an immediate awareness of the brand, and thus has existing confidence transferred to the new product on offer.
- The perceived quality of the existing retail offer is transferred by the customer to the new product.
- A recognisable brand name reassures a prospective purchaser that the retail offer is well supported and hence encourages initial purchases, for example, General Motors or Ford car dealers.

Disadvantages of brand extension

- Brand extension may discourage innovation and may lead to companies producing too many 'look-alike' products.
- The brand extension may weaken the core brand by diluting its appeal, for example Pierre Cardin's extension into too many other product areas.
- The company may waste resources producing products which are very similar to the original, and which may gain their sales at the expense of the original (cannibalisation).
- There is a temptation for the company to rely on the power of the core brand name and hence not give sufficient financial support to the extension.
- Any bad publicity for the original product will affect any other products with the same brand name (spillover). For example, the failure of the Sinclair C5 electric vehicle added to the demise of the company's Spectrum computer range.
- An inappropriate extension in the eyes of the consumer can lead to negative associations, for example Levi's extension into suits, or if a cigarette company extended into health products.
- Research shows that extensions which are successfully launched are seldom as successful as the original brand.

Risks of brand extension

Risk associated with brand extension has two dimensions:

1 the ability of the brand to travel across products;
2 The capability of management to market a new product while not neglecting the core business and overestimating the new brand.

Some markets seem logical and therefore harbour little risk. For example, Paxo's move from supplying dried stuffing mix to other dehydrated food products or Mars' move into ice cream. However, as markets become more competitive, there is pressure for companies to create diverse product portfolios. We have witnessed amazing leaps such as Swatch extending from manufacturing watches to designing cars, and Virgin diversifying into controversial markets such as airline and train transport systems where failure or distrust could have a knock-on effect on other services or products under the Virgin brand name.

Extending successfully

Four brand extension options were identified by Peter Doyle (1989) and are illustrated in the brand positioning grid (*see* Fig. 9.5).

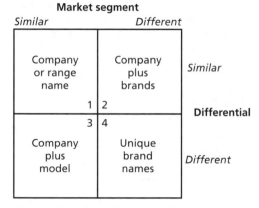

Fig. 9.5 Brand positioning grid
Source: Doyle, 1989

The following is an explanation of the four quadrants of Fig. 9.5.

1 If the brands appeal to the same target segment and have the same differential advantage, then they can safely share the same company name or range. Here, there is consistency in the positioning strategies.
2 If the differential advantage is the same but the target market differs, then the company name can be extended because the benefit is similar. However, it is important to identify the group.
3 If a company has differential advantages, then it should use separate brand names.
4 If both the target customers and the differential advantages are different, then using unique brand names is the most appropriate strategy.

Studies have shown that groups of related products reinforce the brand, particularly where technical expertise is important and perceived to be so. Consumers categorise goods or services in their purchase decision and transfer attitudes associated with a core brand to its extensions. An extension into a separate category has less risk of a resulting negative feedback on the core brand than when the extension is very similar to the core brand. Keller and Aaker (1992) report that high quality brands stretch further than those of average quality. The stronger the brand, the easier it is to extend it into diverse product areas. The question to ponder is how tolerant the customer is if the product differs from the core brand. Toyota did not believe that new product positioning can be achieved by stressing the attributes of the extension; in trying to capture the more luxurious sector of the car market, Toyota believed that a brand extension into a quality position would not be successful. The company, therefore, launched the Lexus brand in order to enter the quality marketplace.

Recent research has shown that a brand name which has a strong association with functional benefits can be extended more readily into product areas which are themselves bought for functional benefits. Similarly, if the original brand is more linked to prestige then it may be extended into a product field also bought for its prestige. For example, a Timex watch which has functional associations would extend readily into stop watches, whereas a Rolex brand might be extended to luxury clocks.

Problems may appear when attempting to move a brand down the income scale rather than up it. However, attempting to move a brand to a higher income group is possibly the most risky form of brand stretching because it involves stretching consumers' perceptions. In such cases the management strategies have to be carefully planned for such a move.

CONCLUSION

In order to maintain a brand successfully, it is essential that its managers thoroughly understand its intrinsic properties – its core values, added value, its positioning, proposition, personality, image, and identity – and constantly update themselves on consumer concepts of their brand in relation to others. Any modification of the store brand or offer must be in line with customer expectations of the original positioning.

Branding is a necessary feature of the marketplace because without brand management there would be no strategies to understand the essence and position of the retail operation. The ultimate aim of management must be that of brand strength and immortality. Such an aim requires adaptation of the brand to the new and evolving demands of customers, competitive moves and the changing marketplace.

New legislation has strengthened the hand of manufacturers in defending their brands against counterfeits and copycat products. However, own-label entrants are one of the most exciting changes taking place. If an own-label brand is very similar in packaging to an existing brand, it does seem unfair to benefit from the reputation of the original brand without having had the expense of development and launching. Another key trend is brand extension. This enables companies to introduce new products and product modifications to new and existing customers. However, their success cannot be guaranteed, and it is important that there is a perceived quality and 'fit' with the core brand. The range of products currently offered may also influence the success of the extension – very similar extensions succeed in narrow ranges, whereas wide ranges can sustain more variety in the extensions. Even the strongest brands have boundaries and the art of brand extension is fully to exploit a brand's possibilities without overstepping the boundary limits.

EXERCISES

The exercises in this section relate to the management of a retail brand. It is advised that you work through them before moving on to Chapter 10.

1 Write down a list of brands or stores you believe you will always patronise. Now refer to the theory you have read to compile a list of reasons for the strength of the brands you have listed.

2 Do you believe that own-brand products will be even more successful in the future, and if so why? What reactions do you think manufacturers will have to these changes in terms of defensive strategies?

3 List all the high street women's clothes stores you can. Then interpret where you believe each of the brands to be positioned and whether some positions are over- or under-subscribed. Does this indicate opportunity or risk for existing retailers?

4 What brands have launched (extension strategy) new products or retail concepts which do not fit easily with the core brand? Were they successful? If not, why not?

5 How does Chanel perfume keep its brand strength – can marketing ensure there is more to a brand than simply a name? Use the following grid as a guide.

Consideration of Chanel attributes:	Identify the marketing approach:
• distribution • promotion • pricing • range and position of products • others (list)	

Now discuss what you have learned about the success, or otherwise, of Chanel which could be applied to a high street fashion retailer.

REFERENCES AND FURTHER READING

Aaker D.A. (1991) *Managing Brand Equity: Capitalising on the value of a brand name.* New York: The Free Press.

Aaker, D.A. and Biel, A.L. (1993) *Brand Equity and Advertising.* Lawrence Erlbaum Associates.

Daneshkhu, S. (1998) 'Growth slows for own-label goods', *Financial Times*, 2 February

Davies, G. (1992) 'The two ways in which retailers can be brands', *International Journal of Retail and Distribution Management*, 20 (2), 24–34.

de Chernatony, L. and Daniels, K. (1994) 'Developing a more effective brand positioning', *The Journal of Brand Management*, 1 (6), 373–9.

de Chernatony, L. and McDonald, M.H.B. (1998) *Creating Powerful Brands.* 2nd edn. Oxford: Butterworth-Heinemann.

de Chernatony, L. and McWilliam, G. (1989) 'The varying nature of brands as assets', *International Journal of Advertising*, 8 (4), 339–49

Doyle P. (1989) 'Building successful brands: the strategic options', *Journal of Marketing Management*, 5 (1), 77–95.

Fagan, M. (1995) 'Virgin steps up cola campaign', *Independent*, 3 January, 26

Hankinson, G. and Cowking, P. (1993) *Branding in Action: Cases and strategies for profitable brand management.* London: McGraw-Hill.

Hollinger, P. (1998) 'Hilfiger sues Tesco over "counterfeit" goods claim', *Financial Times*, 29 May.

IGD (1996) *Brands: Their future on the supermarket shelf. A survey of retailers' and manufacturers' attitudes to brands.* Institute of Grocery Distribution, Watford: IGD Business Publications.

Jary, M. and Wileman, A. (1997) 'Retail brands. Is this the real thing?' *Retail Week*, 11 July, 12–13.

Kapferer, J.N. (1992) *Strategic Brand Management: New approaches to creating and evaluating brand equity*. London: Kogan Page.

Keller, K.L. and Aaker, D.A. (1992) 'The effects of sequential introduction of brand extensions', *Journal of Marketing Research*, 29 (1), 35–50.

Key Note (1993) *Own brands: A market sector overview*. 5th edn. Hampton, Middlesex: Key Note Publications.

King, S. (1991) 'Brand building in the 1990s', *Journal of Marketing Management*, 7 (1), 3–13.

Kotler, P. (1997) *Marketing Management: Analysis, planning, implementation and control*. 9th edn. London: Prentice-Hall.

Meyers, H.M. (1994) 'The role of packaging in brand line extensions', *The Journal of Brand Management*, 1 (6), 348–56.

Monk, H. (1997) 'Gentlemen prefer brands', *Retail Week*, 17 January, 5.

Neely, J. (1997) *UK Fashion Report*. London: EMAP Fashion.

Reid, M. (1995) 'Survey of retailing (4): Make it your own – Own label is good for profits, good for the image and good for consumers. No wonder it is spreading', *The Economist*, 4 March.

Ries A. and Trout J. (1981) *Positioning: The battle for your mind*. London: McGraw-Hill.

Rubenstein, H. (1996) 'Brand first management', *Journal of Marketing Management*, 12, 269–280.

Snowdon, R. (1997) 'No name – just images', *The Times*, 30 September, 29.

Tauber, E.M. (1988) 'Brand leverage: strategy for growth in a cost-controlled world', *Journal of Advertising Research*, September, 26–30.

Vishwanath, V. and Mark, J. (1997) 'Your brands best strategy', *Harvard Business Review*, May/June, 123–9.

10 The applications of IT to retail marketing

This chapter should enable you to understand and explain:

- how retailers add value to their business through the use of IT;
- the use of IT to improve marketing and merchandising performance;
- the role of customer databases in developing effective retail marketing;
- the contribution of data communications to improved retail performance;
- the Internet, multimedia and future IT trends likely to have an impact on retail businesses.

THE GROWING ROLE OF IT IN RETAILING

A visit to any large store will show that information technology (IT) has become a vital part of retailing. The laser-scanners used in most grocery supermarkets and superstores to read product bar codes are among the most distinctive examples of modern computer technology. These are merely the *visible* components of substantial investment by retailers in extensive computer and high speed communications networks which collect and exchange data between stores, distribution centres, suppliers and head offices. Such networks are not the sole preserve of large companies. The relative costs of IT systems have fallen considerably in recent years, enabling retailers of any but the smallest in size to purchase IT.

The use of IT is expected to grow rapidly. Management Horizons (1995), one of the largest retail consultancies, has argued:

> In the next ten years, [information] technology will become a virtual prerequisite to successful competition. Retail-supplier partnerships will depend on technology, substituting information for inventory in the pipeline to reduce costs while improving productivity. Retailers will rely on technology to establish links with customers through electronic retailing and customer relationship marketing. And manufacturers increasingly will use technology to reach consumers directly in their homes and on the selling floor.

The success of many companies may be related to the way they have improved the operation of their business through investment in technology. The significant contributions to efficiency can be directly related to the application of scanning and stock control systems, data interchange and management support systems. Modern technology is transforming the retail environment and has helped many companies expand their operations.

265

INFORMATION TECHNOLOGY – SOME EXPLANATIONS AND DEFINITIONS

IT, or information technology, refers to the

> **technology of the production, storage and communication of information using computers and micro-electronics.**

IT concerns both the *equipment* used to produce, store and communicate information and the business uses or *applications* to which IT is put. It requires '*Hardware*' (the term used for the equipment which handles data, using computer equipment). *Mainframes* are the largest computers used to run major systems, with specialised software often produced by the mainframe supplier or by closely associated companies. *Minicomputers*, as the name suggests, are smaller computers with much of the power of mainframes but which can use commercially available packages, representing considerable savings in cost and development time. *PCs* or personal computers vary in computing power from those which are simply advanced word processing devices to being small computers capable of running an electronic point of sale (EPOS) system or store administration system. Each system will normally have *terminal equipment* (often known simply as *terminals*), which is the equipment at each end of a computer system used to input data (via a keyboard or from reading a barcode) or to display data output on a screen, store it or print it out as text or graphs (paper copies, known as *hard copy*).

There is also *software* which refers to the instructions used to control the way IT hardware will accept data input, and then process, store and communicate that data. Another term also used is *communications*, which concerns the equipment (including any cabling) and software used to transmit data between computers within a store or across a wide distance.

Although the phrase 'information technology' may seem to focus mostly on computer hardware, in this book we follow current usage to cover both computer equipment and the business applications of IT. The context of IT is primarily about how it can be used to help solve retail business problems. A simple case below illustrates the advantages of IT to a retailer of modest size. The bigger the retailer, the more necessary the application of IT.

Example: Grantham Fashions Ltd, Reading

Grantham Fashions Ltd is a chain of five clothing shops. Each store is equipped with a PC which holds information about the stock in the store by item and by range, size and colour. When an item is sold to a customer, the barcode on the label is read by a hand-held device and the item deducted from the shop's stock. Overnight, the sales information on each store's computer is downloaded automatically over an ordinary telephone line to the company computer in the main store.

Every morning the owner of Grantham Fashions is able to review the previous day's sales performance of every one of her stores. When deciding how much to order, she has available the weekly and monthly sales figures for each type of article last year and this year. She is able to spot product lines that are selling very well in the first few days and quickly place 'top-up' orders with her suppliers. She can also reallocate stock between different branches to ensure that every store has an appropriate range of sizes or colours of each range.

The computer is also used to maintain the company accounts, calculate the wages and bonuses of every employee, and holds customer information used to keep in touch with the best customers.

When the owner had only two stores she was able to act as manager for both of them as well as doing all the buying and her own marketing. With five stores she has found that the only way she can keep tight control on all her stores as well as buying is through her computer system, although she still visits every store at least twice every week.

IT FOR COMPETITIVE ADVANTAGE

Grantham Fashions Ltd, like Tesco and Sainsbury, uses IT to carry out basic functions including till systems for selling items, capturing the sales data by item, stock control, buying, management reports, customer information, and accounting. The main uses of IT in retailing are shown in Fig. 10.1. However, the most advanced retailers attempt to use IT to give them competitive advantages over their rivals. For IT to provide competitive advantage it needs to cut costs, differentiate the retailer's service offer, or provide innovation in ways that are prized by the customer.

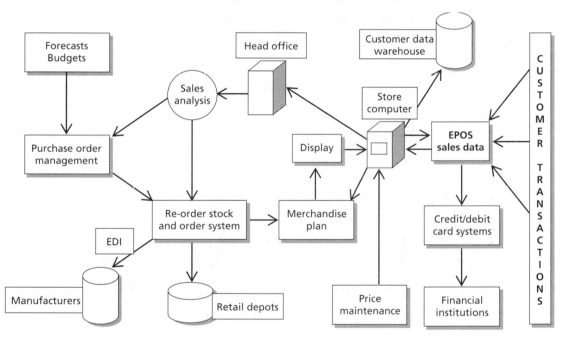

Fig. 10.1 A retail IT system

Lowe and Wrigley (1996) suggest that since the 1970s there have been three main ways in which retailers have used IT, 'positioning themselves at the cutting edge of technological development' compared with manufacturers. These are:

1 investment in IT combined with organisational changes, improved retail logistics, reducing delivery lead times, resulting in a progressive reduction in retailer inventory holdings;

2 better information about consumer demand supported retail policies in own-brand, product development, and the refocusing and redefinition of many of the most successful firms;

3 retailers have cut their labour costs by effective staff scheduling and by using more part-time and casual staff. They were able to use IT to measure staff performance, enabling costs to be further reduced by virtue of the information relating to transactions and performance levels.

IT is having a major impact on the modern retail business. The benefits of article bar coding, combined with the advent of EDI (Electronic Data Interchange), creates phenomenal efficiencies for the retailer, as are listed below.

Cost and productivity benefits:
- efficiency of time/transaction speed increases;
- reduced queuing times;
- operating cost reductions, e.g. less ticketing;
- increased accuracy of all aspects of the sales transaction;
- improved administration/invoices;
- no new keying required;
- shorter lead-times;
- reduction in stockouts and stockholding;
- pricing can be changed easily and accurately.

Marketing benefits:
- improved data – effectiveness of promotions, forecasts of sales, stock records, etc.;
- faster distribution cycle system;
- improved trading partner relationship;
- ability to incorporate faster responses to changing market conditions;
- consumer benefits from efficiencies of the operation, e.g. shorter queues;
- can lead to the building of loyalty schemes and databases;
- additional selling space due to reduced stockholding.

There are a variety of ways in which retailers may seek to gain competitive advantage from IT. The most important are discussed in the following text.

Automating processes

Automating a process may cut costs, increase accuracy, reduce processing times, enable decisions to be made more quickly, and speed up customer service.

Example

Electronic point of sale, or EPOS, which uses scanning systems to charge accurate prices, enables checkout staff to work faster, and, in a food environment, eliminates the need to apply price labels to individual items. All these factors cut labour costs. Accurate 'shopping basket' data can be collected and stored for analysis.

Collecting data about the customer

Data about what individual shoppers buy is collected, collated and analysed. The purchasing patterns of different types of shopper can be analysed, assisting decisions about ranging, product extension or promotions. (*Note*: The Data Protection Act limitations operate across the EU, where data cannot be exported unless the receiving country has an equivalent level of restriction on the processing of the data.)

MINICASE 10.1

The use of IT for retail development

In the increasingly competitive retailing sector, advances in IT systems such as data mining, multimedia kiosks and web-based commerce are helping businesses differentiate their services and enabling them to develop closer relationships with their customers. 'Expenditure on IT in European retail markets is booming as cut throat competition drives retailers to use technology to cut costs and help retain customer loyalty,' said Datamonitor. According to Datamonitor, retailers in the six largest West European countries spent $10.8bn on IT systems in 1997, a figure which is expected to rise to $16.3bn by 2002. Within those totals, retailers in Germany spent over $3bn on IT last year – the highest spending in Europe – but will be overtaken by UK-based retailers who are expected to spend $5.3bn in 1998 on IT. Retailers, already under tremendous pressure on margins, are trying to reduce labour costs, improve customer retention and fine-tune pricing and inventory. To achieve this, they are deploying IT systems ranging from demand forecasting and logistics software, to self-scanners, electronic labelling systems and huge data warehouses. 'There is already a sustained pressure in the retail supply chain to reduce cost and this trend is set to continue,' says IBM, one of the leading suppliers to the retail sector. According to a recent Harvard Business Review study, the cost of carrying inventory for a year is equivalent to at least a quarter of the price retailers pay for the product. Therefore a two-week inventory reduction represents a cost saving of nearly 1 per cent of sales and a significant boost to profits. At the same time, retailers are using IT systems to personalise their offerings and switch from 'demand-led' to 'customer-focused' strategies in an attempt to differentiate their services and retain customer loyalty. IBM has launched a business intelligence initiative aimed in part at helping retailers develop 'relationship management' strategies. Business intelligence involves collecting, cleaning and organising the vast amounts of data available from point-of-sale systems, loyalty cards and other sources into a 'data warehouse', and then using analytical tools to extract real value from the data. At the same time, loyalty cards – increasingly likely to be smart cards rather than magnetic stripe cards – are being used to boost what analysts call 'frequency of shop', especially in the food retailing sector. When electronic point-of-sale (EPOS) systems were introduced over a decade ago, they were mostly used for stock control and inventory management. Now, the data is used to identify trends and target consumers. Retail-based data warehouses, such as those installed by NCR, the market leader, manage the records of transactions from a variety of processing systems and information sources such as electronic cash registers, inventory systems, weather records and customer demographics. They then enable users such as store managers to query the database. Wal-Mart, the US retail chain which claims to operate the world's largest commercial data warehouse, uses the vast amounts of information stored there to guide its business. It is expanding the warehouse, based on the NCR Teradata system, from 7.5 terabytes to more than 24 terabytes – the equivalent of 6bn pages of text. 'Every cost, every item is carefully analysed, enabling better merchandising decisions to be made on a daily basis.'

Clearly, the Internet, and the World Wide Web in particular, represents another emerging channel. Many early entrants in the home shopping arena have been slow to take off or have failed. However, Christmas 1997 saw a rapid increase in Internet-based consumer commerce in the US. A Cap Gemini sponsored survey of European retailers published in March, 1998, suggested over the next decade, 'Internet shopping will steadily build for traditional store-based retailers to 14 per cent of total sales, and just over half of home shopping sales.' If such forecasts prove correct, Web-based electronic commerce could bring about radical changes in retailing.

Source: Paul Taylor, *Financial Times*, 17 March 1998

Example

Loyalty card databases hold customer demographic information and the addresses of cardholders. These entries can be linked to transactions data provided by EPOS to show what particular customers buy. Specific offers can be made to certain types of customer. Boots the Chemist launched its first mail order catalogue, *Mother and Baby*, by sending copies to all loyalty cardholders who had bought baby products from Boots in the previous year.

Feedback on marketing decisions

EPOS data can be analysed to show quickly the effects of promotions, prices, new products, and packaging changes. The impact of changing the layout, or merchandising, of stores can be rapidly assessed in terms of category sales, competitor brands, gross profit and sales elsewhere in the store. New ideas and concepts can be carefully tested against marketplace realities.

Example

The DIY company B&Q has a rigorous policy of using its EPOS data to evaluate its promotions, enabling it to calculate customer price responsiveness for core and seasonal products at different times of the year. This enables the company to plan its promotions more effectively and predict the outcomes with accuracy.

Communications

Stores can communicate with suppliers and send documents such as purchase orders, stock and sales information over third-party communications networks. Once known as electronic data interchange (EDI), the term e-commerce (electronic commerce) is now preferred. Electronic systems are cheaper and faster than paper-based systems, so that many stores trigger immediate replenishing or only need to place their orders 24–48 hours in advance, compared with seven days earlier with traditional ordering methods. Store computers also transmit daily EPOS data and other information to head office so that senior managers are more in touch with the performance of every store and product group, and can respond appropriately.

Example

In the Tesco Stores Group stock replenishment occurs automatically, made possible by a computer system which receives daily EPOS data from each store, generates the next day's stock requirement using a computer model of predicted sales, and sends the requirement electronically overnight to the distribution centre for picking and delivery the next day. The *lead time* (the time between sending an order and receiving the merchandise) has been slashed. This system has allowed Tesco, over five years, to halve the amount of stock it carries and improve the freshness of its product on offer to the consumer.

Tools to plan the business

Sophisticated computer software systems may help retailers to plan, budget and forecast, to choose the most successful locations, and to control their business. Expert systems can model decision making, statistical application can forecast sales, data mining tools can extract and analyse information in a database, and neural networks can 'see' changing patterns in complex data.

Example

Retailers use geographic information systems (GIS), which draw on socio-demographic data by postcode, along with company transaction data, and intelligent analytical tools to forecast the likely turnover of stores in different locations. The large food retailers are so accurate that they expect to hit their initial target and to be trading profitably within the first year.

Adding value to the retail transaction

IT-assisted transactions may be preferred to 'traditional' retailing because they provide at least some customers with the benefits of greater transactional speed, accuracy and convenience. The use by bank customers of automated teller machines (ATMs or 'hole-in-the wall' cash machines) demonstrates that this is not an illusion.

Example

Safeways in the UK and Albert Heijn in The Netherlands are the European pioneers of self-scanning for customers. On entering the store, the customer collects a small handscanner, which is used to read the item bar code before putting the goods into the shopping trolley. Customers can go at their own pace, they can check the accuracy of the prices they are being charged, they can change their minds and replace merchandise back on the shelves, and there are virtually no queues.

When they finish shopping, a quick check on the items purchased may be made, the customer pays the member of staff and leaves the store.

Technologically-enabled shopping

Selling goods over the Internet or from multimedia kiosks is likely to become increasingly important. A kiosk is a free-standing enclosure designed to match the decor of the store or sales area. Inside is a powerful computer operated through a touch screen. The customer can order goods and arrange delivery through the system. Retailers who have derived few competitive advantages from IT so far, will find it hard to trade up into the electronic future. It will need expertise, patience, commitment, and considerable resources to fund long-term development. Selling from the Internet is probably the most exciting new development of recent years.

Example

Amazonbooks.com has become the world's largest retail bookseller selling 2 million different titles only over the Internet. As a *virtual* bookseller it has no stores, only a series of pages on the World Wide Web. It has therefore merged the role of the wholesaler/distributor and retailer. The business strength is that all they need is a massive warehouse and no shops as their business is Web based. The marketing benefit is the lower prices they can pass on to the customer because of their shorter and more cost-effective supply chain. They have succeeded, based upon Porter (1980), due to a generic strategy of industry-wide differentiation and having smaller overheads than their rivals. The company have questioned existing accepted ways of doing business and are specialising in a commodity item market.

Further reinforcement of the powerful role of IT in business has been developed by Porter and Millar (1985). They felt that new technology was transforming the nature of products, processes, companies, industries and even competition itself. Companies could not stand aside from the massive changes that were going on and survive indefinitely. Porter and Millar's *transformational* view of IT is currently widely accepted.

Limits to using IT for competitive advantage

IT was originally used by retailers to automate central services such as finance, payroll, and management accounts. The first EPOS systems appeared in the 1970s, usually in department stores which were large enough to be able to justify a computer installation. The use of EPOS across most retail markets did not occur until the mid-1980s, and even the largest and most IT-committed retailers did not complete the installation of EPOS in all their stores until the early 1990s. Retailing is a highly dispersed business and the cost for retailers of providing elaborate IT equipment in all their stores has been high. Complex systems are required to handle the large number of product lines and the wide range of purposes the systems are to serve. Only the very largest store can afford to employ computer specialists, therefore systems have to be designed which require little maintenance and can be used in stores where no one may know much about computers. Thus the costs, both of routine investment in automating processes (such as EPOS) and the *transformational* IT investment, may be simply too high for many retailers. Moreover, the more adventurous and radical the IT investment, the longer it may take to garner the rewards. Many IT projects fail and the risk of a novel application failing may, again, be too great for many companies to contemplate.

Professor John Dawson (1994) felt that there was little evidence that European retailers made sufficient use of IT to transform their businesses. He argued that large European retailers devoted proportionately smaller amounts of their budgets to IT than manufacturers, and from this stated that many retailers were untouched by significant involvement in IT. It was found that they concentrated on operational improvements rather than transformational ones, and that the expected pay-offs from IT had not been fully realised.

Effective use of IT

IT is not a single event or product and this will also limit the ability of many retailers to gain the maximum competitive advantage from IT. 'Computerisation' is usually dependent upon many other changes in related IT and processes. Getting the full benefits of IT may take a long time while the retailer attempts to *learn* how best to exploit the new systems. Although many UK grocers invested in EPOS in the 1980s, they were able to make little effective use of information about patterns of individual customer shopping behaviour (called 'shopping basket data' in grocery) until the late-1990s when cost-effective ways of creating and analysing masses of data became available. It has taken Tesco seven years of heavy investment and learning from experience to create one of the most advanced IT-based stock replenishment systems, using EPOS sales data, expert forecasting systems, and electronic data communications. Powell and Dent-Micallef (1997) investigated the linkages between information technology (IT) and the performance of firms. Their research examined the IT literature and included a retail study; they found that IT alone has not produced sustainable performance advantage in the retail industry, but that some firms have gained advantages such as flexible culture, strategic planning-IT integration, and improved supplier relationships. This underlines the point that the real advantage lies in people and systems rather than systems alone.

Obtaining the full competitive advantages from IT requires long-term investment in an IT strategy which supports the retailer's strategic direction. It is likely to involve not simply heavy investment in one or two applications but continuous investment and improvement in most functional areas where IT can add value.

CAPTURING DATA AT THE POINT OF SALE

To be able to plan effectively there is a need to collect timely data on retail transactions, which may be fulfilled in a variety of ways.

Retail data capture (or data collection) of every sales transaction at the point of sale is one of the most important elements of retail IT, whether data capture occurs through an EPOS (electronic point-of-sale) device or is directly entered into a computer using a keyboard. It provides accurate information about customer purchases, the sales of individual merchandise lines and other data the retailer wishes to capture, such as how the customer has paid for the item, a loyalty card reference, the time and date of transaction, the sales assistant and amount spent.

This means that for marketing purposes, the likely performance of new product lines can be assessed quickly by using a number of well-located trial stores. The impact of new lines upon the sales of other products can also be measured by comparing how sales of different lines have changed in the trial stores and in control stores. Many retailers offer an EPOS-based service to manufacturers, which allow them to market test the impact of new products in their stores. The effect of a new promotion may be analysed in the same way. There are many retailers with pronounced seasonal sales for whom rapid feedback about new product lines is not merely important, it is vital. To know exactly how well or badly the new season's colours or designs are selling in the first week enables merchandisers and buyers to turn provisional orders into firm orders and to make purchases in the Far East with confidence. Mistakes may still be made, but EPOS data can provide buyers with accurate and timely information.

Extensive, timely and accurate sales data generated by EPOS systems have become a critical source of marketing information for retailers and supplier marketing departments. Data communication is a normal, though not essential, part of an EPOS system. It allows sales and other data to be passed to head office on a daily or even more frequent basis, and price amendments, other data and messages also to flow between the store and head office.

Data capture involves three elements on a practical level:

- a coding system;
- a code symbology;
- the means used to capture the data in a form that can be fed to the computer.

Coding systems

The retailer must decide how merchandise will be coded. In practice, this usually involves the retailer deciding whether to use the dominant European Article Numbering (EAN) system using 13 digits (EAN13), which has become the international standard, or to develop a different one (*see* summary of EAN below). The code structure adopted must uniquely identify every product line to prevent confusion (and pricing errors). *Velocity codes*, now relatively rare, are short codes used for the best-selling lines which are committed to memory by till operators.

Code symbology

How will this code be represented in machine-readable form? Retailers who use EAN will naturally expect manufacturers to deliver merchandise to them already barcoded. The EAN13 code is omni-directional which means that it can be presented to the scanner in any direction and be successfully read in any orientation. Where retailers have adopted their own coding system, they usually adopt a version of EAN13. There are also new symbologies, just starting to be introduced at the end of the 1990s, which can represent considerably more data within a comparatively small space. Such new systems include *snowball*, a two-dimensional symbology that is read vertically as well as horizontally. For most retailers, however, the use of the international standard, EAN, will provide considerable benefits.

Data capture

There are several options available to the retailer in capturing sales data. Although the price of laser scanners has fallen, it is still a considerable investment for retailers to adopt a policy of high-speed automatic data entry. Scanning systems provide the best pay-off in supermarket or mass merchandising environments. These require fast transaction speeds for high densities of relatively low-cost products. Data can also be captured automatically by using a hand scanner or some other portable device (for example, a light wand). Alternatively, the item code can be captured manually by keying the product identification numbers into the cash till or computer keyboard. On each occasion a sale is registered, the retailer will have captured on a decision support system the brand name, size, colour, and price – and perhaps details of the individual if a loyalty card is utilised. This information can be combined with other forms of market research to help the retailer improve both marketing and retail planning decisions.

At the point of transaction, credit or debit cards need to be read. Computerisation of credit card transactions has created a more efficient and secure way for retailers to accept payment. In addition, retailers realise the advantage of increased sales due to accepting credit cards as the higher the cost of the merchandise the more likely it is that a credit card will be used. Credit card and debit card information (and most loyalty card information) is coded on the reverse of the card using magnetic stripe technology (soon to be replaced by smart card technology) which can be read (or decoded) only by specialist devices called card-swipes. As third party cards do not allow the retailer to capture address lists, a phone number or address code is often requested as a means to build lists or add to market intelligence.

Most standard bar codes do not include prices, they simply identify the merchandise. If the merchandise price is kept on file within the EPOS terminal or the central store computer, then the correct price is automatically entered every time the bar code is read. This system of *price look up* (PLU) saves the need to price mark goods and is much faster than entering prices individually. PLU systems make it easier for the retailer to amend prices – only the shelf edge label and the computer need to be changed. Some non-food retailers have taken advantage of this facility to create extra excitement in-store by reducing prices for 30 minutes or an hour. Newer EPOS systems allow multiple purchase promotions to operate automatically – with the EPOS system re-calculating the correct price for a multi-save, buy-one-get-one-free, or linked transactions – thus enabling the retail marketer to be more adventurous with pricing mechanisms.

European Article Numbering Association

The most prevalent coding system is that administered by the European Article Numbering Association (EAN), set up in 1977. There are now 79 national associations covering 85 different countries. These associations allocate random 13 digit codes (EAN 13) to manufacturers and retailers to identify their products. The first two digits represent the issuing organisation (the UK Article Numbering Association (ANA) has the code 50, France is 32, the USA is 00). Digits 3–7 represent the manufacturer or company marketing the product, digits 8–12 identify the product and digit 13 is a check digit to ensure the code has been entered correctly. In North America a 12-digit code (Universal Product Code or UPC) is used, but this is compatible with EAN 13.

Shorter EAN codes have been introduced for particular purposes, such as fashion where 8 digit code labels (EAN 8) are more compact than EAN 13 labels. Some retailers and manufacturers wish to encode additional data, such as batch numbers, sell-by dates, or other information needed by the retailer. There is an agreed EAN standard for coding this supplementary information, using a bar code symbology known as Code 128.

Publishers have a coding system of their own (International Standard Book Number (ISBN)). Prices may be included using a five digit supplementary code. A related system is used for newspapers and periodicals (International Standard Serial Number (ISSN)).

EAN has established many standards including the traded unit code, ITF14, which is used on outer packaging to represent the identification numbers. EAN coding systems and standards are also widely used for exchanging data such as orders and consignment data using a common standard called EANCOM.

DATABASE MARKETING, DATA MINING AND BUSINESS INTELLIGENCE

A database is a computer system used to store and analyse large volumes of data. Data relating to item sales, customer information, and the range of goods bought by customers can be held on a database and used for marketing purposes. A department store can develop a specialised catalogue aimed at affluent customers with teenage daughters. Postcodes uniquely identify a small location and the demographic information available commercially for each postcode area (for example from CACI) will allow the department store to target affluent areas with a degree of precision. Customers of bookshops who mainly buy management books can receive mailings of the retailer's management offerings along with something more frivolous, such as a selection of thrillers or humour. In practice, retailers have found it difficult and expensive to target customers with precision.

Example: Wal-Mart, USA

Analysis of its shopping basket EPOS data stored on its data warehouse showed Wal-Mart that sales of beer and nappies were linked and that joint sales were highest on Friday evenings. The company's reasoning was that males were buying nappies on their way home and were stocking up on beer at the same time. When beer and nappies were merchandised next to each other the sales of both soared. Wal-Mart, America's largest and fastest growing retailer – and its most famous exponent of data warehousing – has the world's largest data warehouse and uses it for marketing and merchandising.

This use of a database to trigger off a large number of mailshots or telephone sales is probably the most typical use of databases at present. However, most large retailers are investing in *data warehouses* (*see* Fig. 10.2). These are large systems collecting *internal* information from inside the company (such as electronic point-of-sale, loyalty cards, and customer services) and *external* information from other organisations (such as third party suppliers, customer profiling tools, competitor information and market research). These data are usually stored in a separate computer system so that the data warehouse does not interfere with normal day-to-day operations. The data then need to be analysed by easy-to-use tools, often in conjunction with other external data. If the analytical tools can mimic normal patterns of thought they will be much easier to use. The retailer hopes that trawling through masses of data may expose key marketing patterns or relationships about types of customer which can be exploited to increase sales or profitability. *Data mining* involves extracting and analysing different types of data to detect patterns that are not immediately obvious and might never be discovered using normal reporting systems.

Data mining and analysis will permit data to be organised to assist customer segmentation. Retailers need to be able to answer the following questions.

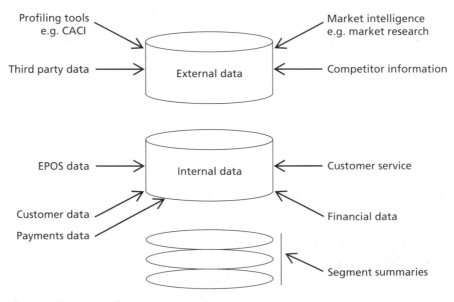

Fig. 10.2 Data warehouse

1 Who are our best customers and what do they buy?

2 Where are they price sensitive and where are there possibilities for price advances?

3 What products do they tend to buy or order at the same time, during a single visit to a store? How much do they spend per visit?

4 What can we do to hold on to these customers and to attract others like them?

Many data warehouses have been poorly designed, making it difficult to access and analyse the data except by specialists. There has often been a tendency to store 'everything,' which is not cost-effective. Several North American retailers, such as J C Penney, have suffered expensive failures with data warehouses, which were badly delayed and failed to provide the business with new insights. However, expectations of the new systems may have been too high. A more cautious approach involves creating what is known as a *data mart* – a smaller data warehouse used for one functional area – and adding new data marts until they can be linked in a data warehouse. This scheme of implementation style may be ultimately more successful than a total approach.

The Data Protection Acts 1984 and 1998 control the use made of personal data held on databases. Retailers who legally hold data provided specifically for one purpose, for example details of applications for store credit cards, may be restricted in their ability to include these data within a second unrelated purpose. This could be related to the building of a customer data warehouse, without the specific permission of the applicants. The position at present is not completely clear, but it seems that the Data Protection Registrar will impose greater curbs on the activities of retailers and others in exchanging data about the personal details of customers.

The growing interest in data warehouses is part of a trend towards developing methods of assessing the massive volumes of data which retailers typically collect every day. Data warehousing is one, big-bang approach towards doing this but there are many other systems, variously called executive information systems (EIS), business intelligence, or decision support systems (DSS). Enterprise-wide business data, often stored in different places and databases, are modified, simplified and stored in what is known as an 'online analytical processing engine' (OLAP). This *moulded* or transformed data may be examined by end users in several different ways, for example in terms of sales by store, by product and product group, and by supplier. Some versions of business intelligence may be interrogated by the manager on a desktop computer, although these have difficulty in handling large quantities of data. Once data are in the right form, decision makers can look at several aspects of the business simultaneously.

Many retailers have only a few years experience of data warehousing, data mining and business intelligence systems and are learning how to configure them to the best advantage. While there will continue to be failures, these systems are likely to be a fundamental method of enabling managers to understand and make decisions about their own company within the retail market.

Example: Allders International

This UK department store group uses data mining to analyse the performance of its 82 stores to identify poorly performing lines and to establish the reasons for problem stores. They have used the system to take out lower margin lines, even though they were selling well, substituting them or adjusting their location within stores.

BUSINESS DATA COMMUNICATIONS

Rapid data communications have been an essential element in the application of new IT systems to retailing. Computer files with the data arranged in a specified way are switched between individual retail stores, depots, head offices and suppliers using a range of networks including ordinary public telephone lines, dedicated networks and secure public data lines, or by satellite link.

What types of data are exchanged? There are four main types of system for data exchange:

- retail data transaction file exchange;
- EDI and e-commerce;
- Extranet;
- Intranet.

Retail data transaction file exchange

Stores and depots transmit EPOS sales data files, financial transactions data, the amount banked, plus a range of other data such as staff hours worked, despatch information and stock levels – all electronically – to head office computers for processing and analysis. Much of this information is transmitted automatically. The store may be *polled* at night by one of a number of central computers and the required data downloaded to head office. In larger stores the store computers automatically exchange data with a central computer several times every day, enabling the merchandise director to view the progress of that day's trading in every store by 11 a.m. the following day. The same systems are used by retailers to update the price files held by stores. The new prices are downloaded from head office to the store computer, often on a Thursday night to take effect the following Monday morning. Depending on exactly how the system is configured, the new price files may finally be passed to every EPOS terminal by the store computer.

EDI and e-commerce

Sending orders to suppliers and to depots electronically saves time and avoids the need to re-key order information. In principle, an order sent by electronic data interchange (EDI) can be received by a manufacturer, accepted, and immediately passed into the distribution system for order picking in the warehouse and subsequent delivery. After processing the order, the supplier or depot can then electronically transmit despatch information to the store (that is, what goods are going to be received) and send an invoice. Further information is provided in the next section.

Extranet

Also termed *Web EDI*, this is a relatively new concept used to describe the way it is thought many businesses will use Internet technology for business-to-business communication (rather than business-to-consumer communications). Normal EDI transactions can be very costly to manage, and many companies have said that EDI is not cost-effective for data exchange with any but the top 100 or top 200 suppliers. Smaller suppliers may use dedicated (that is, closed and secure) Internet services to receive orders from retailers. Specialist companies such as BT/MCI or GEIS will provide high performance Web browsers that retail stores or buyers can use to place Extranet orders and review current and past order delivery schedules.

Example: Extranet and Sainsbury

The UK food retailer Sainsbury has set up an Extranet for its suppliers to help with promotions and other events. Now, one third of suppliers are part of the scheme. It claims that the EQOS Extranet facilities improved joint planning, so smoothing out 'spikes' in supply. Information about regional publicity is shared with suppliers and any differences in perception about start-dates and deadlines are resolved (there had been some earlier problems regarding start dates and product codes from Sainsbury). Also it is possible for comments from customers to be passed on more quickly. The Extranet will permit ECR to be achieved with suppliers.

Intranet

An Intranet is a formal system to permit the electronic exchange of business data within an organisation, mostly between managers and senior staff. Managers may have access to a range of software to create or amend text, spreadsheets and graphs. They should be able to send the documents electronically to colleagues. Staff in the 'field' (that is, visiting stores) can download required information about the store's performance and other documents over a telephone line or even down their mobile phone. This means that staff can have access to current data, whether marketing or logistics, in order to make decisions or provide advice.

EDI

Stockholding (or *inventory*) is one of the retail sector's largest costs. Tight control over inventory – exactly what is in stock, what is on order, what new items are out of stock, what potential problems exist – is a necessary requirement for modern retailers. From a marketing approach it is necessary to improve service and product availability, and simultaneously reduce the stock levels in order to improve profitability. To be able to cut inventory to the minimum at the same time as ensuring that product is never out of stock represents a trading ideal. *Computerised ordering* speeds up the stock ordering process, thereby cutting costs – including the costs of safety stock – and providing more information. The use of electronic data exchange (EDI) provides the electronic administrative management of replenishment through a system of product despatch and returns. The technology allows the retailer to:

- be more efficient due to enhanced merchandise availability;
- have higher stockturn rates;
- incur lower spoilage and shrinkage costs;
- achieve improved merchandise tracking;
- have less need for discounting lines;
- lower administration costs;
- provide fresher products for customers and timely offers in store, particularly valuable for food retailers.

EDI involves data communications between systems, usually (but not always) belonging to different organisations. EDI messages between companies must necessarily conform to a common standard, the worldwide standard being UN/EDIFACT. This defines

1 the core information being exchanged; and

2 where and how that information must appear.

There are many different EDI messaging systems which retailers, manufacturers and shippers use. In the UK, the dominant system is one developed by the UK Article Numbering Association called Tradacoms which resulted from an initiative led by UK grocers. One of the oldest EDI systems is Bookshop Teleordering. There are potentially more than 20 000 different sources of book supply in the UK alone. Bookshop Teleordering enables even a one-shop retailer to have its orders routed overnight to the appropriate suppliers, with confirmation that the order has been sent. Interflora, which is a franchise of independent retail florists promising same-day delivery, uses EDI to transmit orders between outlets. Odette is used by car distributors to order cars and to search for the right model; and EDICE is the EDI system for the consumer electronics industry.

Data communications and merchandise reordering systems

Two *transformational* reordering systems are:

● automatic stock replenishment systems;

● Efficient Consumer Response (ECR).

Automatic stock replenishment systems use daily or weekly EPOS sales data to generate a fresh order for rapid delivery overnight or within the next 48 hours. Sales data are sent electronically to the depot or to the manufacturer by EDI. The order from the store can be automatically converted into a picking list, a despatch note and an invoice without the need to key in the data. The amount sold one day is the amount replenished the following day.

Efficient Consumer Response (ECR) makes EPOS sales data available to suppliers so they can programme their production and distribution systems to ensure that the retailer never runs out of stock. The retailer creates a supplier partnership with key suppliers, using a confidential EDI link to the retailer's weekly or daily sales of relevant merchandise so that suppliers can be responsible for maintaining the target inventory levels of the retail business. ECR is increasingly common in clothing and fast-moving non-food merchandise.

There are currently 20 000 UK users of EDI, but although the Tradacoms standard has come to dominate many retail applications only 5 per cent of Western hemisphere trade is carried out using EDI. Most users are only at the basic stage of transmitting electronic orders, irrespective of the fact that more than thirty different messages – including despatch notes, invoices and financial messages for banks – can now be transmitted electronically. There has been a large increase in the use of EDI at the end of the twentieth century and we can expect this progress to continue. However EDI can be very cumbersome and there has already been some shift towards Extranet-based ordering which is more intuitive and easy to use. It seems unlikely that more than 50 per cent of retail orders will be transmitted to suppliers by electronic means before 2005.

ELECTRONIC RETAILING

Electronic retailing was first developed on a large scale in the 1980s. The area is advancing at a rapid rate with retail organisations realising the growing importance of the sale of products through these new distribution channels. Electronic delivery systems do not necessarily require direct human interaction and, as such, they offer specific advantages. For example, quality can be assured, the costs are lower, there is consumer convenience of access, and distribution can be wider than normal retail channels. The different categories of this major growth area fall into two distinct systems: passive or interactive systems.

1 *Passive systems*. These are non-interactive one-way media, where the retailer can decide upon the content and timing of messages. It includes all forms of one-way communication media such as shopping pages, or clubs on television, or one-way cable systems. The success of the Quality Value Convenience Network (QVC), using such an approach, is discussed below. This form of selling includes video catalogues or electronic media which demonstrate the product in use or provide further information.

2 *Interactive systems*. This type of electronic retailing allows for two-way interaction and includes the Internet or promotional touch-screen booths and kiosks for items such as airline or holiday bookings. Some systems can demonstrate the product in use and, in the case of touch-screens, give printouts or allow further enquiries from the database. A feature of both systems is that a credit card can be used in order to secure the sale.

Passive systems and home shopping

Home shopping through direct mail, agency catalogues, and direct response advertising already account for a significant proportion of spending by European consumers. New technology will add greater variety to the routes that already exist. However, many innovative IT home shopping systems have failed because they were not based on what customers needed but on what the technology could provide. This is surprising as most surveys of customers show they dislike routine shopping for commodities, but this does not mean they welcome technologically-enabled retailing. In practice, service levels are poor, with considerable amounts of time spent staring at unchanging computer screens; lead times are much longer than popping into a shop on the way home; and there are abiding concerns about security. One clear trend that is successful is the growth of the home shopping networks, especially in the USA. These are based upon the use of studio demonstrations of products while a telephone salesforce stands by to receive orders. As the number of calls diminishes, the Network operator is able to demonstrate a new product. The system is therefore characterised by instant feedback on what items are popular and should remain on screen for longer periods or those that should be replaced. In addition, the overheads are low as there is only the need for warehouse storage, a telephone salesforce and the rent of studio time.

In the USA, a number of retailers offer televised home shopping. They include JC Penney Shopping Network, Home Shopping Network, QVC Network, Cable Value Network and Sky Merchant. The USA television retailing marketplace is segmented by product, brand, and price. The Cable and Home Shopping networks are targeting the lower end of the market whereas QVC offers well-known national brands. The different networks are able to offer easy payment plans because they own company credit facilities and use promotional techniques such as direct mail coupons. The means of response is by telephone.

TV-based retailing (for example, home shopping programmes such as QVC in Britain and Germany, and the extended TV advertising called *infomercials*) have proved extremely successful compared to the comparatively slow growth of retail sales on the Internet. Against this background, changes are occurring which may affect the future use of electronic retailing. The introduction of digital TV in several European countries, including the UK, may enable the Internet or home shopping to migrate from the PC to the television. There have been trials of interactive TV in many countries which show that customers will use a variety of services including home shopping, but that the greatest interest concerns entertainment and games rather than retailing. Purchasing video on demand, that is having videos downloaded to the home via the telephone line rather than purchasing or renting them from a store, is thought to be the most likely retail possibility, but the effect of interactive TV on other types of retail demand may be slow to build a critical mass.

MINICASE 10.2

Home shopping in the UK

Littlewoods, the mail order house, and Granada, the broadcasting and leisure group, are set to launch a television-based home shopping channel in a joint venture. The channel will form part of the pay-TV package to be launched this year by British Digital Broadcasting, co-owned by Granada and Carlton Communications. It is understood the TV shopping service will be different from the QVC channel, run by the US-based group of the same name, which has notched up sales of more than £60m since its launch in 1993. It will offer consumers the chance to buy from the 15,000 branded products carried in the Littlewoods catalogue as well as new ranges to be chosen by the joint venture company. QVC focuses on just 250 items a week. For Littlewoods, the UK's biggest private retailer, the deal marks a further step in the strategy of Barry Gibson, the new chief executive, to build a network of joint ventures in home shopping. The group aims to exploit its expertise in mail order logistics and recently concluded a deal with the former Burton Group, now renamed Arcadia, to develop a home shopping business.

Source: Peggy Hollinger, *Financial Times*, 9 March 1998

Interactive systems – the Internet

The Internet is an open worldwide computer network, linking together by fast data communication countless thousands of computers owned by government, education, commercial and other organisations. No one actually owns it. The Internet is a set of protocols governing how data is presented by individuals and organisations wishing to provide information to others. Within the Internet, the World Wide Web (WWW) is a collection of linked documents or pages that span the Internet. They are accessed from the user's own PC or computer terminal by what are called Web browsers, which are software products enabling the user to load and view a document relatively quickly or switch to other related documents.

Most large retailers of any size and many small retailers now have their own Web site, including Marks & Spencer, Virgin, Arcadia, HMV, and Gratton. Setting up a Web site is affordable as costs are relatively low. Once established, the Web site allows a retailer to conduct a targeted business 24 hours a day, 365 days in the year, with a potential worldwide audience. The Web is available and open to anyone with an Internet connection, irrespective of geography, time zone, or computer system. This makes the offer of retail products more accessible to the new global marketplace.

Related to the above features of the Web is its ability to provide a more level playing field for all, where equal opportunity exists to access the market for all types and size of business. The technology also allows sophisticated digital images, video and sound. 'Electronic brochures' could include three-dimensional aspects of the product which the potential customer could explore continuously.

From a marketing perspective, the major benefit of the Internet is the much greater degree of interactivity than other communications media. The most valuable Web applications are those that allow companies to transcend communication barriers and establish dialogue directly with customers. For example, Web sites can contain electronic forms for customer completion and retailers can reply directly via electronic mail (e-mail). This kind of connection will improve customer relations and contribute towards the building of customer loyalty. The Web can give access to a greater store of information than other traditional communication media, and provide visitors with the means to select and retrieve only that which appeals to them. This means that customised promotional material could be produced at the touch of a key. For the modern retailer, it provides a useful tool in the adoption of micro-marketing in this 'age of the individual' and relationship marketing. However, it must be remembered that the true determinant is the willingness of customers to use the Web to make purchases.

Although there are some exceptions, only very small proportions of company retail sales are currently generated via the WWW. A KPMG report found that only 1 per cent of sales were totally WWW based. Nevertheless, surprisingly high estimates of the potential of WWW sales have been made. The respondents to the KPMG report estimated that one third of their sales (£350 billion) would be WWW based by 2002, while the microprocessor company Intel estimated that the Internet market for Europe in 1998 was $681 million which would rise to $15 billion by 2002.

The number of private households already with Internet links is increasing rapidly. In the first half of 1998 40 per cent of Internet accesses in the UK were from households as opposed to 35 per cent from business. Twenty-seven per cent of UK and German households had a PC in 1998 compared to 40 per cent of US households. Twenty-eight per cent of European homes are expected to have PCs by 2000, double the level of 1996. Thus a substantial marketplace is developing, pushed primarily by educational, games/leisure and professional/business needs rather than shopping.

The presence of many retailers on the WWW is still fairly basic and unresponsive. The KPMG report found that much WWW development was funded by spare IT cash. Spending per site had doubled in one year to a 1997 average of £68 000, still relatively small compared to the costs of one television advertisement. Only 20 per cent of retailers found Internet sales more profitable than conventional sales and in 1998 more than one half of retail sites provided information about the retailer and its products rather than allowing transactions to take place. These web sites were geared towards generating additional in-store sales rather than WWW sales. However, this is now changing.

Internet retailing has gone through several stages of development. Initially it was felt that users would prefer to access WWW retailers through virtual shopping malls, with a range of different retail businesses, similar to actual retail shopping centres. In fact these electronic malls have been generally unsuccessful and some important ones, like IBM's World Avenue, have disappeared from the WWW. The most successful Internet retail marketplaces have been those in which the quality is known and customers are searching for low prices, availability, or convenient delivery. Verdict Research found that computer software (purchased by 35 per cent of respondents), books and CDs have been the most popular products sold via the Internet, and a number of specialist Internet retailers have been set up to supply these needs. IGD (1998) provided a slightly different list in rank order listing of sales:

1 PC hardware and software;
2 travel;
3 entertainment;
4 books and music;
5 Gifts, flowers and greetings;
6 Clothing and footwear;
7 Food and beverages.

Amazonbooks.com is the largest bookshop in the world, yet its only existence is on the WWW. Twenty-seven per cent of its sales are to overseas customers. There are comparatively few companies like this. The fact that Amazonbooks.com was not expected to return a surplus until after 2000 may explain why this is so. In contrast, Dell Computers sell $1 million of its PCs every day on the WWW.

Writers such as Cope (1996) suggest that the WWW makes retail location comparatively unimportant as long as the logistics exist to supply the customer. He concludes that the WWW will transfer a substantial proportion of shopping from orthodox stores to the Internet by 2006, routine purchases such as groceries being particularly vulnerable. The experience of Tesco does not suggest that this target is obtainable. By 1998 Tesco delivered groceries to the home from more than ten stores in London and one in Leeds, and will not cover the whole of London until 20 London stores have the system. Poor Internet response times meant that Tesco provided users of its home shopping service with its product file on a CD-ROM. Most customers use a telephone or fax to place orders, but the company found that electronic ordering was higher than expected. The average order size of £90–100 is double their normal supermarket order. The delivery fee of £5 does not cover the costs of the service and Tesco is attempting to find ways of reducing its costs further. Tesco's own estimate is that by 2008 home delivery might be 5–10 per cent of its total business and an unknown proportion of this will occur over the Internet. Other UK grocers including Iceland, Sainsbury and Somerfield have launched major home shopping services but have only a very small, or no, Internet element.

Most surveys show that a major barrier to the use of the Internet for transactions is security. There are now several systems for making payment and credit card details secure, usually involving data encryption. Authorities around the work are currently working on a complex payments security project called *secure electronic transaction* (SET), which will allow cardholder and merchant to authenticate each other during an

Internet transaction. Other problems preventing rapid take-up of the WWW include the logistics of home delivery (particularly a problem for bulky or perishable items such as food), customs duties between countries, and the decision to tax Web transactions.

Limitations of the Web

There are potential problems and limitations that the retail industry must address. The Butler Group suggests that effective Web applications are those that demonstrate an understanding of network limitations, demographics, and culture (URL: *Business on the Web*, June 1996).

Network limitations

The visual impact of the Web site is important, but raises conflicts. Graphics and multimedia attributes require that the customer (client) end has access to a high specification personal computer (PC). Also, the inevitable slowing down of the data transfer can result in customer frustration and even the premature termination of the access.

Demographics

Successful Web applications should demonstrate clear relevance to the customer base. Web sites can be structured so that pages are targeted to specific on-line customer groups. These pages must be dynamic enough to keep pace with the ever-changing interests of such groups. The challenge here is to monitor the interests and to be flexible in responding to them.

Culture

It is important that customers are comfortable with electronic shopping if they are going to purchase via the Internet. Consumers have been reluctant to supply credit card details over the Internet as they judge it to be risky and have a fear of breach of security. Both popular Web browsers, Netscape and Microsoft Explorer, have now incorporated secure payment encryption algorithms. Electronic cash (e-cash) has also been developed by Digicash (URL: http://www.digicash.com) for secure payments over the Internet without having to transmit credit card details. It would appear that users, as potential customers, are not aware that it is often easier for hackers to obtain credit card details passed over a cordless or mobile telephone.

The commercial success of Internet technology depends not only upon connectivity but also the fundamental question of social acceptance. Electronic commerce will flourish if users of technology are motivated to become customers and to change their patterns of buying. Shopping by catalogue, TV and phone marketing, and phone banking are increasingly accepted as part of the way society works. While the home PC market is growing at speed, the home Internet market is also set on an upward trend. This means that society is becoming more familiar with technology, and in particular with PCs and the Internet. Therefore, the retail industry has an opportunity to deploy the Web as an effective marketing tool, providing it is able to respond to the demands of Internet commerce by being responsive, agile and innovative.

Example: Pinault-Printemps-Redoute

A number of European mail order retailers have started issuing their catalogues in CD-ROM format mainly because of slow access speeds on the Internet. Pinault-Printemps-Redoute, one of the largest French mail order companies, uses what it terms a multi-channel approach on the basis that no current technology is clearly superior. Orders can be sent in through the post, or placed by telephone, Minitel (the pioneering French videotex system) or the Internet. The Company carries 110 000 book titles, 80 000 record titles, 8000 videos, and 2000 CD-ROMs.

Many commentators on the WWW believe that, in addition to the competition conventional stores face from Internet retailers, manufacturers of heavily branded goods may also start to use their Web sites to bypass retailers and supply WWW customers direct. CDs, jeans, videos, cosmetics, perfumes, cameras and so on could all be sold over the WWW by manufacturers who have invested heavily in their brands, such as EMI, Levi, Warner Bros, Estee Lauder, J-P. Gaultier and Kodak.

FUTURE TRENDS

IT has already had a tremendous effect on the retail sector. A number of new IT innovations lie in store for shops. There are many different possibilities. The main difficulty is to assess how quickly these new IT products will be used in stores. The Internet has generated a tremendous level of excitement and sensational predictions have been made with regard to the future of electronic commerce. However, it is argued by Burke (1997) that the Internet is only one of many tools available to manufacturers and retailers for advertising, selling, and distributing their products to customers. He indicates that marketers are most likely to use the Internet in cases where its unique characteristics make it a viable and attractive substitute for the functions of traditional channel intermediaries. He suggests that, because of its ability to transform information quickly and inexpensively, the Internet will have the greatest impact on marketing communications, a moderate effect on sales transactions, and a minimal impact on logistics.

Some of the trends predicted for the future of IT innovations in retailing are discussed below.

Smart card

Smart cards equipped with a silicon chip are likely to replace magnetic stripe credit and debit cards and loyalty cards by 2005. The Association for Payment Clearing Services (APACS) announced that British credit and debit cards would begin to incorporate microchips from 1999 onwards. However, they will also carry a magnetic strip to allow them to be used abroad. Before the new smart cards replace other forms of transaction, retailers will have to invest in equipment that can make full use of the card's stored information. The smart card will be more secure than conventional cards and can carry additional information. Smart loyalty cards could include the customer's name and address, preferences, points awarded and be capable of being used across a number of retail companies and services. It is believed that smart cards will reshape banking in the same way that automatic teller machines did twenty years ago. Smart cards will enable consumers to transfer money easily and provide the benefits of accurate and secure cash free transactions in the same way that ATMs liberated consumers from having to queue in banks during lunch breaks.

By the mid 2000s, it is thought that smaller versions of smart cards will be applied to many articles in the form of 'smart tags', to provide full information about their manufacture (essential for food or pharmaceutical products), monitor their progress down the supply chain, provide stock control in the stores, and may be a partial replacement for ANA codes at the checkout. These smart tags will provide proof of ownership and may help to combat theft in-store as well as helping householders to protect their goods. Retailers may be able to charge a premium for goods that are protected by smart tags. A tagged domestic TV or video playback equipment can be protected from unauthorised use in the home (for example, by children when the parents are away). Similarly, without knowledge of the code or the activation device, such products would be unappealing to burglars because

- the goods could be used only by the legal owners;
- the legal owners of goods can be identified;
- stolen goods can thus be returned to their owners.

The price of silicon chips, which are the key ingredient of smart cards and smart tags, are falling rapidly, suggesting that the next few years will see a considerable growth in the use of these products.

E-cash

E-cash or electronic purses consist of smart card systems which can be used in the same way as cash or debit cards with retailers whose stores are equipped with special card readers. Users of the scheme 'deposit' funds into the cards, which are then debited every time they are used until further deposits are made. The pilots carried out in Britain and other European countries show that the technology works but that there is not yet a widespread consumer acceptance of the scheme. Development is, therefore, likely to be slow.

Multimedia kiosks

Multimedia kiosks placed in stores, shopping malls, libraries and railway stations are likely to become increasingly important over the next few years. For the retailer, they will add value in a number of ways. The kiosk can be used by loyalty cardholders when entering the store to receive details of special offers, check the number of points they have, receive updates about new products, and spend their points. In DIY or gardening, heavy or cumbersome items could be ordered electronically and be assembled ready for collection in 15 minutes. The retailer could use multimedia to cross-sell related products, for example, a session with a beautician may be booked in a healthcare store; customers can book holidays, arrange insurance, purchase tickets for the cinema, or check and book concessionary train fares.

Example: Service Merchandise Inc.

Service Merchandise Inc. is the USA's largest catalogue retailer with over 400 showrooms across the southern states. It has a customer database of 27 million people and segments them by lifestyle. Over the last five years it has spent millions of dollars in developing customer-friendly kiosks which people would use to buy their goods without the need to involve staff. Current versions use touchscreen technology, show pictures and video clips of the product, and allow customers to compare different items through a comparison screen. Customers can place their orders and pay by credit card for home delivery. These have been so successful that Service Merchandise is now starting to locate single kiosks into shopping malls and airports.

Customer specific offers

Customer specific offers is another possibility in the grocery store of the future. The customer's loyalty card (loaded with customer preference information) inserted into a card reader on a shopping trolley would trigger individualised offers at different parts of the store. Some offers would attempt to induce the customer to buy different ranges of product; others might reward a highly loyal customer. Yet others might attempt to retain the custom of a consumer who has become less loyal than before.

Electronic body scanners

Electronic body scanners are devices that can provide an exact set of measurements for the perfectly fitting pair of jeans, underwear or suit. This allows customers to be scanned 'in the round' when they place their order. The goods can then be ready for them about 30 minutes later.

Other ideas being discussed or developed include the virtual reality store (to mimic shopping, but used by home delivery companies). Virtual reality stores may also be used to help with space planning and the positioning of checkouts and new gondola designs in retail outlets; 100 per cent customer self-scanning stores with no staff; and the integration of smart tags into products to provide information about product integrity, prices, and to act as an anti-theft device. Also available are Electronic Shelf Edge Labels (ESELs) which are liquid crystal modules that replace paper labels on the shelf front. These ESELs may be automatically linked to the head office EPOS system and so enable the changing of all prices on outlet shelves to coincide with scanned prices at the checkout.

CONCLUSION

We have seen how IT has transformed the operation of retail marketing by providing accurate sales data and a mass of high quality information about customers. Fast data communications have enabled retailers to make their merchandise re-ordering systems more responsive to customers at the same time as cutting the costs of inventory. Data communications are also at the heart of the development of the Internet, which will have a considerable effect on retailers of all kinds – even if the hopes of its greatest supporters prove over-optimistic. A major task facing retailers is to discover new opportunities in the customer and product data now being held on databases and data warehouses. Retailers are attempting to be more customer-focused and hope to use customer information and loyalty systems to increase the average amount spent, and to understand consumer sensitivities about pricing and ranges. The costs of investing in the new IT systems and getting the most from them, and the penalties of *not* investing, will continue to make retailing a high risk area.

EXERCISES

The exercises in this section are related to the applications of IT to retail marketing. It is advised that you work through them before moving on to Chapter 11.

1 Taking the short-, medium- and long-term trends, how is electronic retailing going to displace the current patterns of retail purchasing? Relate this to different segments such as business to business as well as consumer sub-groups. In addition, comment on the implication for electronic advances in retailing and the changes which may occur in the social aspects of shopping.

2 What is the supportive role of IT systems for retail (such as EDI) and how can any of the systems you have identified be used by retailers to improve further the management and cost-effectiveness of their operations?

3 Look up the Web sites listed in the grid below and record your impressions of them.

Company web site:	Note your impressions of the Web pages:
Blackwell www.blackwell.co.uk/bookshops Co-op www.co-op.co.uk Iceland www.iceland.co.uk M&S www.marks-and-spencer.co.uk Sainsbury www.sainsbury.co.uk/company Tesco www.tesco.co.uk Top Shop www.topshop.co.uk	
Note others you looked up:	Note your impressions of the Web pages:

Then explore the Internet for the retail methods of selling different types of merchandise such as automobiles, travel and CDs, or visit foreign sites such as www.carrefour.fr. Report which Web sites you visited and again note your impressions, particularly recording any differences you find.

4 Discuss, with reasons, what you believe to be the most important future applications of IT to retail marketing and retail operations in the next twenty years.

REFERENCES AND FURTHER READING

Alba, J., Lynch, J., Weitz, B. and Janiszewski, C. (1998) 'Interactive home shopping: consumer, retailer, and manufacturer incentives to participate in electronic marketplaces', *Journal of Marketing*, 61 (3), 38–53.

Barnatt, C. (1994) *The Computers in Business Blueprint*. London: Blackwell Business.

Branigan, L. (1998) 'The Internet: the emerging premier direct marketing channel', *Direct Marketing*, 61 (1), 46–8.

Burke, R.R. (1997) 'Do you see what I see? The future of virtual shopping', *Journal of the Academy of Marketing Science*, 25 (4), 352–60.

Comer, J.M., Mehta, R. and Holmes, T.L. (1998) 'Information technology: retail users versus nonusers', *Journal of Interactive Marketing*, 12 (2), 49–62.

Cope, N. (1996) *Retail in the Digital Age*. London: Bowerdean Publishing.

Curtis, G. (1995) *Business Information Systems: Analysis, design and practice*. 2nd edn. Wokingham: Addison-Wesley.

Davies, G. (1995) 'Bringing stores to shoppers – not shoppers to stores', *International Journal of Retail and Distribution Management*, 23 (1), 18–23.

Dawson, J. (1994) 'Applications of European management in European retailing', *International Review of Retail, Distribution and Consumer Research*, 4 (2), 219–38.

The e centre, 11 Kingsway, London WC2B 6AR, Telephone 0171 655 9000, Website http://www.ana.org.uk

Fidler, C. and Rogerson, S. (1996) *Strategic Management Support Systems*. London: Pitman.

Haeckel, S.H. (1998) 'About the nature and future of interactive marketing', *Journal of Interactive Marketing*, 12 (1), 63–71.

IGD (1998) *Grocery Market Bulletin*. Institute of Grocery Distribution, Watford: IGD Business Publications.

Gonyea, J.C. (1996) *Selling on the Internet: How to open an electronic storefront and have millions of customers*. Maidenhead: McGraw-Hill.

Hogarth-Scott, S. and Parkinson, S. (1994) 'Barriers and stimuli to the use of Information Technology in retailing', *The International Review of Retail Distribution and Consumer Research*, 4 (3), 257–75.

Hollinger, P. (1998) 'Littlewoods in TV-based home shopping move', *Financial Times*, 9 March.

KPMG (1997) *Home Shopping Across Europe: Experience and opportunities*. KPMG Publication 5670.

Lowe, M. and Wrigley, N. (1996) *Retailing, Consumption and Capital: Towards the new retail geography*. Harlow, Essex: Longman.

Management Horizons (1995) *Retailing 2005*. New York: Management Horizons.

Margolis, B. (1996) 'Digital commerce: the future of retailing', *Direct Marketing*, January, 41–6.

Mulhern, F.J. (1997) 'Retail marketing: from distribution to integration', *International Journal of Research in Marketing*, 14 (2), 103–24.

Packaged Facts Inc. (1994) *The Electronic Retailing Market*. New York: Wiley.

Porter, M.E. (1980) *Competitive Strategy: Techniques for analyzing industry competitiveness*. New York: The Free Press.

Porter, M.E. and Millar, V.E. (1985) 'How information gives you competitive advantage', *Harvard Business Review*, 63 (4), 149–60.

Powell, T.C. and Dent-Micallef, A. (1997) 'Information technology as competitive advantage: the role of human, business, and technology resources', *Strategic Management Journal*, 18 (5), 375–405.

Rhodes, E. and Carter, R. (1998) 'Electronic commerce technologies and changing product distribution', *International Journal of Technology Management*, 15 (1, 2), 31–48.

Rogers, D. (1998) 'Barclays offers on-screen links', *Marketing*, 21 May, 2.

Rowley, J. (1996) 'Retailing and shopping on the Internet', *International Journal of Retail and Distribution Management*, 24 (3), 26–37.

Schwartz, E.I. (1997) WEBECONOMICS – *Nine Essential Principles for Growing Your Business on the World Wide Web*. Harmondsworth: Penguin.

Taylor, P. (1998) 'The electronic revolution: making close links with shoppers', *Financial Times*, 17 March.

11 Consumerism and ethics in retailing

This chapter should enable you to understand and explain:

- the different pressures for companies to become more socially responsible;
- what would be deemed constraint of trade or unfair methods of competition;
- the criticisms levelled at different aspects of marketing;
- the societal marketing approach.

It is not uncommon for reports to reach us of unacceptable service, poor quality, shoddy goods, marketing malpractice and the belief that a company has no interest apart from the profit motive. The situation is currently being managed far better by retailers, however. This is because there is the growing awareness that long-term customer satisfaction and the building of a positive image is a prerequisite for success. In light of this understanding companies are discovering the need to identify and react to the new wave of consumerism and its associated values.

As indicated, the problem of negative attitudes to the modern business world is associated with faceless, large companies attempting to increase their profits. We should, however, be made aware that companies are made up of people similar to us and the problems may not be divorced from what we all do. Some studies have highlighted that up to one-third of middle managers have submitted deceptive reports to their supervisors and that even more would bend the rules to gain personal advancement. We know of companies that can be viewed as 'bad barrels' because they have 'bad apples' working for them. To be successful, retail companies need to discover approaches to the marketplace that will build a socially responsible and ethical company culture. There is a need to understand the following three basic issues.

- *Consumerism.* This is organised group pressure, by all consumers, to protect and benefit consumer groups and the environment. This means it is not solely those consumers buying from a company, it is a broad movement to bring about improved exchange relationships.

- *Corporate social responsibility.* This is the decision of a firm to conduct its business in the interest of society as a whole as well as its own interests.

- *Ethics.* This involves personal decisions on the moral principles of what would be the right or wrong activity for individual employees. These decisions will be linked to the values and culture of the organisation.

THE DIFFERENT PRESSURES FOR A COMPANY TO BE SOCIALLY RESPONSIBLE

The concept on which to base the ensuring of long-term satisfaction is not a straightforward one. Consumer satisfaction is linked to aspirations and these may change in relation to political systems, and the products and services other consumers enjoy. For example, the basis of satisfaction of consumers in Eastern European countries prior to and since 1989 will be totally different. Similarly, America will not have the same cultural values as less industrialised countries. Satisfaction is based upon personal concepts of acceptability of the type of products available, the potential to purchase them, and how companies act in the transaction process of creating and supplying products or services.

One major change in values can be traced to the widespread realisation that the world needs to have its environment protected. Green issues are creating more awareness of the environment in Western societies. Pollution due to acid rain, the motor car and leaded petrol, nuclear waste, chemicals in farming and untreated sewage are topical concerns. This has led to the emergence of the 'green' consumer who will seek out and buy environmentally friendly products. The same consumer will expect a retail company to adopt responsible attitudes in terms of the way it carries out its business. This could be related to the organisation of waste recycling, energy conservation and some control of the products it stocks or sells. There is the further concern that financial services institutions should work with acceptable political regimes and provide loans only for ethical business ventures. In the late 1990s, various retailers were accused of exploiting workers in developing countries. The recognition of the power of the consumer, based upon emerging values which deem unethical processes unacceptable, has led companies to adopt more socially responsible policies. The recognition by different companies of the need to be more aware of the personal values of those in society is primarily due to consumerism.

Consumerism

This is organised group pressure which has become a set of values held not only by the consumers of a company's products but also within the wider society. Hence consumerism has the objective of protecting all consumers from organisations with which there may be an exchange relationship. As a movement, it attempts to influence the policies and behaviour of organisations and groups to minimise the likelihood of disbenefits being inflicted on individuals, society or the environment. The values of the movement are based upon scepticism of the motives of businesses. There is a belief that businesses are more likely to maximise their profits than think about issues of public interest. This leads to a large number of individuals believing that retailers combine with producers to ensure they, the consumers, are 'ripped off'.

In recent years, the consumer has not been passive. Consumers have realised their economic power and have used this to bring about change. Consumerism has been used for political ends with purchasing power being applied to influence the policies of different governments. The boycott of goods from South Africa prior to the change of government is one example of this. Similarly, there has been concern over the sale of fur products, genetically modified foods, or the use of cheap child labour in developing countries. In 1996 a boycott took place related to retailers sourcing in Burma, a country where the military regime abused human rights. A campaign was targeted on the fashion retailer, BHS. In this instance BHS promised to sever their connections with the country by the following year. However, other companies such as Levi withdrew more quickly.

Ralph Nader is an influential individual in the history of the modern consumer movement. His book on the automobile industry of America, *Unsafe at any Price*, focused consumers' minds on the need for large companies to be more responsible to the users and to society in general for the products they make. Whereas each individual is relatively powerless against large companies, the consumer movement champions the needs of individuals through a collective voice. President Kennedy, following the tradition of Thomas Jefferson with his 'inalienable rights' in the Declaration of Independence, signalled the need for organisations to recognise the rights of the consumer when he incorporated the following four areas into his 'Consumer Bill of Rights':

1 *the right to safety* – that there are no hidden dangers;
2 *the right to be informed* – that there should be honest communications;
3 *the right to chose* – that there should be real competition among sellers;
4 *the right to be heard* – that there should be channels or bodies for complaints.

The protection of the consumer and supplier is often represented by pressure groups. Consumerism as a movement is often based upon the activities of a number of pressure groups who influence government, the media and affect the values within society – groups such as ASH (Action on Smoking and Health) who have organised and promoted national non-smoking days and sensitised the public to the problems of smoking; CAMRA (Campaign for Real Ale) who have forced significant changes on the brewers of beer; and ROSPA (Royal Society for the Prevention of Accidents) which has improved safety regulations in various industries. The self-financing Consumer's Association has been in operation since 1957 and has done much to improve standards through its publication of *Which? Magazine*, which provides comparative information on different products.

The idea of a free marketplace seems, at face value, to be good for the consumer. However, complete freedom in the marketplace is not in the interests of consumers or suppliers. Complete freedom can lead to monopoly situations, may restrict competition and allow price fixing. Consumers are most concerned when a monopoly situation exists. Where effective competition cannot be provided – as was the case with the privatisation of many of the UK public utilities in the 1980s – other means of control are needed. The result has been the creation of a number of regulatory bodies that can determine the level and structure of charges made by these utilities. The utilities of telecommunications, water and gas are controlled by Oftel, Ofwat and Ofgas respectively. In the case of British Gas, Ofgas regulations allow the company to raise gas supply prices in line with energy prices but the price for ancillary services, such as standing charges and repairs, can only rise in relation to the rate of inflation. However, some groups argue that the regulatory bodies are not as powerful as they should be as they cannot insist, by statutory requirement, that the utility companies will meet with their recommendations.

The Monopolies and Mergers Commission, The Office of Fair Trading, trading standards officers and different government departments are consistently ensuring that the consumer has some protection from unfair methods of competition and selling. There is also an EU minister responsible for competition. In recent years that minister has ruled on anti-competitive practices ranging from financial services to airlines, and forced companies to alter trading practices. The Monopolies and Mergers Commission in the UK is an independent body whose members are drawn from a variety of backgrounds including lawyers, economists, industrialists and trade unionists. This commission has the power to take action to remedy or prevent harm to the marketplace. Their power is able to be applied if the marketplace changes where at least a quarter of the supply is controlled from a single source and leads to a distortion of competition. Historically, much of the regulation of retailing has been designed to encourage and maintain competition and to limit or end deceptive or unfair business practices. What is required is control of restraint of trade and unfair methods of competition.

Restraint of trade

1 Retailers should not be able to place pressure on manufacturers to prevent them from selling products to their competitors.

2 Retailers should not acquire their competitors with the intention of substantially lessening competition or creating a monopoly.

3 Retailers should not conspire to fix prices at levels which are unfair.

4 Retailers should not price their products lower in some areas with the objective of driving some retailers out of business so that they can then raise average prices.

5 Retailers should be allowed to sell foreign imported products if they compete fairly with domestic supplies.

Unfair methods of competition

1 Retailers should not use deceptive labelling, advertising, pricing or sales techniques. Consumers believe the most misleading forms of selling are those by telephone, followed closely by direct mail techniques.

2 Prices of certain products such as drinks, ice creams, etc. should be displayed so that customers can check on what they have been charged. Prices have been removed from the items in many food retailers, with the prices being marked on the aisles and shelves only, due to the use of computerised checkouts which scan pre-marked bar codes. Some groups believe this process to be deceptive as it makes it harder for consumers to judge if the final total is correct or not.

3 Advertised special offers should be available so that the initial customer request is fulfilled.

4 Credit practices should be fair and unambiguous.

5 Warranties should be clearly written with an affirmation of a guarantee to the performance of the product and freedom from defects.

6 If a customer enters into a contract it should have clear wording about cancellation and liabilities. The contract should be written in easily understood terms.

7 When a product is ordered there should be no long-term delay in its delivery.

8 Deregulation of services should occur if it is in the interest of the consumer to have wider choice. For example, building societies moving into banking is a change with positive repercussions for the consumer due to increased competition.

Rights

When considering the above points, it should be realised that both the retailer and consumer have certain rights.

Sellers have the rights to:

- sell any product determined by the retailer as long as it is not injurious to health and safety and has a description or label as to the correct use and contents;

- price products at any level provided that there is no discrimination among similar classes of buyers;

- claim any points about the product in their promotions as long as it is not dishonest and misleading;

- utilise whatever level of promotional expenditure they wish, based upon incentive schemes or other means of increasing sales, as long as these schemes are classed as fair competition.

Buyers can also be considered to have demonstrable rights:

- not to frequent a store or purchase the products offered them. The silent vote of consumers is to demonstrate consumer sovereignty by staying away from stores which create consumer problems. This is a very powerful sanction;

- to expect that a supplier will have ensured the product to be safe. With the increasing amounts of artificial additives in foods and the alarmist coverage of the press, this is a major concern. The whole food chain is under suspicion from worries of carcinogenic effects of food substitutes or additives to the worry over diseases which can be transmitted through fresh meat and other products. To ensure their fast food did not suffer from health hazard scares, McDonald's reformulated the cooking process of its french fries in order to make them more healthy and Dunkin' Donuts spent two years in an attempt to remove egg yolks and reduce levels of cholesterol in its doughnuts. The question is whether these are only minimal health improvements. These issues are discussed further in the section on product misuse and safety issues;

- to expect that the product will be essentially the same as the seller has represented it. This means a fully informed buyer should be able to make a rational decision.

Criticism of the exploitation of workers

Western retailers are accused of attempting to make maximum profits through the exploitation and manipulation of suppliers in Third World countries. Whether it be a fruit farm worker in South Africa, a toy worker in China or a factory worker in Bangladesh, Sri Lanka or Pakistan, many are on subsistence wages; some are forced to work unpaid overtime, may be fired or even beaten if they cannot keep up with the production schedules. An Oxfam leaflet (1996) shows how a banana from the Caribbean costing 10p provides 4p to the retailer, 2p to the importer/wholesaler, 3p for shipping and handling charges and only 1p for the picking and growing.

The criticism is not confined solely to overseas labour; the National Group on Home Workers estimates there are currently a million home workers in the UK on extremely low wages. Whatever any retailer believes about the current situation, a number of pressure groups are now quite vociferous regarding the terms and conditions of different workers who are considered to be exploited and lacking in bargaining power. It is not just the small companies who are held up as examples of bad practice; Marks & Spencer were at the centre of a *World in Action* TV programme in January 1996 regarding the ethics of retailers and Toys Я Us have featured in the *Wall Street Journal*.

CRITICISM OF MARKETING ACTIVITY

As we move towards the twenty-first century there is a growing concern for ethical practice which leads to business policies that aim to sustain the earth's resources. The new values emerging are placing pressure on the underlying concepts of marketing. This is creating a great deal of debate around the ethical standpoint of marketing. In examining criticisms of marketing it is important to distinguish between micro (the individual firm) and macro (how the whole system works) levels of marketing. Some complaints are only directed to one level, say the advertisements of Benetton. Other types of criticism, however, may be levelled at the industry as a whole – for example that society is over-materialistic due to the actions of the advertising industry in its prolific use of promotional techniques. Some of the most significant criticisms are discussed in the following subsections.

The disregard of the effects of promotion

The marketing concept can lead to a tunnel vision focus on potential retail consumers without consideration being taken of the wider society. Promotion targeted on a specific segment may be criticised by other groups who may find it annoying, insulting, misleading or socially unacceptable. Promotional campaigns are often judged adversely to affect others due to the insensitive nature of marketing policies. Many women are offended by the use of the female body to sell products. It is argued that this indirectly creates symbols and meanings which bear no relationship to the place of women in modern society. While advertising is recognised as a powerful medium, it is criticised because it is not used in a socially responsible way. The critics often feel that individuals are manipulated by promotion to buy products that they do not need – and often products that, critics feel, should not exist. It is difficult to know whether the critics or consumers should lead on this. For example, some critics would ban many recreational products such as private boats and planes as well as motorcycles and some pets. On the other hand it is argued that marketing can only inform people and stimulate interest, it cannot manipulate people.

In addition, pollution and damage as a by-product of retail activities is treated as an environmental and social cost carried by the whole of society and not simply the company's consumers. Marketing pollution is the over-abundance of promotion which makes an area less attractive. There are roadside poster sites, advertisements on taxi cabs and buses, messages painted on buildings, and leaflets are given away which are then discarded – all of which create invasive pollution. There is also a trend to produce advertisements which aim to shock, such as those of Benetton, and there are others which offend, such as the amount of promotion for sex-talk telephone numbers. The overall effect of these trends is to lead the general public to mistrust marketing generally and to suspect the motives of advertisers.

In 1990 Benetton accepted the earlier emphasis of Oliviero Toscani to create a unified corporate trademark approach of reflecting the different nationalities of its customers throughout the world. This culminated in the launch of the 'United Colours of Benetton' campaign, where the company's communications were replaced by a series of advertisements related to social concern. Critics condemned the programme due to its ultimate goal to sell more products rather than to deal properly with the issues it raised. The management of Benetton responded by pointing out that other retailers simply provided a 'perfect world' style of advertising which was based upon an association that buying products leads to happiness. Toscani took the stance that if consumers were concerned about the world situation, they would be better to shop at Benetton. The use of large billboards to publicise the company and to bring about change was not fully accepted by major sections of the public – but this did nothing to stop the Benetton communication campaign. Such images as a priest and nun kissing on the lips; a bloody newborn baby with uncut umbilical cord; David Kirby dying of AIDS surrounded by his family; human body parts, marked like a side of beef with an 'HIV Positive' stamp; these are just a few examples of images taken from the campaign. This type of controversial advertising is not new. Calvin Klein has been accused of projecting images of child pornography based upon images of young people in seductive and vulnerable poses.

Changing values related to retail consumer issues

The UK government has produced a code of practice to crack down on misleading 'green' claims on consumer products. The new rules, which will ban terms such as 'environment-friendly', set standards for retailers and manufacturers. Claims will have to be accurate, capable of being substantiated by hard evidence, relevant to the product in question and used in an appropriate context. So boasting that a deodorant does not contain CFCs would not be allowed because CFCs are already banned by law. Nor could greeting cards be advertised as 'biodegradable', because all paper is over the longer term. Such claims have helped generate cynicism among consumers. But the government has ignored calls from consumer groups to make the code

legally-binding. The National Consumer Council, which demands statutory rules, will monitor products to see whether the code has any impact. The environment, regions and transport department, which is publishing the code after a year of consultation, hopes retailers will take it up voluntarily. 'The code's effectiveness will depend on how enthusiastically it is taken up by retailers,' the NCC said. B&Q, the DIY chain, said the company is to make the code mandatory for its suppliers. It has also changed the labelling of some of its products to make them comply with the rules. As a result, labels on insulation materials had already been changed to read: 'This product helps conserve energy.'

Source: Leyla Boulton, *Financial Times*, 17 February 1998

An overemphasis on profitable products

The marketing concept dictates that products should only be offered to the marketplace when they are profitable. This has culminated in the axing of bus and train transport routes and the disregard of low spending individuals. The loss of the supporting services of transport may affect poorer individuals disproportionately and, in turn, will have an

Retail Marketing Management

impact on their choice and selection of retail outlet. Where a want exists and the marketing opportunity cannot deliver the required profit return, then a retail offer is seldom developed. The market-based system is guided by self-interest and profit motivation, therefore consumer preferences are only accounted for if an ability to pay is demonstrated. These values are represented by a lack of concern for those who cannot afford to purchase certain items, travel to cheaper priced stores or obtain credit. In addition, it is widely questioned whether retailers want to cater for those who are disadvantaged or disabled. Facilities for blind and disabled people are of low priority in most business planning.

Marketing is sometimes blamed for the drive to the development of monopolistic competition. It is often felt that marketing is the catalyst in the constant attempts to create monopolistic competition. Retail price control by manufacturers has led to the domination of markets and is taken to be a key marketing strategy in order to create premium prices, obtain greater control and make higher profits. The question remains, however, as to the choice or alternatives different consumers have. Accordingly, it can be asked whether some are disadvantaged by the way retailing is organised. The report by the Monopolies and Mergers Commission discussed in Minicase 11.2 highlights this problem.

MINICASE 11.2

The Monopolies and Mergers Commission is about to demand an end to the use of recommended retail prices by electrical appliance makers

After one of its longest and most expensive inquiries, the Monopolies and Mergers Commission has decided to ban recommended retail prices (RRPs) across a wide range of electrical goods. The commission has concluded that appliance manufacturers have used RRPs to fix the prices at which televisions, video recorders, hi-fi systems, camcorders, washing machines, tumble dryers, dishwashers and refrigerators are sold. Leading manufacturers will be required to promise not to seek to control prices or refuse to supply discount retailers. 'We are very concerned at the approach taken by the commission', says Malcolm Wellings, Sony's company secretary in Britain. 'We have not had a fair hearing', complains Peter Hamblin, the managing director of Panasonic UK. Other manufacturers, such as Aiwa, appear to have decided to pre-empt the report's conclusions by unilaterally abandoning RRPs.

The MMC's evidence of price fixing is based on a five-week survey of transaction prices of electrical goods sold by all major retailers operating in Britain. An additional sample of 440 smaller independent retailers without sophisticated electronic point-of-sale systems was also surveyed. The pricing study, according to parts of the draft MMC report found that most electrical appliances were sold at or close to the manufacturer's RRP. Nearly 90% of sales of the best-selling washing machine on the market, Hotpoint's WM22, were within 5% of its RRP. The MMC also conducted a survey of mail-order prices charged by five leading companies – Grattan, Empire, Littlewoods, GUS and Freemans. It found that 29 out of 36 different washing machines, 8 out of 12 tumble dryers, 18 out of 29 freezers and 5 out of 7 dishwashers were listed at an identical price in their catalogues. The MMC report also claims to have uncovered evidence that manufacturers have used RRPs to confuse consumers. It reveals that electrical manufacturers use two types of RRPs, one that is disclosed to the public and another, much lower, that is confidential. The higher nominal RRP allows the retailer to boast of offering 'discounts'. But the manufacturer also dictates the real RRP, the lower price at which the goods are actually sold at 'discount'.

Source: © *The Economist*, London, 31 May 1997

There is greater profitability to be gained by developing in new site areas. Therefore, there is growing concern over the demise of the high street due to the relocation of large retailers to out-of-town sites. The large retail companies have continuously developed new out-of-town areas, forcing out smaller alternative retailers, and creating change without due regard to the cost of environmental or social impacts on the area and local population. The concern over the pollution and waste of resources due to the increased use of the motor car may heighten the pressure on the development of future out-of-town sites or may lead to the introduction of parking fees which could subsidise other forms of transport.

The invasion of privacy

The power of modern computers allows companies to capture a complete range of personal information for use in targeting direct mail campaigns. As retail companies such as Tesco begin to spend more on loyalty programmes, there is a growing database of information which can be utilised by retailers for different purposes. Also, there is a greater use of telephone and high street interviews to collect information. If this is for a reputable survey, there are no problems, but a number of companies use the disguise of research to collect information on individuals who are then targeted with specific insurance or financial offers or for fund-raising activities.

The waste of resources on retail marketing

Marketing is seen as a waste of money due to the large amounts of money spent on promoting products. The money given over to retail promotion is often associated with convincing consumers to buy merchandise which it is believed they do not want. It is believed that the most disadvantaged of consumers are the ones most likely to be influenced by high expenditure on retail marketing promotional campaigns. Promotion is often criticised as a wasteful cost. In addition, competitive advertising is argued to be responsible for higher costs and subsequently higher prices. It is therefore argued that if advertising were reduced, or did not exist, there would be more competition based upon price and service. The consumerist standpoint is that it would be better to spend the money on informative advertising rather than competitive advertising. It is interesting to note, in this context, that when the US government banned cigarette advertising the sales did not fall significantly and the relative market share of the cigarette manufacturers remained very similar.

The levels of marketing expenditure are often blamed for changing consumer attitudes and bringing about a materialistic society where status is derived from the number and type of products we own or consume, the number of shopping trips we undertake, or what areas we shop in, rather than how good we are as a caring member of society. There is little doubt that marketing panders to materialistic values. However, the question is does marketing create these values or simply appeal to the values already within society? It is found that the most simplistic of societies have members who want to accumulate possessions. In many tribal societies status comes from the number of animals or possessions an individual owns. On the other hand, marketing may well enhance or reinforce the appeal of materialism.

Need for more protection of children

Children are often believed to require protection from different products. While there is an age ban on certain products which are thought to be harmful to the young – alcohol, tobacco and gambling – it is often believed retailers' profit motives lead to sales to those who are often under age. Also, it is thought that the way scratch cards and the lottery product is offered alongside sweets and other pleasure purchases will lead to the young having a weakened set of values related to gambling.

Some retailers are careful to ensure that products such as toys or games are not sold to inappropriate age groups. The retailers take the responsible action of insisting on age labelling to ensure the safety of younger children. They also help individuals to purchase presents which will provide higher satisfaction for the recipient.

The targeting of children with advertisements can be seen to be unfair rather than misleading. This is because children often find it difficult to understand the advertising messages. The important questions in respect of children that need to be asked are:

- can children tell the difference between commercials and the programmes they are watching?

- do children understand that advertisements are attempting to influence them to buy?

- can commercials make children want products that are of no benefit to them?

MINICASE 11.3

Consumer issues – investigation of supermarkets by the Office of Fair Trading

Only one real issue is at the heart of the Office of Fair Trading's decision to investigate the profitability of the big four supermarkets in the UK: are they making too much money at the expense of customers and suppliers? Industry watchers will know the debate has been fuelled by two simple facts. First, that the big four retailers dominate food retailing in the UK, with an estimated 47 per cent of the £83bn-a-year food market, and are expanding their share at the expense of smaller players. Moreover, their growing dominance has allowed them to cut costs in part by getting lower prices from their suppliers. Second, the big four UK food retailers – Tesco, J Sainsbury, Asda and Safeway – appear to enjoy disproportionately high margins and sales densities compared with those of international counterparts in their own countries.

'We have had a strong pound so arguably prices should have been slipping,' says Robert Clark of the consultancy Corporate Intelligence in Retailing.

But few observers expect any of the big four to jeopardise the situation with a price war. Such a move would be a 'no-win situation', says Keith Wills, food retail analyst at Goldman Sachs, as it would be immediately copied by the others.

Retailers, of course, claim competition is more intense than ever, and the stable environment is simply a reflection of an efficient market. As for their market dominance, they claim the government is partly responsible for thwarting competition by clamping down on out-of-town superstore development. They also say other European markets are more concentrated than the UK. In France, for example, Goldman Sachs estimates the top five have 56 per cent of the market, and in the Netherlands the top two have more than 60 per cent. Moreover, they claim bigger UK returns are partly due to a greater proportion of more profitable own-label products.

Source: Peggy Hollinger, *Financial Times*, 31 July 1998

PRODUCT MISUSE AND SAFETY ISSUES

The most dangerous aspect of any purchase concerns the way the customer uses the product. In fact, the most dangerous aspect of any purchase often relates to the type of consumer utilising it. Most of us realise that electrical appliances in the bathroom can be extremely dangerous or that electrical garden tools have to be used with care; such dangers have prompted public policy makers to urge or insist on safe designs and testing. However, there is a limit to the precaution notes which can be presented on a label and a manual or leaflet may often be discarded without due notice to safety hints. Consumerism would like greater safety but individuals may easily misuse products simply because of the type of user they are.

1 *Enthusiastic users* may focus more on using the product as early as possible than on studying the directions for use. There is also a problem in the assembly of products whereby care in construction and checks are not carried out in the rush to use the product.

2 *Desensitised users* are often unaware of the consequences of their action, or they may carry out the activity routinely and thus become less vigilant and alert. In addition, when the consumer takes risks which do not lead to problems – they 'get away with it' – they may be more prone to risky behaviour.

3 *Hedonistic users* focus on the fantasy and fun of using products and are less likely to assess the risks of their actions. The use of alcohol, or even glue, may also lead to misuse and abuse.

Critics of the safety of products believe that thousands of accidents could be avoided if companies made better use of improved design and safety standards. The Consumer Product Safety Commission (CPSC) is the federal US agency with major responsibility for product safety in about 15 000 product categories. The CPSC can exercise its powers to:

● require products to be marked with clear warnings and instructions;

● issue mandatory standards that may force firms to redesign products;

● require manufacturers and resellers to notify if they find a product has a defect that would create a substantial risk of injury;

● require manufacturers to conduct reasonable testing programmes to make sure the products conform to established safety standards.

When the CPSC finds a product that may be a potential danger, it can issue an order for the firm to bring the product into conformity with the applicable safety rule, repair the defect or exchange it for one that meets existing safety standards. They can also insist the original price is refunded. Firms found breaking the safety rules can be fined, and executives are held personally liable and can be fined or jailed for up to a year. The CPSC may also instigate product recall – where the product recall can be ordered to occur so that the product can be modified or discontinued.

Consumers in the US have the right to sue the maker or seller of an injurious product, in addition to the powers held by the CPSC. These are so-called class-action suits and there are over 100 000 in the USA each year.

GREEN ISSUES

There is a green consumerism movement which expresses a preference for less environmentally harmful goods and services. Of course, environmentally friendly is a non-specific term and, in reality, no mass-produced good can be entirely environmentally friendly. Such misleading terminology has allowed considerable freedom for retailers to declare their operation or processes as being green. At the same time, there has been a rise in the awareness and concern of green issues due to pressure group activity, increased media coverage of the issues, and the adoption of new legislation. The trend is strong throughout Europe, with Germany leading the way with all organisations having a formal environmental policy. The Germans are also keen to introduce schemes whereby scientific testing takes place to assess the claims of various products that they are environmentally friendly. The German consumer is seen as being more environmentally conscious than other European consumers. Sriram and Forman (1993) found 82 per cent of German supermarket consumers make decisions on environmental considerations. This can be compared to 67 per cent in the Netherlands, 55 per cent in the UK and 50 per cent in France. However, the key question is whether the consumer will be willing to pay higher prices for green products. There is a segment of about one quarter of the population which is willing to pay higher prices but this is affected by times of recession, competitive pricing and the media. The retail industry may also be affected by the use of more friendly chemicals in products. If the new ingredients are perceived to be inferior in terms of achieving the results required by the consumer, the implication is that the consumer would sooner buy the more harmful product if it is thought to be superior. There is another segment which believes that the retailer will claim the products are green on the basis of wanting to charge higher prices. The cynical view held by many is that greenness is a way to exploit the consumer through:

- making only marginal or cost-free shifts in the responsibility of the company towards the environment;
- saving on costs by using cheaper packing or other measures;
- using so-called greenness simply as a public relations exercise;
- disguising the prime objective of achieving higher profits behind a mask of social responsibility.

Some companies, such as The Body Shop, who follow EU Eco-Management guidelines and Boots the Chemist, are being proactive in the area of environmental responsibility. Others merely jump on the bandwagon and offer recycled or disposable packaging without examination of their own environmental practices and policies within the organisation or giving any consideration to wider ethical concerns. Sainsbury have taken bold initiatives in the writing of an environmental policy and undertaking a constant review of policies. Their initiatives included the early removal of CFCs from own-label products, refrigeration equipment, a plastics and waste recycling facility for the company and customers, new energy management systems – plus a wide range of environmental and organic products.

THE ACCEPTABILITY OF A SOCIETAL MARKETING APPROACH

It has been argued that the pressures affecting the image of marketing need to be taken into account. This has culminated in the movement toward a societal concept of marketing which stresses the enhancement of the needs of society as well as of the consumer. The importance of any changes a company makes to improve society has to be balanced with how much else could be achieved. Some companies, such as brewers and distillers, are creating campaigns to warn people of the excesses of drinking but it is questionable whether they are as worried about the customer as they are about the legislation which could affect their operations. While some companies may pay lip service to a societal concept for PR purposes, in a competitive situation many of the problems related to retail, and its marketing, will continue. It is also important to recognise that consumers are now better educated and informed, and are competent enough to select products which are not creating undue problems for society. If companies or their products do create problems, there are articulate pressure groups and government legislation is available for consumer and environmental protection. A truly societal marketing approach is problematic due to the need to resolve multifaceted decisions over profit, pollution, and environmental concerns such as energy and land use. However, some companies perform their marketing activities better than others and are judged in positive terms by the public. The disposition of the public to buying and promoting the brands of retailers is an important aspect of contemporary marketing. The image of retailers, based upon the expectations of the public and the behaviour of the company, may lead to different patterns of negative or positive demand. It is therefore important for companies to adopt a more societal stance by showing they are ethical and considerate in their marketing and planning. This is important for both retailers and marketers who should accept responsibility for any consequences of their activities and actions. Good business managers are being urged to put themselves in the consumer's position with regard to how they or their family would feel they should be treated by others. The following points are relevant in this context.

1 Good business managers should be socially responsible to all stakeholders (customers, employees, suppliers, shareholders, society, etc.) related to the company or retail offer so as to minimise social costs. They should also have regard for laws or regulations, and be ethical in management decisions. For example, not selling certain products such as alcohol and tobacco to children or placing sweets at the checkout counter.

2 Managers should be honest in claims and promotions, not be deceptive or agree to misleading advertising. They should show fairness to third parties. In addition, there should not be any hidden costs – identify extra costs which may be applicable.

3 The retail products offered should not cause harm when in use or on disposal and managers should communicate any risks which are known to be associated with any product.

4 Marketers should undertake not to adopt sales techniques or fund-raising under the guise of it being research. Also, it is unfair and unethical to use promotions as research when adequate stock is unavailable because the research is being used as a method of deciding on the stock requirements.

Some retail companies such as The Body Shop have attempted to become benefactors of the local environment in which the stores are located, so as to bring about improvements to inner-city neighbourhoods and communities. This is a proactive approach to social responsibility. Community relations programmes may include:

- ensuring that all retail outlets do not limit or hinder access for disabled people;
- demonstrating an ecological approach by clearing up packaging and the local environment as well as recycling waste;
- supporting local charities, and young and old people's centres;
- setting up links with local colleges and schools;
- training and employing local residents;
- giving special promotional offers to senior citizens or disadvantaged groups.

Cause-related marketing

The use of sales promotion techniques is not always well accepted when such techniques are used under the guise of helping the community. There is a proliferation of schemes aimed at schoolchildren – encouraging their families to patronise certain retail chain outlets so that the children's school will receive some benefit. Tesco have used computers for schools, WH Smith have offered books for schools and Boots, sports equipment. Teachers have shown some concern that the underlying purpose of the retailers' ventures is to benefit themselves in the long run in terms of improved profits and improved image. However, there is also some public concern as to the true purpose of such schemes.

The strength of 'good cause' related marketing is that the majority of parents as well as children are more interested in buying a company's products if they are associated with a charity. Mintel found in 1998 that over three-quarters of those questioned about cause-related marketing would be likely to purchase a product which supported a good cause. The public, especially females, were even willing to pay higher prices for products which were linked to charitable causes. Camelot, Virgin and The Body Shop were the companies most frequently associated with charitable causes. Apart from these, there were few other companies mentioned. Therefore, the use of cause-related marketing can play an important role in the marketing of a retail company to enhance its corporate image and increase sales.

MINICASE 11.4

Iceland – socially responsible or utilising marketing promotion?

Iceland, the frozen food retailer, challenged the food industry yesterday to follow its lead in refusing to accept genetically modified ingredients in own label products. The group has pledged that all own label products would be manufactured without soya, or any of its derivatives, which have been genetically modified to resist weedkiller. It also revealed it was exploring the possibility of eliminating all processes involving genetically modified products in the manufacture of its own label ranges and will seek to use meat from animals fed only on non-modified products. Malcolm Walker, chairman, said the introduction of genetically modified soya into the food chain represented unquantifiable risks to consumers. It was 'even potentially more devastating ... to health and the environment than BSE'. 'Genetic engineering is an issue which should concern us now. We urge all other food retailers, manufacturers and farmers to campaign for crop segregation and tighter safety legislation,' he said.

However, the big food retailers said it would be impossible for them to follow Iceland's example. 'You cannot equate a niche frozen food retailer with a supermarket as the quantities required are so different,' said Safeway. Four supermarket groups – Asda, J. Sainsbury, Tesco, and Safeway – have volunteered to label products containing genetically modified ingredients. Although EU and US authorities have declared modified soya safe, some scientists are concerned that the long-term effects are unknown.

Source: Peggy Hollinger, *Financial Times*, 19 March 1998

CORPORATE SOCIAL RESPONSIBILITY

The issues of corporate social responsibility cover a company's approach not only to its markets but to its employees, the local community, suppliers and the way it treats the environment. This places a duty on the organisation to seek social approval for its policies because of the potentially detrimental effect on the quality of life of others. Many companies are attempting to provide a green, caring image for their organisations and project the message that they have a social conscience. Sponsorship for the arts, the environment or worthy causes is taking a growing share of marketing budgets. The Body Shop is entering into a long-term plan to have partnership agreements with staff and managers in nearly half its 40 stores; Thomas Cook is funding local hospital construction; Butlins is offering day visits for underprivileged children; and ICI is transforming redundant sites into nature reserves. Kentucky Fried Chicken is co-operating with the Tidy Britain Group to remove litter and educate people on how to improve the environment. The cynics of all this argue that it is impossible for companies to provide for society without an accompanying high environmental cost such as global warming, damage to the ozone layer or a waste of scarce and non-renewable resources.

Some companies are offering to give donations to good causes in order to improve their image. The Leeds Visa card has made it into the Guinness Book of Records twice for its charitable money-raising efforts. By March 1995, it had donated £6.1 million to three charities – the British Heart Foundation, Mencap and Imperial Cancer Research. Some 20p is donated for every £100 spent using the card. In addition, those spending more than £1500 a year on their card have their £12 annual fee refunded or £7 refunded and £5 given to charity.

Many retail companies are leading the field in environmental concern by the participation in recycling initiatives. Reusing newspapers, aluminium cans, bottles and packaging is a saving on resources and does not add to the ever-increasing need for landfill sites. Collection banks for different types of refuse and return policies on carrier bags for reuse are to be seen in most advanced countries.

The different company initiatives explained above are part of a wider need for companies to have a posture which gives them comparative marketing advantage over their competitors. Companies now need to be doing things better than their competitors if they are going to survive and prosper. To be socially responsible, it is not enough to have a hidden agenda of saving on costs – although improved quality management will often reduce wastage and management time. Today's consumers are able to judge the actions of retailers. There is often a need to undertake a strategy which may have cost implications but which should lead to longer-term increases in profitability. The actions of companies have to link their performance into medium- and long-term benefits. The best strategies being adopted are often proactive and honest and are not knee-jerk reactions to pressure groups. They include:

- integrated management policies aimed at protection of the consumer and environment;
- a policy for the continuous process of improvement in relations with all stakeholders as shown in Fig. 11.1;
- a continuous education programme for all staff in order to train and motivate them into conducting all company activities in an ethically agreed way;

- a system to check all retail products and services are safe, fairly priced and promoted with full information. Where possible to assess the possibility of the products and packaging being recycled, reused or having directions related to safe disposal;

- advising and, where relevant, ensuring that there is provision of information to customers, suppliers and the public in the safe use, transit, storage and disposal of retail products. This may be stipulated by the retailer as a condition to the supplier;

- running the operation in an energy efficient way and to minimise the problems of waste disposal and impacts on the environment;

- supporting and conducting research which identifies the ways and means of improving the retail product and services in relation to preventing adverse impacts and improving quality;

- promoting partnership principle relationships with suppliers so that they also adopt a consistent approach to socially responsible policies;

- having contingency plans and emergency preparedness in case a hazard or health risk is associated with any of the company's products.

Figure 11.1 illustrates the relationship factors which need to be considered when contemplating the benefits of adopting a socially responsible approach to the marketplace. The way some retailers approach strategic planning to achieve the advantages of social responsibility are discussed in the following sections.

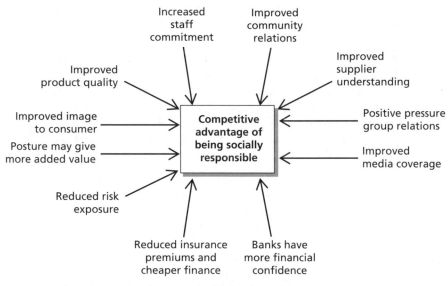

Fig. 11.1 The relationship factors of social responsibility

Finding merchandise which is environmentally acceptable

The chemical compounds chlorofluorocarbons (CFCs) are/were used in the production of aerosols, packaging materials, refrigeration and air-conditioning plants. It is widely recognised that there are long-term dangers to the ozone layer from CFCs which could culminate in a greater number of skin cancers and other wide-ranging problems. Many companies have taken a responsible attitude and voluntarily found alternative chemicals to CFCs. This has led to far greater pressure on those companies who did not change quickly to new compounds. Most aerosols have now adopted more benign chemicals which – given the diversity of range of spray applications, from hair sprays to furniture polishes – has provided strong evidence of the speed at which companies can adopt the above guidelines.

One of society's main problems is based upon the lack of space to dispose of refuse. This makes the disposal of non-biodegradable materials such as plastics and styrofoam packaging a major problem. It also makes the sale of products such as disposable nappies a long-term environmental problem. In the USA, a number of states have banned the use of all plastic packaging in stores and restaurants. This trend has caused problems for McDonald's and other fast food restaurants which have had to find alternative forms of packaging. McDonald's has changed to wax-paper packing rather than attempting to dispose of polystyrene from the estimated 22 million customers it serves each day. Some firms are recycling plastic to make the most of the relatively recent concerns about environmental issues. Procter & Gamble market cleaning products in recycled plastic bottles. The important question to be posed by retailers, however, remains whether the customer will be willing to pay higher prices for products that are less harmful to the environment. There is also a supplementary question: will the consumer be satisfied with lower quality recycled packaging? There is no clear answer to this as some consumers will accept these changes but others will not. The young and the affluent are more likely to accept pro-environment changes irrespective of whether they lead to higher costs and changes.

Self-regulation

The setting up of voluntary codes of practice is valuable for the consumer and creates benefit for those companies who join such an initiative. Once a code has been agreed companies are more likely to abide by the code because they will be in danger of being judged to be a deviant if they contravene the procedures agreed by every other company. Voluntary codes do not protect the consumer from companies that are determined to stay outside of such schemes. The Office of Fair Trading is a useful arbitrator in consumer or trade disputes as one duty of the Office is to approve, monitor and revise codes. The advertising industry set up the British Code of Advertising Practice in 1962. Any complaint is brought before the British Advertising Standards Authority whose job it is to ensure advertisements are 'legal, decent, honest and truthful' and that any advertisement is produced with 'a sense of responsibility to the consumer'. The US Direct Marketing Association has a code of ethics. The main directives are:

- all offers should be clear, honest and complete;
- offers suitable for adults only should not be made to children;
- sweepstakes prizes should be advertised in a clear, honest and complete way so the consumer may know the exact nature of the offer;
- merchandise should not be shipped without first having received the customer's permission;
- telemarketers should remove the name of any customer from their telephone lists when requested by the individual.

Self-regulatory programmes have certain advantages over government laws and regulatory agencies. They are usually less expensive to establish and implement, and the guidelines which make up the code are normally more realistic and easier to apply. In addition, self-regulatory programmes reduce the need to expand government bureaucracy and costs. However, with some trade associations, the worst offenders are not members and therefore are not required to abide by the code. When an association attempts to revise its members' actions it may find it has little authority to enforce guidelines. Therefore, self-regulation is often less strict and has less sanctions than would be the case if the regulation were applied by a government office.

The Body Shop was one of the first retailers to adopt a company policy against the testing of products on animals. The company has raised public awareness on the issue of animal testing over many years, having worked closely with the British Union for the Abolition of Vivisection. While such policies are now commonplace, almost three million experiments on live animals took place in Britain in 1994 and as such this will remain a contentious issue. A leaflet from The Body Shop states:

> The Body Shop never has, and never will, test ingredients or final products on animals or authorise such tests on its behalf. We adhere to the BUAV's five year rule – every six months, our suppliers and manufacturers must sign a declaration stating that they are not testing our ingredients on animals and have not done so within the last five years. This dynamic policy is proving successful in changing the practices of suppliers and manufacturers who used to test on animals.

The strategic options for any company policy are as follows.

Non-compliance

Companies who have poor long-term planning and 'tunnel vision' may choose non-compliance with the new trends and regulations sweeping the world. Alternatively, there are those companies which will decide that because of cost constraints they are not able to change their policies or products.

Compliance

Companies which pick up pressures from their operating environment are going to be more reactive to the demand by legislators and consumers for changes in the methods and organisation of business practices. Compliance as a posture will not achieve competitive advantage as the company is more likely to be a follower than a leader in social and environmental concerns.

Proactive compliance

Companies which are well aware of their operating environment due to the systems they apply to understanding the environment ahead of the need for legislation or change will be more proactive. These companies will be the first to introduce policies and change, and this may enhance their image and reputation.

Social and ethical leadership

These companies will strive for best practice in all their standards of business. They will be the leaders in their sectors, with environmental management and social responsibility being a pivotal basis for their business. The Co-operative movement and The Body Shop are examples of this type of organisation.

CONCLUSION

Consumerism is a growing, powerful force which has to be treated seriously. Clearly the retailer's reaction to consumerism must reflect the changing attitudes of the customer. The benefit of living in a pluralist society is that pressures are brought to bear on organisations to encourage them to be more socially responsible. Retailers need to be increasingly sensitive to the needs of society and to practice improved community relations. The demands made by the consumer are often realistic and should be an indicator of what needs to change. The dilemma from the retailer's perspective is how to bring about change while still being able to compete with other stores. It has been argued here that there are advantages in being responsive to consumer pressures. In fact, retailers should actively encourage and seek feedback on consumer issues to ensure that they are abreast of the trends.

The change in different individual and pressure group values toward the acceptability of business actions creates the preconditions for a change in strategic planning within retail companies. This change needs to address the ethical concerns of different stakeholder groups and provide for assessment of policies related to society and the environment. We cannot expect any dramatic voluntary short-term change by companies; we can, however, expect a gradual and continuous adjustment to the need to satisfy not only existing consumers but members of the wider society.

EXERCISES

The exercises in this section relate to consumerism and ethics in retailing. It is advised that you work through them before moving on to Chapter 12.

1 Having read this chapter what ethical guidelines, if any, would you now recommend to a chain of children's clothes shops?

2 With regard to ethics, think about the future issues for retailing and write down what you believe are the most important aspects of concern for an improvement in the way UK retailing or business will operate in the next twenty years. Use the grid below as a guide.

Business operations/interfaces:	Issues to be faced in next twenty years:
• retail marketing • purchasing from stores and electronically sourcing and buying • local community • EU and government legislation • pressure groups • others (list)	
Issues identified as of most concern:	**How you believe these will be resolved:**

3 Explain all the different pressures there are for a retailer to become more ethical. Can you explain why a retailer or the retail industry is so resistant to pressures for change from consumer groups?

4 It can be said that consumerism provides the ideal business opportunity for retailers. What is meant by this statement and do you believe it is valid?

5 What can be done to improve the safety of retail products? What are the cost and other implications of your argument?

REFERENCES AND FURTHER READING

Body Shop (1996) *Measuring Up: A summary of The Body Shop values report 1995*. The Body Shop Consumer Literature.

Boulton, L. (1998) 'Ministers to publish guidelines for "green" labelling', *Financial Times*, 17 February.

Chryssides, G. and Kaler, J. (1993), *An Introduction to Business Ethics*. New York: Chapman & Hall.

DeGeorge, R. (1986) *Business Ethics*. New York: Macmillan.

Economist (1997) 'Upheaval on the high street: The Monopolies and Mergers Commission is about to demand an end to the use of recommended retail prices by electrical-appliance makers. A wave of discounting could follow', *The Economist*, 31 May.

Eadie, A. (1995) 'Money: if you want a new Vauxhall, get a GM card', *Independent*, 24 June.

Hollinger, P. (1998) 'Iceland challenges rivals on genetic soya', *Financial Times*, 19 March.

Hollinger, P. (1998) 'Probe into profitability set to fire a warning shot at the big four food retailers: inquiry by Office of Fair Trading may signal that any further concentration of power among supermarket groups will only be acceptable if customers see benefits', *Financial Times*, 31 July.

Packard, V. (1960) *The Wastemakers*. Harmondsworth: Penguin.

Simms, C. (1992) 'Green issues and strategic management in the grocery retail sector', *International Journal of Retail and Distribution Management*, 20 (1), 32–42.

Suchard, H.T. and Suchard, J.C. (1994), 'Corporate environmental marketing: an environmental action model', *Business Strategy and the Environment*, 1 (1), 25–34.

Sriram, V. and Forman, A.M. (1993) 'The relative importance of products' environmental attributes: a cross cultural comparison', *International Marketing Review*, 10 (3), 51–70.

12 International retailing

This chapter should enable you to understand and explain:

- international retailing;
- differences between national retail structures;
- motives underlying retail internationalisation;
- the direction of expansion;
- different market entry methods;
- typologies of international retailing.

THE MOVE TO INTERNATIONAL RETAILING

Retailers have long operated on an international basis yet it is only within the last decade of the twentieth century or so that they have done so on any significant scale. In the past, companies trading outside their home market were rare by comparison with the number of retailers operating solely within the domestic market. This meant that international operations were usually a much smaller part of the business than domestic trade. However, the larger retail companies that have successfully developed their marketing strategy and human resource base in a domestic market are well suited to extend development into international markets.

A common trend for retailers who have internationalised is to be found in the luxury goods sector where companies have sought to serve a consumer niche. This is exemplified by Harrods who opened a store in Argentina in the early twentieth century in order to meet the needs of colonial expatriates. Around the same time, in 1909, Woolworth (then FW Woolworth) expanded from the US to Europe with its variety store concept. At the end of the twentieth century we are increasingly seeing retailers from a diverse number of sectors operating internationally. International retailers are often perceived as companies with a strong brand image, such as The Body Shop or Benetton; however, mass merchandise retailers are also moving across national borders, as exemplified by Tesco's move into continental Europe and WH Smith's and Sainsbury's entrance into the US market.

This is not to say that we have witnessed significant international expansion by retailers on a large scale. Even today, it is noteworthy that many retailers remain essentially domestic operations. In addition, many of those retailers we might perceive to be developed internationalists, or indeed global operators, receive only a minority of their turnover and profit from their operations outside the home market. Thus, it might be suggested that while the process of retail internationalisation has increased at a substantial rate, particularly since the late 1980s, international retailing is still at a relatively early stage in its development.

Case 12.1 Overseas turnover: examples of European retailers

Retailer	Origin	Ranking	Percentage turnover from overseas operations
Tengelmann	German	1	56
Carrefour	French	4	31
Aldi	German	7	20
J Sainsbury	UK	9	12

Source: Eurostat, 1993

Case 12.2 Overseas turnover: Marks & Spencer

Market	Store type	No. of stores	Turnover (£)	Operating profit (£)
UK	M&S	289	6.70bn	936.7m
Europe	M&S Franchise	37 53	538.2m	32.8m
Far East	M&S Franchise	10 33	128.3m	18.3m
Americas	M&S Canada M&S/franchise/Brooks Bros Kings Supermarket Other franchise	43 191 22 5	606.2m	16.8m

Source: Marks & Spencer *Annual Report*, 1998

Why do retailers chose to enter new geographical markets? The motivations underlying the strategy to internationalise have often been explained as relating to *saturation*, namely that retailers in developed markets such as the UK are forced to move into new markets due to limited opportunities at home. While this is certainly a factor, it is only part of the reason. Increasingly the forces driving the process of internationalisation are seen as a complex interplay of push and pull factors. The trend towards increasing retail internationalisation is illustrated by the fact that not only are more retailers operating internationally, but increasingly they are moving into markets that are distant – both geographically and culturally. As part of this change retailers must also assess which market entry method is most appropriate. Their selection will be the outcome of the interplay of a number of different factors such as the nature of the host market, the sector of retail activity, and the nature of the organisation.

THE DEVELOPMENT OF INTERNATIONAL RETAILING

This chapter examines the concept of retail internationalisation by uncovering some of the variations within Western European retailing. The motivation question is then explored. While in the past much prominence has been placed on a reactive interpretation of internationalisation, namely that retailers only move outside the domestic market when there are severely limited opportunities for growth at home, more recently a more proactive stance has been taken. In recent years this has been based upon the notion that retailers actively seek opportunities outside the home market, regardless of the potential for growth within it. These two schools of thought are discussed below and a contemporary interpretation is drawn.

We will consider both the direction of expansion and the method of entering a market. Emphasis is placed upon the different requirements of retailers operating in different sectors or with various retail offers, and we also explore the problems of retail growth in such expansionary moves.

Prior to examining the nature of the contemporary international retail arena, we will discuss the factors that restrained retailers from operating on an international basis in the past, and how those influences have changed to promote the modern international retail environment. Manufacturers and retailers are at opposite ends of the distribution channel (*see* discussion in Chapter 1). They may also be viewed as dichotomous in other ways. Until recently, manufacturers have dominated retailers within the channel of distribution. Coca-Cola, as a supplier, has had the advantage of utilising the expertise of overseas distributors who were familiar with local consumer attitudes and preferences. However, US companies such as Sears had major problems in Belgium and Spain, and JC Penney were not successful in Italy and Belgium. Many of the problems of these US companies have been related to their lack of awareness of the European consumer. In fact, the problems have been multi-faceted. There was a lack of awareness of the market and its infrastructure.

Conditions constraining the international development of retailers

1 Retailers have traditionally been perceived as operating in a localised manner and to hold limited market power, whereas many manufacturers have long since had an international presence.

2 While manufacturers have been characterised as large companies with sophisticated organisational structures, retailers have been perceived as small scale and unsophisticated in comparison.

3 Manufacturers have established brands, while it is only recently that retailers have created strong brand images capable of international transfer.

4 There has been a lack of understanding of the consumers in foreign markets.

Before discussing the motivations leading to internationalisation, it is important to have an understanding of the structural changes that have occurred in the retail industry in the last few decades. Although these trends have not in themselves caused internationalisation to occur, they may be considered as prerequisites to significant levels of retail internationalisation.

As was discussed more fully in Chapter 1, there have been major changes in the retail environment since the Second World War. While to some extent these structural shifts have occurred throughout Western Europe, they are most apparent in the advanced retail markets of the UK and Germany, and particularly within the food sector.

Structural changes in post-war retailing

1 Retailers have grown in strength relative to manufacturers and in some cases are now characterised as dominating the distribution channel.

2 Traditional independent retailers and co-operative societies have lost market share to multiple retail organisations.

3 Increasing consolidation of the retail sector measured by increasing rates of market concentration and claims of saturation.

4 Higher profitability of major EU and US retailers and subsequent ability to embark on expansionist strategies into foreign markets in order to achieve growth.

Each of these structural shifts have allowed, or indeed promoted, the process of retail internationalisation. The fact that retailers have grown in size and strength has given them the capability to operate on an international basis. Intrinsically linked to this is the dominance of the multiple organisations. Their sheer size has given them the necessary financial resources and backing required to move internationally and as they have grown in size so they have developed in terms of organisational structure. The multiples, therefore, have the management expertise and sophistication which allows them to operate internationally which smaller, more traditional, firms have not.

The first two structural change trends listed above are prerequisites for international retailing, but the third has provided the prompt. If retailers are to continue to grow in a concentrated market then they must look to diversify from their core activities. While some may follow a strategy of diversifying their activities within the home market – for example, the move of J Sainsbury from food into the DIY sector with Homebase – others look to transfer their offer to a new market, for example Tesco's move into France and, latterly, Eastern Europe.

The following description of the strategic concerns of retailers when considering whether to internationalise, or not, relates to some of the sections at the end of this chapter.

The type of decisions made, whether to internationalise or not, will be based upon the following strategic concerns.

The strength of the 'push' factors of:

● saturation of the home market or over-competition;

● national economic recession or limited growth in consumer spending;

● a declining or ageing population which will affect the market size;

● strict planning polices on store development which will constrain growth;

● operating costs which are considered too high (labour, rents, taxation);

● shareholder pressure to maintain profit growth;

● inability to find any further competitive advantages in the home market.

The strength of the 'pull' factors of:

● international opportunity due to the underdevelopment of some markets or weak competition;

● strong economic growth or rising standards of living;

- population growth in relation to the target market of the retailer;
- a relaxed regulatory framework of employment and retail site development;
- favourable operating costs (labour, rents, taxation, etc.);
- a geographical spread of trading risks;
- the opportunity to innovate, in new market conditions.

INTERNATIONAL RETAILING: A DEFINITION

Prior to our continuing to discuss retail internationalisation, further consideration is needed to define the actual process. Within the body of the academic literature, no single comprehensive definition is used. There are numerous attempts to describe the process and, although they have obvious similarities, distinct differences between them exist which can make discussion of the topic confusing.

The term 'retail internationalisation' may seem clear enough, yet a number of complexities underlie it. For example, does internationalisation encompass only the operation of stores outside the domestic market or does international sourcing count as international activity? Should a company with one store in a neighbouring market be differentiated from retailers with a global strategy operating in many diverse markets? Is a company with a portfolio of different brands/fascias going through the same process as a retailer which operates a single brand around the world?

Alexander (1997) has highlighted the varying conditions that international players operate in, suggesting that retail internationalisation is:

> **the management of retail operations in markets which are different from each other in their regulation, economic development, social conditions, cultural environment, and retail structures.**

Perhaps the most obvious definition of retail internationalisation is the transfer of retail operations outside the home market; indeed, much of the research into retail internationalisation is concentrated precisely on this. However, it is more sensible to consider it as a wider and more complex process than merely the transfer of stores. It may involve the international transfer of retail concepts, management skills, technology and even the buying function. Based on this we would suggest a usable definition for retail internationalisation is:

> **the process of a retailer transferring its retail operations, concept, management expertise, technology, and/or buying function across national borders.**

These factors are discussed in the following subsections.

Operations

A literal interpretation of retail internationalisation is the expansion of a retailer's operation into a foreign market. The type of operation may or may not be similar to that in the home market, and even if it is all but identical, it may well trade under a different brand/fascia. For example, Marks & Spencer operate stores in numerous markets using their domestic brand/fascia. Additionally, they acquired Brooks Brothers, a US fashion store not dissimilar in terms of retail offer, and also operate Kings supermarkets in New England – a different brand and a different format to their domestic operation.

315

Concepts

Retail concepts include innovations in the industry, such as the self-service concept which first emerged in California in 1912, with the later establishment of the first supermarket in New York in 1930. This concept was transferred to a number of international markets within the next two decades; for example, to Sweden and Germany in 1938, and France in 1947. Similarly, the convenience store format, which originated in the USA in the late 1920s was subsequently the focus of internationalisation with its transfer to Europe in the 1970s (Sternquist and Kacker, 1994).

The process of internationalisation may introduce new retail formats into markets. For example, the hypermarket was initially developed by Carrefour in France in 1963. The format was subsequently transferred to foreign markets – some extremely successfully such as Spain and Brazil, others with less success such as the UK and USA (Dupuis and Prime, 1996). Retail concepts also encompass particular retail offers focused on niche consumer segments. The internationalisation of The Body Shop brought with it the idea of environmentally sensitive products and a socially responsible organisation. The success of such concepts has meant they have been adapted and adopted by competitors in the markets The Body Shop has entered.

The transfer of retail concepts may be carried out by the retailer who originally developed the concept or it may be copied. One scenario is when a retailer sees a successful concept in a foreign market – whether a style of retailing, a particular format or a niche retail approach – and then transfers the concept into its own home market. Although it may not have experience of operating that particular concept, it would have knowledge of the domestic market and the prevailing conditions. An example of this includes Sainsbury's (among others) importation of the supermarket format from the USA to the UK in the late 1940s.

Conversely, concept internationalisation may be carried out by a retailer who is operating a particular retail concept and perceives that a similar format would be successful in a foreign market. Examples of such actions include niche retailer IKEA who felt their concept was strong enough to transfer into other markets. They perceived their offer was not reliant on particular market conditions, and hence could be successful in non-domestic markets. Rather than targeting a mass market, IKEA seek to target a specific niche market, but one that is evident in a number of countries.

Example: Aldi develops new outlets across Europe

The majority of UK grocery retailers have relentlessly moved into middle to upmarket positionings with their retail offers. They have concentrated on developing own brand offers, improving quality and service levels, and designing large outlets with car parking and other facilities. The budget sector position has been left to a few limited line, no frills service providers which concentrate on manufacturer brands. However, Aldi, the German heavy discounter, which is one of the largest grocery retailers in Europe, entered the UK market in the last decade. Aldi is also a no frills retailer with little spent on store fittings and atmospherics.

The way Aldi and other Global players gain advantage from being international is:

- *system transfers* – planning, budgeting and distribution systems which have been tested in different markets can be implemented easily;
- *people transfers* – skilled people can be assigned across national borders, thus drawing upon an international experienced workforce;

- *economies of centralisation* – rather than duplicating the main company systems functions across different countries, they can be centralised thereby developing greater competence and reducing costs;
- *global perspectives* – international retailers are well positioned to understand the different opportunities and retail changes which may benefit the whole of the business given the right strategies.

Management expertise

The transfer of concepts is related to the internationalisation of management expertise. This includes the internationalisation of skills and techniques used in the management and running of the company; also included is the transfer of characteristics of the culture of a company. An increasingly important means of transferring management functions is by the formation of alliances. Retail alliances were once seen as primarily a means of achieving economies of scale in buying; modern international alliances go much further than this. Retailers' motives for joining alliances include: operational synergies, buying economies of scale, increased retailer power with manufacturers, the development of own labels, joint defence building against the market entry of foreign competitors and an outcome of the growing trend of globalisation. Successful alliance management requires close co-operation, communication, synergistic performance measures and an agreement to common objectives.

Technology

The scale and sophistication of retailers, especially those operating internationally, means they require the use of technological advancements to remain competitive. The introduction of IT has also allowed the development of new techniques and systems used in the central management of retail operations to improve decision making in functional areas such as finance, personnel and logistics. These areas are increasingly complex functions for international players. Technology is also implemented at the operational level, for example EPOS systems in stores.

Internationalisation may not always involve the introduction of state of the art technology, but generally will involve employing technology that is relatively advanced. Retailers may justifiably feel that it is preferable to move into a market where they have a technological advantage. In such a situation the technological advantage would confer a competitive advantage over indigenous retailers. Thus, though technology may be employed for the purposes of efficiency and cost savings, it may also be used as a form of competitive advantage in itself.

The implementation of technology to many aspects of the retail industry internationally has numerous implications. Notably, a changed working environment is imposed upon the recipient country. The process of internationalisation can result in changes in the retail environment of the host country. This is particularly the case when a retailer originating from a developed market moves into a country with a less-developed retail structure. It is not just the introduction of specific formats or new technological tools that impacts on the host; the use of sophisticated management structures may also have a significant effect on the host country. For example, a study of non-indigenous retailers on the Greek market suggests that the major impact is not the introduction of new forms of retailing, but 'the diffusion of modern management thought and practices' (Boutsouki *et al.*, 1995).

Buying

Finally, as in retail operations, management expertise and technological know-how are being increasingly transferred across national borders, so is the function of buying – indeed it is sourcing that has had the greatest impact in terms of internationalisation. In the post-war era many manufacturers have grown in size and have become transnational corporations. In many cases this has resulted in retailers, even those whose retail operation is based solely in the domestic market, dealing with manufacturers and wholesalers in foreign markets.

One of the major motives for retailers to join an alliance is still the efficiencies and leverage they can attain in sourcing. When dealing with transnational manufacturers, the benefits of joining together to increase their size are evident: namely, to use their collective influence with suppliers to reduce prices and improve quality. For example, the European alliance EMD explicitly stated their aim of exerting the combined purchasing power of its members: 'In unity there is strength. In international unity even more strength' (Retail Intelligence, 1991, p. 18).

It is suggested that internationalisation of one function of a retail company often follows the internationalisation of another aspect. For example, if a retail company internationalises its product sourcing, this may lead to the international transfer of certain technologies and management functions. This in turn develops the experience and confidence of the retailer in operating in the international environment, which may act as a catalyst to them following a growth strategy of internationalising their operations. It is therefore possible for us to consider the process of retail internationalisation as following a learning curve.

INTERNATIONAL RETAIL STRUCTURES

While we may talk of a global retail environment there remain fundamental differences between national retail markets. Despite the existence of truly global retail brands which are found throughout the world, such as the ubiquitous McDonald's, we can still find traditional retail structures in many parts of the world. Informal retailing, such as open trading markets, characterise developing regions. Even though modern forms of retailing are emerging in such markets, traditional retail styles remain an inherent part of the market structure and are inescapably bound to the local culture and lifestyle. For example, even in Singapore with its sophisticated shopping malls and variety of international retailers, shopping for produce at markets remains a daily way of life for many people.

Measuring retail structures

So what do we actually mean by the term retail structure, and how do we measure it in order to compare markets? The structure of the retail environment generally refers to the nature and characteristics of the market: for example, the type of retail operations, the variety of retail offers, store location and nature of ownership.

In terms of measuring the retail environment, levels of market concentration are often used. Higher levels of concentration are associated with more developed markets. For example, the top three retailers account for 46 per cent of the market in Germany and 43 per cent in the UK, indicating that these are both highly developed retail environments.

Compare this with market concentration levels of just 20 per cent for Spain and 11 per cent for Italy, illustrating their less developed retail industries (ACNielsen, 1997). This is explained by the fact that, as retail industries develop, so multiple organisations begin to take market share from traditional independent and co-operative retailers; thus, a smaller number of larger organisations are taking a greater proportion of the market.

It is suggested that retail structure development can be measured not just by the number of retail organisations, but also the number of stores (Davies and Whitehead, 1995). As illustrated in Fig. 12.1, as a demand-led retail market begins to develop the number of stores, and also the number of retail companies, increases. As the market becomes more structured, the number of retail organisations begins to drop off due to the dominance of fewer but larger multiple organisations. The number of stores begins to decrease due to the fact that the size of individual shops has increased, whereby one store can serve a larger group of the population. The number of employees per retail business or per store also increases since traditional retail businesses are characterised as small scale, and employ few people per outlet and per company. As the retailer develops, the size of the store tends to increase as does the number of outlets per business. Hence, more developed retail industries have more employees per business and more employees per store.

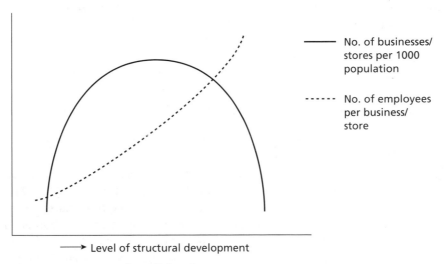

No. of businesses/ stores per 1000 population

No. of employees per business/ store

Level of structural development

Fig. 12.1 Measures of retail development
Source: Adapted from Davies and Whitehead, 1995

The number of consumers per store is a useful measure as it takes account of the number of outlets and the size of the market by using a per capita ratio. The implication is that more developed markets will have a higher number of consumers per store because the stores are larger and more sophisticated. For example, the advanced markets of the UK and Germany have 202 and 196 inhabitants per outlet respectively, while the traditional structures of Italy and Greece are illustrated by having 91 and 61 people per outlet (Retail Intelligence, 1997).

Tordjman (1995) has divided the markets of Western Europe into a four-stage matrix of structural development. The *advanced* markets of the UK and Germany are characterised by having the highest levels of concentration and a clearly segmented

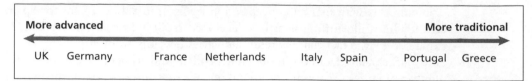

Fig. 12.2 A Continuum of European retail structures
Source: Adapted from Tordjman, 1995, p. 25

market. Next are the *structured* markets of France and the Netherlands, followed by the *intermediary* markets of Spain and Italy and, finally, the *traditional* retail structures of Portugal and Greece. Rather than regarding these as unchanging distinct phases, it is perhaps more useful to consider these markets as being at different points along a continuum of retail development (*see* Fig. 12.2).

The retail environments of former centrally planned economies (CPEs) may appear similar to other developing markets, however, there are fundamental differences. For example, the Russian retail industry is based on a legacy of a supply-led, not a demand-led economy. Retailing has traditionally been perceived as an unproductive link in the channel of distribution. The outcome of this is that concepts such as marketing, product advertising or the role of the salesperson were previously unknown – or at least absent. While many foreign operations are moving into former CPE markets due to consumer demand and limited indigenous competition, the former state-owned operations are finding it difficult to transform themselves.

It is important to note that the above description does not fully explain the structure of CPEs and former CPEs. With a retail industry based on supply rather than demand, the pattern of growth in terms of size and number of retail businesses does not follow the same rules. The nature of the economy dictates that increased consumer demand is not met by more stores or the development of multiple organisations, thus former CPEs need to be analysed separately.

The following section has characterised markets by their national borders which suggests that there are various differences between national retail markets. While we fully support this assertion, it is also necessary to point out that there may be similarities between markets – retail characteristics do not necessarily change abruptly at national borders. For example, it may be difficult to distinguish differences between retailing in West Germany and conditions across the Dutch border. It is also true to say that conditions may vary considerably within national markets; indeed, this was a point made by Hollander (1970) in a seminal study of international retailing. He suggested that differences between retailing on the East coast of the USA with conditions on the West coast far outweighed variations between the retail environments of North-east USA and Canada, despite the national border separating them. This concept, that variations may be greater within a market than between them, has also been supported in a European context (Dawson, 1994; Myers, 1996).

MOTIVES AND REASONS FOR INTERNATIONALISATION

A question fundamental to the discussion of retail internationalisation asks why retailers follow such a strategy. Invariably operating in a new market is a high cost and high risk method of growth. Indeed, it has been suggested, 'Global retailing demands huge investment and gives no guarantee of return' (quoted in Lamey, 1996).

While there are certainly successful international retailers, there are many examples of failure. Some retailers have not succeeded in transferring their operations into a new market for what are, undoubtedly, a series of complex and interrelated reasons. For example, although a successful domestic retailer, Boots the Chemist, has also entered Canada, New Zealand and France only to subsequently retreat. It is now tentatively pursuing opportunities in South-East Asia. In other cases, retailers already enjoying success in some markets may fail in others. For example, Tesco entered Ireland in 1978 only to pull out in 1986 after incurring substantial losses. As well as operating in Eastern Europe and Asia they have recently re-entered and now have 109 stores throughout N. Ireland and the Irish Republic (Tesco, 1998).

Growth strategies

If it is assumed that retailers want to grow their company, then they have three options (Pelligrinni, 1994; Treadgold, 1991).

1 From operating their core offer in the home market they may choose to follow a strategy of *sectoral expansion*, whereby they move into new formats, retail sectors or even outside the retail industry.

2 The second growth strategy open to retailers is to remain with the core offer and to transfer this into *new markets*. The advantage of this is that they are experienced in the operation; however, they may need to learn about and adapt to new market conditions.

3 The third method of growth is to use a *combined strategy*, whereby a company may move away from its core offer and also internationalise. If this strategy is taken to its extreme, the company then becomes an international portfolio or holding company.

Case 12.3   Growth strategies

Sectoral expansion

Although J Sainsbury have operations in the US which they acquired in the 1980s, they have predominantly followed a growth strategy of sectoral expansion. They have moved into hypermarket operations and convenience formats with the fascias Savacentre and 'Local' stores. They have also moved outside the food retail sector with their DIY operation, Homebase, and into personal banking. The advantage of such a strategy is that they are familiar with the home consumer market and their brand image is strong enough to transfer into other activities.

International expansion

An example of such a retailer is the German 'hard discounter' Aldi. The company was founded in the immediate post-war years with an orientation on heavily discounted limited lines of generic products. Since the 1960s Aldi has moved into numerous European markets and also the US, using a method of organic growth. Although a number of alternative fascias are used, all stores are practically identical. This generates vast economies and efficiencies of scale. Despite moving into a variety of markets, Aldi has made the very minimum of adaptions to its retail offer.

Combined sectoral and international expansion

Great Universal Stores operates in retailing and other industries such as financial services and direct marketing in a number of countries. The advantage of this strategy is the array of opportunities; however, it also increases the problems associated with working in unfamiliar markets and in unfamiliar sectors. It is a strategy perhaps more appropriate for experienced companies.

Reasons for internationalisation

The motivations underlying the decision to internationalise have been addressed in a number of ways. One of the first studies, by Hollander in 1970, proposed five reasons for retail internationalisation:

1 inadvertent internationalisation;

2 non-commercial motives;

3 commercial objectives;

4 government regulation;

5 capitalise existing or potential sales opportunities.

By *inadvertent* internationalisation Hollander was referring to political instability. Changes in the demarcation of national borders may mean a retail company is operating in a different market although its stores have not physically moved. This is exemplified by changes in Eastern Europe. The US retailer Kmart entered Czechoslovakia and within a year found itself operating in two distinct markets, the Czech and Slovak Republics (Alexander, 1995; Loker *et al.*, 1994).

Milton Friedman (1970) controversially suggested that the only responsibility that businesses have is to increase their profits. However, Hollander (1970) perceived that some retailers may move into new markets not to make money but for reasons of *political, personal, ethical or social responsibility*. For example, retailers may move into markets for reasons of social and environmental responsibility, notably The Body Shop's 'Trade not Aid' sourcing policy, or to help develop infrastructures in order to stabilise economies, such as in Eastern Europe.

Commercial objectives include entering a market in order to establish a presence before a competitor, to gain important market knowledge before moving in on a larger scale, or to learn about innovations to transfer elsewhere.

The impact of *government regulations* is perhaps more likely to influence the choice of market rather than be a prerequisite to internationalisation. Retailers are obviously more likely to enter markets with less restrictions on their growth. If regulations at home are severely restricting growth plans it may be the catalyst that pushes them into the international arena. A prime example of such a situation is the Loi Royer in France, which severely restricted the development of large out-of-town stores. The outcome was that French hypermarkets turned to less restrictive markets, such as those in Spain, to continue their expansion.

Hollander's fifth suggestion is probably the most obvious. Retailers are businesses seeking the best *growth potential* possible, therefore if they perceive significant enough opportunities in overseas markets they are likely to capitalise on them despite the risks involved.

The proactive–reactive debate

The strategic focus of retailers is shaped by a set of underlying forces. If a retailer expands by moving into foreign markets, it is due to the influence of a set of specific conditions in both the external environment and internal factors within the company. Traditionally, internationalisation has been viewed as the outcome of forces pushing the retailer from

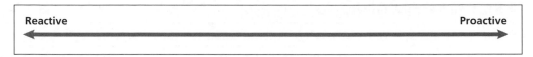

Reactive   Proactive

Fig. 12.3 The proactive–reactive continuum

the domestic market. It is proposed that if market conditions make it increasingly difficult for retailers to continue to expand, then they will be forced to seek opportunities for further growth in a new market. This has been termed the *reactive* school of thought.

The other perspective suggests that retailers internationalise not because of limitations at home but rather because they seek opportunities in other markets. This has been defined as the *proactive* response. The debate about these two ideas continues. In many cases, it is true to say that retailers internationalise due to a combination of both push and pull factors. If this is indeed the case, it is perhaps more appropriate to view motivations for internationalisation not as dichotomous forces, but rather as two ends of a continuum (*see* Fig. 12.3).

Forces acting to push retailers from continuing to expand within the home market include:

- *structural* conditions that inhibit the development of further growth – for example, competitive pressure from increasing rates of market competition, concentration, and the proximity of saturation levels;
- *legislative* factors, for example, the impact of planning restrictions controlling the development of large scale out of town food stores;
- *political* issues, such as the unstable environment of Eastern Europe;
- *social* and *demographic* factors, such as the effect on consumer demand of an ageing and declining population;
- *economic* issues, an example being the impact of a recession on consumer spending power.

Pull factors are the opposite. In some respects they may be considered to be the reverse side of the coin. For example, a market that has comparatively unrestrictive legislative measures concerning such issues as store opening hours may serve to highlight the potential for growth. A retailer faced with a restrictive environment in its home market may therefore seek to move into one with less regulation. A market with a growing population may appear attractive to retailers from countries with ageing demographic structures. Similarly, a market with a high amount of consumer expenditure is likely to be more attractive than one where consumers have limited spending power (*see* Table 12.1).

The traditional interpretation of internationalisation is the reactive school of thought. Primarily based on observing the actions of retailers in the 1960s, 1970s and early 1980s, it suggested that the underlying motives for increasing numbers of retailers moving into foreign markets were push factors, namely the lack of opportunities at home (Kacker, 1985; Salmon and Tordjman, 1989; Treadgold, 1988). It was considered that retailers would not undertake a high risk and high investment strategy of internationalisation unless prospects for continued growth within the domestic market were severely curtailed and they had few options or opportunities for domestic growth.

In contrast, it has been suggested that pull factors motivate retailers actively to seek and identify opportunities in foreign markets. Proactive internationalisation occurs when

Table 12.1 Push and pull factors

Factors	Push examples	Pull examples
Structural	Maturity of superstore in UK	Competitive advantage of importing hypermarkets to Indonesia
Legislative	Planning restrictions for large out-of-town stores in France	Laissez-faire regulations in Spain
Political	Instability in Eastern Europe	Stable political environment in Germany
Social/demographic	Declining population in developed Western markets	Increasing and unfulfilled consumer demand in Europe
Economic	Economic recession in Japan	Increasing consumer expenditure in Latin America

perceived opportunities in foreign markets outweigh the associated risks and high investment necessary for internationalisation, regardless of the opportunity for continued growth in the domestic market. It is a more aggressive strategy, and potentially more successful as it may be implemented more slowly and with less initial investment. There is also less risk as there is still growth within the home market. Even within the reactive school of thought, the influence of pull factors is not ignored. Instead, it is suggested that rather than being a reason for retailers seeking to internationalise, pull factors are an important influence in the choice of one market over another.

In contrast to research based on observing retailers' actions suggesting a reactive view, empirical work conducted in the early and mid-1990s proposed a proactive interpretation (Alexander, 1990a, 1990b; Williams, 1992a, 1992b; Myers and Alexander 1996, Myers, 1996). Alexander (1995) suggests that the degree to which a retailer is willing to exploit opportunities in the international arena, namely the extent to which they are proactive internationalists, is partly dependent on the operation's format and merchandise as well as saturation levels within the domestic market. While the reactive school of thought proposes that retailers internationalise when there is a high level of market saturation, despite the fact they operate formats with low levels of global relevance, the reactive interpretation suggests that retailers internationalise when operating a format with a high degree of global relevance despite there being low levels of saturation within the home market.

The importance of the proactive debate in the latter research does not necessarily contradict the reactive school of thought, but simply provides an analysis of the perceived motives for internationalisation in the 1990s. It may be viewed as a continuum along which the motives underlying international expansion can be placed. It would appear that at different times and to different extents for individual retailers, factors of both a reactive and a proactive nature work in conjunction as underlying motives in the decision to internationalise.

Driving forces

In addition to analysing environmental influences such as economic growth and legislative conditions, *internal factors*, for example the opinion of senior directors and management philosophy, are also considered part of the complex array of factors

MINICASE 12.1

European expansion problems and plans

Europe's leading retailers are finding it more difficult to expand organically in their own markets. European retail sales have hardly moved ahead in the past two years, according to consultants Corporate Intelligence on Retailing, hovering at about $1.9 trillion. Goldman Sachs estimates that the top 10 European retailers account for 56 per cent of the region's total retail sales and the next 40 generate a further 40 per cent. To grow, the big retailers have to look for ways of targeting the highest spending customers, according to retail strategists. 'In the past business was simple,' says Peter Scott of consultants Booz Allen and Hamilton. 'Retailers cut costs and got the right mix and off they went. But retailing on a European basis is much more complex. European retailers are being forced by the saturation in their home markets to move abroad in growing numbers. A study by the Oxford Institute of Retail Management for property consultants Jones Lang Wootton found that the number of cross border moves made by retailers in the past seven years was almost double that during the 1980s. Although the favourite destinations for foreign retailers were the UK, France, Germany and Spain, almost one-third of the moves were to the former eastern bloc countries of Poland, Hungary and the Czech Republic. But increasingly retailers are choosing to move even further afield – to the Far East or Latin America. Sir Geoff Mulcahy, chief executive of the UK retail conglomerate Kingfisher, argues that any retailer which is not making plans to move into such developing markets may have missed the boat for future growth. The drive for globalisation came relatively late to the retail sector and has largely been led by supermarket and hypermarket operators. Although food is regarded as the most difficult product to transfer to new markets, due to widely differing eating habits, operators such as Carrefour of France and Tengelmann of Germany were among the pioneers of international expansion. They have been successful partly because as hypermarket operators they have a product range wide enough to be adapted for local tastes. But they and others are also succeeding because consumer tastes are beginning to converge, according to Keith Oates, of Marks & Spencer. For example, in fashion, 'everyone is wearing the same thing,' he says. 'So it makes selling clothing in different markets easier.'

Source: Peggy Hollinger, *Financial Times*, 17 March 1998

underlying the motives for retail internationalisation. McGoldrick and Davies (1995) have constructed a model of the driving forces of internationalisation. This is a development of the dichotomous push–pull theory. In addition to analysing the effects of environmental factors, consideration is also given to the impact of various influences within the organisational sphere. Defining and understanding the factors of influence within the organisational sphere is particularly useful as they are more easily controlled, unlike the environmental factors which are often beyond the control of retailers.

Environmental factors include those that:

- *promote* international activity, such as the availability of suitable targets for acquisition and lower political and economic barriers;
- *push* retailers from their home market, elements such as domestic trading restrictions and market saturation. In addition to environmental influences, the framework gives prominence to influences within the organisational sphere;
- *inhibit* the implementation of a strategy of international expansion, such as start-up costs and fear of shareholder reaction;
- *facilitating* factors, for example, and the effect of international alliances and the bandwagon effect.

As illustrated in Fig. 12.4, findings from an empirical study of the international activity of the largest European food retailers supported McGoldrick's model (Myers, 1996).

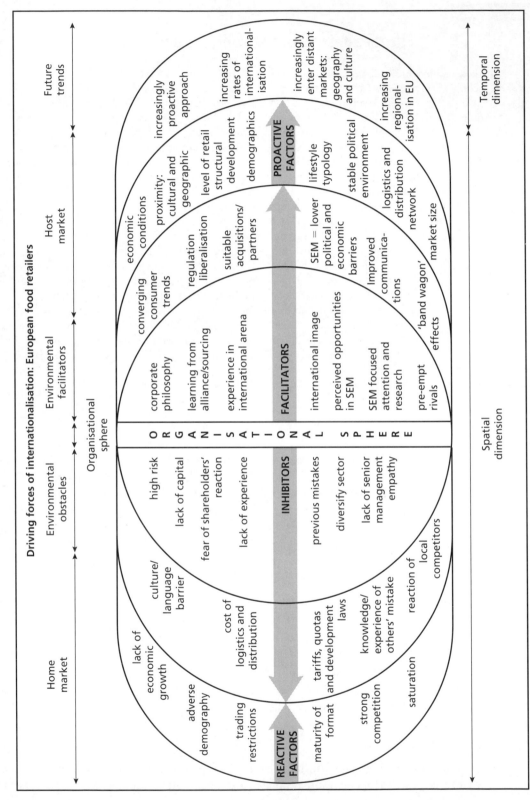

Fig. 12.4 Driving forces: European food retailing

Source: Myers, 1996; adapted from McGoldrick, 1995

Trends in global retailing

Retailers as brands are supplanting many of the traditional manufacturer brands on the world stage. This has not always been the case. Until the mid-1970s, the extent of retail internationalisation was limited and there were many failures. However, some of the most prominent internationalists go back many years. Many trailblazers were American. Woolworth went to the UK in 1909, although it is not now American owned; British Home Stores (now BHS) was incorporated in 1928 by two Americans; Safeway crossed over to the UK in 1963 but was taken over by Argyll (now Safeway plc). The prominent European retailers were generally much less ambitious. An exception was the Netherlands-based C&A, which expanded throughout Europe between the First and Second World Wars. In the 1970s, UK chains Marks & Spencer and Boots both expanded into Canada but have since been judged to have failed. Carrefour, the French supermarket chain, entered the UK in the mid-1970s but quickly withdrew and sold out to Gateway, which later sold its stores on to Asda. European retailers came into their own during the 1980s. This was a period of 'border hopping', when many companies from all sectors of the industry expanded into adjacent markets. In the first half of the decade the process was led by fashion retailers. Some of these – such as Benetton, Laura Ashley and to a lesser extent Stefanel – tried to build global businesses instead of merely border-hopping. Expansion in the second half of the 1980s was dominated by the big food retail companies. French hypermarket operators (Auchan, Carrefour, Promodes) began pouring into Portugal and Spain and the German deep-discounters (such as Aldi and Lidl and Schwarz) began expanding westwards. Similar activity took place in North America. Wal-Mart, the giant US general merchandise trader, expanded into Canada. The new US power-retailers – for example Toys Я Us, Home Depot and Staples, the office supplies company – also crossed borders. These companies are also known as 'category killers' because of their dominance over particular categories of trade.

In the Far East two Hong Kong retail companies, A.S. Watson and Dairy Farm, also began hopping into neighbouring countries with their supermarket and pharmaceutical chains. Japanese department store companies such as Takashimaya and Isetan became established in Singapore. There was a sudden escalation of franchising of Western retail brands such as Benetton, The Body Shop, Marks & Spencer and fashion designer brands. The border-hopping of the 1980s has accelerated in the 1990s. The number of cross-border moves by retailers within Europe between 1990 and 1997 has been almost double the number made during the whole of the 1980s despite the mid-1990s recession. The most conspicuous example of expansion into adjacent territories has been the movement of German companies (for example, Metro, Rewe and Tengelmann) into the Czech Republic, Hungary and Poland. These mainly food-based companies have often established joint ventures with former socialist co-operatives.

Growth in the scope of internationalisation, in the sense of companies entering many markets besides adjacent ones, has been another characteristic of the 1990s. Three of the big food retailers in western Europe – Tengelmann (Germany), Ahold (Netherlands) and Delhaize Le Lion (Belgium) – now generate more sales and profit from their foreign activities than from their home markets. Each trades extensively in the US, has established chains in central Europe and is now entering the Far East. UK retailers, particularly Marks & Spencer, The Body Shop and Laura Ashley, have played a significant part in this wider international activity. The UK has also been prominent as a major importer of foreign brands. Tesco and Sainsbury are the only two UK food retailers with full-line grocery operations overseas. Many US companies (such as clothing chains Talbots and T.K. Maxx) have seen the UK as a bridgehead into continental Europe. More and more retail companies will begin to see themselves as global players. For many, this will be a deliberate strategy – to build their brand as a world brand. For others, in more diversified sectors, the strategy will be sales driven. In the UK, the clearest expression of the brand-led strategy must be The Body Shop. For the sales-driven strategy it might be Kingfisher, although it has a long way to go in the international arena. Encompassing both might be Marks & Spencer, a company building its brand strength throughout Europe, the Middle East and the Far East but building sales through acquisitions of food and fashion chains in the US. Marks & Spencer is one of the few global retail aspirants to use all four of the principal methods of market entry: acquisitions and joint ventures (as in Spain); organic growth (as in France); and franchising (as in the Far East). Metro, the biggest of all the European companies, trades in 17 countries, including Greece, China and Romania. Ahold trades in 12 countries, including China, Malaysia and Thailand. The leading companies are Ikea (from Sweden), trading in 28 countries, and Toys Я Us, trading in 27. Wal-Mart, too, is a dominant international retailer with stores across the Americas, Canada, Argentina, Brazil, Mexico, Puerto Rico, China and Indonesia. It has also recently acquired Wertkauf, a German hypermarket company.

Niche retailers are particularly prominent in the UK, represented by The Body Shop which trades in 46 countries, Tie Rack in 30 and HMV in nine. Many of the niche retailers have expanded rapidly through franchising but HMV has taken an 'organic' route and, in some respects like the power retailers, has sought to dominate a new market rather than feed off high pedestrian flows. In addition, designer brand companies, primarily in fashion and drawn principally from the US and western Europe.

Most have been very international for some time but mainly as concession outlets in department stores or hotels in capital cities around the world. In the past few years, however, brands such as Donna Karan and Ralph Lauren have been opening large flagship stores, again in capital cities, that mainly sell upmarket fashions rather than haute couture. These stores are not judged purely on their contribution to local profit but promote brand awareness in their wider markets.

Source: Ross Davies and Megan Finney, *Financial Times*, 13 March 1998

While structural factors in the home market – such as the maturity of domestic food retail formats – push retailers to internationalise, demographic conditions in potential host markets may pull retailers into the market. Environmental factors such as the establishment of the Single European Market promoted the opportunities available in other markets, while obstacles such as language and culture barriers had a negative effect. In terms of internal factors, though lack of experience may have held retailers back from making an international move, the image of wanting to be perceived as international was an important factor promoting international activity.

DIRECTION OF EXPANSION

The direction of international expansion taken by retailers has received a good deal of attention in recent years. Much of the recent research on internationalisation describes either the development of new markets or the invasion of home markets by foreign competitors. Burt (1993) suggested that the initial direction of international retail expansion is primarily determined by three factors:

1 *cultural* proximity;

2 *geographical* proximity;

3 the *stage of development* of the retail market.

Retailers, at least in early stages of international activity, tend to choose markets that are *spatially* close. Borderhopping has obvious advantages in terms of logistics and distribution. A retailer may be able to service international stores from a domestic distribution warehouse, which is a more efficient and less costly and risky option than setting up an entirely new distribution chain. For example, Marks & Spencer are able to service some of their stores in France from their regional distribution centre in Kent. This type of activity provides retailers with the option of moving into a market on an incremental scale, perhaps building their stores at a slow pace as they learn about the market.

When first operating internationally, retailers will often try to move into markets they consider *culturally* similar. Knowledge of both the consumer and business culture is important to success. Defining cultural similarity may not be as easy as assessing levels of geography and structural development, not least because culture is not necessarily dependent on national boundaries. However, culture might well be one of the most salient factors; this being the case, the difficulties of defining and analysing its impact should not result in culture simply being ignored. The following indicates the significant cultural considerations in internationalisation.

It has also been assessed that retailers usually prefer to enter a market that is less *structurally* developed than their home market in order to have competitive advantage over indigenous players. While there are many examples of such strategies, such as HMV moving into Hong Kong or Makro moving into South East Asia, it is not always so straightforward. For example, the UK is characterised as one of the most competitive food sectors in the world, yet a number of European retailers have entered the UK despite knowing that they are moving into a market equally or more competitive than that in their home market.

The social and cultural environment

- Buying processes vary between different cultures. The role of women may differ on an international basis.

- Different family structures may place more emphasis on the family producing some of the retail goods that would otherwise be purchased in developed societies.

- Services that are taken for granted in one country may be rejected in another; for example, interest charges levied on a store credit card scheme will not be acceptable in some Muslim cultures.

- Attitudes between cultures differ when promotions are utilised. Symbols, colours and product claims can be perceived in different ways. In most of the Arab world a woman's cleavage should never be utilised in promotions and bare arms are not acceptable in Thailand and Malaysia. In addition, merchandise which is bright in colour may not be acceptable in a number of countries, including Japan.

- The knowledge of the importance of 'face' and the need for the development of social connections in business transactions in oriental countries is a key to success.

Case 12.5 Entry into the UK food retail sector

The UK is one of the most concentrated markets, the top three companies taking about half of all sales. The primary format in the food sector is edge-of-town superstores. They are characterised as providing ease of access and car parks, high levels of service, a large proportion of quality own brand lines, a strong retail image, an increasingly wide range of goods and services and the ability to command high profit margins.

Failure

The French company Carrefour transferred its hypermarket format to the UK only to subsequently withdraw. The venture failed for a number of reasons, not least its unacceptability to British consumers. For example, shoppers were not used to buying high priced non-food items from food stores and thus profit levels were hit. Superstores were already beginning to offer the advantages of a hypermarket, namely ease of access and parking and longer opening hours, and shoppers preferred higher levels of service and the familiarity of the trusted UK retail brands.

Success

Continental 'hard discount' operation Aldi entered the UK in 1989. Again, the format was heavily price orientated and with a limited service. Typically they offered generic brands at prices one-third cheaper, made possible by limited lines – typically 550 – and high sales volumes. Discounters account for 9.3 per cent of the UK food sector and non-UK 'hard discounters' are taking a larger proportion of it; for example, Aldi increased their share from 0.4% in 1994 to 0.9% in 1997 (IGD, 1997) and now operate over 200 stores. Their success is based on their strategy of not competing head on with the big three superstore chains, but rather their offer is complementary.

Retailers can be successful by not only entering markets that are less developed than their home market, but also by filling a gap in the market. In terms of the wheel of retailing (McNair, 1958; Brown, 1987), the UK food sector had traded up from its price orientation to service and quality. Consequently a gap had been left at the bottom of the market which was filled by the hard discounters.

While the factors of geography, culture and market structure are fundamental to an understanding of the direction of expansion and are observable within the commercial environment, it is dangerous to assume that attitudes toward the direction of expansion remain static. Consequently a fourth factor, which alters perceptions of international opportunities, should be considered; it is *time*. This fourth factor has been recognised by Treadgold (1991) who suggests that retailers, while initially *reluctant* to follow the high risk and cost strategy of internationalisation, over time become less *cautious*, more *ambitious*, and are inclined to seek expansion outside the confines of the markets implied by those factors.

> **Stages of international retail development**
>
> 1 **Reluctant**
>
> 2 **Cautious**
>
> 3 **Ambitious**

The underlying logic of Treadgold's (1991) model (*see* Fig. 12.5) is that retailers are initially reluctant to internationalise due to the high investment and high risk involved. At the time Treadgold assessed Tesco to be in the category of *reluctant* internationalist. The argument suggests that once they moved into the international arena, most likely as a result of push factors from the domestic market, their experience in operating on an international basis grew and they became *cautious* internationalists. J. Sainsbury was

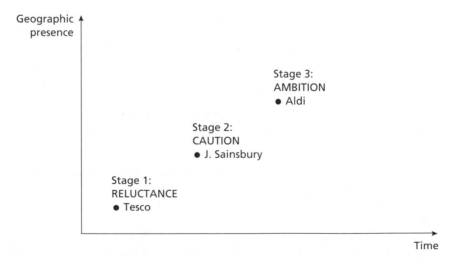

Fig. 12.5 Stages of international development

Source: Adapted from Treadgold, 1991, pp. 20–1

cited as an example of a retailer in the second stage of internationalisation. Over time, they are likely to move into markets of increasing geographical distance from home. The third stage in Treadgold's model is when retailers have significant experience in the international arena and have a wide geographical presence. Carrefour and Aldi are quoted as *ambitious* internationalists.

Retailers do not necessarily develop along this line of expansion and, once they have reached a certain stage, it is possible for them to retreat as well as progress. Almost a decade after this work was carried out it is interesting to evaluate whether the positions of these companies have changed. Tesco is now certainly an accomplished international company with 109 stores in Ireland, 41 in Hungary, 32 in Poland, 7 in Slovakia and 6 in the Czech Republic (Tesco, 1998). Thus, currently we might assess Tesco as being cautious but moving towards the ambitious stage. And what of Sainsbury? They still operate only in the US. Perhaps we could now categorise them as cautious going towards reluctant internationalists. Carrefour have operations throughout southern Europe and Latin America and are concentrating their efforts on South East Asia. Thus they are ambitious and becoming global. Aldi continue to roll out their stores in the more developed markets of Europe and the US, perhaps a more cautiously ambitious strategy.

MARKET ENTRY METHODS

Retailers may enter new markets in a number of ways. Although various terms are used, the basic choices are between *shareholding, acquisition, joint venture, organic growth* and *franchise*.

Common market entry strategies

- *acquisition* – taking over a retail company already established in the market
- *joint venture* – establishing a company with a partner, most usually one who is indigenous to the market or who has experience of operating there. 7-Eleven entered Japan utilising this method due to needing a partner who understood the complexity of the Japanese distribution systems
- *organic growth* – opening new outlets using their existing brand/fascia or creating a new one
- *shareholding* – acquiring shares of a retailer already operating in the chosen market
- *franchise* – allowing entrepreneurs to open outlets under a single brand/fascia which are operated under certain controlled conditions. US fast food giants such as KFC, Burger King and McDonald's are key exponents of this approach. In the non-food sector, Benetton is a good example.

Each one of these methods of market entry offers particular advantages and is subject to specific disadvantages (*see* Table 12.2). The choice of market entry method is dependent upon a number of issues. The *sector* of retail activity will influence the way in which a retailer enters a new market. For example, food retailers are somewhat restricted in their choice of entry strategy because they generally need to enter on a substantial scale due to distribution requirements. In contrast, niche retailers with a strong brand image have

Table 12.2 Market entry methods

Market entry method	Example of advantages	Example of disadvantages	Retail example
Acquisition	Fast substantial market presence	High cost and risk	Tesco's acquisition of Kmart in Eastern Europe
Joint venture	Each brings own skills, e.g. market knowledge and format experience	Need suitable partner	Carrefour JV with PT in Indonesia
Organic growth	Incremental process, can learn and adapt as you go	Slow growth, delay before returns against investment	Aldi's growth in the UK since 1989
Shareholding	Reduces risk, can learn about company from the inside and decide if to invest further	Culture clash between teams of management	JS shareholding of Shaws in USA in 1984 leading to full acquisition in 1987
Franchise	Very fast and low cost way to roll out stores	Limited control, need suitable franchises	Toys Я Us in Indonesia

the option of franchising or using licensing agreements. Thus, they may achieve a widespread presence fairly quickly but at a lower cost and risk than many other strategies.

Conditions within a new *market* will shape the decision on how to internationalise. In markets that are economically and politically stable, retailers may feel it is safe to develop quickly by utilising a high cost strategy such as acquisition. In more risky environments retailers may favour a less costly strategy such as franchise and proceed at a more controlled pace. The geographical and cultural distance of the host market will also influence the decision. In markets perceived as distant, a slower more incremental entry strategy may be used in order that the company learns about market conditions and adapts accordingly. Acquiring a company outright in a culturally distant market is a very risky option, and one that may be extremely costly if the retailer subsequently withdraws.

The *size* of the company is also a determinant of market entry method. Large powerful companies have the financial backing to follow high investment strategies such as merger or full acquisition. Smaller companies are obviously not in a position to follow the same path. Private companies also have the freedom of perhaps taking a longer-term view of expansion as they are not restrained by the opinion of shareholders. Linked to

MINICASE 12.3

Food retailing expansion plans

Tesco, the UK's leading supermarket group, plans to invest £150m in Thailand over the next four years to develop the Lotus hypermarket chain. Tesco is paying £200m for a controlling stake in Lotus, which, with 13 hypermarkets, is the country's second largest chain. Tesco's deputy chairman, said the acquisition had only been possible because of the crisis. 'In normal times, it would have been unlikely for stores of this quality to be available.'

Source: Peggy Hollinger, *Financial Times*, 19 May 1998

this, the *management* culture often influences strategy. While some retailers have a clear mission to be global or international players and will take risks to achieve this central aim, others are not willing to consider such strategies. The opinion of senior management often determines whether a retail company becomes international or not. Research suggests that it often takes a main board member to champion the idea of going international for it to occur (Myers, 1996). As a result, financial analysts place great importance on the opinions of senior executives.

The degree of *control* required is also a major factor shaping the way in which a retailer will internationalise. Some retailers require very high levels of control and are willing to use more costly and often risky strategies to ensure they maintain it; for other retailers it is more important to establish a diverse international presence. A rapid and lower cost method such as franchise might be used, despite the fact they have only limited control over international operations. The length of *time* over which the process is to take place is also a constraint on some entry methods. If a retailer wishes to establish international operations very quickly, it may choose to acquire an existing company, or to internationalise the retail brand it may develop concessions or use licensing agreements. However, if a retailer prefers to take a slower pace of internationalisation it may open stores on a incremental basis, providing the advantage of learning about the market and adapting the offer as a presence is built in the new market.

Factors determining market entry strategy

- retail sector
- market conditions/level of competition
- company size/capital
- management culture/philosophy/calibre of staff
- degree of control
- time scale
- capital available

Perhaps the best way to consider market entry strategies is to work from a realisation that there is not a 'best way', rather some methods are more appropriate for some retailers than others. For example, food retailers tend to use strategies of acquisition or shareholding. This is a high cost option; however, logistical requirements of food retailers mean they need to operate on a substantial scale to be competitive. There are exceptions, however, such as the hard discounter, Aldi, which is growing organically. This option is preferred by them because they are a very large private company and can take a very long-term perspective that other retailers would be unlikely to use due to shareholder reaction.

Some entry method decisions may be made on opportunistic grounds. For example, a company may enter a particular market not because of specific conditions within it but because of finding an appropriate company for a joint venture or an acquisition. Thus, the direction of expansion and market entry method choice are very much interlinked in the decision-making process. There is no perfect strategy of retail internationalisation.

Each method has specific advantages over others and each has particular disadvantages. Retailers use a strategy that is most appropriate given the nature of their operation, the organisation and the host market.

TYPOLOGIES OF INTERNATIONAL EXPANSION

Terms such as global, international, multinational and transnational are often used interchangeably and without much regard for the differences in implication. While on one level they all suggest the movement of retailers into new markets, they also imply differences in terms of the nature of international activity. Classifications of retailers have been determined partially by their direction of expansion and market entry method. For example, Salmon and Tordjman (1989) categorise three types of international strategy:

- investment;
- global;
- multinational.

Investment is often used by companies with diverse portfolios that are seeking new growth opportunities and want to spread their risk of investment. Attaining shares in a foreign company or acquiring the entire company allows swift expansion and may allow the transfer of know-how from the indigenous retailer. Unlike the other two classifications, it is a strategy implemented by both retailers and non-retailers. It implies no real international marketing strategies as the companies are treated autonomously within the portfolio.

Global retailers replicate a concept in a new market. Typically they have a strong brand such as Marks & Spencer, IKEA and Benetton. The replication of the retail offer implies a standard global marketing strategy which allows savings from economies and efficiencies of scale due to the replication of factors such as assortment, store designs and advertising. There is opportunity for vertical integration in terms of design, production and distribution. However, the lack of autonomy as a result of a centralised management structure requires, and leads to, the development of excellent information and communication systems. Global retailers are then likely to achieve the greatest rates of international expansion due primarily to efficiencies of operation.

With the third category, *multinational* retailers, the basic concept is unchanged in the international transfer, but the offer is adapted to suit local conditions, as exemplified by C&A. Although the concept is replicated, the marketing mix is adapted to suit local demand. The store decor, service and pricing are similar throughout the world, while the assortment and advertising are subject to local determinants. The management structure is decentralised, providing operations within different markets with a significant degree of autonomy. This is an important source of the transfer of knowledge from one market to another, but the philosophy of adapting to local conditions means that there are few savings from economies of scale on a global level. Although multinational retailers are set to expand within the global arena, it is thought unlikely that such expansion will be to the same extent as the global retailers.

Treadgold (1991) divides retailers into categories of:

- multinational;
- transnational;
- global.

There is a great deal of similarity with Salmon and Tordjman's (1989) model in that the position of a retailer within the typology is dependent upon the level of local responsiveness and the degree of benefits from integration. An example of a multinational retailer is Vendex of the Netherlands. It employs a high degree of adaptation to the local environment and subsequently has few benefits from integration because it has a variety of diverse retail formats. Global retailers are at the other extreme. They provide the same offer in every market with limited, if any, change made to suit different environments. This does, however, provide them with savings from economies of scale, an example of this is The Body Shop. The third category, transnational retailers such as Carrefour and Marks & Spencer, are in the middle ground and show a degree of responsiveness to local conditions and achieve limited benefits of integration.

SUMMARY AND CONCLUSION

This chapter has set out to define the term retail internationalisation, suggesting it includes not only the transfer of retail operations across national borders, but also the international transfer of retail concepts, management expertise, technology and sourcing. Retailers operating on an international scale are still in a minority and for most companies the domestic market remains a far larger proportion of their business than international operations. The internationalisation of retailing is still a relatively recent phenomenon and it is suggested that it is a process likely to continue to increase.

Retailers who internationalise may be characterised as doing so for predominantly reactive reasons – because they are being pushed out of the home market due to lack of growth opportunities – or for proactive reasons, that is they are actively seeking international opportunities irrespective of growth potential in the home market. The extent to which a retailer is reactive or proactive depends upon conditions in its sector of the home market, relevant international opportunities, and/or the culture of the organisation. It is important to realise the position on the proactive–reactive continuum may change over time.

Retailers tend to move into markets that are geographically and culturally close, and those that are less developed than their own. As they develop into experienced internationalists, they are more likely to move into more diverse markets. Their choice of market entry strategy is dependent upon the type of operations, the organisational structure and culture, and the nature of the host markets.

More and more retailers are developing their experience of internationalisation and increasingly we are witnessing retailers from all sectors moving into more distant and diverse markets. While for many retailers from developed markets conditions at home are becoming increasingly competitive, other opportunities are opening up. For example, developments within Eastern Europe are offering opportunities for expansion that were previously impossible. The advent of the Single Market of the European Union is also facilitating intra-European expansion. Retail internationalisation is a growing phenomenon and one that is set to characterise retailing at the beginning of the new millennium.

EXERCISES

The exercises in this section relate to international retailing. It is advised that you work through them before moving on to Chapter 13.

1 Think of four non-European markets that might be characterised as advanced, structured, intermediary and traditional. What are the factors that can be used to classify them?

2 Select a retail company with an international presence. Consider what might have motivated this company to internationalise. In order of importance, list five factors that you think motivated the retailer to internationalise. For each factor decide whether it is an internal or external force and to what extent it was a push or a pull factor. Overall, to what extent do you consider your chosen retailer to be a reactive or proactive internationalist? Use the form/grid below as a guide.

Company name:

Home market:

Host market(s):

Motive	Internal-1-2-3-External	Push-1-2-3-Pull
1		
2		
3		
4		
5		

3 Select two companies, each active in a different retail sector. For a destination of your choice, decide which would be the most likely market entry method for each. Justify your answer with reference to the nature of the retail sector, the company and market conditions.

4 It has been suggested that retailers are initially reluctant to internationalise, but over time become cautious and finally ambitious. Using examples of retailers from more than one sector, discuss the extent to which you agree with this theory.

REFERENCES AND FURTHER READING

ACNielsen (1997) *The Retail Pocket Book 1998*. London: NTC Publications.

Akehurst, G. and Alexander, N. (1996) (eds) *The Internationalisation of Retailing*. London: Frank Cass.

Alexander, N. (1990a) 'Retailers and international markets: motives for expansion', *International Marketing Review*, 7 (4), 75–85.

Alexander, N. (1990b) 'Retailing post-1992', *Service Industries Journal*, 10 (2), 172–87.

Alexander, N. (1995) 'Internationalisation: interpreting the motives' in McGoldrick, P.J. and Davies, G. (eds) *International Retailing; Trends and Strategies*. London: Pitman.

Alexander, N. (1997) *International Retailing*. Oxford: Blackwells.

Boutsouki, C., Bennison, D. and Bourlakis, C. (1995) 'The impact of retail internationalisation on the host country: a case study of Greece', *CESCOM 8th International Conference on Research in the Distributive Trades*, Universita Bocconi, Milan, September 1–2, A7.11–A7.18.

Brown, S. (1987) 'Institutional change in retailing: A review and synthesis', *European Journal of Marketing*, 21 (6), 5–36.

Burt, S. (1991) 'Trends in the internationalisation of grocery retailing: the European experience', *International Review of Retail, Distribution and Consumer Research*, 1 (4), 487–515.

Burt, S. (1993) 'Temporal trends in the internationalisation of British retailing', *International Review of Retail, Distribution and Consumer Research*, 3 (4), 391–410.

Davies, G. and Whitehead, M. (1995) 'The legislative environment as a measure of attractiveness for internationalisation', in McGoldrick, P. and Davies, G. (eds) *International Retailing; Trends and strategies*. London: Pitman.

Davies, R. and Finney, M. (1998) 'Retailers rush to capture new markets', *Financial Times*, 13 March.

Dawson, J.A. (1993) 'The internationalisation of retailing' in Bromley, R.D.F. and Thomas, C.J. (eds) *Retail Change: Contemporary issues*. London: UCL Press.

Dawson, J. (1994) 'Internationalization of retail operations', *Journal of Marketing Management*, 10, 267–82.

Dawson, J. and Burt, S. (1989) 'The Evolution of European retailing', *Report for ICL*. Vol. 4. Institute of Retail Studies, Stirling: University of Stirling.

Dupuis, M. and Prime, N. (1996) 'Business distance and global retailing: a model for analysis of key success/failure factors', *International Journal of Retail and Distribution Management*, 24 (11), 30–8.

Eurostat (1993) *Retailing in the Single European Market 1993*. Commission of the European Communities, Brussels.

Friedman, M. (1970) 'The social responsibility of businesses is to increase profits', *The New York Times Magazine*, 13 September.

Hellferich, E. Hinfelaar and Kasper, H. (1997) 'Towards a clear terminology on international retailing', *The International Review of Retail, Distribution and Consumer Research*, 7 (3), 287–307.

Herman, G. (1995) *The Impact of Information Technology in Retail: Globalisation and customer focus*. A Financial Times Management Report. London: James Capel and Company.

Hollander, S. (1970) *Multinational Retailing*. East Lancing, MI: Michigan State University.

Hollinger, P. (1998) 'Survey of retailing', *Financial Times*, 17 March.

Hollinger, P. (1998) 'Tesco to invest £150m in Thailand', *Financial Times*, 19 May.

IGD (1997) *Grocery Retailing*. Letchmore Heath: Institute of Grocery Distribution.

Kacker, M. (1985) *Transatlantic Trends in Retailing*, Westport, CT: Greenwood.

Lamey, J. (1997) *Retailing in East Asia*. Financial Times Management Report. London: Financial Times.

Loker, S., Good, L. and Huddlestone, P. (1994) 'Entering eastern European markets: lessons from Kmart', *Recent Advances in Retailing and Services Science Conference*. Banff, Alberta, Canada: 7–10 May.

Marks & Spencer plc (1998) *Annual Report and Financial Statements 1998*. London: Marks & Spencer.

McGoldrick, P.J. and Davies, G. (1995) (eds) *International Retailing: Trends and strategies*. London: Pitman.

McNair, M.P. (1958) 'Significant trends and developments in the post-war period' in Smith, A.B. (ed.) *Competitive Distribution in a Free High-Level Economy and its Implications*. Pittsburgh, PA: University of Pittsburgh.

Myers, H. (1996) 'Internationalisation: the impact of the European Union. A study of the food retail sector', Unpublished PhD Thesis, University of Surrey.

Myers, H. and Alexander, N. (1996) 'European food retailer's evaluation of global markets', *International Journal of Retail and Distribution Management*, 24 (6), 34–43.

Myers, H.A. and Alexander, N. (1997) 'Food retailing opportunities in Eastern Europe', *European Business Review*, 97 (3), 124–33.

337

Pellegrini, L. (1994) 'Alternatives for Growth and Internationalization in Retailing', *The International Review of Retail, Distribution and Consumer Research*, 4 (2), 121–48.

Retail Intelligence (1991) *European Retailing in the 1990s*. London: Retail Intelligence Research Publications.

Retail Intelligence (1997) *The European Retail Handbook*. London: Retail Intelligence Research Publications.

Robinson, T. and Clarke-Hill, C. (1993) 'European retail alliances: the ERA experience' in Baker, M. (ed.) *Perspectives in Marketing Management*. Vol. 3. Chichester: J. Wiley.

Robinson, T.M. and Clarke-Hill, C. (1995a) 'International alliances in European retailing', *International Review of Retail, Distribution and Consumer Research*, 5 (2), 167–84.

Robinson, T.M. and Clarke-Hill, C. (1995b) 'International alliances in European retailing' in McGoldrick, P.J. and Davies, G. (eds) *International Retailing: Trends and strategies*. London: Pitman.

Salmon, W. and Tordjman, A. (1989) 'The internationalisation of retailing', *International Journal of Retailing*, 4 (2), 3–16.

Sternquist, B. and Kacker, M. (1994) *European Retailing's Vanishing Borders*. Westport, CT: Quorum Books.

Tordjman, A. (1995) 'European retailing: convergences, differences and perspectives' in McGoldrick, P. and Davies, G. (eds) *International Retailing; Trends and strategies*. London: Pitman.

Treadgold, A.D. (1988) 'Retailing without frontiers', *Retail and Distribution Management*, 16 (6), 8–12.

Treadgold, A.D. (1991) 'The emerging internationalisation of retailing: present status and future challenges', *Irish Marketing Review*, 5 (2), 11–27.

Whitford, F. and Hope, A. (1994) 'The grocer's tale', *Sainsbury Magazine, Sainsburys 125 Years: Celebration Supplement*. London: New Crane Publishing Ltd.

Williams, D. (1992a) 'Motives for retailer internationalization: their impact, structure, and implications', *Journal of Marketing Management*, 8 (2), 269–85.

Williams, D. (1992b) 'Retailer internationalization: an empirical inquiry', *European Journal of Marketing*, 26 (8/9), 8–24.

13 The future of retailing

This chapter should enable you to understand and explain:

- the future retail environment due to consumer change;
- prospective retail development;
- learning curves and their benefits;
- the advantages of retail as opposed to manufacturer brands;
- some of the key variables affecting the future of retailing.

Shopping has existed since the advent of civilisation. Communities grew and prospered due to local markets at suitable places on fixed days. Markets have always attracted different groups of purchasers who had either money or the means to barter. While the need for disposable income is an important prerequisite for successful retailing there is little correspondence between the early beginnings of retailing and the modern marketplace. The changes taking place are dramatic; and the pace of change in the modern business world is intense – change takes place at rates which would be incomprehensible to the retailers of the 1950s and 1960s. The last thirty years of the twentieth century witnessed dramatic increases in the power and scale of major retailing organisations, with the relentless trend of power changing from the locus of the manufacturer, moving first to the retailer and then through to the consumer. By the later half of the 1980s, the consumer was dictating a whole series of improvements in the retail service offer as well as expressing the need for price and value for money to be carefully managed. In response to the growing power of the consumer, retailers expanded product lines, became concerned with the strategic issues of discounting, but then needed to move on to everyday low pricing and then value retailing.

During the 1990s, recessionary times meant that retailers had to ensure that they had to be more effective in the management of their retail offers. At the same time there was the need for greater productivity to ensure that costs were controlled and efficiencies could be passed on to the consumer. This heralded the adoption of a systems approach to retailing where computer applications and EPOS were pivotal in the development of all strategic improvements. At the same time as these changes were taking place, the retailer had to contend with the emerging values of concern for the environment and the need for more user-friendly products. The changes are continuous throughout society. There are new economic constraints, rapidly changing attitudes and new business relationships. The future is never clear but we can say, with some certainty, that the retail structure will continue to respond and evolve. Change will take place in relation to the pressures and trends in the internal and external environments of retail organisations. Retailers will need to ensure they have strategies which will relate to changes in consumer demand, social trends, government legislation, improvements in technology and competitor actions. The future will require innovative ways of structuring and carrying out business. This may involve improving the productivity of existing businesses, increasing or improving direct selling methods, and development of partnership and loyalty schemes. All this is going to happen within the constraints of greater government and EU involvement in retail planning and employment issues.

IMPROVED CONSUMER UNDERSTANDING

The main emphasis of this book is that the consumer has to be at the centre of any decision making carried out by retailers. Modern consumers are very different from those of the 1970s and 1980s. In the UK the youth market has declined dramatically while, at the same time, the student population in higher education has almost doubled to 1.2 million. This has produced a ready part-time workforce for retailers and a growth in the consumption of education and leisure-related products. Consumers as a potential market are easy to predict even until the year 2020 as they are already born. Given the rise in the number of older people in society and the values of individualism, there will be a growth in smaller households which will be higher than the population growth rate. However, the population of the UK is set to decline by just over 100 000 by 2036 and by just over 150 000 by 2046. This is due to a general trend in lower birth rates throughout developed countries where the population will ultimately decline. Long before this happens there will be a high number of older consumers with specific needs in relation to retail consumption. The growth rate of ethnic minority groups in the UK offers opportunities for retailers. In the UK the consumption potential of the various ethnic minority groups will become more important as these groups numbered over 2 million in 1995 and represent a substantial market for retailers, especially in inner city areas. A further background to the consumer marketplace is the emerging economic situation in world markets, as discussed below.

1 The establishment of a common currency among most EU member countries – European Monetary Union – and further relaxation of trade restrictions. This should further stimulate retail trade. In addition, national debts are better controlled in European countries due to the needs of monetary union.

2 There are growing concerns over the ability of some geographical areas to solve their financial problems in the short term – South East Asia, former Soviet Union countries and South America. If banks in countries such as Japan solve their bad debt problems, these countries may recover in the new millennium. However, all the geographical problem areas are desperately attempting to bring more order and stability to their economies.

The proportion of women working will increase in the first decade of the next century, with a resultant increase in household income. This financial boost, however, will be accompanied by a decrease in available time to shop and make decisions over household choices. There are changes already occurring, with food retailers considering opening smaller stores, or specialised retail environments, in working districts where convenience is important. There will also be an increase in the available time to shop, correspondingly longer opening hours and the employment of part-time staff. The impact of more women working is going to result in many women making a trade-off between convenience and making economies. The trend will also proffer opportunities for more fashion-oriented outlets aimed at dressing the working woman and providing for leisure wear. We have yet to find out if technology will provide the impetus for more direct sales or ordering of food and other retail related items. Perhaps the trend will be to regularise routine purchases by the use of technology, while leisure shopping and recreation will be combined as a more pervasive form of retail. We can only indicate that this seems to be the trend but the evidence is too sparse, at the moment, to forecast more precisely what the shape of retailing will be in the years up to 2010.

It is clear that social values are changing. We are witnessing the widening acceptance of debt, especially by the young, who are now taking loans to fund their education or to purchase more freely. An indicator of this is the expansion of the use of credit card facilities (*see* Table 13.1).

Table 13.1 Percentage of cards in use in the UK by percentage of population

Percentage of cards by year for UK population over the age of 16	1989 (%)	1993 (%)
ATM/Debit card	43	62
Debit card	30	52
Credit/charge card	37	38
Any plastic card (including cheque guarantee card)	67	76

Source: Association for payment clearing services

As the consumer learns to be more sophisticated in purchasing habits, they will also acquire the values from the media and pressure groups about environmental and consumer issues. This consumerist movement is often treated as a concern and many firms react defensively, as if consumerism were a major threat to the retailer rather than an opportunity. In fact, because of the overt nature of the movement, the retailer can often be over-defensive. Taking a marketing approach, then the type of concerns expressed by the general public are an indicator of the wishes of the customer and these should trigger changes in the business policy of retail operations. We have discussed the ways that companies have approached social responsibility in an earlier chapter. We discussed the need for companies to adopt policies for continuous improvement in respect of recycling, directions on product use, storage, energy usage, partnerships with third parties, responsible decision making, and employee education in the adoption of more socially responsible procedures. The issues which will be more important in the future relate to expectations regarding the quality of the product and retail service, the after-sales service component as part of added value, acceptable containers and packaging, as well as fairness in business practices.

In most developed countries the retail industry is becoming more and more concentrated and better at carrying out its business. The advantages gained by location decisions and the application of technology are important technical aspects of the

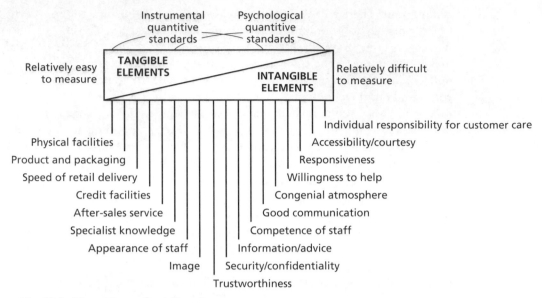

Fig. 13.1 Dimensions of retail customer care

Source: Based on Carson and Gilmore, 1989

business. However, the ultimate winners in the marketplace will be those companies that can harness their workforce's energy and motivation to deliver a world class service – which is why we provided a great deal of theory and discussion on managing service in earlier chapters. Service excellence is important in the retail product amalgam and the ability of retailers to differentiate on service will be of greater significance in the future. Non-price aspects of the marketing mix will grow in importance and, as such, more research and emphasis will need to be placed on understanding the attitudes and beliefs of the retailers' target market. Figure 13.1, which has been compiled from the marketing of services literature, indicates the full range of skills and functions required by retail operations. This emphasises the ideas and concepts discussed in Chapter 4 on service and quality in retailing.

MORE EMPHASIS PLACED UPON BRAND, IMAGE AND POSITIONING

In order to take full advantage of the efforts retailers will place on both functional and service improvements, there is a need to distil the retail offer into a clear proposition based on the retail product, brand image and positioning. Each brand will need to be reassessed in light of the changing nature of the retail marketplace. We have discussed in great detail the important trends and concepts behind branding, especially those of own-brand developments. As the retail market continues to mature, it will be interesting to monitor the use of advertising by the different retail organisations to identify those which are attempting to alter the perceptions of consumers to their offers. It may be a while before we witness an expansion of the majority of the 'big players' into advertising campaigns based upon the type of marketing carried out by McDonald's. Whatever happens, all this will take place against a backcloth of manufacturers' attempts to hold on to the strength of their own brands and products, while at the same time the power of the retailers will continue to grow. There are going to be a number of challenges in the

The future of retail shopping

It is Saturday morning and Mary Duffy is getting ready to do the weekly grocery shop. She goes to the kitchen cupboard and has a quick look. The kids have been at the biscuits again and three packets stand half empty. She picks up a pen and runs the point over the bar code on the biscuit packets. The brands are automatically added to an electronic shopping list via the scanner built into the pen. The list will also include products which, once used, have been thrown into a bin specially adapted to read radio signals emitted by intelligent labels. She splashed out on the Trashscan just two months ago, but was annoyed to discover there are still some bugs: such as when the baby repeatedly lifts rubbish out of the bin and puts it back in again. Frustrating, but it is simply a matter of adapting the shopping list, which has been downloaded on to the interactive television or the family's personal computer. Both now use a Microsoft-designed Windows navigation system. Although Mrs Duffy usually has the groceries delivered, this Saturday she decides to shop herself. So after adapting the list on the PC, she sends it to the store. Everything but the fresh fruit and meat will be waiting for her when she gets there. She, like most customers, prefers to choose these items herself. On the way she remembers at least three things she forgot to put on the list. No problem. The voice-activated personal computer fitted into the dashboard of her car will send an updated list. Mrs Duffy's shopping trip sounds far-fetched, but all the items she used can be purchased today. The penscanner is available from Symbol Technologies of the UK, interactive television will launch in the UK this year, and leading car manufacturers such as Mercedes and BMW are planning to launch models with voice-activated computer screens. The only fantasy item might be Trashscan, developed by ICL, the computer services company, two years ago. Technology is the new battleground of retailing.

As she wanders round the store to get ideas for the dinner party tomorrow night, she notices a special offer on compact discs. Pressing the trigger on the keyring given to her by the supermarket chain after she built up 100,000 points, the CD's electronic price tag flashes up a further 10 per cent off just for her. The price looks good, but just to double check, Mrs Duffy runs the scanner in her mobile phone across the album's bar code. It dials up the bargain hunting search engine on the internet and lists the 10 retailers who sell the CD at the lowest prices. Only one is cheaper than the supermarket's offer, so she decides to buy it.

Source: Peggy Hollinger, *Financial Times*, 3 April 1998

future retail marketplace. Manufacturers will attempt to reorganise the shape of the market to ensure that they continue to have some influence over the marketplace. This may mean a trend to the use of categories, as brands become less important. Whatever happens the manufacturer will not be able to counteract the power of the retailer and this may lead to the need for manufacturers to assess their portfolio of brands in order to rebrand or dispose of those brands which may not survive a prolonged battle. The ultimate threat of powerful retailers to delist a manufacturer's products is a very serious threat that all suppliers will need to take more and more into account as specific retailers continue to grow in size and power.

Corstjens and Corstjens (1995) have offered the concept of a battle for mindspace of the retail consumer. They have uncovered a number of arguments regarding advantages to the retailer and the manufacturer of their specific branding exercises. A number of these are summarised in Fig. 13.2.

The retail organisation of the future will have to be poised to take a much more proactive stance to the retailing and shopping behaviour of its customers. To have a greater understanding of the dynamics of consumer behaviour will provide an advantage for retail managers. A great deal more research should be carried out into understanding satisfaction or dissatisfaction with the whole service delivery process. The use of techniques such as critical incident technique (CIT) will enable companies to uncover the

Retailers	Manufacturers
Ownership of the stores which provides or means:	*Critical mass and specialisation which provides or means:*
• ability to communicate directly with customer	• specialist manufacturing technology
• full control of retail marketing mix	• use of media communications and advertising to influence customer
• timely and accurate feedback and information	• use of market research in order to understand the consumer
• ability to be efficient with new product introductions and to reinforce the store image	• advantage of image especially for quality
• staple food products can be own-branded without worry of prestige or need for communication, e.g. spaghetti	• advantage of ubiquity of the brand and potential placement in all outlets
• advantage of habitual, low interest purchases occurring and therefore brand acceptability is not difficult	• can develop a whole range with great deal of variety which provides for a sense of choice
• high margin sales will attract competition	• outside of the retailer versus retailer battle and would benefit from overcapacity
• sales are more likely to occur when the retailer is of a mass appeal level	• able to be sold through a variety of different channels

Fig. 13.2 Comparison of branding advantages between retailers and manufacturers

hidden factors which may lead to disenchantment with the existing retail business operation and its products. Research by Bell, Gilbert and Lockwood (1997) at a Tesco store indicated how CIT can be utilised to improve the management of retail operation. There is a need to know more about store choice, shopping habits, and in-store behaviour and decision making. Consumer behaviour studies are set to be a more important aspect of retail management. We have attempted to cover the fundamentals of consumer behaviour in this book (*see* Chapter 3) because we believe it is a key area of retail management.

This is because:

• improving customer satisfaction is a key to gaining store or brand loyalty;

• knowing what to provide, so as to deliver value for money, will become more important. As such, premium price policies can exist on the basis of the willingness of a customer to pay higher prices because of the image and value delivered;

• there is a need to deal with customer dissatisfaction, but first it has to be uncovered and understood;

• with a hyper-segmented store clientele, there is a need to understand the range of customer needs;

• customer satisfaction surveys will not easily uncover the complexities and subtleties of customer reactions to the existing and future business.

MINICASE 13.2

Futuristic links between banking and retailing

Barclays Bank became the first of the big UK banks to launch 'screenphone' banking with a service that includes innovative links with retailers. The service is provided via a larger version of a normal phone, featuring a built-in 8cms by 5cms screen. Information is carried over a fixed telephone line. Customers using the device will get access to their Barclays and Barclaycard accounts and a variety of other services, including shopping, ticket purchasing, weather forecasts and local information. They will be able to check balances, view mini statements and search for past transactions. More complex transactions, such as switching money between accounts and paying bills, will involve speaking to an operator. Barclays has linked up with a number of providers including Victoria Wine; Entertainment Express, part of Kingfisher, the retailing group; Scoot, the business directory service; Ticketmaster and the Meteorological Office. Entertainment Express will deliver CDs and videos to homes at a £1 discount on high street prices. 'This takes the banks closer to retailing, just as retailers are pushing further into financial services,' said one analyst. Donald Rankin, Barclays' director of personal banking, said the service was 'positioned between telephone and pc banking'. A pilot scheme involving 2,000 customers will run for six months, with plans for a national roll-out. The screenphone costs £99 and there is a £5 a month service charge.

Source: Christopher Brown-Humes, Financial Times, 20 May 1998

EMERGING TRENDS IN IT

Retail and information technology are inextricably linked. Some changes will be directly related to the new technologies entering the industry or based upon the way retailers utilise existing technology within their retail operations. IT may also serve to stabilise the future retail industry structure because current applications – and the need to specify and invest in new systems – make for barriers to entry and exit.

The trends emerging in relation to IT are:

- an increased level of intelligence being incorporated into computer systems;

- the increased availability of multimedia technology. As television, telecommunications and audio systems converge, there will be interactive multimedia systems developed to provide exciting new opportunities for retail developments;

- an increased usage of IT to improve levels of retailer productivity;

- miniaturisation of electronic systems will continue. It is already possible to fit the processing power of an early mainframe computer into a space smaller than the average briefcase. The electronic wallet will be available soon. It will allow electronic payments and carry a wealth of information, including shopping lists;

- the back office workforce will be able to work at home via special modem and computer links. This will place more pressure on rural rather than city properties as the need to commute will become less necessary. This trend will be reinforced through the policies of local authorities, who are keen to cut down on traffic congestion in city centres;

- stand-alone sales kiosks which can provide voice recognition communication and real comprehension of queries and transaction processes. Ultimately holographic projection will be possible to enhance the sales experience.

Recent IT applications allow for extremely high levels of sophistication and intelligence. The diverse situations to which they can be applied range from operational analysis to decision support systems. This development has been paralleled by an array of software tools known as artificial intelligence (AI). AI includes many different branches of computer technology which are designed to mirror the human thinking, reasoning and decision-making processes. These can be *expert systems*, which contain a knowledge base and decision-making protocols so as to provide the type of answers an expert may suggest if given a similar situation. Expert systems contain an inference engine which has been programmed to tolerate uncertainty. They do this by incorporating probabilities into their logic which is often referred to as 'fuzzy logic'. On the basis of this, the system can take into account a number of uncertainties such as the weather, consumer tastes and environments. Expert systems can be developed into neural networks which, through the identification of patterns, will allow the system to learn as it operates. This can have applications to the calculation of complex pricing policies, diagnosis of operational problems within the organisation, or decision-making support for managers to plan the staffing requirements during any time period. The systems will be able to learn from financial reports and returns and from demand patterns how to change and allocate space to different items and brands.

Robotic technology is another branch of IT. *Robotic systems* can help with the manipulation of objects by picking them up and moving them to where they need to go. Robots are different from automatons in that they can be programmed to perform a variety of tasks. The system allows for motion to let the robot move around, sensory processing by use of infrared, ultraviolet or sonar scanning to recognise shelf or stockroom areas, and it also allows actuation to lift and move items whether by electric hydraulics for light movement or pneumatics for heavy objects. Robotics could be used in the future to replenish shelves, clean shop floor areas, collect trolleys, or replace the non-skilled work carried out by retail employees.

In the future, consumers will be able to use robots which will use a card or could learn to pick their regular shopping items for them while the consumer carried out some other task. The checkout will be automated and an electronic fund system will allow for the debiting for the merchandise. In the home, the packaging of food items will have information able to communicate directly with the microwave or cooker to ensure perfect cooking. Finally, *multimedia systems* will increase the marketing facility to transmit information and communicate with potential and actual customers, employees and suppliers. Use of the Internet and other systems has been discussed in Chapter 10, along with the realisation that there is global connectivity for retail businesses.

THE PHYSICAL ASPECTS OF RETAILING

Some predictions indicate that stores as we know them will disappear, to be replaced by interactive modules or kiosks which can display the product, provide for a series of questions, take an order by capturing information from the customer, make the transaction by way of a credit card and then create a confirmation printout. All this has been available for some time but has not been fully developed. The store of tomorrow may well look different to that of today, but all indications for the short term suggest that technology will be harnessed to make retailers more productive rather than radically to alter the way consumers shop. As automation can be expensive, its increased use favours the larger organisations who will be able to utilise it to create a competitive advantage. There will be the use of technology at head office to automate the business and reduce the number of personnel, and to provide improvement in information so that less profitable lines can be discontinued, inventory control improved, more room be given to selling space rather than for stock items, workforce planning improved, etc. It has become a vital part of modern retailing. These changes are described in Chapter 10 on IT applications to retail. Relationship marketing, by the capture and use of database information, will become increasingly important along with the development of Internet retail possibilities.

MINICASE 13.3

Dynamics of change affecting the British high street

For the second time in two decades, the shape and feel of the British high street is being transformed. In the early 1980s, the high street – the traditional centre of Britain's towns and cities – was changed by the arrival of national chains of retailers, building societies and US-style fast-food outlets. This, as any foreign visitor will testify, made British high streets all look the same. Boots, J Sainsbury, McDonald's and The Body Shop seemed to be everywhere. Many of these companies then moved on at the start of the 1990s, either because of retrenchment or because they were seeking greener pastures. Their places are being taken by up-market pubs, restaurants and cafes. Britain's high street is turning into a kind of Upper Street, the centre of north London's fashionable Islington. Upper Street is lined with giant glass and stripped pine bars and a variety of international restaurants. The same combination can be seen all over provincial cities.

The face of the high street is reflecting a variety of forces all the way from changes in what people want to spend their money on to the increased economic importance of students and even new policing techniques. 'Twenty years ago, you couldn't really conceive town councils giving planning permission to pubs and restaurants like this,' says Neil Blake, research director at Business Strategies, a consultancy that analyses regional economic trends. Mr Blake says the introduction of eating and drinking outlets in town centres has been more or less forced on councils. The earlier invasion of the 1980s had crowded out the traditional high street shops, such as butchers and greengrocers. Then the big chains left for new shopping centres, often out of town – leaving councils with the prospect of their central business districts becoming ghost towns.

Source: Richard Adams, *Financial Times*, 21 February 1998

COMPANY LEARNING CURVES

The concept of companies experiencing the benefits of learning curves is widely accepted. It is believed that as companies gain more experience of increasing the size of the business they will develop specific efficiencies which can be exploited in the market. Therefore, as retailers expand their business they are able to deliver better value and be more profitable due to the experience gained. The form of the learning or experience may differ, as some companies emphasise improving technology and the development of technological know-how whereas others may focus more resources on research and understanding the customer. Companies make strategic decisions in order to move them down the cost curve to provide added value. In the footwear market, Adidas and Puma invested in setting up large-scale European manufacturing capacity. On the other hand, Nike and Reebok used the learning curve to gain cost advantage from Far East manufacturing locations which had the ability to switch designs quickly – enabling these companies to introduce a flexible fashion element to their marketing. Large retail companies are able to use the learning curve to improve productivity as this is one of the easiest ways for them to prosper. The larger companies are well positioned to harness the benefits of the learning curve. This places a barrier on the entry of new competitors in different retail sectors.

As retailers prepare for the future they have to form a vision and scenario of what the future may hold. This has to take into consideration competitive benchmarking of the business against the best examples in the wider business world. This will push them into improvement and repositioning to become best in class. The exciting aspect of marketing is that there are always a number of alternatives available. The choice has to be made on the basis of the existing company resources, the expected changes in the environment, consumer trends and the most logical direction. The following section lists just some of the possibilities.

POSSIBLE AREAS OF CHANGE

The areas of possible change which retailers need to decide on are:

- increased access and variety through vending machines and kiosks as well as the development of Internet sites and virtual stores;
- more precision marketing through telesales and specialist catalogues. The use of portable stores based in mobile truck or van units could be taken into specific neighbourhoods. The less mobile and rural communities are a key area for the expansion of specific ranges of merchandise;
- greater customisation of stores to suit niche markets;
- increased market coverage through cable and tv shopping networks or extending opening hours;
- improved turnover through the development of new areas of retailing such as financial services, specialist merchandise within department stores, or franchising;
- reduction in staff, and therefore costs, through the application of technology, with computerised sales information, inventory and display control, increased security and anti-shoplifting devices, improved scanning systems;
- reappraising the size and location of stores with a more balanced approach to small-scale development in key locations due to future legislation and working trends;
- creating longer-term retention of customers through relationship marketing and loyalty programmes;
- improve information database through introduction of smart card technology, EPOS developments etc.;
- decide upon international expansion strategies in order to realise the opportunities in countries such as India with 850 million people and a growing middle class or China with a population of 1.2 billion – 300 million of whom are adults living in just 95 cities. Forecasts of growth in these countries indicate that a huge market will exist in the near future. That is why Wal-Mart and Carrefour have built stores in China, on the basis of learning how to harness the predicted improvement in the Chinese economy and political situation.

As a background to the changes taking place, there are development trends involving the renovation of older retail areas or the redevelopment of large areas to create major new shopping areas in urban locations. At the same time it is becoming more difficult for retail developers to dictate what their requirements are. Government legislation introduced in 1996, as described in Chapter 8, creates problems for retailers who may want to expand into new greenfield site developments. Retailers may need to examine other ways to expand but there are few true innovations as the risk is quite high.

If there are to be major changes in store design then we should expect the development to favour the niche markets. If a more specialist form of targeting takes place, there is a need to offer a more customised approach. This means that the stores will need to have a format that will target clearly defined segments – for example, more age-specific or lifestyle and cultural-specific design innovations. The 1990s are witnessing stores which have an ecological influence in their format, with products aimed at helping wildlife and reminding us of the environment. The atmosphere of the store is enhanced by countryside sounds, such as bird calls, and the range of merchandise is carefully selected to complement the store's market positioning. This is indicative of the efforts made by some retailers to bring the ambience of the store closer to their target customers. Other forms of this approach can be found in the way merchandise displays can be planned to become a retail attraction in their own right. The Disney stores, with their use of costumed characters, movies and videos, create an entertainment leisure environment which relaxes and pleases the customer, which in turn leads to themed purchases.

CONCLUSION

This book has been structured so that the reader will have been exposed to the underlying logic of a marketing approach to retailing. The concepts that you should have mastered from reading the chapters create a useful framework of approach. However, any company adopting these ideas has to be both flexible and adaptable in order to take the course of action with the highest expected value outcome. Retailers will need to react consistently to the environment by ensuring that their offer meets current and future needs. This may mean giving up the established positioning of the brand. Kentucky Fried Chicken became KFC so that it could offer more than simply chicken meals and British Home Stores become Bhs to appeal to younger consumers. There is no short-cut route to deciding on the future. It requires a great deal of analysis of emerging trends and the signals of change. Retailers who create a company culture which seeks to understand and manage change are the ones who are best suited to survive and prosper.

EXERCISES

The exercises in this section are related to the future of retailing – the issues discussed in this chapter.

1 What are the key changes which you expect in retail markets in the next decade and what are your reasons for your beliefs? How should current retailers start planning for these expected changes?

2 What is going to happen in the battle between retail and manufacturer brands? Are alternative distribution channels or other changes going to affect the power struggle?

3 What will be the key skills and knowledge requirements of retail marketing managers in the next decade? What are the reasons for and implications of your ideas?

REFERENCES AND FURTHER READING

Adams, R. (1998) 'Cafe society comes to the high street', *Financial Times*, 21 February.

Bell, J., Gilbert, D. and Lockwood, A. (1997) 'Service quality in food retailing operations: a critical incident analysis', *International Review of Retail Distribution and Consumer Research*, 7 (4), 405–23.

Brown-Humes, C. (1998) 'Barclays to launch "screenphone" service', *Financial Times*, 20 May.

Burke, R.R. (1997) 'Do you see what I see? The future of virtual shopping', *Journal of the Academy of Marketing Science*, 25 (4), 352–60.

Carson, D. and Gilmore, A. (1989) 'Customer care: the neglected domain', *Irish Marketing Review*, 4 (3), 49–61.

Corstjens, J. and Corstjens, M. (1995) *Store Wars: The battle for mindspace and shelfspace*. Chichester: Wiley.

Ernst and Young (1991) 'Survey of retail information technology expenses and trends', *Chain Store Age Executive*, September, Section 2.

Hasty, R. and Reardon, J. (1997) *Retail Management*. London: McGraw-Hill.

Hollinger, P. (1998) 'The microchip moves into the supermarket. Imagine a dustbin that knows what you've thrown away and what should go on the shopping list', *Financial Times*, 3 April.

Keh, H.T. and Park, S.Y. (1997) 'To market, to market: The changing face of grocery retailing', *Long Range Planning*, 30 (6), 836–46.

Index